# NEW ENGLAND
# BOUND

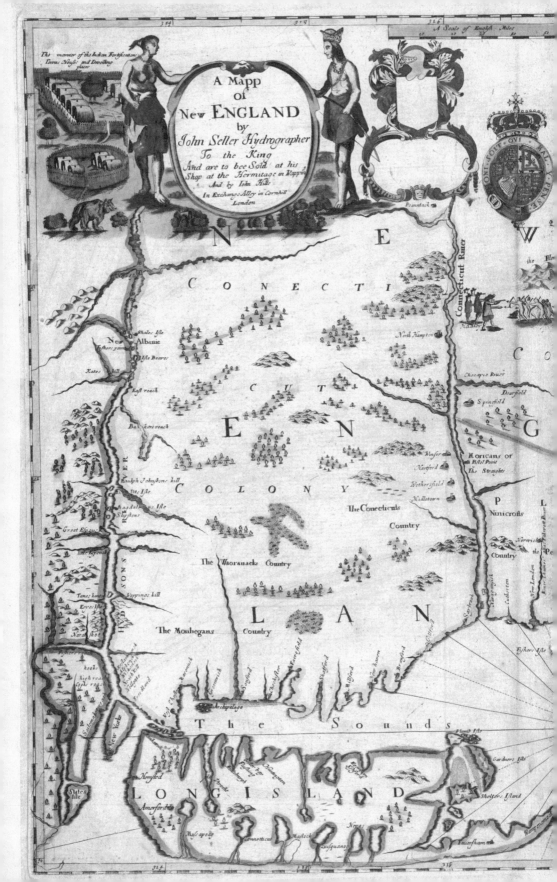

The manner of the Indian Fortificatons, Townes, Houses and Dwelling places

A Mapp
of
New ENGLAND
by
John Seller Hydrographer
To the King
And are to bee Sold at his
Shop at the Hermitage in Wapping
And by John Hills
In Exchange Alley in Cornhill
London

N    E    W

HONI · SOIT · QVI · MAL · Y · PENSE

A Scale of English Miles

Pasantack

CONECTI

Schates Isle
New Albanie
Esherpens
Isle Beares
Kates hill

North Hampton

Connecticut River

Radby

Chicapsye River

Dearfield
Springfield

CVT

East reach

Back oversreach

E    N

Waser
Hartford
Wethersfield
Nidletown

Moricans or
The Passe Point
The Straights

G

Radulph Johnstons kill
Potts Isle
Magdalena Isle
Shystons

COLONY

The Conecticuts
Country

P

Ninicrofts
Country

Norwich
the Pe

Great Esspous
the Espous

The Waoranacks Country

Tans house
Rupings kill
Kaelysse
Narath hoss

HUDSONS RIVER

The Mouhegans    Country

L    A    N

New London River
Cathorten

Eshers Isle

Fishers
hoeke
high read
Cape read

Sandy point

Greenwich
Stanford
Norwalke
Fairfield
Stratford
Milford
New Haven
Branford

New York

The        Sounds

Plumb Isle
Gardners Isle

Stales Isle

Hemsted

Sheltors Island

L    O    N    G    I    S    L    A    N    D

Amersfort

Massapeag    Conecticut    Mastock    Cushquans    Noyes    Faiersham

# NEW ENGLAND
# BOUND

## Slavery and Colonization

## in Early America

# WENDY WARREN

**Liveright Publishing Corporation**
A Division of W. W. Norton & Company
*Independent Publishers Since 1923*
New York • London

For information about permission to reproduce selections from
this book, write to Permissions, Liveright Publishing Corporation,
a division of W. W. Norton & Company, Inc., 500 Fifth Avenue,
New York, NY 10110

For information about special discounts for bulk purchases, please
contact W. W. Norton Special Sales at specialsales@wwnorton.com
or 800-233-4830

Manufacturing by Quad Graphics, Fairfield
Book design by Lisa Buckley
Production manager: Anna Oler

ISBN 978-0-87140-672-9

Liveright Publishing Corporation
500 Fifth Avenue, New York, N.Y. 10110
www.wwnorton.com

W. W. Norton & Company Ltd.
Castle House, 75/76 Wells Street, London W1T 3QT

1 2 3 4 5 6 7 8 9 0

*to*

*my parents, and my children,*

*and to*

*Joseph*

When the thought of New England is regarded not from a New England or even from an American point of view, but is seen as what in truth it was, a part, and an important part, of the whole thought of the seventeenth century, exemplifying the essential characteristics and struggling with the most importunate problems of the epoch, then and only then can both the provincial and European scene be illuminated.

—Perry Miller, *The New England Mind: The Seventeenth Century*

# CONTENTS

# NOTE ON SOURCES

*New England Bound* is based on seventeenth-century sources. In order not to lose the sense of a world that had irregular spelling, grammar, and punctuation, quotations remain as they appear in the original text, except that superscript letters have been lowered, and abbreviations that would not be intelligible to the modern reader have been expanded or spelled out. Readers may find that passages that seem opaque become clearer if they are read out loud, as was indeed the practice of many early modern readers. All dates have been aligned with the modern calendar, with the year beginning on January 1.

Biblical passages cited in the following pages are from the King James Bible (KJV). While the Geneva Bible could be found throughout the colonies, English Puritans in New England largely preferred the KJV, or "Authorized" version.[1] Each chapter begins with a quotation from Ecclesiastes, a book of the Bible that fascinated, among others, the preeminent Puritan colonist, John Cotton, who was interested always in what he called "mans perverse subtlity in inventing wayes of backsliding."[2]

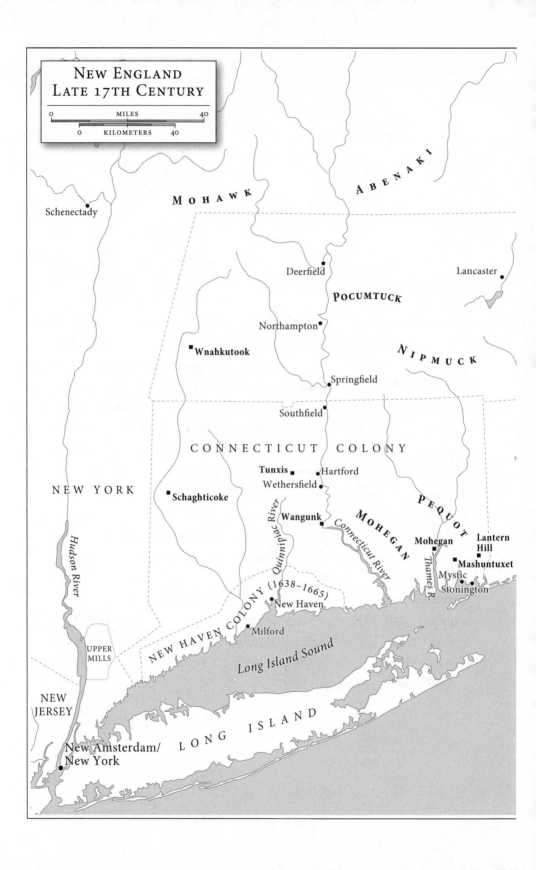

## NEW ENGLAND
## LATE 17TH CENTURY

0 — MILES — 40

0 — KILOMETERS — 40

MOHAWK

ABENAKI

Schenectady

Deerfield

Lancaster

POCUMTUCK

Northampton

Wnahkutook

NIPMUCK

Springfield

Southfield

CONNECTICUT COLONY

Tunxis    Hartford
Wethersfield

NEW YORK

Schaghticoke

Wangunk    MOHEGAN    PEQUOT

Mohegan    Lantern
Hill

Mashuntuxet

Mystic
Stonington

Hudson River

Quinnipiac River

Connecticut River

Thames R.

NEW HAVEN COLONY (1638–1665)

New Haven

Milford

Long Island Sound

UPPER
MILLS

NEW
JERSEY

New Amsterdam/
New York

LONG    ISLAND

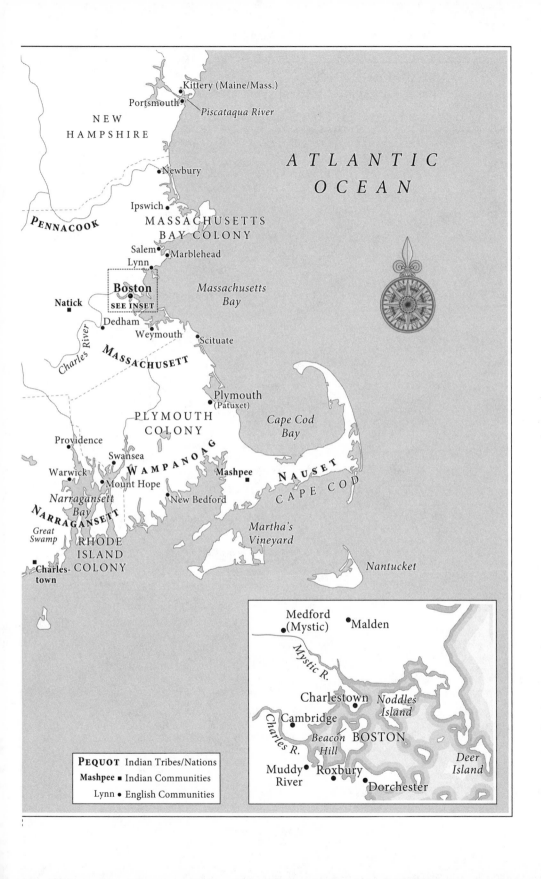

NEW HAMPSHIRE

Kittery (Maine/Mass.)
Portsmouth
*Piscataqua River*

ATLANTIC
OCEAN

Newbury

Ipswich

PENNACOOK

MASSACHUSETTS
BAY COLONY

Salem Marblehead
Lynn

Boston
SEE INSET

*Massachusetts Bay*

Natick

Dedham
Weymouth
Scituate

MASSACHUSETT

Plymouth
(Patuxet)

*Cape Cod Bay*

PLYMOUTH
COLONY

Providence
Swansea

WAMPANOAG

Mashpee

NAUSET

Warwick
Mount Hope
New Bedford

CAPE COD

NARRAGANSETT

*Narragansett Bay*

*Martha's Vineyard*

*Great Swamp*

RHODE
ISLAND
COLONY

Charles-
town

*Nantucket*

**PEQUOT** Indian Tribes/Nations
**Mashpee** ■ Indian Communities
Lynn ● English Communities

Medford
(Mystic)     Malden

*Mystic R.*

Charlestown  *Noddles Island*
Cambridge

*Charles R.*

*Beacon Hill*  BOSTON

Muddy  Roxbury
River

Dorchester

*Deer Island*

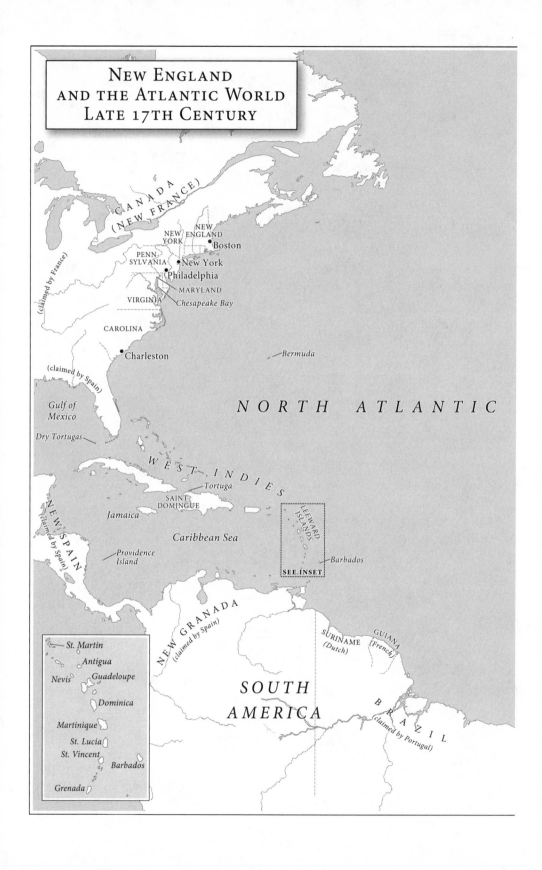

# NEW ENGLAND
# AND THE ATLANTIC WORLD
# LATE 17TH CENTURY

CANADA
(NEW FRANCE)

(claimed by France)

NEW
YORK
NEW
ENGLAND
• Boston

PENN-
SYLVANIA
• New York

• Philadelphia

MARYLAND

VIRGINIA
Chesapeake Bay

CAROLINA

• Charleston

Bermuda

(claimed by Spain)

Gulf of
Mexico

Dry Tortugas

NORTH ATLANTIC

W E S T   I N D I E S

Tortuga

SAINT
DOMINGUE

Jamaica

NEW SPAIN
(claimed by Spain)

Caribbean Sea

Providence
Island

LEEWARD
ISLANDS

Barbados

SEE INSET

NEW GRANADA
(claimed by Spain)

SURINAME
(Dutch)

GUIANA
(French)

SOUTH
AMERICA

B R A Z I L
(claimed by Portugal)

St. Martin

Antigua

Nevis    Guadeloupe

Dominica

Martinique

St. Lucia

St. Vincent

Barbados

Grenada

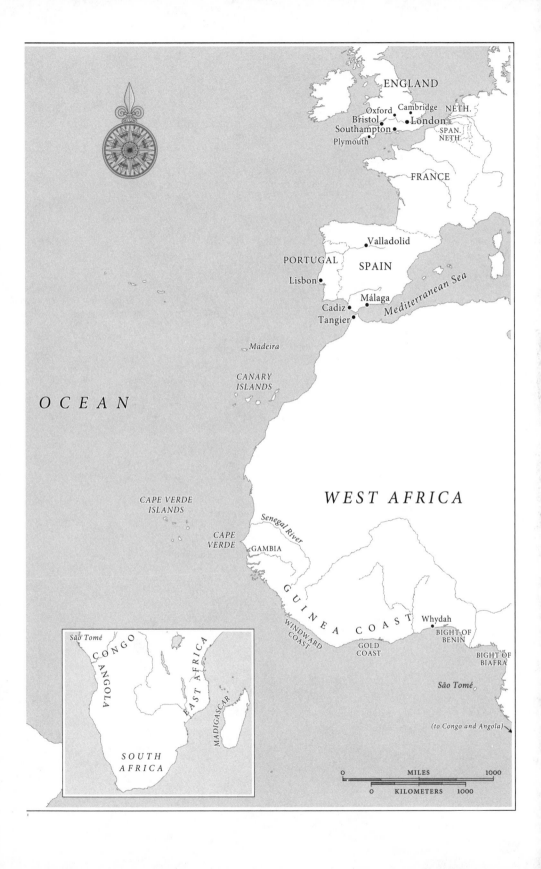

# NEW ENGLAND
# BOUND

# The Cause of Her Grief

For *there is* not a just man upon earth, that doeth good, and sinneth not.
—Ecclesiastes 7:20

T his is a book about two of history's most violent enterprises: slavery and colonization. Both of these problems of course continue to afflict the world, but in the centuries following the Columbian "discovery," they were among its most prevalent features. Between the sixteenth and nineteenth centuries, a period that roughly coincides with the colonial periods of North and South America, nearly thirteen million Africans were enslaved and shipped west across the Atlantic, while two to four million Native Americans were enslaved and traded by European colonists in the Americas.[1] In fact, though, this pairing was no coincidence. Slavery and colonization went hand in hand. Without colonies to grow staple crops like sugar, rice, and tobacco, and to proffer wealth in the form of valuable minerals, there would have been much less need for slaves. Without Indian and African slaves, there would have been no labor to grow the crops or to extract those minerals—at least not labor cost-efficient enough to create the profits that made the whole system viable. It was a deadly symbiosis.

1

That symbiosis fostered the European colonization of all the Americas, including a small region known as New England, a cluster of colonies perched on the edge of England's fledgling North American empire. Colonized in the early seventeenth century by stern people wearing black hats and somber clothes, the popular story goes, New England became an exceptional land of hard work and bountiful crops and thrift and curtness and fervent religiosity. Puritans, we call these fabled people, a sort of shorthand used to describe a motley array of Protestants interested in reforming a Church of England they considered too encumbered by vestiges of Roman Catholicism.[2]

Between the years 1620 and 1640 alone, more than twenty thousand English colonists emigrated to the northeastern coast of North America, where they founded in quick succession the colonies that would become jointly known as New England: in 1620, Plymouth (a colony that later joined with Massachusetts); in 1630, the Massachusetts Bay Colony; in 1636, the colonies of Connecticut and of Rhode Island; in 1637, the New Haven Colony (eventually joined to Connecticut). Some of these colonists were Separatists (that is to say, they sought to separate totally from the Church of England), while some were considerably less radical, but most shared a dissatisfaction with the current state of affairs in English society. In New England they famously, even infamously, sought to live in ways that more closely hewed to a notion of spiritual purity than seemed possible to them in England—they established more than forty meetinghouses in the first two decades alone.[3] By the end of the century, the New England colonies were established, even thriving.

But more than the spirit moved English colonists who went to New England. In fact, historians in recent decades have told a more complicated story, one that highlights how the famed devotion of these colonists coexisted with their very real pecuniary desires, how piety and profit worked hand in hand in the region. And scholars have also long pointed out that English colonists were not all Puritan, and that the English were not the only characters in the story. More recent narratives have emphasized that native people in the region played an equal and crucial role in the colonial encounter, trading commercial goods, religious visions, and agricultural practices with the English, and also warring with them, all groups vying for control of the region's plentiful land and propitious waters.[4] In these ways, the colonization of New England has come to seem more like the colonization of the rest of the Americas.

And yet, even as our understanding of the colonial process in the region has grown more complicated, there has remained something exceptional in both the popular and the scholarly understanding of early colonial New England, an exceptional absence. Put plainly, it is this: the tragedy of chattel slavery—inheritable, permanent, and commodified bondage—the problem that dominates the narrative of so many other early English attempts at colonization in North America and the Caribbean, hardly appears in the story of earliest New England.[5] The following pages demonstrate why it should.

The shadow of an Atlantic slave trade darkened even the earliest interactions between Europeans and Indians in New England, because before there was any large-scale English settlement in the region, there was already enslavement of Indians by English.[6] Take the story of Squanto, the famed Indian guide and translator for the even more famous Pilgrims of Plymouth Colony, those intrepid voyagers on the *Mayflower*. They struggled through their first long winter of 1620 at their rudimentary outpost of Plymouth, along the western shore of Cape Cod Bay, but were approached, fortuitously, in the spring by a Patuxet Indian man named Squanto (Tisquantum, perhaps), who showed them where to find food and game.

How, we might ask, had this deus ex machina learned to speak English well enough to approach the Pilgrims in 1621? The answer is grim: Squanto had been kidnapped in 1614 by Thomas Hunt, captain of a ship under the general but not direct oversight of Captain John Smith, of Pocahontas fame.[7] About Squanto's capture, Smith later recounted that Hunt had "betraied foure and twenty of those poor Salvages aboord this ship, and most dishonestly and inhumanely for their kinde usage of me and all our men, carried them with him to Maligo, [Málaga, Spain] and there for a little private gaine sold those silly Salvages for Rials of eight." Smith was not pleased by this act of kidnapping. He noted that whereas amity had once prevailed, the Indians now had cause for animosity.[8]

Sir Ferdinando Gorges, an early English investor in colonial endeavors, also related the story of Hunt's kidnappings with disdain, and he explicitly identified Hunt's victims as slaves. "It happened," he wrote in his account of the early English explorations of the region, that "there had beene one *Hunt* (a worthlesse fellow of our Nation) . . . who (not content with the commoditie he had by the fish, and peaceable trade he found among the Savages)," kidnapped some of the Indians with whom he had been trading, in such ways acting "more savage-like then they." Having lured them onto the ship, Hunt secreted them in the hold and took them to Europe, "where hee sought to sell them for slaves, and sold as many as he could get money for."[9]

But Squanto escaped that fate. Gorges explained that when it became known where the Indians had come from, Spanish priests intervened and took some of the captives "to be instructed in the Christian Faith," thus thwarting Hunt's hopes for profit with his "new and divelish project" of slave trading. Gorges also noted that Hunt's actions had wider consequences back in North America. Two other Indians, who heard of the kidnapping, "presently contracted such an hatred against our whole Nation, as they immediately studied how to be revenged; and contrived with their friends the best means to bring it to pass."[10] Unsurprisingly, enslavement created enemies. This was a lesson that colonists in New England would repeatedly learn.

Squanto proved adept at navigating Atlantic currents and somehow made his way from Spain to England. There he fell into servitude to John Slaney, the treasurer of the Newfoundland Company, a group chartered to establish a colony that might take advantage of Newfoundland's abundant fishing possibilities. While with Slaney,

Squanto apparently learned English and also looked for an opportunity to return to North America. When his ship sailed, and Squanto finally did return to his home, he found most, if not all, of his family and village dead of smallpox. In a brutal irony, captivity abroad had protected him from the epidemic.[11] But the captivity and the epidemic, of course, derived from the same sources.

Already, then, before the Pilgrims had endured their first winter in the Plymouth Colony, the interlocked gears of colonization and enslavement had forced a Patuxet Indian man across the Atlantic and back, into chattel slavery and out, through two empires' motherlands and, finally, perhaps wiser and certainly worldlier, back to a village that was no longer home because no one was there. William Bradford, governor of Plymouth, later described with delight that "Squanto continued with them and was their interpreter and was a special instrument sent of God for their good beyond their expectation."[12] The Christian God, Squanto might have thought, worked in mysterious ways.

That no colonist ever took the time to marvel at the amazing experiences of Squanto *before* the Pilgrims arrived underscores that such a life was not marvelous, or noteworthy, at least not to the English. So many of New England's initial colonists had experience in overseas ventures, had traveled to North Africa, and had encountered people of various races and ethnicities and nationalities in various forms of freedom and bondage that the man's story probably seemed unremarkable. Before coming to America, the Pilgrims themselves had migrated once already to the Netherlands, a cosmopolitan country full of strangers, and it was from there, not from England, that they departed for New England; many of them spoke Dutch by the time they set out for North America. More to the point, the movement of enslaved and captured people around the Atlantic world also was, by the seventeenth century, an accepted reality.

But if Europeans found Squanto's experience unremarkable, Indians were understandably less sanguine. The Plymouth colonist, and frequent governor of the colony, Edward Winslow, later wrote of encountering an old woman in a nearly empty village who burst into "very grievous" tears upon seeing the English. She cried when she saw them, others explained, because she was the mother of some of the other unlucky men who had been kidnapped with Squanto and who had *not* escaped the fate of slavery. Hunt had taken three of her sons to Spain, "by which means shee was deprived of the comfort of her children in her old age." Winslow's party apologized to the woman, assuring her that they "were sorry that any Englishman should give them that offence, that *Hunt* was a bad man, and that all the English that heard of it condemned him for the same." The Englishmen took pains to distinguish their methods from those of Hunt, promising they "would not offer them [the Indians] any such injury, though it would gain us all the skins in the Countrey." And then as salve, they "gave her some small trifles, which somewhat appeased her."[13]

In historical hindsight, the woman seems quite within her rights to have been only "somewhat appeased," for surely this was a terrible bargain: children for trifles. Though Squanto had survived and returned, this old woman had not shared his luck; she lost three sons in one stroke. Winslow and his fellow Englishmen spoke soothing words and gave paltry gifts, and they presumed to have— "somewhat"—appeased the elderly woman by promising her that they would not engage in such dealings. But their promises proved to be trifling, because over the century English colonists would repeatedly offer such injury to Native Americans they encountered. "Hunt was a bad man" at the moment for Winslow. Really, he was just a man ahead of his time, since decades later Winslow would himself sell an indentured Indian servant to a Barbadian merchant.[14] Still later, members of Winslow's own family would expand the quarry, trading captured African slaves.

They were hardly alone in doing so. The enslavement of Africans began in New England soon after the start of English colonization, proving to be the mirror process of Indian removal. The first documented shipment of enslaved Africans arrived in 1638, eighteen years after the *Mayflower*'s journey. The arrival of those Africans merited a brief mention by Governor John Winthrop, who noted in his journal that the Salem-based ship *Desire* took captive Indians to the West Indies for sale as slaves, returning with "some cotton and tobacco, and negroes, etc., from thence, and salt from Tertugos," thus describing the first known slaving voyage to *and* from New England.[15] It came to seem, to the English at least, a convenient swap.

In that very same year, a man named Samuel Maverick, an ambitious New England colonist, embarked on a related economic venture. He was already the owner of the "fruitful" Noddle's Island, a hilly and marshy landmass of 660 acres in the middle of Boston's harbor, so lush with trees that inhabitants of Boston went there in boats to cut firewood.[16] Maverick had been one of the first Englishmen to settle in the area, and he was among the first in another dubious category: in 1638, he owned three enslaved Africans, two women and one man, and saw cruel possibilities in the grouping. "Desirous to have a breed of Negroes," an acquaintance recounted, and "seeing [that the woman] would not yield by perswasions to company with a Negro young man he had in his house," Maverick ordered that "negro man," whom he also owned, to impregnate her, or try to, by force; the man obeyed. In other words, when the woman would not willingly couple with the man, Maverick ordered her raped. After the attack, the distraught woman came to the window of another Englishman she could hardly have known well—John Josselyn, a temporary houseguest of Maverick's on Noddle's Island—and complained in a "very loud and shril" voice about the assault. The woman "took" the attack, Josselyn noted with concern, "in high disdain beyond her slavery," and it was "the cause of her grief."[17]

Her story demands a pause: only eight years after the founding of the famed Massachusetts Bay Colony, less than two decades after the celebrated Pilgrims founded the equally mythologized Plymouth Colony, an enslaved African woman on an island in Boston's harbor was anguished because another slave had raped her upon their mutual owner's orders, so that he might own a "breed of Negroes."[18] In taking the time to write down her story, Josselyn showed himself to be an at least momentarily sympathetic listener. But the very next paragraph of his narrative recounted, in humorous tones, his first encounter with a ferocious North American wasp. It seems that little was done in response to the woman's complaints. Here, as with Winslow, a woman had expressed her "grief" to an English observer. Here again, that sorrow proved no impediment to colonial determination.

Rather, a grievous process became entrenched over the century. Colonial wars and settlement continued to plunder Indian land, populating the newly acquired territory with English colonists who brought with them the institution of chattel slavery in the form of enslaved African bodies. By the end of the century, enough enslaved Africans had arrived in far-flung New England that the prominent New England colonist Samuel Sewall felt compelled to write that "the Numerousness of Slaves at this day in the Province, and the Uneasiness of them under their Slavery" had led him to conclude that the institution should be abolished altogether. Published in 1700, Sewall's essay, *The Selling of Joseph*, was New England's first antislavery tract. It generated attention at the time, though less for its novelty than for the standing of its author. Samuel Sewall was a Harvard graduate, wealthy Boston merchant, and chief justice of the Massachusetts Superior Court. Only seven years prior to publishing *The Selling of Joseph*, he had served as one of the presiding judges at the Salem witch trials, which had led to the execution of twenty accused witches. These trials and the horrors they wrought still figure somewhere near the heart of the collective memory of colonial New England. Less central to that memory is the fact that prominent among the accused, and crucial to the trials' proceedings, were an enslaved Indian woman named Tituba, possibly from Barbados, and at least two enslaved Africans.[19]

This book focuses on the roughly sixty-year period between the *Desire*'s voyage and *The Selling of Joseph*'s publication, demonstrating how slavery worked in a fledgling colonial society, how it looked, in other words, at the beginning of the English colonial enterprise in North America. In explaining *how* slavery worked at this time, *New England Bound* also emphasizes *that* it worked at this time. Slavery was in England's American colonies, even the New England colonies, from the very beginning. In the seventeenth century, leading colonists like Samuel Maverick, Samuel Shrimpton, Cotton Mather, and John Winthrop Jr. owned slaves, sold slaves, had daily interactions with them, and wrote about the institution of slavery. And while such wealthy New Englanders were more directly invested in the Atlantic slave economy than were their fellow colonists of lesser means, slavery was an ever-present reality even for many of the colony's common craftsmen, sailors, and farmwives.

From Massachusetts to Rhode Island, slavery appeared in the simplest acts of everyday life: enslaved people wore shoes made by local cobblers, they helped English farmers harvest crops, and they worked alongside merchants and traders at the mundane tasks of their occupations. Most colonists in seventeenth-century New England knew of enslaved Africans or Indians. For colonists who lived in larger towns, or near a port, the actual sight of such people might have been a daily one. "You may also own negroes and negresses [in New England]," wrote one European traveler to the region in 1687, for "there is not a house in Boston, however small may be its means, that has not one or two."[20] But slavery was never limited to port towns like Boston; it extended into the New England interior. Indeed, among the first people to die in the famed Deerfield massacre of 1704, wrought on a small town on the western edge of English colonial settlement, were two enslaved Africans.[21]

One of the chief ambitions of this book is to recover some of the lives of those hundreds, even thousands of individual slaves who found themselves living and working in seventeenth-century

New England, unwilling foot soldiers of the initial English colonization campaign, set apart by race and religion from the English, but
brought together by the exigencies of labor. The clearing of trees,
the planting of crops, and the catching of fish that enabled "New
England" to become a real entity, rather than a colonial dream,
required labor, and in New England as elsewhere in the Americas, a
not insignificant portion of that labor was enslaved. Alongside Puritans and Anglicans and Quakers from England, enslaved people not
from England formed families, worked, and struggled, sometimes
for their freedom.

Among them were an enslaved African who worked a side job as
a con artist, an elderly man who sold some of his owner's property
and fled to New York to die among friends, enslaved people who
married and loved and had children, enslaved Indians who protested their banishment to sugar plantations, slaves who set fire to
their owners' houses, and some who stole their owners' silver. Some
enslaved people in the region spoke English, and some did not; some
had Anglicized names, and others carried African or Indian names
their whole lives. Slaves in New England rode horses, managed warehouses, worked as nurses, dug wells, sailed on ships, and toiled in the
fields. By the end of the century, when the English population was
somewhere around ninety thousand people, there were probably fifteen hundred enslaved Africans in the region, and a roughly equivalent number of Indians in some form of captivity, while hundreds
(at a minimum) more Indians had been exported as slaves to English
colonies in the West Indies and elsewhere.[22]

In describing the lives of these people, *New England Bound* deepens
the story of the beginning of colonial North America and the story of
chattel slavery on the continent. The skewing of the study of slavery
in North America toward a relatively short period of time in the continent's long history has created a false impression that slavery and
the antebellum South were synonymous, and that American slavery
was *only* the enslavement of people of African origins. When I ask my

students to describe North American slavery, they inevitably bring up cotton, plantations, the U.S. Civil War, and abolition. But the cotton gin was invented in 1793, and the Civil War began in 1861, meaning that King Cotton reigned for only one human life span of the roughly three centuries that the Atlantic slave trade affected North America. Narratives of American slavery that center on the antebellum era, and culminate in emancipation and abolition unfortunately elide the fact that most generations of enslaved people never saw political freedom enacted. This project instead joins a growing body of work asserting the importance of the preceding two and a half centuries to scholarship on American slavery.[23] The gaze here is on a time when, as one scholar has neatly noted, slaves were mostly "seized, not born."[24] Such a focus underscores that the nineteenth-century divide of a slave south and a free north does not hold for the early colonial period. In fact, in the mid-seventeenth century, the northern English colonies had more slaves than those in the Chesapeake, at least in part because neither, yet, held very many at all.[25]

The great historian of slavery and race Winthrop Jordan once mused, "In considering New England Negro slavery, it might well be asked not why it was weakly rooted there, but why it existed at all."[26] The answer to that question is that the New England colonies were intimately tied, early on, to English possessions where slavery was a central feature of the society, such as Barbados and, later, Jamaica. A huge amount of New England's economy—though sketchy records elide the exact numbers—had direct ties to the West Indies and their sugar plantations. By the 1680s, more than half of the ships anchored in Boston's harbor on any given day were involved in West Indian trade, and almost half of the boats trading in the West Indies had set sail from New England home ports. Profits from West Indian trading helped build, for example, Salem's famous House of the Seven Gables.[27] But these trading trips mattered beyond their economic implications. It turns out that the same colonists trading with the plantation societies in the Caribbean also often had family there, or owned property in both places, and often that property took the form of slaves. New England's early colonists were no strangers to slavery. In fact, the region in many ways depended on plantation slavery—those plantations were simply offshore.

This is not to say there were no differences between the Caribbean colonies and the New England colonies; of course, there were. Most obviously, slavery in New England was, throughout the colonial period, far less deadly than the horrifying form of bondage practiced on Caribbean sugar plantations. But so, too, generally, was slavery in South Carolina and Virginia and New York and Pennsylvania less deadly than sugar slavery. As the historian Michel-Rolph Trouillot has pointed out, when it came to slavery, it was the style of labor that caused great mortality, not the slaveholder's ideology.[28] In fact, slavery in New England had much in common with slavery in other places. Slavery in early New England was most predominant in urban centers, but urban slavery existed in other locations, too. Slavery in early New England largely consisted of smallholdings of individual slaves in individual houses, but that was also true of much slavery throughout colonial North America, and throughout much of history. Indeed, the desperate loneliness of that common situation is a crucial theme running through this book.

Really, almost nothing about early New England's practice of slavery was unique to the region. Chattel slavery worked there as it worked elsewhere in the colonial Americas: people of non-European descent were forced to labor against their will. Their bodies were owned, and their children were owned, and all were sold as commodities at the will of their owners. New England colonists did not invent slavery, but they embraced it. After all, the first known attempt in North America to "breed" African slaves happened in Boston, in 1638, and already the preceding year Indians from New England had been sold into the Caribbean as chattel slaves. The first legal codification of chattel slavery in North America, the paradoxically named Body of Liberties, was written in New England in 1641. And, less famously, more locally, in 1670, a despondent and enslaved African man took a stolen gun to the woods behind his owner's house, stood the gun on its butt, placed his chest on its barrel, and then pulled the trigger. His suicide, by means of a bullet through his heart, happened not in the West Indies, not in Virginia, and not in South Carolina. Instead, his final act—whether a defiant demonstration of his autonomy in the face of a brutal system, or of his submission, or of something else—took place in early New England.

In 1630, John Winthrop wrote what would become the most famous articulation of the Puritan mission to New England, a sermon purportedly delivered to his fellow passengers aboard the *Arbella* sometime as they sailed west from England to North America. Before they ever set foot in their new world, Winthrop warned his listeners that there would be no escaping the importance of their project, for they were headed to New England on a journey for God. And given that, he famously admonished them, "wee must consider that wee shall be as a citty upon a hill." Cities built on hills, of course, cannot be hidden, since their lights shine for all around to see. But such visibility came with a steep price. Winthrop noted, "If we shall deal falsely with our God in this work wee have undertaken, and soe cause him to withdrawe his present help from us, wee shall be made a story and a by-word through the world." A byword: a joke and, worse, a failure. Such was the fate that awaited colonists who faltered in their mission. The stakes could not have been higher.

To avoid that end, Winthrop told his congregation, "we must bee knitt together, in this worke, as one man." Rather than striving for individual glory (a reference to previous methods of colonization, his listeners would have understood), "wee must entertain each other in brotherly affection." In the Massachusetts Bay Colony, he said, no one would be left behind. As members of a community, he reminded them, "we must delight in eache other; make other's conditions our owne; rejoice together, mourne together, labour and suffer together." The result of this communal sacrifice, Winthrop promised, would be divine approval. If the congregation could stay true to its mission, "Wee shall find that the God of Israell is among us, when ten of us shall be able to resist a thousand of our enemies; when hee shall make us a prayse and glory that men shall say of succeeding plantations, the Lord make it likely that of *New England*."[29]

Scholars and the public have long seized on Winthrop's sermon as an exemplar of the pious sentiments of New England's colonists, and of their communal ethos.[30] But emphasizing the communal aspects of the speech requires ignoring the exclusive nature of those crucial words "we" and "us." Winthrop spoke to and for a self-selected group of religiously motivated colonists: "members of the same body," to be sure, but not members of a universal body. Theirs was a necessarily limited group. Without *others*, without people outside the community, who would be left to gaze in awe at this new city on a hill? Whence the point in climbing a hill, if no one remains at the foot to watch? What is the value of salvation without the existence of the damned?[31] And, more pragmatically, how would the colony survive?

The last question was key. As it turned out, it came to be that standing all around the base of that holy hill were numerous enslaved and colonized people on whose backs the holy city was in myriad ways constructed. Messianic impulses alone could not and did not sustain New England; the Atlantic system required more. Colonists like Samuel Maverick, John Winthrop, Samuel Shrimpton, and Cotton Mather came soon enough to learn that lesson, and so too, reluctantly, did the many people whose bodies were traded to and from New England in the process called colonization. A great historian of colonial America once called the "central Puritan dilemma, the problem of doing right in a world that does wrong."[32] What the experience of colonial New England perhaps shows best is the futility of that quest, the impossibility of keeping clean hands in a dirty world. As Ecclesiastes had warned, *"that which is* crooked can not be made straight."[33]

# PART 1

# A
# WORLD
## THAT DOES
# WRONG

# NEGONNE OOSUKKUHWHONK *MOSES,*

## Ne asoweetamuk

# GENESIS·

### CHAP. I.

Eike kutchissik *a* ayum God Kesuk kah Ohke.

*Psal.*
*33.6.*
*& 136.*
*5.*
*Act.14.*
*15.*
*& 17.*
*24.*
*Hebr.*
*11.3.*
*b 2Cor.*
*4.6.*

2 Kah Ohke mô matta kuhkenauunneunkquttinnœ kah monteagunninno, kah pohkenum wolkeche mœnôi, kah Nashauanit popomthau woikeche nippekontu.

3 Onk nœwau God *b* wequaiaj, káh mô wequai.

4 Kah wunnaumun God wequai ne en wunnegen : Kah wutchadchaube-ponumun God noeu wequai kah noeu pohkenum.

5 Kah wutunoweetamun God wequai Kesukod, kah pohkenum wutusoweetamun Nukon : kah mô wunnonkœœk kah mô mohtompog negonne kesuk.

*Psal.*
*136.5.*
*Jer.10.*
*12. &*
*51.15.*

6 Kah nœwau God *c* sepakehtamœudj nœeu nippekontu, kah chadchapem œudj nashauwet nippe wutch nippekontu.

7 Kah ayimup God sepakehtamóonk, kah wutchadchabeponumunnap nashaueu nippe agwu, uttiyeu agwu sepakehtamóonk, kah nashaueu nippekontu uttiyeu ongkouwe sepakehtamóonk, kah monkô n nih.

*d Jer.*
*51.15.*

8 Kah wuttiuoweetamun God *d* sepakehtamo onk Kesukquash, kah mô wunnonkœœk, kah mô mohtompog nahohtoeu kesukok.

*Psal.*
*33.7.*
*& 136.*

9 Kah nœwau God mœmœidj e nippe ut agwu kesukquashkah pasukqunnau, kah pahkemoidj nanabpeu, kah monkô n n h.

*Job 38.*
*8.*

10 Kah wuttiuoweetam n God nanabpi ohke, kah mœemœ nippe wuttisoweetanun Kehtoh, & wu naumun God ne en wunnegen.

11 Kah nœwau God deanuekej ohke noskeht,moskeht kannémunaœk kannéununash, nish noh pasuk neane wuttinnau suonk, kah mahtug meechunmœok, ubbuhkunminnaœk et woikeche ohke, kah mônkô n nih.

12 Kah ohke deannegenup moskeht, kah moskeht kannenennaœk k n nemunash, nish noh pasuk neane wuttinau suonk, kah mahtug meechunmœok, ubbuhkunminnaœk wuhhogkut nish noh pasuk neane wuttinnusuonk,kah wunnaumun God ne en wunnegan.

---

13 Kah mo wunnonkœœk, kah mo mohtompog shwekesukod.

14 Kah nœwau God, *f* Wequanantégi-nôhettich ut wusepakehtamœonganit kesukquash, & pohshehettich ut nashauwe kesukod, kah ut nashauwe nukkonut,kah kukkineatuongaûûhettich , kah ut œcheyeûhettich, kah kesukodtûœwuhhettich, kah kodtumœœwuhhettich.

*f Deut.*
*4.19.*
*á 36. 7.*

15 Kah n nag wequanant´ganuóhettich ut sepakehtamœwonganit wequaiumôhettich onke, onk mô n nih.

16 Kah ayum God neesunash missiyeuash wequanantéganssh, wequananteg mohtag nananun o nœ kesukod, wequananteg peassk nananananomœ nukon, kah an œgqlog.

17 Kah uppônun God wusse pakentamœongtnit kesukquash , woh wequohsumwog ohke.

18 Onk wohg wunnananu wunneau kesukod kah nâkon , kah pohthénœ nashauet wequai, kah nashaueu pohkenum, kah wunnau nun God ne en wunnegen.

*g Jer.*
*31.35.*

19 Kah mô wunnonkœœk kah mo mohtompog yaœu quiaukok.

20 Kah nœwau God, mœnahettich nippekóntu po-no nutcheg po nantamwae, kah puppinihaduisog pu nunahettich ongkouwe oaket woikeche wusepahkehta nœonganit kesukquash.

21 Kah kezheau God matikkenunutche a Pœtâbpoh, kah nish noh po nantamóe ôsas noh pompâ nayit uttiyeug mœnacheg nippekontu, nish noh pasuk neane wuttinnusuonk, kah nish a oh œnuppohwnunin puppisthaath, nish noh pasuk neane wuttinnusuonk, kah wunnau nun God ne en wunnegen.

22 Kah œnaiu noh nihhog God nœwau, Misénee[tu]onictegk, *b* kah muttaanœok, kah nunwapeg k nippe ut kehtohhannit,kah puppin shsog mattianhettich ohket.

*b Gen.*
*8.17.*
*& 9. 1.*

23 Kah mo wunoikœ o k kah mo mohtompog napanna audtahshikquinukok.

24 Kah nœwau God, Pasœwaheonch ohke ôsas po nantamwaeu, nish noh pasuk neane wuttinau sin, neetasuog, pa nayéch g

A     kœ

# CHAPTER 1

# Beginning

Is there *any* thing whereof it may be said, See, this *is* new?
It hath been already of old time, which was before us.
—Ecclesiastes 1:10

C aptain John Smith, world traveler and world weary, seems
the first to have used the name New England, in a narrative
of his initial travels to the region. "In the moneth of Aprill,
1614," he began his account, "I chanced to arrive in *New-England*,
a parte of Ameryca." But it wasn't really chance. Smith was on a
scouting expedition, sanctioned and paid for by the English crown.
Though England came to colonization later than did Spain and Portugal, in the early seventeenth century its efforts gained speed. The
great English trading companies had already been founded: the Turkey Company (which later became the Levant Company) in 1581, the
Muscovy Company in 1555, and the English East India Company
in 1600, among many others. But those companies had looked east-
ward for profits; the opening of the Americas to English colonization
meant that investors could now look west. They did so quickly, reset-
ting their sights on newer, American ventures like the Newfoundland

Company, the Virginia Company, and the Plymouth and Massachusetts Bay Companies.[1]

It was in this context that Smith, already famous for his encounter with Pocahontas, wrote his treatise on New England. Smith's *Description of New England* offered prospective investors a seductive tour of the northeastern coast of North America; even his rhetorical flourishes showed colonizing tendencies. His dedication entreated Prince Charles, heir apparent to the throne, to "change [the region's] Barbarous names, for such English, as posterity may say, Prince Charles was their Godfather." Charles seems to have listened. Thus for Europeans did "Accominticus" become "Boston," and "Aumough-cawgen" become "Cambridge."[2]

"What's in a name?" Shakespeare had asked only two decades earlier. In regard to colonization, the answer was clear: the future.[3] Spain's Queen Isabella had already discovered this in 1492, when presented with a Spanish grammar book, the first such for a modern European language. Upon asking what it was for, she was told, *"Siempre la lengua ha sido compañera del imperio"*—language has always been the companion of empire.[4] Those being colonized still wondered at such presumptuousness long after the Columbian voyages. "Why," one 1647 document records some Massachusetts Indians having asked, do "the English call them Indians, because before they came they had another name?"[5]

While unnaming and renaming were perhaps the easiest part of colonization, fulfilling the dream inherent in the words "New England" was harder. Smith himself pointed out, "It is not a worke for everyone to manage such an affaire as makes a discoverie, and plants a Colony." Such work demands "all the best parts of Art, Judgement, Courage, Honesty, Constancy, Diligence, and Industrie, to doe but neere well."[6] The man knew whereof he spoke, having witnessed the great debacle that was early colonial Virginia, a fiasco that left overly hasty and optimistic colonists dying in Jamestown mud. It was that experience that caused Smith to quickly disabuse readers of any belief that New England offered quick riches and easy sources of profit, such as gold or silver.

Smith insisted instead that the most profitable aspect of the New England lay in its ocean. "The maine Staple," he predicted, "is fish; which however it may seeme a mean and a base commoditie: yet who will but truely take the pains and consider the sequel, I think will allow it well worth the labour." For those who doubted him, he gave the example of the stalwart Dutch, who fished, Smith noted with admiration, "at a great charge and labour in all weathers in the open Sea." These hardy fishers then sold their catch to members of the Hanseatic League, receiving in return products like lumber and tar and rosin, which Dutch merchants then sold to the French, English, Spanish, and Portuguese empires, which needed to build more ships. In the process, the Dutch became "so mighty, strong and rich, as no State but Venice." But the real wonder, to Smith, was that they achieved this great wealth and power as mere middlemen. He marveled that it could be fairly asked of the Dutch, "What Voyages and Discoveries, East and West, North and South, yea about the world, make they?" None, was the answer, nor had the Dutch an army. And still, "never could the Spaniard with all his Mynes of golde and Silver, pay his debts, his friends, and army, half so truly as the Hollanders still have done by this contemptible trade of Fish." The sea, Smith argued, served as a Dutch mine.[7]

New England had plenty of fish to net, too. The problem, as Smith pointed out, was that contemptible cod had no glamour, and it failed to entice many of the people most inclined to risk their lives on colonial ventures three thousands miles from home. That demographic— young, single men—seemed more apt to prefer to seek the glorious sort of immediate wealth that too often proved chimerical, to devastating results, as had happened before Smith's eyes in Jamestown. There, far too many of the early arrivals had been gentlemen well dressed but ill suited to the kind of labor required to create a new colony. Their gentility proved their downfall; unwilling to till the earth and plant the crops, they starved and died. Letters sent back to England were filled with scenes of absolute horror, detailing lives of fighting and starving. One young man wrote to his parents in England, "And I have nothing to Comfort me, nor ther is nothing to be gotten here but sicknes and death."[8] Roughly six thousand English colonists went to Virginia in the first two decades of colonization. Only twelve hundred were living there at the end of that period.[9]

John Smith had little patience with lazy gentlemen looking for easy profits. "More are choked then well fedde," he noted caustically, "with such hastie hopes."[10] As a result, first on his list for success in New England was stamping out the notion of immediate wealth, of quick riches. Hence, his insistence that colonists in New England follow the Dutch example—they would be the suppliers of those empires fortunate enough to have mines and metals and cash crops. They might become rich by association, literally, but that wealth would come from prosaic labor: fishing and farming and loading and selling and shipping. England was not yet "a nation of shopkeepers," but John Smith presciently suggested at least some of its colonies might be.[11] Even the name New England had both grandeur and earthiness. The adjectival portion pointed to lofty ambitions, but the noun was rooted in intimately familiar, if not quotidian, kinds of lives. "England" was, to Smith's readers, a known land of known things, of farmers and miners and fishers and sawyers and coopers and hunters and good wives and tailors and cooks. In the rich soil of such grounded mundanity, he promised, would grow the seeds of success. But what he failed to explain to his seventeenth-century readers, perhaps because he himself did not know, was that success depended on the existence of the slave societies of the West Indies.

Perhaps even more than other voyagers of the time, John Smith had traveled the world with his eyes open. For over eighteen years, he reminded his readers, "I have beene taught by lamentable experience, as well in Europe and Asia, as Affrick, and America, such honest adventures as the chance of warre doth cast upon poor Souldiers."[12] Such travels had offered him a savvy perspective, and if Smith thought New England's profits would derive from cod, sturgeon, and millet, he was probably right. But therein lay the fly in the ointment.[13] It was, and remains to this day, an extraordinary thing to uproot, pack up a life, and move to a new place, one fraught with danger. It was an even more extraordinary thing for middling English families to do, many of whom were farmers, tillers of the land, some of whom had never been aboard a boat. Leave aside the two to three months of harrowing and cramped sailing conditions, the sort of perilous journey that even a century later led to Samuel Johnson's pithy precept "No man will be a sailor who has contrivance enough to get himself into a jail; for being in a ship is being in a jail, with the chance of being drowned."[14] Earlier, an English wit had observed of a trip to New England, "A Man on Board [a ship] cannot but be thoughtful on two Destinies, *viz.* Hanging and Drowning," for ropes were all over the inside of a ship, and water all around the outside.[15]

Moreover, leave aside the dangers faced upon arrival, the hostile inhabitants, the unknown predators, the weather, and the illness, and consider instead the intrinsic emotional cost of moving, of severing the bonds that created safety in an increasingly uncertain world. To take leave in the early modern period meant truly to leave. Long-distance communication was slow, at best, in the seventeenth century. News of the death of a loved one back home might take months to arrive, and a response might take months more to return. Good-byes to aged parents, unwilling or unable to make the trip, could be permanent. Children might never know their extended families. Were the profits of cod worth the costs of such a move? Could people really be persuaded to start lives on unknown continents in hopes of earning wealth as intermediaries in a complicated Atlantic trade? Common sense might say no.

But colonization relies as much on hope as on sense, and the English who eventually colonized New England were famously hopeful, optimistic that their way of colonizing would avoid the mistakes and sins of colonists preceding them. Many of them, though not all, were Puritan, interpreting their move to the Americas in religious overtones and chiliastic terms as an "errand into the wilderness," so described in one famous retrospective rendering of their aim.[16] Like many who do errands, they made lists of how to succeed. "Three things," wrote the Plymouth colonist Edward Winslow (and three-time governor) in 1624, "are the overthrow and bane . . . of plantations." The first, he warned, was "the vaine expectation of present profit," and that expectation's "principall seate in the heart and affection," a position ahead of affection for God. Second, he noted the too-common flaw of "ambition in their Governours and Commanders, seeking onely to make themselves great, and slaves of all that are under them." A sense of community, in other words, would be required.

Finally, Winslow noted the folly of sending too many untested and unfaithful colonists, who were often "endued with bestiall, yea, diabolicall affections." Puritans, he implied, had reason, understanding, and holiness in abundance, and thus they could succeed where others, bestial and diabolical, had failed. Perhaps he was right, though it was also true that New England had little else to offer those English who might incline to devilishness. Its land in terms of precious minerals was barren; its fields could grow none of the cash crops desired by the world market. It turned out to be instrumental that New England was known to hold no easy riches, no immediate profits. In the region, piety and environment seemed a perfect match.[17]

Edward Winslow was hardly the only colonist to New England to espouse such lofty hopes. In 1630, before he even set out for America, John Cotton, the famed Puritan minister (for whom his grandson Cotton Mather, another famous Puritan minister, would be named), traveled down from his home in Boston, Lincolnshire, to Southampton's bustling port. There he offered his blessing and advice in, of course, the form of a sermon, to those colonists, John Winthrop among them, about to head out in the first expedition to found the Massachusetts Bay Colony.[18] Cotton addressed any potential concerns that might be lingering among his listeners. "But how shall I know," he suggested a prospective colonist might ask, "if I be well where I am, what may warrant my removeall?"[19] (That archaic spelling of "removal"—to remove all—underscores the drama of the decision to migrate.) It was a fair question: the Puritans who went to New England were generally from the middling ranks, neither starving nor desperate. Why move?

John Cotton, a man of method, had enumerated answers for his hypothetical hesitant colonist. His first response was that colonists might move to North America simply to gain knowledge. But the accumulation of knowledge, as many scholars can attest, is rarely glamorous or lucrative. Little wonder, then, that Cotton's second and third reasons quickly moved on to address the pecuniary value of colonization. Some, he noted, might go for "merchandize and gaine-sake," a motivation that Christ himself had approved.[20] Along those same lines, others would go simply to find more room, "to plant a colony" because England had become too crowded for them to prosper. Removing for this reason, too, was biblically sanctioned.[21] These were all financial motivations, pragmatic to their core. His last reason, however, spoke of spiritual justifications for colonization.

> Fifthly . . . there be evills to be avoided that may warrant
> removeall. First, when some grievous sinnes overspread a
> Country that threaten desolation. *Mic.* 2. 6. to 11 verse: When
> the people say to them that prophecie, *Prophecy not*; then verse
> 10. *Arise then, this is not your rest.*[22]

"Arise then, this is not your rest," these were the very words the crowds of nervous English people waiting to journey to New England wanted to hear—that they were divinely, the adverb being key, called to remove themselves, to "rest" elsewhere. Add to this the belief of many that England under Charles I had become corrupt and restrictive of the Puritan religion. Cotton was hardly subtle when he alluded to the worship of false idols, a clear reference to the remnants of Roman Catholicism that lingered in the Church of England's ceremonies and rituals, and to the restrictions on Puritan preaching ("when people say to them that prophecie, Prophecy not"). The right decision was clear: departing for a new place was not only preferable, according to Cotton, but also necessary for the two strongest possible reasons: God and profit.

Those were inspiring reasons, but the possibility of failure was high. Shattered dreams and lowered aspirations were common not just in Virginia but all around the early modern Atlantic world. New Englanders knew well that other Europeans had dreamed of a neat spiritual conquest of the Americas. The Spanish, for example, after getting over their surprise at the existence of the Americas, had famously espoused lofty goals of converting the "heathen" souls that populated the continents. But their pious intentions and words did not lead to mass conversion, or to a guilt-free colonization. Nobody, not even Puritan colonists, could dismiss out of hand the failures of such predecessors. It was a tall order, this mission: to establish a successful colony for "gaine-sake" even while establishing a new Jerusalem. Given what colonization involved—the taking of land claimed by one people for the use of another—how could a successful colony be created in combination with a religious mission?

One quick and true answer is that it could not and did not, even in New England, most notably because the Indians in the region were understandably reluctant to give up their land through purchase, or suasion, or violence, to English interlopers. Their own "removeall" needed to occur before the English settlement could solidify, and so their removal became more and more a matter of force. And even if there hadn't been those twenty thousand Indians with prior claims to the region (a neat match for the twenty thousand English who came in the Great Migration), the next and bigger problem to solve would have been the same: how to make the profits that would provide the engine for the colonization process. Where would the money come from, after the initial wave of migrants arrived and settled? Or, how to follow Captain Smith's advice?

Even the historian Perry Miller, once the dean of Puritan studies, dismissed the idea that "piety . . . should have driven its votaries
in solitary flight to the desert and attired them in the hair shirt of
repentance." He explained that the practice of Puritan faith should
in no way be associated with abstemiousness; "in everyday life Puritanism did not mean that because Puritans were virtuous there
should be no more cakes and ale."[23] John Smith, as always, got there
first: "I am not so simple, to thinke, that ever any other motive than
wealth, will ever erect there a Commonweale; or draw companie
from their ease and humours at home, to stay in New England to
effect my purposes."[24] Profits and piety could and needed to go hand
in hand. It would be slavery that made firm that grip, in New England
as across the American colonies.

Captain Smith had perhaps overmanaged expectations, leaving it to
colonists like William Wood, a proponent of colonial New England, to
promote the region and assure prospective immigrants in 1634 that
life in North America held little danger. Wood hastened to insist that
though discouraging reports from the heavily forested region suggested the land harbored "horrible apparitions, fearefull roarings,
thundering and lightning raised by the Devill," such reports were
entirely spurious. A firsthand witness, he promised readers that he
had never seen or heard of any signs of the devil in New England.
Even more tellingly, Wood emphasized that no Indians had reported
such sightings—this despite Indians' notoriety among the English
for being naïve and superstitious. Indeed, he chortled that the only
Indians recently reporting an encounter with the unholy were simply scared at the unexpected sight of a lost "Black-more in the top
of a tree" who had climbed high into the branches to try to spy his
path. The startled Indians, encountering the man, "surmised he was
*Abamacho* or the Devill, deeming all Devils that are blacker than
themselves." The sight of this devil was so alarming to the Indians,
Wood reported, that they entreated some English colonists to find the

evil spirit and somehow to return it whence it came. Those intrepid colonists, girded to find the devil, instead found only "the poore wandring Black-moore, [and] conducted him to his Master."[25]

Wood intended potential colonists to read this story and feel reassured: how silly those Indians! (And thus how harmless!) But this narrative from early New England is far more revealing than what Wood intended. Even if his point was that the scared Indians' demon was simply a black man, in this story, the devil is in the details. Despite Wood's intent, his story nonetheless says, for example, that while the sight of an African was not common in New England in the 1630s to an Indian, Wood himself was not confused or surprised. Instead, the success of his story depends on the existence of English familiarity with Africans, on the shared knowledge between author and his readers of the ridiculousness of the Indian reaction. The story depended on English people's knowing what and who Africans were and, more importantly, what and who they were not: the devil. It required that its readers understand why an African would be atop a tree in the middle of a Puritan colony that had no cash crops, no minerals to be extracted, and none of the features of an economy that might demand chattel slaves. It required, in other words, readers who understood and accepted the existence of enslaved Africans throughout the English Atlantic world.

William Wood's readers did understand this, and quite well, for enslaved Africans were hardly unfamiliar to the English by the start of the seventeenth century. Familiarity had already bred contempt. As early as 1596, Elizabeth I had complained about the numbers of "blackmoores brought into the Realme," noting that there were "all ready to manie [already too many]" and ordering that they be "sent forthe" from the country.[26] The world had become smaller, and to see Africans in New England was no more a surprise than to see them in London, and indeed probably made perfect sense, for it was well known that colonies required labor and that enslaved Africans could provide it.

Not all of it, of course. At first, indentured servants, contracted for specific terms of service, were sufficient, and they came over, as in Virginia, to serve the needs of wealthier colonists. But there were only so many indentured servants who could be convinced for only so long that working crops in the Americas was better than staying home, and only so many who could be dragooned into coming against their will.[27] Attempts to enslave Native Americans for labor in North America proved inefficient and insufficient. The Indians of northeastern North America weren't arranged in large-scale sedentary empires, like those in Central America—they were instead loosely allied groups of disparate peoples, and so far from ideal as a labor force.

The solution was found in other bodies: slowly, all over the colonies, the English started to trade in Africans, including, in small numbers, in New England. By the time of English colonization in the region, an African slave trade had existed for centuries, consisting of African elites enslaving, buying, and selling captured Africans in local networks. Europeans, explained one historian, "remained in profound ignorance of what lay beyond the greater part of the coast." Indeed, coastal African merchants also had "little to do with the trade of the interior, which was in the hands of middlemen."[28] Evidence suggests that Islamic traders from North Africa, aided by their shared language and literacy, controlled most of the complicated and elaborate trans-Saharan slave trade that had already exported millions of enslaved Africans to Europe and Asia and others regions of Africa by the time the English arrived. That institution of slavery looked and was quite different from what would develop in the Americas, but the trade patterns and practices already in existence helped facilitate additional routes to the Atlantic slave trade.[29]

Portuguese explorers and traders entered into preexisting trans-Saharan slave trade networks more than two centuries before the time of English colonization in North America. Strong and skilled sailors with easy access to the Atlantic, the Portuguese began exploring the coast of Africa in the early fifteenth century, hopeful of circumventing North African control of lucrative gold, ivory, and slave trades. African merchants quickly funneled some of the trans-Saharan slave trade to these new buyers. It was a growing market. By 1441, large-scale shipments of African slaves had arrived in Portugal from that region, and throughout the fifteenth century the country received eight to nine hundred slaves a year, destined to work in sugar production or in domestic service. By the middle of the fifteenth century, enslaved Africans formed as much as 10 percent of Lisbon's population, thus continuing a long-held tradition of having domestic servants from Africa. While previously North Africans had dominated these positions, by the mid to late sixteenth century, sub-Saharan Africans formed the majority of domestic slaves.[30] Also by midcentury, the Portuguese had sugar mills in Madeira and on São Tomé, Atlantic islands off the coast of West Africa, worked by more than two thousand enslaved Africans.[31]

As sugar production increased in the African islands and Portuguese colonies in South America (Brazil), so did agricultural slavery.[32] By the 1550s, more than half a century before the English landed in Jamestown, Brazil's sugar production was growing, already heavily dependent on imported Africans as a workforce.[33] Indeed, at the very moment that Europe was generally eliminating slave labor within its own borders, the system was flourishing in European colonies elsewhere, thanks almost entirely to Spanish and Portuguese trade; those Iberian countries were, one scholar has noted, "the transitional link between slavery as it had existed throughout history and slavery as it developed in America."[34] By the seventeenth century, the English were ready to take advantage of that link, joining the rush for land and resources.

That the English had not been in a position to join in the colonization enterprise of the fifteenth and sixteenth centuries should in no way be taken as evidence that they did not want to, or that they were unaware of the progress of their Catholic rivals. Some enterprising English merchants and adventurers even engaged in the African trade while it was still dominated by the Spanish and Portuguese. One historian has estimated that at times in the first decades of the seventeenth century, as much as one-third of the members of England's House of Commons were somehow implicated in colonial endeavors.[35] English traders and merchants, along with the crown, showed intense interest in the use of slaves to further their respective goals.[36]

The prime example is John Hawkins, a merchant cum slave trader well ahead of his time. Born in 1532 in Plymouth, England, Hawkins was the son of a merchant who had led trading voyages to the western coast of Africa and Brazil as early as 1530. Young John Hawkins followed his father's path. Already in 1564, Hawkins described his second slaving trip to Africa as involving stopping on "certain daies, going every day a shoare to take the Inhabitants, with burning and spoiling their townes."[37] He consulted with more seasoned Portuguese traders about the best place to take slaves, hearing in one case of a town that held not only gold but also forty men and a hundred women and children, enough "that if he would give the adventure uppon the same, he might gette a hundreth slaves."[38] Such a ruthless calculus, such a stark assessment of the ratio of defenders to defenseless in the village, suggests both how early the Atlantic slave trade dehumanized Africans and how willingly some English joined that predatory process.

On his third slaving trip, three years later, Hawkins again went to West Africa, again "hoping to obtaine some Negroes." There he and his sailors allied with an unnamed king embroiled in local wars who wished their help in the fighting. They joined him, and took human prizes as their spoils. Having thus "obtained between 4 & 500. Negroes," Hawkins noted, "we thought it reasonable to seeke the coast of the *West Indies*; and there, for our Negroes, and other our merchandize, we hoped to obtaine whereof to countervaile our charges with some gains." Hawkins did successfully obtain his desired gains, by selling the slaves to eager Spanish buyers in the Caribbean, thus completing a transatlantic slave-trading voyage seventy-one years before Samuel Maverick owned and bred slaves in New England.[39] At the end of his second voyage, Hawkins had been granted a new coat of arms featuring, among other images, an African lion and a black slave tied with rope, showing both royal cognizance and approbation of what the man had been up to.[40] Nor was Hawkins the only Englishman who made such expeditions in the sixteenth century. Between 1555 and 1558, for example, the English merchant William Towerson completed three voyages "to Guinea," expeditions marked by repeated encounters with hostile and friendly "negros," and with great fear of the Portuguese.[41]

Such voyages were well known in England, spread by word of mouth and subsequently published in Richard Hakluyt's famous and widely read *Principal Navigations, Voyages, Traffics and Discoveries of the English Nation*, in which narratives about Martin Frobisher, Walter Raleigh, and Francis Drake all described trips to West Africa, and the capture of Africans featured prominently in their accounts.[42] Hakluyt's volumes were followed by the even more popular compilation of travelers' stories from around the world, arranged by Samuel Purchas, an Anglican cleric. John Smith shared manuscript maps of Virginia with Purchas, who also knew early colonists to Bermuda, and who had interviewed Englishmen who had been captured by Indians.[43] By 1617, a third edition of Purchas's work on English colonization attempts had been printed; it described, among other things, links from the slave trade in Angola to lucrative sugar plantations in Brazil.[44] Such narratives had broad appeal and served to instruct the English reading public on the economic relation between high seas adventure, colonial possession, and enslavement. Three years after Purchas's third edition, the *Mayflower* pulled anchor in Hawkins's hometown of Plymouth and set sail for North America.

By the decade of the 1630s, English merchants and mariners were frequent explorers of the west coast of Africa, mostly, it seems, unimpressed by what they saw. Thomas Herbert of London noted, "The Afrique shore runs on in divers names, *Congo* in 6. degr., *Angola* In 9 . . . [all] full of wretched black skin'd wretches; rich in earth, but miserable in demonomy." This negative sensibility carried through his observations, where Herbert clearly showed little love for the Africans he saw. "Let one character serve them all," he said. "They look like chimney sweepers; and are of no profession, except rapine, and villany makes one."[45] This kind of opinion did not bode well for English and African interactions.

But regarding one matter, Herbert was correct: rapine and villainy could and did make a profitable profession, for the English. By midcentury, some independent and private English traders had finally garnered a small piece of the profitable Atlantic slave trade. Slowly, those traders became more insistent, and their advances against their continental competitors culminated in the Royal African Company's charter in 1672, which gave the company a legal monopoly over the entire English slave trade.[46] By 1673, lists of ships freighted by the Royal African Company included some from New England. Historians have cautioned against the false belief that the Royal African Company's monopoly ever existed anywhere but in the minds of the charter's author—competition from private traders and foreign carriers always existed. But the legal act of creating a charter certainly speaks to the crown's feelings about the legitimacy of the slave trade.[47] Indeed, in 1687, a trader at the Royal African Company's fort in Whyddah, on the west coast of Africa, could brag, "It will sound best that this Factory where more Slaves is shipt off then from any one place in the world should be maintained by the Royall Company."[48]

That there was no general English aversion to slave trading and slave owning does not, of course, speak to the specific situation of the English in the New England colonies, many of whom had emigrated precisely because they disapproved of much of the contemporary English culture. So the question remains: did the New England colonists disapprove of slavery? The answer is a resounding no. Puritan theology had no existential distaste for slavery, no more than did Anglicanism, the religion of Samuel Maverick and John Josselyn, among others. In 1617, Paul Bayne, a prominent Puritan author in England, described various forms of servitude, noting that "service" in general was a natural "state of subjection, grounded partly in the curse of God for sin; partly in Civill Constitution." Some people in that state of subjection, he noted, were "more slavish" than others, especially those "whose bodies are perpetually put under the power of the Master, *as Blackmores with us.*" That kind of slavish servant, Bayne explained, sometimes fell into bondage "forcibly, as in captivity [and] sometime voluntarily, as when one doth willingly make himself over [and] sometime naturally, as the children of servants are borne the slaves of their Masters."

Here, then, in 1617, was a Puritan minister articulating the legitimacy of slavery, in stark opposition to a term servitude, which he called the "most frequent kinde of service," in which people served only for set periods, under agreed-upon terms, "such are our Apprentises, Journeymen, maide-servants, &c."[49] His terminology is worth noting, as well. English people in the early seventeenth century only sporadically used the word "slave" to describe people of African or Indian descent in perpetual servitude, in New England or elsewhere. More often, the words "negro" and "negro servant" and, in some cases, "Indian servant" demarcated chattel status for Africans and Indians in the English Atlantic colonies. Counterintuitively, where "slave" was used in New England records during the seventeenth century, it generally referred to English captives held in North African slavery, or even as a figure of speech to connote some sort of debased state.[50] This slowly changed over the century; more than sixty years later, an observer on Barbados would note, "These two words, *Negro* and *Slave* being by custom grown Homogeneous and Convertible; even as *Negro* and *Christian, Englishman* and *Heathen,* are . . . made *Opposites.*"[51]

Semantics aside, early in the century, Bayne already knew and accepted the notion that some people were "perpetually" in service—enslaved—and the example that sprang to his mind was that of "Blackmores," and their situation "with us." Such permanence did not rule all social life for Bayne. The political theorist Michael Walzer has pointed to Bayne as an exemplar of a distinctly Puritan system of

radically contingent thought, in which Puritans' belief in divine calling challenged a traditional political world of "natural hierarchy" by
insisting on the potential impermanence of positions of servitude:
thus Bayne wrote, "When God doth orderly leade us to more free and
comfortable conditions, we are rather to use them."[52] Not so, though,
with slavery. Slavery was perpetual.

Even if a prominent thinker like Bayne could endorse a measure
of social mobility, no Calvinist or any right-minded early modern
English person believed that humans, a category that unquestion-
ably included Africans and Indians, were equal among themselves.
The world, they knew, was organized hierarchically, with God above
and beyond the social order. The rest of humanity and the world lay
below, in the graduated order both natural and necessary for a functioning world. The Massachusetts minister William Hubbard, one of
Harvard College's first graduates, noted that it was not "the result of
time or chance, that some are mounted on horse-back, while others
are left to travell on foot. That some have with the Centurion, power
to command, while others are required to obey."[53] Slavery fit neatly
into this scheme, forming the bottom rung of a ladder that led all the
way up to God.

No less an authority than the Bible confirmed such beliefs. Deuteronomy allowed for the possibility of lifetime servitude, albeit in
the unlikely case of a willing subject.[54] Leviticus gave more explicit
advice, explaining, "Both thy bondmen, and thy bondmaids, which
thou shalt have, *shall be* of the heathen that are round about you; of
them shall ye buy bondmen and bondmaids," and adding that these
servants would serve forever, as would their children.[55] In this view,
so long as the slaves were foreign, they were legitimate.

Undergirded by the Bible and validated by ministers, Puritans
embraced slavery, as did other English colonists, where and when it
seemed appropriate. The clearest example of this embrace occurred
on Providence Island, a Caribbean colony founded in 1630, the same
year as the Massachusetts Bay Colony, by many of the same people.

Puritans looked to the West Indies as well for potential colonies, and with equally lofty ambitions. Some hoped that Providence Island would become the foremost example of Puritan society, a city on a hill with good weather and fertile soil. On that temperate island, proprietors hoped to use slave labor to grow goods destined for a European market. Colonists in Providence Island maintained frequent contact with their peers in New England, comparing growth and progress.[56]

From Providence Island's inception, slaves were crucial, as the founders hoped to grow cotton and tobacco on large plantations. Accordingly, its colonists imported slaves in relatively large numbers; by 1638, when Samuel Maverick was attempting to breed slaves in Boston's harbor, captured Africans made up almost half of Providence Island's population. That racial balance only exacerbated the insecurity the English planters felt in their precarious position, isolated in the western Caribbean, surrounded by Spanish territorial claims. As it happened, they felt insecure because they were. Slaves took advantage of their numbers to flee into the island's hilly interior, settling above its plantations. And then they grew bolder. On May 1, 1638, Providence Island slaves carried out the first slave rebellion in any English colony. Soon afterward, frightened authorities began selling slaves off the island. But despite the sales, when the Spanish conquered the island in 1641, they found 381 slaves and 350 English colonists; the preceding year the governor had warned that the island's slaves threatened to "over-breed us."[57]

New England's colonists, Puritan and otherwise, could not grow the crops that flourished in Caribbean soil, and they never came close to having the proportion of slaves in their population as had existed on Providence Island. Still, they encoded the institution of slavery into their laws almost as soon as there was time to do so. Consider the Body of Liberties from the Massachusetts Bay Colony, written in 1641. Explicitly based on the Magna Charta, the document announced, "It is ordered by this Court and the authoritie thereof, that there shall never be any bond-slavery, villenage or captivitie amongst us; unless it be lawfull captives, taken in just warrs, and such strangers as willingly sell themselves, or are solde to us."[58]

The word "unless" has seldom carried more baggage. Slavery was forbidden *except* for such capacious and ill-defined categories as war captives and legal sales. The Body of Liberties legislation was a joint creation of the prominent colonists John Cotton and Nathanial Ward at the request of Massachusetts's General Court. In the nineteenth century, the historian George Henry Moore observed of this law that it was intended to confirm what was already obvious: the buying and selling of people was a legitimate act, as legitimate as the status of being enslaved. He saw the law as descriptive of a situation that existed, and saw its purpose as "sanction[ing] the slave-trade, and the perpetual bondage of Indians and negroes, their children and their children's children."[59] Despite the legislation's lofty title, the Body of Liberties inscribed bondage into law. This slave code predated and formed the basis for similar laws in places as varied as New York, Virginia, South Carolina, and Barbados.[60]

Nor was Massachusetts the only New England colony to legalize slavery. Connecticut put the institution into its laws less explicitly only five years later. The Connecticut Code of Laws of 1646, published in 1650, made reference to Indian and African slavery as a legitimate form of punishment for wrongdoing.[61] Upon order from magistrates, a "convenient strength of English" could go to an Indian town and "seize and bring away any of that plantation of Indians that shall interteine, protect, or rescue the offendor, onely women and children to be sparingly seized, unless known to bee some way guilty." Ever aware of the potential costs and damage towns faced when they had to feed and clothe criminals, and aware also that Indians who escaped English prisons often "prove[d] more insolent and dangerous" after their experience of incarceration, the lawmakers placed additional strict limits on how long such prisoners could be detained. The magistrates explained that if, after a trial and a guilty verdict, satisfaction for the crime was not rendered promptly by the accused's community, colonial authorities could then deliver the guilty person to their alleged victims, "either to serve [them] or to bee shipped out and exchanged for neagers, as the case will justly beare."[62]

This law made explicit the same painful presumptions that sustained the Body of Liberties. Like the Massachusetts authorities who established that legislation, the Connecticut authorities here did not intend their law to create a new Atlantic slave trade, but rather to describe the one that already existed, and then to use that trade to rid themselves of troublesome Indians. Note what the code takes as unquestioned: the plausibility of a two-way trade, Indians for Africans, and the existence of reliable connections between the region and West Indian colonies, whence the "neagers" would presumably come. Note also that, already in 1650, a rough equality between "neagers" and Indians existed in the minds of some colonists. The one might be exchanged for another, at least according to the Connecticut legislature. It was an aggressive law, with race-specific penalties (English people were not being exchanged for Africans), indifferent to the severing of family connections, and willing to describe humans as cargo to be "exchanged" and "shipped."

If slave codes such as the Body of Liberties and the Connecticut code of 1646 did not create a slave trade, they nonetheless acted to shape their home societies. The legal scholar Christopher Tomlins has argued that during the development of each English colony in North America, something about each settlement changed in parallel order: "the simple presence of *slaves* turns into the presence of *slavery*," and the colony then creates a "regime" to handle the institution.[63] The code of 1646 pointed to a moment in that process in Connecticut: Indians had acted in unruly ways, and their erstwhile rulers then shipped them into Atlantic slavery. In doing so, they started to establish, perhaps unintentionally but not unsuccessfully, a nascent slave regime.[64]

Indians were exported and Africans were imported; early on, New England's ships transported people as chattel goods outbound and homebound again. Smith's advice to the English to be carriers for other nations and colonies may not have been intended to refer to participation in the slave trade, but this too happened.[65] In 1644, for example, three New England colonists, Robert Shopton, Miles Casson, and James Smith, agreed to sail in three ships for Cape Verde, and then to the west African coast, in search of "whatsoever negars, or goods, gold, or silver, or other quality or vallew shallbe equally divided tunn for tunn, and man for man, in each severall ship, in the Country of Ginny." After leaving Africa, they further agreed that they would stay together until they arrived on Barbados, where they would sell their goods and presumably divide the profits. At least one of the ships did successfully return the following year, earning the notice of the Massachusetts Bay Colony's governor, John Winthrop. He duly noted the ship's return in his journal entry of April 1645: "One of our Shipps which went to the Canaryes with Pipestaves in the beginninge of November last, returned now, and brought wine and Sugar and salt, and some tobacco, which she had at Barbados in *exchange for Africoes*, which she carried from the Ile of maio."[66] Winthrop's initial diary entry demonstrated no particular interest in the ship or its exchange of chattel goods for chattel persons. Instead, he seems to have viewed it as just one of many vessels returning to Massachusetts from an Atlantic port with goods for sale.

But the story soon proved to have been far more complicated than Winthrop's bare summary suggested. The governor returned to the voyage in his diary several months later, observing with some disapproval, "The said mr James Smithe with his mate keyser [in the ship the *Rainbow*] were bonde to Guinye to trade for Negroes: but when they arrived there, they mett with some Londoners, with whom they consorted." These London men had claimed to have been assaulted by some Africans on shore, and wanted assistance in seeking revenge. Accordingly, the New Englanders had helped the "Londoners" invite those Africans and others on board their ships "upon the Lordes daye," and then kept them prisoners, an act reminiscent of the subterfuge that had brought Squanto into slavery more than

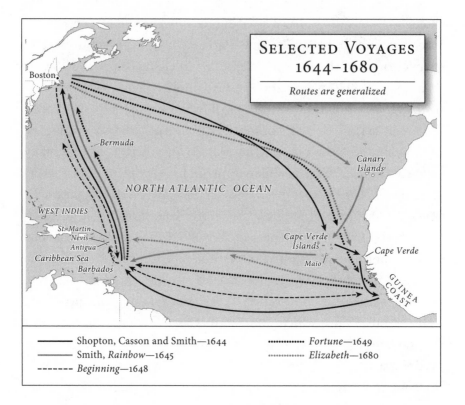

two decades before. While the prisoners were kept on the ships, the English brought a cannon ashore and fired on a town, thus "kill[ing] many of the people." African reinforcements from inland eventually arrived to aid the coastal inhabitants, causing the New Englanders to flee the area with at least two captives on board, leaving in their wake more than one hundred Africans murdered.[67] For all the economic and market-driven aspects of the Atlantic slave trade, such massacres as this one in an African coastal village demonstrated, with deadly spectacle, that there was as much cruelty to the slave trade as cupidity. There was no need to fire on the town, and no coin in this killing, and yet there they were, the hundred dead.

After the massacre, the ship sailed to the tiny island of Barbados, the easternmost of the Lesser Antilles, and first stop for most English ships crossing the Atlantic. There, after an unexplained falling out among the original group of New Englanders, the mate Thomas

Keyser seized the ship and returned to New England without Captain Smith, there to settle the question of goods and bounty. In doing so, the ship and the African captives became Winthrop's headache, because it quickly grew apparent that the captives might have been seized illegally. Richard Saltonstall, the nephew of a former lord mayor of London and now a wealthy New England colonist, outlined the salient facts of the situation: that the ship's captain and another had chased and captured certain "negers," that they had killed many whom they did not take captive, and that all this was done on a Sunday. Saltonstall deemed all of these acts to be illegal for what he saw as obvious and clear reasons. First, both murder and theft, of people or goods, were illegal according to divine and civil law. But, most importantly, he argued that doing any of this "upon the sabbath day (being a servile worke and such as cannot be considered under any other head) is expressly capitall by the law of God." Saltonstall concluded that the parties involved should be swiftly jailed and punished, so that "the sinn they have committed may be upon their owne heads, and not upon ourselves (as otherwise it will)."[68]

Winthrop seemed in full agreement with Saltonstall's assessment of the situation. "For the matter of the Negroes," he observed, "whereof 2: were brought home in the Shippe, and neere 100: slaine by the confession of some of the mariners, the magistrates tooke order to have those 2: sett at Libertye, & to be sente home."[69] Justification for the repatriation relied heavily on Smith's own confession to the court, that "the negroes . . . were fraudulently and injuriously taken and brought from Gynne."[70] One of these men had been sold to Francis Williams, a prominent early colonist to whom Sir Ferdinando Gorges had granted vast lands of Williams's choosing on which to establish a colony; he chose Strawberry Bank (soon to be renamed Portsmouth) at the mouth of the Piscataqua River. In his landmark *History of New-Hampshire*, Jeremy Belknap wrote that Gorges, along with his partner Mason, appointed Williams governor of this short-lived plantation/colony. Another early history suggests that Williams arrived to run the saltworks. Regardless, within months of his attempted purchase of Keyser and Smith's enslaved man, Williams sold his plantation at Strawberry Bank and sailed for Barbados, where eventually he died.[71]

In addition to rectifying what they saw as the illegal kidnapping of these two African men, members of the court further declared themselves "bound by the first opportunity to bear witness agains the haynos and crying sinn of man stealing." To this end, they ordered specifically that one of the returned captives, whom they referred to as the "negro interpreter," carry a letter with him expressing the apologies of the colony.[72] One can only imagine what the inhabitants of the west coast of Africa would have made of such a letter, and what would have happened to a man returned to a slave fort on the coast of Africa with a letter in English from colonial authorities in New England. That probably was not the surest road to freedom. On the other hand, it is hard to think of an easy or better way people might have rectified a transoceanic assault and kidnapping.

It was at least possible to return stolen goods and even people, but the one hundred dead posed a trickier injustice to resolve. Winthrop outlined it thus: as for "the slaughter committed, they [the Massachusetts judges] were in great doubt what to doe in it, seeinge it was in another Countrye, & the Londoners pretended a Just revenge."[73] The enslaving of prisoners and the killing of combatants in a "just war" were of course permitted by the Body of Liberties, and by English law in general, but Winthrop's rhetoric seemed skeptical that there had been a just war, whatever the Londoners pretended. In any event, the matter of African reparation seems to have been dropped.

It would probably be a misreading of this case to use it to assert that New Englanders were inherently averse to slavery. Elizabeth Donnan, an early scholar of slavery, cautioned about the trial that "though Massachusetts protests against the slave trade began at an early date it is hardly possible to ascribe them to this episode, as do some writers." Instead, she contended that the objections to the 1646 events focused on the "violence by which the slaves had been acquired," and that if they had been purchased in the usual way, no furor would have developed.[74] The historian Lorenzo Greene similarly noted that "the alleged repugnance of Massachusetts to slavery is based on [this] single incident," and he further argued that "careful reading of the records reveals that the offense of Smith and Keyser was not slavery but man-stealing." Like Donnan, Greene believed that "had the Negroes been lawfully acquired in exchange for rum, iron, or trinkets, probably no protest would have been made." Making matters worse for the accused, he pointed out, "was the fact that Smith and Keyser, by attacking, killing and kidnapping Negroes on Sunday, had desecrated the Sabbath."[75] Both Donnan and Greene held that this case was an exception rather than the rule, and that slaveholding and trading continued after the case, without a pause. The *Rainbow*, after all, had been openly and legally outfitted in New England for the purposes of slave trading.

But it may also be that Donnan and Greene were too quick to dismiss the significance of the trial. Even as history demonstrates that New Englanders did in general participate, avidly and effectively, in the slave trade, this trial may underscore that the inhumanity demanded by a system such as chattel slavery did give individual colonists pause, even in a world like the early modern world, built on hierarchies of power and violence. And if the existence of Providence Island makes implausible the idea that Puritanism as a system was inherently antislavery, such moments of questioning as occurred in this trial suggest that individual people at times might have had their own doubts, given the right circumstances. Rather than the first stirrings of a long tradition of New England aversion to slavery, the *Rainbow* affair might be seen as a fleeting emergence of conscience that lay mostly submerged in the immensity of the Atlantic slave trade.

So perhaps it matters that in the middle of the seventeenth century some colonists in New England took exception to the task of unloading a ship that had on it two enslaved Africans captured in a violent raid. It matters that, for some reason, the sight of those two enslaved men gave some English colonists pause—certainly it ultimately mattered immensely to those two men. Just so, it mattered that John Josselyn had once hesitated in the face of an enslaved woman's grief over her rape. Whether that hesitation lasted only for a moment or gnawed at him for his entire life, we don't know; but his at least momentary concern caused him to write down her story and entreat her owner on her behalf. Other examples of individuals' wincing in the face of similar cruelty exist as well. Consider the English merchant in West Africa who in 1623 expressed his reluctance to buy enslaved people. Upon being offered as slaves "certaine younge blacke women, who were standing by themselves, and had white strings crosse their bodies," Richard Jobson answered, "Wee were a people, who did not deale in any such commodities, neither did wee buy or sell one another, or any that had our owne shapes."[76] And yet the trade went on, and cruelly so. What was Puritan about the trial was the insistence on rigorous adherence to the law, what was English about the trial was the series of events that led to it, and what was human about it, just maybe, was that it left some people disturbed.

Or perhaps such a optimistic view of humanity is naïve and modern. Contemporaries understood a darker world. "This is the condemnation," the Gospel of John explained, "that light is come into the world and men loved darkness rather than light."[77] The slave trade continued and even flourished. In 1648, only a few years after the *Rainbow*'s crew killed one hundred people in West Africa, the ship *Beginning* departed Rhode Island on a trajectory for Barbados, then to Africa, and from there back to Barbados, then to Antigua, and finally to Boston.[78] The itinerary alone strongly suggests slave trading was intended to be part of the voyage. The next year, the ship *Fortune* set sail for Guinea and then for Barbados, before returning to New England.[79] Again, the route and the calls of port were those of a slave ship, and records show that the following year the *Fortune* did carry at least one slave, a "Negro boy cleare of all Charges."[80] The *Fortune* was owned by one John Parris, a Charlestown (Massachusetts

Bay Colony) merchant. He appears several times in the scattered seventeenth-century records, directly involved with the outfitting of ships to obtain slaves. In 1650, the same year the *Fortune* sailed, he supplied the *Gift of God*, a solid ship of 120 tons, with orders to follow the same general triangular route, with the contractual caveat that none of the sailors on the ship be allowed to "trade for any Negro or Negroes whatsoever." But the captain, as opposed to the sailors, was held to no such rule. Instead, the contract provided that he could "have foure Negroes frieght free, provided he there buy them with his owne goods."[81]

Many outfitters specified that a ship's crew could not buy slaves for personal profit. Without such a prohibition, sailors might distinguish among the human cargo in the hold by feeding their own slaves better, and they might assume a sense of ownership inappropriate to their status. It was much better, from the point of view of an investor, to have all slaves uniformly held by one owner, in this case by Parris (save the four allowed to the captain if the trip was successful). The level of specificity and detail in the *Gift of God*'s 1650 contract thus reflects the sophisticated understanding at least some New England colonists had of the Atlantic slave trade, already in the middle of the seventeenth century.

Even attempts to stop the practice of slave trading and buying serve as reminders that such activities were frequent in the region. Rhode Island colonial authorities, while attempting in 1652 to ban slavery within their colony's borders, acknowledged that they were swimming against the tide. "Whereas," they noted, "there is a *common course* practised amongst English men to buy negers, to that end they may have them for service or slaves forever," they nonetheless sought to ban the practice by ordering that people could not be kept in perpetual slavery. After ten years of service or after an individual's twenty-fourth birthday, the legislature demanded, masters were to set all such servants free, "as the manner is with the English servants." The legislators even instituted a punishment for an owner who felt inclined to ignore the law, decreeing that owners who kept slaves permanently, or sold them away into permanent slavery, would be fined forty pounds.[82] But, like so many laws written contrary to common custom and without strong force behind them, this one was largely ignored.

Why the law, we might again wonder? Was it aspirational, stemming from some antislavery impulse particular to Rhode Island? Was it self-interested, attempting to keep out foreign bodies from the colony? Some scholars have argued that the law was a product of factions in Rhode Island that had less connection to the slave trade than did some inhabitants of its port towns, meaning that it should not be viewed as the colony's general stance.[83] Whatever its origin, the act had no teeth. Rhode Island colonists, like colonists elsewhere in New England, kept African slaves throughout the colonial period. And they kept Indians, of whom the 1652 law made no mention, as slaves as well.

In fact, throughout the remainder of the century, New Englanders steadily increased their role in the Atlantic slave trade. In 1680, Sir Henry Morgan, the famous Welsh pirate cum Royal Navy admiral reported back from Jamaica to the privy council that a New England ship had arrived in port with only two men on board. Those men had testified to Morgan, on oath, that they had traveled from New England "to Guinea, where they loaded with negroes, elephants' teeth, and dust gold, and sailed for Nevis." On their way back, they stopped to resupply at French-controlled St. Martin's, an island on the Atlantic edge of the Caribbean Sea, where their goods were seized. The rest of the crew remained in Jamaica, where the captain was seeking redress for the wrong. Presumably it was his fault they had stopped to reprovision at an unfriendly island.[84]

The very next year, a group of prominent Boston merchants, clearly anxious, to say the least, sent orders to look out for the ship *Elizabeth*, captained by William Warren. The merchants noted that they had outfitted the *Elizabeth* the preceding year for Guinea, giving it orders to return to Swansea, in Plymouth Colony, a port town very close to Providence, Rhode Island. The merchants had heard rumors that colonists in Rhode Island intended to seize the ship and its cargo, and they implored a representative to go to assess the situation and if possible to get Warren to return to Massachusetts. Above all, they ordered the man to make sure to get off the ship "such negroes etc. as he hath of [ours], and come up in the night wth them giveing us notice thereof," adding, "We shall take care for their Landing." Their priority was the slaves, ahead even of securing the ship, perhaps because the human cargo was contraband. The Royal African Company had recently been granted a monopoly on slave trading, meaning this was essentially a smuggling voyage.[85]

Monopoly or no, voyages continued. A ship's doctor from Boston named William Hews shared a grim tale of a 1694 voyage from New England to "the Coast of Guiney." Once there, after engaging in some light fire with a hostile ship from another colonizing European power and taking captives, the ship left for Bermuda and finally arrived in Rhode Island.[86] Along for part of the journey with Hews "were several women on board the ship which they tooke, they were of a swarthy colour, as the men were."[87] Hews did not mention what happened to these captives; he did not need to. Such "man-stealing" may have disturbed New England hearts forty years earlier when the *Rainbow* had made port with its captives taken on the Lord's day, but by century's end, this was ordinary business.

All told, at a bare minimum at least nineteen documented trading voyages in the seventeenth century followed the telltale slaving route of New England to Africa to the West Indies and back.[88] Many more must have gone undocumented, and even more trading voyages carrying slaves went back and forth between the Caribbean and New England, a slow but steady influx. In 1680, Governor Bradstreet, fellow passenger in the fleet that had brought John Winthrop to Massachusetts, and widower husband of Anne Bradstreet, answered a Committee of Trade and Plantations inquiry about the state of slavery in the colony. By this time nearly an octogenarian, Bradstreet declared, "There hath been no Company of blacks or Slaves brought into the Country since the beginning of this plantation, for the space of Fifty years." He could remember only one ship in all that time docking with any substantial number of slaves aboard, a small boat returning from Madagascar that "brought hither betwixt Forty and fifty Negro's most women and Children."

Aside from that one large-scale importation, Bradstreet insisted, the importation of slaves had been slow and sparse. "Now and then," the old governor admitted, "two or three Negro's are brought hither from Barbados and other of his Majesties plantations, and sold here for about twenty pounds apiece." As a result of these sporadic trans-actions, Bradstreet estimated that "there may bee within our Gov-ernment [Massachusetts] about one hundred or one hundred and twenty" slaves.[89] But despite the disinterested tone, Bradstreet was an interested party. Nine years later, when he composed his will, among the chattel goods he listed were two enslaved African women, Hannah and Bilhah.[90] His estimates were almost certainly too low.[91]

In 1708, Rhode Island's Governor Cranston responded to ques-tions from the Board of Trade in London with his own summary of the trade situation in that colony. He held that ships sailing directly between Africa and Rhode Island were rare (he described just one such voyage). Instead, he informed the board, "the whole and only suply of negroes is from Barbados, from whence is imported, one year with another, betwixt 20 and 30, and if those arrive well and sound, the generall price is from £30 to £40." A general "dislike" for imported slaves existed among planters, he claimed, "by reason of theire turbulent and unruly tempers." But there was no need to import, it turned out, because New England's slave population was numerous enough by then to reproduce naturally. Those planters who might have been inclined to purchase slaves, Cranston noted, "are already supplyed by the offspring of those they have already, which increase daly." Anyway, he explained, the "inclination[s] of our people in generall are to imploy servants before negroes."[92]

Cranston probably hoped to exonerate Rhode Island from par-ticipation in the African trade, which was legally controlled by the Royal African Company. But his casual references to various voyages, along with his mention of the reproductive abilities of the slaves, instead underscored that the trade was well established in the colony (and that Samuel Maverick's dream of "breeding" had become reality in some New England colonies). As for the "general dislike" that he described, it stemmed not from a distaste for the institution of chattel slavery but rather, according to him, from the distemper of the "turbulent and unruly" slaves who arrived in New England. Merchants and slave owners there, on the perimeter of an empire, knew that they rarely got first pick of a slave cargo. It turned out to be fortunate, for them, that they could prosper even with the leftovers.

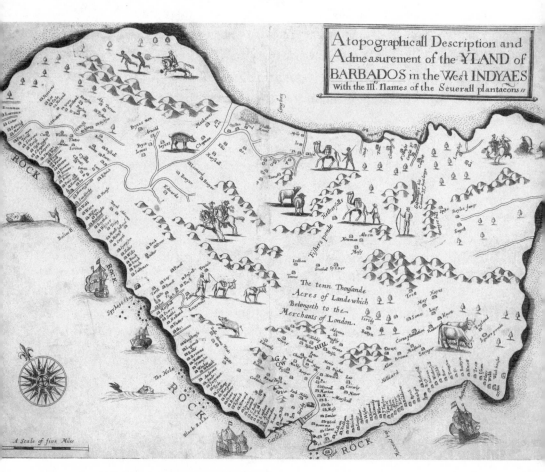

A map of seventeenth-century Barbados, from Richard Ligon's *A True and Exact History of the Island of Barbados* (London, 1673). In the upper left corner, slaves flee a colonist on horseback. *Courtesy of the British Library Board.*

# CHAPTER 2

# The Key of the Indies

All the rivers run into the sea; yet the sea *is* not full;
unto the place from whence the rivers come,
thither they return again.
—Ecclesiastes, 1:7

In 1648, only one year before his death and only eighteen years after he first proposed building a city on a hill, John Winthrop faced the problem of how the colony could pay for his vision. Winthrop, an inveterate diarist, observed to his journal that a recent prohibition on trading guns to Indians, intended to prevent Native American enemies of New England's colonies from improving their military capabilities, had had an unwanted effect: a markedly decreased willingness on the part of local Indians to trade beaver pelts to New Englanders. This created a problem. Indians wanted guns, and when the English stopped offering them, they turned to the French and the Dutch, who would still trade. The unexpected turn of events left New England's colonists empty-handed in their trade with merchants from the mother country, who wanted furs above all else. Winthrop described the situation in stark terms: "Our meanes of Returnes for Englishe Commoditys were growne very shorter."[1]

This specific obstacle was only one in a series that created a general economic malaise in the region during the 1640s. Perhaps the largest problem was the abrupt end to the huge influx of immigrants from England. Starting in 1620, Puritan emigrants, troubled and threatened by the political situation in England, had flocked to American colonies, bringing their liquidated English assets. In 1629, when Charles I dissolved a hostile Parliament, a trickle became a flood. More than thirteen thousand Puritans came to New England between 1630 and 1640. Only when the king was forced to reconvene Parliament in 1640, to raise money for his war against Scotland, did the flow return to a trickle; with Parliament back in session, presumably, Puritans no longer needed to travel three thousand miles to create a new world.[2] Their decision to remain meant that New England's economy could no longer rely on continual injections of capital from new arrivals purchasing the necessities of beginning life in a new country. The historian Bernard Bailyn has argued that the "ending of the Great Migration also destroyed the embryonic economy of the Puritan Commonwealth."[3]

This destruction, however, proved only temporary. Though the diminished trade with Indians meant that New Englanders had less to offer for English goods, and though the decrease in colonists meant capital was suddenly more limited in the colonies, disaster was averted by the emergence of a new source of commerce. The delighted John Winthrop noted that disaster was averted, when "it pleased the Lorde to open to us a Trade with Barbados and other Ilandes in the w[est] Indyes."[4] Down in the Caribbean, the potential profits of sugar were becoming clear, and colonists on the island were forgoing the planting of food and raising of animals on the land that could grow the amazing crop. New Englanders, unable to grow sugar, could instead serve as surrogate farmers and fishers for West Indian planters. The Lord had worked in mysterious ways.

Truly that foreign trade seemed a perfect and providential fit for New England. With the West Indies as seller's market, New England merchants could sell their cattle and fish in exchange for commodities like sugar and tobacco, products that in turn helped them pay debts back across the Atlantic, in England. In a display of perhaps unchristian glee, Winthrop reported that a drought in the summer of 1648 ruined almost all the food crops of the West Indian colonies, so London ships trading in the islands could not have been provisioned for the trip home "if our vessells had not supplyed them." This situation helped New England's reputation as well as its pocketbook, for whereas before "many of the London Seamen were wont to despise New England, as a poore, barren Country," they were now fed with its produce and thus "releived by our plenty."[5] New England had once been disparaged as a region unable to produce a cash crop. Now, as John Smith had predicted, its people proved to be the provisioners and carriers for those islands too busy to provide and carry for themselves because they were so busy making money from the growing profits of sugar, produced by growing numbers of slaves.[6]

Slavery bridged the ocean between New England and the West Indies. The historian Ira Berlin has argued that a crucial marker for understanding the first two hundred years of European settlement in North America is the distinction between a "society with slaves" and a "slave society." In the former, slavery was not necessarily kinder or gentler, but it was "marginal to the central productive processes," making the institution just "one form of labor among many." In "slave societies," by contrast, "slavery stood at the center of economic production, and the master-slave relationship provided the model for all social relations." Using this distinction as a template for understanding North American history, Berlin then argued that "slaves were few in number and marginal to commerce and agriculture in New England and the Middle Colonies."[7] But slavery was only "marginal to commerce" in seventeenth-century New England if the region is examined in isolation.[8]

Examining New England's actual trade flow from beginning to end demotes colonial borders—borders between colonies—from their usual place of importance. Tracing economic connections instead of intercolonial boundaries offers a new understanding of New England's relationship to slavery. To understand New England not only by the labor done within its colonies but even more by the commodities that came and went is to understand New England as John Winthrop did, by its place in its world. To think of the labor behind these commodities—wherever that labor was done—is to understand New England's place in a slave economy. Whether these economic ties between the West Indies and its sugar plantations were fastened consciously or unconsciously, they tugged at all of New England. The vast majority of colonists in seventeenth-century New England lived in port towns on the Atlantic coast or on major rivers, and even farmers who lived inland were often close to major ports and sold their surplus harvests there.[9] The waves of Atlantic commerce lapped far beyond the ocean's shores.[10]

This is not to say that New England and the Caribbean were the same, nor is it to assert that the experience of day-to-day life in New England was identical to that in the West Indies or elsewhere. The regions were different, and, in general, to be an African or Indian or English person in New England was an experience different from that of being an African or Indian or English person in other parts of the globe. The climate was milder in the northern colonies, and so the crops and the labor system were dissimilar. New England blizzards were not at all like Barbadian hurricanes. The towns and markets had their own peculiar sounds and looks, in large part because the human demographics were jarringly distinct: in New England there were more English persons than in the West Indies, fewer Africans, many more Indians.

More noticeable still, to be enslaved in the West Indies was often to have been given a death sentence. The astonishing profits to be made from sugar were perhaps matched only by the mortality rates of the people who grew the crop. From the hazards of cutting the cane, barefoot and with machetes, to the pressures of harvesting, to the dangers of the boiling houses, the plantation production of sugar was among the deadliest innovations known to humanity. As early as 1636, the governor of Barbados declared, *"Negroes* and *Indians,* that came here to be sold, should serve for Life, unless a Contract was made before to the contrary."[11] Such laws were necessary at least in part because the crop was so deadly that no laborer would stay on the island unless forced to do so. Though more than a quarter million enslaved Africans were imported to Barbados, Jamaica, and the Leeward Islands in the second half of the seventeenth century, only one hundred thousand were there in 1700—more than half had died. Sugar made an unyielding master.[12]

But those tangible distinctions between the West Indies and New England do not change the reality that the English Atlantic colonies were part of one economic system, and that the people who lived there also experienced them as such.[13] What made this Atlantic world one was slavery—"what moved in the Atlantic in these centuries," in one historian's words, "was predominantly slaves, the output of slaves, the inputs to slave societies, and the goods and services purchased with the earnings of slave products."[14] And yet, the system made for uncomfortable bedfellows. Even as the English colonists in New England profited from slave labor in the West Indies, they judged their partners. At midcentury a correspondent warned John Winthrop Jr. to be careful how he sent his messages. "I wish," he said, that "you sende your letter per way of London to my sonne and not to trust any that comes this way from Barbados for they are a skum of nations the most part in whom little honesty."[15] This was the contempt of familiarity. But the disdain was probably unfair, for by that time such distinctions between New Englanders and Barbadians had blurred. Thousands of West Indian colonists came to New England during the seventeenth century, including more than one thousand in the years 1643–47 alone.[16]

Colonists in New England and up and down the Americas quickly realized that the West Indies meant money. So did authorities in England. At midcentury, England, working under a general theory of mercantilism—that English trade and money should stay in

English hands—passed a series of Navigation Acts, the first of which appeared in 1651. These acts created a system of trade that excluded other European powers from English markets.[17] Drafted particularly to limit Dutch trade to the English colonies, but never perfectly enforced, the Navigation Acts passed over the century nonetheless gradually benefited the growing colonies in New England by increasing their opportunities for trade and restricting their competition. The passage of such laws again highlights just how integrally New England's growth was helped by a larger imperial design, and also how emphatically the seventeenth century was a time of scrambling for control over, among other things, the Atlantic trade. The colonization of the Americas thus involved not only colonial wars, that is, offensive wars against colonized people, but also imperial wars, that is, competitive wars against other empires that wished to colonize. Between 1652 and 1674, the English engaged in no fewer than three wars against the Dutch involving control of colonial territory and concomitant trade.[18]

Also in the mid-1650s, Oliver Cromwell, ardent Puritan and Lord Protector of the short-lived Commonwealth of England, launched his "Western Design," a plan to capture Spanish colonies in the Caribbean, the better to further both commercial opportunities and Protestantism.[19] In 1656, Cromwell asked the New England colonist Daniel Gookin, recently returned to England, to help in his aims. Gookin published a broadside calling for New Englanders to move to Jamaica, a colony that English forces led by William Penn (the future Pennsylvania founder's father) had recently seized from the Spanish. Gookin offered strong encouragement to potential West Indian colonists, noting that Cromwell's religious sympathies with New England caused him to desire that Jamaica be "inhabited by a stock of such as know the LORD." To that end, Cromwell offered ships and large tracts of land to any New England colonists willing to uproot, as well as "Protection (by God's blessing) from all enemies; [and] a share of all the Horses, Cattle, and other beasts, wild and tame upon the place freely."[20] Some New Englanders took Gookin up on the offer, but most did not. Perhaps as significant as their numbers is the gist of the broadside, which describes a Jamaica safe and familiar, in a West Indies reachable and tamed.

Such schemes to strengthen imperial networks of trade helped New England. By midcentury, the situation could hardly have been better for the region, a place rich in the very commodities needed by the West Indian colonies, where, one observer marveled already in 1647, the English planters were "so intent upon planting sugar that they had rather buy foode at very deare rates than produce it by labour, soe infinite is the profitt of sugar workes after once accomplished."[21] Sugar, like spices in a different trading arena, meant wealth, which was almost better than food, but not quite; colonists could not eat profits, at least not directly. But if New Englanders would grow the mundane crops and catch the fish, West Indian colonists could use slave labor to get on with the job of growing first tobacco and then that most lucrative crop, sugar.[22] With the profits of sugar, English colonists in the Caribbean could buy what they needed to feed themselves and the slaves who produced the sugar that made their wealth.

And so it was that New England merchants and fishers and farmers provisioned the great sugar colonies and over the seventeenth century turned substantial profits in the process. They were savvy exporters, for it turned out that some of the fish they sold to the West Indies was not considered worth eating in Boston. They shipped to the islands the cod rejected by both the local and the European, markets. The exported cod did not improve any from its shipping time to the West Indies, but it went to a captive market—slaves could not easily regulate or reject foodstuffs. In no uncertain terms, then, New England merchants were by midcentury racializing food: products understood to be beneath English standards were deemed sufficient for enslaved peoples in the West Indies. Rotting fish, however unappetizing to European stomachs, was a relative bargain for the feeding of slaves, for it cost so much less.[23] Colonists could pocket the difference.

But the economic bridge between the regions was cemented by more commodities than putrid fish. Samuel Maverick, years after his breeding experiment on Noddle's Island, served as a royal commissioner to Charles II, charged with advising the crown on how to control the Puritan colonies. In a report back to England, Maverick described the strong ties Massachusetts had to the West Indies. "The commodities of the Country [Massachusetts]," he noted, "are Fish, which is sent into France, Spaine, and the Streights." But New England also produced an abundance of other valuable items, including "Pipe-staves, matts, Firr-boards, some Pitch and Tarr, Pork, Beif, Horses and Corne, whch they send to Virginia, Barbados, & take tobacco and Sugar for payment, which they (after) send to England." The Anglican Maverick, who had by then been run out of the colony, bore no great love for colonists still in Massachusetts—"their way of worship is rude and called Congregationall; they are zealous in it, for they persecute all other forms"—but he gave them their due, acknowledging that they controlled the entire coastal trade. Massachusetts, he complained, "has engrossed the whole trade of New England, and is therefore the richest," keeping too much of the profits to itself.[24] But the region itself was very well placed for trade "from and with all parts of the West Indies, and may in tyme on that Account, prove very advantagious to the Crowne of England if Regained, and as prijudiciall if not."[25]

With more enthusiasm, the New England colonist (and unabashed partisan) Edward Johnson reported much the same about the region at midcentury, noting that it could essentially build its own boats, for the land provided tar and masts, as well as food for the provisioning of seagoing vessels. Johnson asserted with a booster's cheer that whereas the area around Boston had been, as he saw it, a wilderness, it was now "wharfed out with great industry" and full of grand and beautiful buildings built, in the wake of experiences with devastating fires, with "Brick, Tile, Stone and Slate," all placed nicely along orderly streets. Johnson directly attributed the continual growth of Boston to its proximity to Atlantic trade, declaring with approval and pride, "This Town is the very Mart of the Land, *French, Portugalls*, and *Dutch* come hither for Traffique."[26]

What delighted Johnson alarmed London. Another report said of the region that its increased autonomy and wealth posed a problem for the English economy. The engrossment of commerce, the author pointed out, "is hugely distructive to Ingland; in many respects which people are in their trade, and navigation; distinct from us; and cannot be called sound members of our nation; in respect to they keepe all the increase of their labors to them selves, and carry away our people."[27] A decade earlier, another English captain returning from Massachusetts, named Thomas Bredon, had already remarked on the same alarming tendencies toward autonomy. He noted that the New England colonies "Looke on themselves as a free state [and deny] having any dependence on England." His observation, made 150 years before the American Revolution, suggests how deep ran the roots of the colonists' independent thinking.[28]

At some point, historians have generally argued, the concept of mercantilism gave way to a nascent system of capitalism. Looking closely at the trade records of midcentury New England indicates just how that transition happened in the daily lives of people living in the rollicking Atlantic world. The captain who complained about New England's ascendancy saw its merchants as enterprising free agents outmaneuvering the mercantilist state. The New England merchants drew their power by bucking the state-imposed economic order and operating instead as the market rewarded. Though the metropole may have regarded the New England colonies as peripheral to the real economic action, it turns out that those peripheral colonies may in fact have driven the move to full-fledged capitalism.[29]

Economic transformation aside, the New England colonists' success had an immediate effect on their sense of duty to the mother country. It seemed obvious to many on both sides of the ocean that it was a small step from economic clout to political disobedience. And that sort of local political impertinence, Captain Bredon warned, was only the tip of England's troubles. Unless the New England colonies were brought under, he argued, they would have too much economic power, for "they being the *key of the Indies* without w[hi]ch Jamaica, Barbados & the Caribee Islands are not able to subsist." He thought England should take command immediately, by making merchants swear allegiance to the crown and he even wondered whether trade from New England might best be embargoed for the time being.[30] This man knew that money equaled power, and that New England was getting the former and thus the latter from the West Indies.

The "key of the Indies" remains such a wonderfully apt metaphor. New England trade opened to commerce what had long been immured, while the commodities New England had to offer served to open the gates to West Indian commerce. This became a comprehensive economic system of products and surpluses and profits, and even in the seventeenth century interested observers saw that New England held the key to the entire enterprise. Likewise, seventeenth-century New England is still a key, now, to making sense of the enslaved labor system of the West Indies. If the logic of the new American market meant that West Indian planters profited by producing ever more sugar, and laying out ever more mono-cropped rows across ever more razed land, these profits were made possible only by Maverick's "commodities of the Country"—the New England beef, pork, peas, and putrescent fish always appearing in time for the West Indian planter class to return its attention to what it knew best. New England commodities provided the energy that was consumed and then burned calorie by calorie in slave labor, converted ultimately into a commodity perfect for the world market.

Despite its global reach, the English Atlantic system began to come together in the most local of ways: through family connections. Indeed, while capitalism often seems distinct from family economy, in this instance and in most of the early modern world, family and trade and money were inextricable.[31] One prime example was the influential Winthrop family, a clan that spread throughout New England and the Caribbean in the seventeenth century. The Winthrops were headed by John Winthrop, who had been born in 1588 into a prosperous English family living comfortably in the small town of Groton, just beyond the bustling orbit of London. Winthrop fell sway to Puritanism early—where and why is unclear—and his religion marked his life in obvious ways, not the least of which was his decision to uproot his family and replant it on a distant continent. In 1630, at the age of forty-two, he left behind his beloved and pregnant (third) wife, their two-year-old son, and various other children and family members, and boarded the *Arbella* to establish the Massachusetts Bay Colony across the Atlantic.[32] Its first years were marked by arduous labor, the cutting and plowing and building always required in any new settlement, and by the martial reality of colonization: that it required wars.

Still, the Winthrop family thrived. In New England, its members cropped up seemingly everywhere. John Winthrop Jr. eventually joined his father, becoming a man of nearly equal prominence, in New England and old, serving as governor of Connecticut for almost two decades and gaining membership in the Royal Society of London.[33] By the age of twenty-four, he had already lived in England and Ireland, and had traveled to Turkey and Italy and around the Mediterranean. His travels had somewhat jaded him; he wrote to his father that he had by then "seen so much of the vanity of the world" that he "in the best, or in the worst, findeth no difference." To his father's idea of moving to New England, Winthrop Jr. simply replied, "I shall call that my country, where I may most glorify God."[34]

John Winthrop Jr.'s own son Waitstill (he preferred to be called Wait) Winthrop became a prominent merchant and magistrate in Massachusetts; Wait's brother Fitz-John Winthrop also served as governor of the Connecticut colony.[35] The elder John Winthrop's second son, Henry Winthrop, emigrated to New England soon after his father and died tragically just a day after arriving. But prior to that, Henry Winthrop had spent time on Barbados. Indeed, key to the Winthrop family's success was that its members not only spread across New England but reached beyond it. John Winthrop's twelfth child, Samuel Winthrop, eventually moved to Antigua, establishing one of the first large-scale sugar plantations on that island. Proof of his prosperity was in his estate; he died owning sixty-four slaves.[36]

John Winthrop. *Courtesy of the American Antiquarian Society.*

John Winthrop Jr. *Courtesy of the Massachusetts Historical Society.*

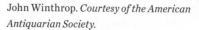

The Winthrops joined the colonial trade early. The first mention of Barbados in the voluminous Winthrop family correspondence came in 1626, four years before the voyage of the *Arbella,* as Forth Winthrop, John Winthrop's third son, asked for news of his brother Henry's trip "to the Indes"—"what place he hath or how and with whome he goeth, for my father wrote to me that he was goinge."[37] This was more than fraternal duty, because family members relied on such news to direct their own decisions. Had Henry found fortune? Forth wanted to know. Or, more to the point, was his venture worth emulating?

Henry was a part of the first English settlement on Barbados. Years before his father was vaunting the Massachusetts Bay Colony's destiny as a city on a hill, Henry Winthrop was writing of Barbados's great prospects. In a 1627 letter to his uncle, he noted that he intended, "god willing," to stay on Barbados to plant tobacco, "which [in] 3 yeres I hope wilbe very profitable to me." He described the island, so far as he saw it, as overwhelmingly English, "save a matter of 50 slaves of Indyenes and blacks." Note his phrasing, and the perhaps reflexive religiosity of the phrase "god willinge," as he imagined himself improving his station.[38] Any prosperity would depend not only on his—and his servants'—hard labor over the coming years but also on the inscrutable will of the Lord.

Note, too, his equally reflexive dismissal of the slave population as insignificant, worthy of mention only as an afterthought, simply a qualification on his point that Barbados was an English island. Alongside imported Africans, many of the first laborers on Barbados were Indians, at least some of whom were brought from the Dutch colony of Guiana. The English captain Henry Powell, whom Maverick may have encountered in Virginia, brought "25 or 26 Indians, men, women, and children, to worke there."[39] Richard Ligon's 1657 account of Barbados included the sentimental story of an "Indian maid" named Yarico who followed her lover, an English youth, from the American mainland to Barbados, where he "sold her for a slave, who was as free born as he."[40] The historian David Brion Davis has pointed out that in eighteenth-century editions Yarico was tellingly transformed into "a Negro virgin."[41] By then, the demographics of Barbadian slavery had changed, and so its folklore had evolved accordingly. But in his 1627 letter Henry Winthrop did not seem to distinguish between Indian and African slaves. There was no need to do so. To his mind, they fit neatly into the same category.[42]

Henry was the family ne'er-do-well, in both love and money. In England, he wooed without permission Elizabeth Fones, the daughter of one of his uncles, letting the courtship proceed so far, the uncle, Thomas Fones, complained in a letter to John Winthrop, that the two had gotten engaged without his "knowledge or consent." Though Thomas Fones remained purposefully unspecific about Henry and his daughter's romance, he minced no words regarding Henry's extravagant tastes, noting with disdain that the young man wore "a skarlet suit and cloke which is lined through with plush which I believe he owes for besydes." Worse, Henry Winthrop was disrespectful: he had told his horrified uncle, "plainly [that if] he cannot have my good will to have my daughter he will have her without."[43] With big dreams and little talent for achieving them, Henry Winthrop fit perfectly the popular perception of Barbadian colonists. "If all whoremasters were taken off the Bench," one contemporary asked with asperity, "what would the Governour do for a councell?"[44]

On Barbados, councillors, whoremasters, and slave masters were often the same men. But young Henry Winthrop, in debt, dressed in scarlet, and pitching unpermitted woo at his cousin, was still the offspring of upstanding people. Were his Barbadian aspirations a repudiation of his family's respectability? Not at all. While the plush-lined cloak and the illicit love back home might have been the bane and the shame of John Winthrop, Henry's dreams of success on Barbados dependent upon slave labor were not. Indeed, the elder Winthrop might have been proud of Henry's accomplishments in the Caribbean, except that there weren't any. He wrote to his son with some frustration in 1629 about some tobacco Henry had sent. The rolls were, he said, "verye ill conditioned, fowle, full of stalkes and evil coloured, and your unckle Fones takinge the Judgement of divers Grocers, none of them would give five shillings a pounde for it."[45]

Low-grade tobacco certainly was not going to ingratiate Henry with his paramour's father. Still, it is worth noting that though both Fones and his own father presumed to lecture Henry on his failures, neither of them was well versed in the constantly fluctuating tobacco market. The prices Fones cited were absurdly out of scale with the 1629 tobacco market, since, as sometimes happened, the bottom had temporarily fallen out of the market.[46] If Henry had been a thrifty young man, divine providence might have been faulted for such misfortune. As it was, John Winthrop wasted no time scolding his prodigal son: "I pray God, make you more wise and sober."[47] Poor Henry never did grow wiser. He died two years later while trying to swim across a river in New England only a day after his arrival, leaving behind his pregnant wife, the successfully courted Elizabeth, Fones's daughter.[48] He had survived the vicissitudes of Barbados only to sink in New England's rough waters. "My sonne Henry, my sonne Henrye, ah poor childe," John Winthrop sadly wrote to his wife.[49]

Henry Winthrop was hardly the only member of the Winthrop family to show enthusiasm for slavery. The Winthrops' early and eager participation in the West Indian market soon led to slave owning and trading. West Indies planters even reached out to the Winthrops to replenish their pool of slave labor. While in Boston, the Bermuda-based colonist William Berkeley wrote to John Winthrop Jr., Henry's brother, regarding a scheme to grow sugar in Bermuda, and asked whether Winthrop couldn't somehow "procure any Indianes to goe over with mee, and send them alonge with this bearer."[50] Procure, not hire. The verb was deliberate, for there would be no pay. It wasn't the first time Berkeley had raised the point with Winthrop. Only two weeks prior, upon telling him that a ship was soon to be sheathed and fitted "to goe for our Iland," he had said, more delicately, "For the Indianes I leaue it to your farther Consideration to doe as you shall thinke fitt."[51]

Not only was he a man who could deliver enslaved Indians, John Winthrop Jr. owned enslaved Africans and also was in direct contact with family, including his brother Samuel, in the West Indies. One in-law, George Downing, wrote to the younger Winthrop in 1645 that Barbados was flourishing, and that the colonists there had "bought this year no lesse than a thousand Negroes; and the more they buie, the better able they are to buye, for in a yeare and halfe they will earne (with gods blessing) as much as they cost." Downing added that a colonist on the island would ideally bring indentured servants at first. With such servants, he explained, "you shall be able to doe something upon a plantation, and in short tim be able with good husbandry to procure Negroes (the life of this place) out of the encrease of your owne plantation."[52] The mastery of indentured servants, Downing understood, was only a step toward the more lucrative goal of owning slaves and the profits that such ownership could bring. Only ten years later, an observer of Barbados wrote that it was populated with all sorts, including "Ingones [Indians] and miserabell Negors borne to perpetually slavery[,] thay and Thayer seed."

He further called the island the "Dunghill" on which England "cast forth its rubidg," offering a less positive view of Downing's thriving planters.[53]

Nonetheless, that dunghill was important to New England. John Winthrop Jr. paid close attention to news from the West Indies, passing it on to friends and relatives in letters and noting it in his diary. He once wrote to a correspondent with the sad news that a ship recently arrived in Boston from St. Christopher's reported the island had been attacked by the French, who "by the helpe of 900 negroes armed by the French they did much spoyle upon the English especially that part upon which the barbarous Negroes fell upon."[54] Winthrop's letters are filled with such details. Part of his interest stemmed from his fear, commonly held and quite warranted, of the French and Spanish, in the Caribbean and elsewhere. Another factor was probably his also widely held and quite rational concern that enslaved people might rise up and throw off their bonds by violence, in the West Indies and possibly also in New England. Even the New Englander who would eventually pen the region's first antislavery tract, Samuel Sewall, knew Caribbean slaveholders and followed West Indian news, taking the time to note in his diary, when a 1686 motion was introduced in London, "that the K[ing] should motion to have all the negroes at Jamaica baptized."[55] In moments like this, when an old Puritan in Boston dipped his pen into ink to write about his king's decree from London regarding enslaved Africans in Jamaica, the Atlantic world could seem very small.

More often, though, it probably felt big and unwieldy, and the most successful way to bridge the divide was through the use of extensive family networks. The Winthrops were hardly the only family to realize this. The Hutchinsons of Boston were perhaps the most notable family of slave-owning merchants. The family's heads of households included two sons of Anne Hutchinson, the famous dissident, and their two nephews, all prominent merchants. Samuel, Edward, Elisha, and Eliakim Hutchinson, along with Samuel and Edward's brother-in-law, Thomas Savage, conducted an almost continuous trade with the West Indies, sending provisions and cattle to the islands in exchange for cotton and sugar, which they sold through a relative in London. Another cousin, Peleg Sanford, a former resident of Barbados and later the governor of Rhode Island, worked as their agent, shipping the Hutchinson family's cattle directly from Rhode Island to his brothers on Barbados.[56] This complicated trade carried on for decades.

Predictably, many family members not only traded with the islands but also owned slaves. Thomas Savage, in 1675, left a will listing as property, among other items, sheets, a silver jug, and an enslaved woman.[57] The father-in-law of Peleg Sanford owned an abundance of "negro" slaves in Newport. They were given small legacies in his will: Abraham received four pounds; Anthony, forty shillings; Ziporah, twenty shillings; Rose, thirty shillings; Samson, twenty shillings; and "my Indian Edom," twenty shillings. Abraham and Anthony, however, were not only recipients of Sanford's estate; they were part of it, for his will granted them their freedom and an additional five pounds, five years after his death, provided they served dutifully and obediently in the interim. His will also mentioned another prominent colonist and friend, as he left livestock to the more famous "Mr. Roger Williams of Providence," no strings attached.[58]

The Winthrops and Hutchinsons were only two of a whole stock of merchant clans to rise in New England's first decades. These families relied on each other for their mutual prosperity. In his landmark history, *New England Merchants in the Seventeenth Century,* the historian Bernard Bailyn describes a startling amount of intermarriage among early colonial merchants:

By the marriages of the ten children of the immigrants William and Edward Tyng those venerable merchants became related to the Bradstreets, Whartons, Brattles, Dudleys, the Searles of Barbados, the Savages, Ushers, and Gibbonses—all merchant families. The Winthrop, Jr. children married into the Palmes and Corwin families, the latter already connected to the Browne, Lynde, and Wolcott clans. Elizabeth and Charles Lidget, children of the mast merchant Peter Lidget, married respectively John Usher, son of old Hezekiah the bookseller-merchant, and Bethiah Shrimpton, daughter of the immigrant brazier Henry Shrimpton. Through the Ushers and the Shrimptons the Lidget family gained kinship associations with the Tyng tribe as well as with the Hutchinsons, Breedons, and Stoddards. The Sheafe and Gibbs families were linked with the Corwins, Brownes, and Winthrops. . . .[59]

And so Bailyn continues for two pages, concluding that the merchant grandchildren and great-grandchildren of those colonists who had arrived during the Great Migration had, through intermarriage, become one extensive family, which in many ways formed the backbone of New England's society, economically and culturally.[60]

Family ties inevitably became slave-owning bonds, since so much of these merchants' energy was spent in the West Indies. Samuel Shrimpton, for example, whose family figures prominently in Bailyn's description of networks, was a powerful merchant and a judge on the superior court. He owned land throughout Boston, including, eventually, Beacon Hill, a small rise in Boston that even in the early 1630s had a signal beacon on it. In 1670, he purchased Samuel Maverick's old home of Noddle's Island, where the enslaved woman had been raped. Shrimpton owned a ship of "one hundred tunns" called the *Elizabeth*, one-sixth of a ship called the *Dolphin*, and one-eighth of a ship called the *Barron*, which had twenty-six guns; he had interests throughout the Atlantic world, and he also owned slaves, including one, "Will Negro," whom he apprenticed to a ship captain, making Will at once a slave and an apprentice.[61]

Shrimpton owned many slaves, in fact. Though in 1677, he duly paid wages for one day's labor to a hired "negro," ten years later he purchased lifelong labor, buying "one negro woman called & known by the name of Betty to have and to hold . . . during the term of her naturall life," along with a copper furnace.[62] More than a decade after that, court documents recorded Shrimpton on the streets of

Boston with yet a different enslaved man. Shrimpton's wife paid a tailor more than four pounds in 1698 for making "negro" clothes.[63] In 1699, a ship captain, John Helden, wrote to Shrimpton in Boston regarding the availability of a slave in Nevis: "I have nott seen any Negro man fitt for that purpose as yett that is to be sold butt hear is expected ships from Guinney dayly & then I shall nott fail to supply you in what is needful from it."[64] The inventory of Shrimpton's estate in 1703 mentions at least one slave boy, worth twenty-five pounds.[65]

Samuel Maverick was one of the first Boston-based merchants to engage in a triangular transatlantic trade. In 1641, Maverick purchased items in Bristol through an agent there, via credits from another agent and other transactions in Spain.[66] Maverick also had strong West Indian ties, even family ties. By the 1650s, his son Nathaniel had gone to Barbados, and from there remained in close contact with his father throughout his life. Maverick's circle of friends included many merchants who did West Indian business, among them William Vassall, an early colonist, also Anglican, who moved to Barbados, and John Parris, the prominent Boston merchant, who contracted in 1652 to deliver a "negro in may next" to Adam Winthrop.[67] Maverick, moreover, did business with Richard Vines, another Barbadian transplant from New England, who in turn traded with Parris.[68] All these men in this close-knit business circle owned enslaved Africans. It was, it seemed, hard to trade with the West Indian colonies without eventually trading in slaves, and it seemed easy, once one traded in slaves, to possess them as well. Even the captain who had possibly carried Mr. Maverick's Negro woman to Boston, Salem's William Pierce, traded and kept slaves.[69]

Shrimpton and some of the others, like Maverick, in the tightly knit merchant circle were, in fact, not Puritan but Anglican. In the slave trade, however, there was no neat divide between Anglican slave owners and traders and their Puritan peers, for they plied the same waters. Simon Bradstreet, the Puritan merchant and sometime governor of the Massachusetts Bay Colony, was a wealthy and powerful colonist, a respected magistrate. He was married twice; his first wife was Anne Bradstreet, the poet. Though Simon Bradstreet's commercial interests were largely centered in New England, he also co-owned a trading vessel with Richard Saltonstall, the merchant who had found fault with Keyser's Sabbath man-stealing. Eventually a lord of some means, Saltonstall returned to England but kept tight ties to both New England and the West Indies. His principled stance aside, his grandson and great-grandson would both make fortunes in the slave trade.[70] Unsurprisingly, given his wealth and his connection to the West Indies, two African slaves appear in Simon Bradstreet's will written in 1689, to be left as property to his second wife, similarly named Ann. She was to receive his "negro woman Hannah and her daughter Bilhah now living with" him, with the caveat that they could not be sold out of the family. Three years later, he amended this will by removing all limitations to the sale of his slaves, granting Ann Bradstreet the right to do as she pleased with them.[71]

Why the initial caveat? Perhaps Simon Bradstreet had intended the initial restriction as an act of benevolence, even a gesture of paternalism, toward Hannah and Bilhah. He recognized Bilhah as Hannah's daughter, Bilhah then as her mother, the two then as a family. His first wife had tenderly written about the raising of her own children.

> I nurst them up with pain and care,
> Nor cost, nor labour did I spare,
> Till at the last they felt their wing,
> Mounted the Trees and learn'd to sing.[72]

Set against such sentiment, the caveat's later redaction seems particularly cold. Whatever the cause of Simon Bradstreet's revision, such codicillary uncertainty underscored the provisory nature of chattel enslavement.

For slavery was a cold business, no matter who managed it. In 1680, the colonist John Winslow wrote a letter to the Governor's Council in Boston, in which he asked permission "to bring up his Negros to Boston." They had been removed from Massachusetts, "ordered to bee sent down into the Islands" to recover from small-pox. Winslow wanted permission to bring them back, not because of any sentimental attachment but for pragmatic reasons. Having both recovered, they were now costing him money: "as they lye yon-der [they] are at a very great charge, damage, and hinderance to your petitioner in the sale of them."[73] In just a short petition lies so much information: the clear implication that New England authorities felt comfortable ordering people to send their slaves to the Caribbean, away from any family and community, for convalescence, while English colonists stayed home to convalesce, despite the identical risks of contagion that they posed. In a sense, the West Indies had become New England's charnel house, for slaves at least.[74]

Missing in his letter is a discussion, or a hint of concern, about how it felt to be an enslaved, sick person sent from New England to the terrifying West Indies. Surely stories of what it meant, in prac-tice, to labor on a sugar island circulated among the enslaved com-munity in New England, and surely enslaved people understood what it signified to be sent there to perish. Smallpox symptoms included, in addition to the obvious lesions and blisters, fever, painful joints, exhaustion, headache, and nausea. It would have been no small mat-ter to board a boat to the West Indies in that condition, dependent for care on Atlantic sailors hardly known for tenderness. We might wonder how it felt to be lucky enough to have survived smallpox, and then to be summoned back to New England to serve the very people who had shipped you off to die. We might ask what it meant, in other words, to be read as disposable and then be repossessed, to be among the select group of people who had traveled to hell and back, and yet still were not saved.

Indeed, the stress of the back and forth or, more commonly, the forth and forth and then forth even more, from West Africa to the West Indies to mainland North America, is too often lost in the terse annotations of these trips, whose quick descriptions belie the dif-ficult undertaking. African slaves left their home continent only after spending, on average, three months in coastal forts where they awaited purchase by ships of various European empires. Their mortality rates even while captive in Africa were extremely high; one in five died before they ever boarded a boat to the Americas, and the experience must have been disorienting, as they were thrust into groups of strangers. Richard Ligon, an early visitor to Barbados, explained why more slaves did not revolt, despite their horrific treatment: "They are fetched from severall parts of Africa, who speake severall languages, and by that means, one of them understand not another."[75] This was in fact a deliberate strategy on the part of slavers. In 1689, another English observer remarked that the way to "keep the Negros quiet, is to choose them from severall parts of the Country, of different Languages; so that they find they cannot act jointly . . . in soe farr as they understand not one an other."[76]

And yet understanding or at least solidarity of some sort was forced upon African slaves during the next stage of their trip.[77] Mortality rates for the middle passage in the seventeenth century ranged from 20 percent to 30 percent during the roughly eight-week journey across the open Atlantic Ocean, as slaves were crammed into the holds of wooden ships. In temperatures sometimes rising above one hundred degrees, the captives jostled for room and somehow steeled themselves for the nightmarish weeks and months to come—though surely none knew just how long they would be on board the boat.[78] Rather than face the unknown horrors ahead and the known terrors at hand, some opted for the only escape available: they threw themselves into the swells, a grim display of human independence.[79]

Most slaving voyages from Africa not headed straight for Brazil stopped first in the West Indies. There slavers attempted to disguise the effects of the transatlantic crossing on their human commodities. Dehydrated, weakened, possibly abused, slaves were brought on deck in the bright tropical sun, where some had their sores masked with a mixture of iron rust and gunpowder. Some slavers hid the omnipresent diarrhea caused by poor and insufficient rations by inserting oakum—hemp treated with tar and used for caulking seams in wooden ships—far into an afflicted slave's anus, far enough to avoid detection during the invasive bodily inspections potential buyers inflicted on the human goods.[80]

Amid these violations and indignities, surely some enslaved people raised their heads and looked in astonishment at the tiny islands on which they found themselves. Barbados, in particular, is a mere speck of land, hilly, wooded, and tropical; an early English traveler to the island, Sir Henry Colt, compared the placement of Barbados in the Atlantic Ocean to a "sixpence throwne downe upon newmarkett heath." To stand on its eastern shore and gaze across the Atlantic is to gaze into an expanse so immense as to be indescribable—there is no landmass at all between Barbados and Senegal, only thousands of miles of rolling gray swells. After facing that immensity, one could turn around and encounter the most mundane of irritations: the land itself, Colt explained, harbored hordes of biting gnats and stinging ants.[81] And still, enslaved Africans quite possibly felt relief to have stayed alive; any land at all probably felt welcoming after the grim, dank sea.

Ship captains were also relieved when slaves survived the trip, and were eager to rid themselves of their cargo as quickly as possible, in order to maximize profits and limit expenditures in the form of food and water. Richard Ligon described sales of slaves in Barbados this way:

> When they are come to us, the Planters buy them out of the Ship, where they find them stark naked, and therefore cannot be deceived in any outward infirmity. They choose them as they do Horses in a Market; the strongest, youthfullest, and most beautifull, yield the greatest prices. Thirty pound sterling is a price for the best man Negro; and twenty five, twenty six, or twenty seven pound for a Woman.[82]

It was surely a terrifying experience to be once again inspected and purchased by strangers. And for some it must have been emotionally draining to see shipmates carted off in different directions without any hope of seeing them again.

But for the enslaved people who wound up in New England, the journey had not ended on Barbados. Most of them had at at some point been forced to board yet *another* boat, this time headed north. We might imagine the horrors people felt upon reboarding a ship, and the memories it must have brought back of the horrendous Atlantic passage that many had already endured. Surely, terribly, some of these reluctant world travelers believed they were going home, having paid their dues in sweat and blood, and so boarded the northbound ships mistakenly believing they were about to repeat the horrendous middle passage. And certainly some must have feared that the next stop would bring even worse than what they had suffered on the sugar islands.

It seems safe, too, to assume that their arrival in New England marked the first time that enslaved Africans were such an undeniable minority of the population, a situation that must have been frightening in its own, different way. How can one assess the emotional toll of such isolation or the pain of such loneliness? In a world where kinship and connections meant everything, what did such solitude feel like? Some contemporaries knew such questions were unanswerable. "It is with God," observed the Puritan colonist John Norton, "that knoweth the heart of exiles to comfort exiles."[83]

These sorts of experiences underlie the impassive detailings of voyages found in account books from the period, such as the listings of the New England merchant Robert Gibbs, which included prosaic costs such as "the hire of the ketch Beaver to Barbados, Mr. Faireweather Master," an abundance of lumber and fish sent down to the island, and additional goods sent to Jamaica. They also listed costs for "two negro girles," as well as debts owed in the form of "an Indian."[84] Another account book briefly mentions "Negros for acct of Mr. John Usher," arriving in New England, and costs including payment to the captain for "passage of 6 negros" (two pounds, five shillings); "Cash for rum and provision for s[ai]d negros" (nine shillings); and Usher's commission (seven pounds, six shillings). The slaves were spoken for before arrival: one colonists bought a woman for twenty-five pounds, another bought one man and two women for seventy-three pounds, and a third took a man and a woman "that he is to have upon tryall for 2 months to pay when accepted," allowing himself a trial period with his new property. In total, they were priced at forty-eight pounds.[85]

The passage between New England and the West Indies was a corridor governed by self-interest, and any other claim of authority was difficult to enforce upon the high seas. A petition by Ruth Knoll, a colonist in Charlestown, protested the seizure of some of her goods in May 1690 by the captain of a ship called the *Swan*. He had, she claimed, carried away to Barbados her "negroman Sambo, by name being young, strong, & able," a loss that caused her severe financial difficulties. The colony's authorities granted Knoll the estimated value of the slave, believing that she had indeed been harmed.[86] Stealing slaves in one colony and spiriting them away to another was fairly common. In 1694, Abraham Samuel, Peter Bowdon, and Erasmus Harrison all stood bound in Boston on charges that Samuel had taken from the island colony of St. Thomas "a Negroe boy named Polydore." The child ended up far north, where he was sold for thirty-five pounds.[87] The accused were all from Massachusetts, placing the crime under that colony's jurisdiction. As in this case, juries often found themselves adjudicating incidents that had happened far from where they sat in judgment.

Sometimes even sales of slaves took place thousands of miles away from the actual physical location of the person being purchased. In 1676, the Boston merchant Edward Bushell sold to Nicholas Shapleigh, of Kittery (Maine), a "Certaine Negro man Called Coffe now in the Custody of John Holder Senr. Living in Scotland on the Island of Barbados." Shapleigh bought the right to "Have and to hold the said Negro called Coffe . . . during the terme of the naturall life of him the said Coffe."[88] In other words, two New Englanders struck a deal in New England for an enslaved man living in a town called Scotland on Barbados. Distance proved no impediment to trading and selling him, though Coffe may somehow have found for himself a bit of stability in Maine. Some twelve years later, the probate record of Nicholas Shapleigh listed "Two Irish boys, one to serve about two yeares and one 3 yeares," valued at ten pounds, and "4 Neagers 3 men one woman and one little Neager all at ninetie pounds."[89] Perhaps one of those men was Coffe. But even if Coffe did find some constancy in Kittery, an enslaved person could, of course, never count on that in this mobile world.

Records, though sporadic and scattered, do hint at a progression: that the first merchant families helped introduce slavery to New England through their close ties to slave societies, and that this introduction then facilitated the slow spread of slavery throughout the region and down through the social ranks.[90] Wealthy merchants, called "gentry" by one historian, had the connections to send Indians into the West Indies, and they used those connections to bring enslaved Africans back to New England as needed.[91] But even if Atlantic commerce and the concomitant slave trading began on the coast, in time colonists not closely related to these merchant clans, and located far from the coast, purchased enslaved Africans.

Bernard Bailyn identified different market regions in existence by 1660. The first were the exceptionally bustling port towns of Boston, Charlestown, and Salem, with powerful merchants who were in constant contact with their peers back across the Atlantic, and whose gaze was directed out of the colony. These trade towns were dominated both economically and politically by such merchants. But there was also a secondary economic world, consisting of smaller port towns, sometimes upriver from the coast, sometimes in lesser harbors. These towns were less imposing in terms of both population and amount of trade, and though such places also engaged in West Indian trade, their size and relative lack of wealth meant that merchants did not dominate the social scene to the same extent. Nonetheless, all those towns, big and small, were supplied by inland market centers where the surplus crops from farmers in the vicinity were collected to be scattered across the Atlantic, including upon the slave societies in the West Indies.[92] Through such webbed connections, the market suffused even inland English communities.

If the Winthrops were typical merchants of the first order, the prosperous merchant John Pynchon, son of William Pynchon, was an exemplar of the last. He lived in Springfield, which his father had founded, relatively far inland from the Atlantic coast, and he continued his father's work of trading inward, into the continent's interior.[93] He also owned at least five African slaves between 1680 and 1700.[94] His position on the Connecticut River facilitated his trade connections with merchants on the coast and in the Caribbean (he traded food for rum), and his ownership of African slaves serves as a reminder that the Atlantic world extended far into the North American continent.[95] The interior trade inevitably traced the long-established trade systems of the Indian people who lived in the region before any Pynchon had planted his feet on North American soil. Not only did the extension of New England trade transform the interior; the indigenous economic and social systems encountered there exerted their own force on the outward-facing aspect of the New England trade system. Transatlantic trade, too, fed on Indian knowledge and experience.[96]

Like the first, powerful coastal merchants, Pynchon possessed vast personal wealth. Given that, and given that large-scale plantation slavery never developed in New England, chattel slavery in New England might be seen as a vanity project of the very wealthy. But it is perhaps a universal truth that the many strive for what the wealthy few already possess. Accordingly, the extension of slaveholding to less prominent families proceeded apace. Logically, wealthy colonists alone could not account for the increasing numbers of slaves in the region as the century wore on, since almost no New England colonist owned more than ten slaves in the seventeenth century. Instead, the population of enslaved Africans swelled because, increasingly, ordinary colonists owned at least one. Slave ownership grew, in a sense, commonplace. Indeed, as trade with the West Indies became the backbone of New England's economy, connections to the West

Indies—and concomitantly, slavery—became a feature of its social landscape. Centuries later, Thomas Pynchon, the famous, reclusive novelist and direct descendant of John Pynchon, would write the following resigned dialogue for one of his characters: "Slavery is very old upon these shores,—there is no Innocence upon the Practice anywhere, neither among the Indians nor the Spanish nor in the behavior of the rest of Christendom, if it come to that."[97] The novelist wrote what his ancestor lived.

Seventeenth-century records are numerous but sketchy; pieced together they create a image of a New England well connected to the West Indies. One contested will involved the Salem colonist Obadiah Antrum, who set out on a voyage to Nevis, from which he never returned, "whereupon it was supposed that he was lost." Since Antrum had a "considerable estate" in New England that required care, the court ordered it taken into custodianship.[98] The settling of the estate of Henry Ball entailed sending clothing and money to Barbados.[99] The Massachusetts will of William Painter, a merchant in Barbados, left property in the form of land and houses and servants, including slaves, in Barbados and Carolina to his wife. He also bequeathed twenty pounds to his mother in Bristol, another twenty pounds to his mother-in-law in London, and books and clothes both on Barbados and in Massachusetts to his brother. His "two Negroes, by name Muddy and Yando," received a suit of clothes and "their freedome for ever," after his wife's decease.[100] The difference in the fates of Muddy and Yando and that of the unnamed "negroes" on Barbados and in Carolina stemmed perhaps from their location in New England, closer to and therefore more familiar to their owner, or perhaps from the disparity between plantation slavery and a more domestic servitude.

Whereas a need for a slave within a home might end with an owner's death, a plantation's need for labor outlasted any individual owner. James White, a Boston merchant, updated his will in 1666. He left to his nephew all his West Indian plantations, including land on Barbados and "all the stocke [and] negroes" belonging to the land.[101] Thirty years later, the probate inventory of Sir William Phips, the first royal governor of New England, and a member of Cotton Mather's church, included part of the ship *Friendship* and "One negro man, boy & woman."[102] Phips kept a hand in the trade with his ownership of the *Friendship*, and he apparently kept a souvenir of his time in the Americas in the form of three slaves. The will of John Hill, "late of Barbadose," ordered that when he died, the inventory be sent to John Winslow in New England, where he wanted his estate's proceeds distributed.[103] Hill's will tied Barbados to Winslow's New England, and a commitment to enslaved labor tied James White to the knighted William Phips.

The West Indies were probably far more key to New England's prosperity than New England was to that of the West Indies. Quantitative studies support this: one argues that "of colonial shipping trading to Barbados in 1686, 80 percent of tonnage was registered in New England, more than a third of it in Boston."[104] A Boston merchant's account from 1688 included charges from England, Boston, and Barbados.[105] The 1679 inventory of the estate of Captain Paul White enumerated both assets in the form of a slave worth thirty pounds and debts owed to his estate on Barbados.[106] Nathaniel Mighill's estate, inventoried in Salem, listed goods in New England, including sundries such as "eleven pair of freench heeld shooes," and goods on Barbados, including sugar, a bed, a chest, and some bedding.[107] John Jones, a ship's carpenter from Newberry in Essex County, Massachusetts, detailed in his will all his goods in New England and one-third of a plantation in Barbados, which he had in turn inherited from his father.[108] The estate included sugar and livestock. William Pearce died in 1678, and in his middling estate in Marblehead were seven barrels of mackerel, to be sent to Barbados; his trade connections outlived him.[109]

Real people facilitated these connections. William Robinson of Salem offered a pittance in his will to his son Joseph, who had moved to Barbados and achieved success there or, as the elder Robinson phrased it, had been "blessed with a liberall competency for his owtward Subsistance." His success on the island reduced the younger Robinson's inheritance from his father, who noted that his sons who had stayed in New England had not made as much money and so now "want more help than he doth." Ultimately, his father left him a mere twelve pounds, to be paid only if the son came back to New England in person to request it.[110] In this case, the father does not appear to have been pleased by his son's removal to Barbados, even if it meant increased riches and prosperity. The Atlantic's colonial trade and plantation slavery provided the engine for prosperity in the colonies, but it also made an old English colonist in Salem die without his son at his side. In this way, if in no other, Robinson's experience mirrored that of millions of African fathers.

And yet, Robinson's disapproval aside, the West Indies clearly provided a safety valve with which New England might vent its idle young men. Indeed, it became the place to send sons, so that they might in turn send money. Eunice Maverick (Samuel's sister-in-law) explained in 1671 that while "riding to Boston with her son Timothy Roberts, they met with Richard Hollingworth upon the road, who inquired for a man to go to sea with him." Barbados seemed appealing to the young man; he accepted the offer and shipped out on an intended itinerary from Boston to Barbados to Virginia to England and then home again.[111] Roberts's lighting out for the sea without hesitation was anything but an unusual choice for an enterprising New England man with few prospects at home—indeed, it may have been a good way to make the necessary connections for a successful merchant life. The trip was not profitable, though, for Roberts, who returned injured after being ordered to work in roiling weather, and had to sue for his wages.[112]

Such stories of misfortune must have been common, and yet, throughout the century, young men went to the Caribbean to make their fortune, with the understanding that they were to send their gains back home. Those who did not share their profits elicited disapproval: a 1659 letter to New England from a mother in Ireland to her daughter in Massachusetts complained that her son "lies at Barbados and sends noe Retorns butt spends all, [and so] his father will have no mor goods sent to him." Sons on Barbados became prodigal by keeping Barbadian profits for themselves. This woman wrote that she was "disolat In a strang land and in dept [debt] by Reason of [Simon's] keeping the Returnes from barbadous."[113]

Colonists (mainly, but not only, merchants) in New England counted, and counted on, the profits of West Indian estates. In a 1672 case involving goods improperly withheld from a Boston estate, the guardians of the estate's heir, John Hands, sued the agent Thomas Clarke for failing to pay for goods received from London in exchange for the sale of "five butts of sugar shipped from Barbados by Daniell Burr."[114] The convoluted nature of this debt network—Boston, London, Barbados—suggests the complicated life experience of those involved, but did not encapsulate it: before his death, the elder Hands had also traveled to and traded with colonists in Virginia and Holland.[115] Noteworthy, too, is the expansion of credit through the advancement of loans to people living across the Atlantic. Some of these goods and people were paid for sometimes with money, currency existing almost entirely of gold and silver coins, but more often they were bought and sold on credit.[116]

To make these exchanges, colonists had to know whom to trust. For the wealthy, this was relatively easy: they had powerful friends and family accustomed to dealing with far-flung business transactions.[117] For the middling ranks, doing such business was harder, and they relied on friends to serve as agents and attorneys.[118] For example, in 1655, William Williams of Barbados contracted his friend Abraham Hagborne, a shoemaker from Roxbury, in the Massachusetts Bay Colony, as his attorney to handle the receipt of any debts coming due to him from people in New England.[119] In such ways were even New England cobblers implicated in the sugar trade.[120]

Attorneys or agents, professional or not, were of great use for such far-reaching transactions. In 1685, Richard Lord empowered his attorney in New England to sue Samuel Willis in Hartford, while both Lord and Willis were living in Antigua.[121] The same year, an Antiguan merchant, John Lucas, signed a contract promising to pay the prominent New England merchants John Pynchon, Samuell Wyllys, and Richard Lord "eighty thousand pounds of good merchentable Muscovado Sugar payable on demand, at the Common place of payment Att willoby Bay."[122] That a bay in Antigua might be a "common place of payment" for transactions with New England merchants only underscores the familiarity of these deals.

Even so, the spiral of debt here was complicated and penetrating: Lucas owed money to both Lord and Willis, and Willis owed Lord. Eventually, Lucas paid off his debts to Willis and Lord by signing back to them an Antiguan plantation called Cabbage Tree that he had leased. In addition to the Cabbage Tree plantation, the court also ordered Lucas to pay Lord and his heirs more than ten thousand pounds of sugar and to return one more crucial bit of property: "four Negro children which were Left upon the Plantation by the sd Willis and Lord."[123]

The New England Puritans' plain style of speaking was never more plain than in such moments, in the blunt designation of children as collateral, not only commodified but also securitized, made into human derivatives in a system that expected repayment of debt.[124] The court even dutifully itemized Lord and company's reparations by name: "one Negro Girle called Combo[,] three boys named Mingo[,] Dick[,] and Jack." We might wonder how old they were, where their parents were, how they had come to be left upon that Antiguan plantation. But the contracts do not address those questions.

What the documents do speak to is the nature of Combo, Mingo, Dick, and Jack's commodification, a more complex issue than their simply being the personal property of a master on a plantation. Rather, a vast system of merchant capitalism made claims on them from far beyond Cabbage Tree plantation. Whether Willis and Lord understood themselves as the absentee masters of Combo, Mingo, Dick, and Jack, or whether they had transferred title to Lucas, they were able to demand the slaves' delivery back to themselves when Lucas proved unable to turn a profit on the plantation. The relationship of creditor and debtor recasts the relationship of master and slave—or at least it serves as a reminder that enslavement occurred at the hands of multiple actors, many of them other than the slave's immediate master.

Similarly, the sale of the four children and the rest of the capital exchanges took place in New England's courts, among men who considered themselves first and foremost New Englanders despite their investment in property, human and landed, on Antigua and Barbados. John Pynchon's role among Lucas's creditors suggests much about the relationship of New England and the Atlantic system of slavery. To think of Pynchon holding slaves in upriver Springfield at the century's end, six decades after Samuel Maverick's breeding experiment in Boston's harbor, is to picture the ocean's slave trade seeping into the country, first in the oceanside port cities and then upriver, far inland. But to think of John Pynchon in Springfield, Massachusetts, holding the power of the purse over a plantation on Antigua, is to imagine instead how the Connecticut River's trade flowed into the Atlantic Ocean and down to the Caribbean. That current allowed Pynchon, along with his fellow New England creditors, to call in an Antiguan plantation's debts when it failed to deliver eighty thousand pounds of that good sugar.

More to the point, yes, John Pynchon owned enslaved Africans in Springfield, Massachusetts, just as Samuel Maverick held slaves on Noddle's Island and the Saltonstalls kept slaves in Boston. But while such personal slaveholding makes for plain evidence of New England merchants' participation in the institution of chattel slavery, it doesn't encompass the scope of their involvement. To examine Caribbean slavery from the documents of a debtor's court in seventeenth-century New England is to ask for whom exactly the children Combo, Mingo, Dick, and Jack labored on that Antiguan plantation.

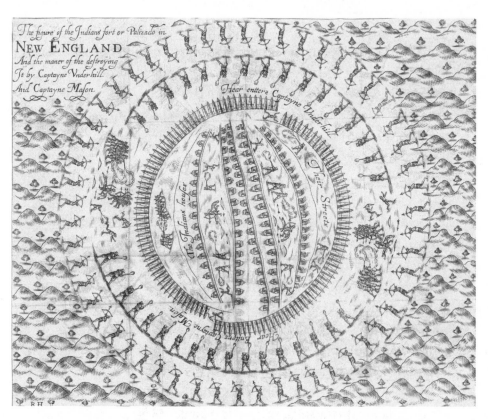

A depiction of the attack on a Pequot village near the Mystic River, as published in John Underhill, *Newes from America* (London, 1638). *Courtesy of the Department of Rare Books and Special Collections, Princeton University Library.*

# CHAPTER 3

# Unplanting and Replanting

A time to plant, and a time to pluck up *that which is* planted.
—Ecclesiastes 3:2

In 1675, a Royal African Company official stationed in Tangiers wrote to administrators in London to ask for instructions regarding an unusual situation. The official, Thomas Hamilton, explained that a ship from New England had recently arrived with "some 30 Indians" on board. Though it was unexpected, Hamilton had accepted the shipment, only to find that nine of the passengers were ill and close to death as a result of poor treatment, leaving only twenty-one likely to survive. The survivors would, he thought, "prove very good men and in my opinion as good if not better than the Moorish slaves." In fact, the shipment's grim mortality rate hardly proved daunting to Hamilton's entrepreneurial dreams. He noted with some eagerness, "If there were every yeare a Recruit from those parts . . . itt might be very advantageous for his Majesties service."[1] This English agent, then, understood that the Atlantic trade in human bodies need not only flow west. He was hardly the first to come to that understanding. By 1675, New England's inhabitants—Indian, European, and African—had known it for many decades.

Before European colonization began, somewhere between 126,000 and 144,000 Indians lived in the area that John Smith would call New England, divided into hundreds of polities, and at least five different language groups.[2] Daniel Gookin, the superintendent of Indian affairs in Massachusetts, described the native people of the region as such: "The principal nations of the Indians, that did, and do, inhabit within the confines of New England, are five: 1. Pequots, 2. Narragansitts; 3. Pawkunnawkuts; 4. Massachusetts; and 5. Pawtuckets."[3] To accept Gookin's conclusion of five distinct nations (a conclusion that radically underplays the number of nations that existed at the time Gookin wrote) is already to glimpse a situation far more complex than "Indian" versus "English." The northeastern coast of North America was in fact populated by many people relatively foreign to each other long before any Europeans arrived.[4] In a sense, then, the arrival of Europeans to the area simply added one more group to an already diverse region. But that new group came with the ambition of colonization, a motivation that made their arrival a very different sort of encounter.

The term "colony" is old, derived from the Latin *colonia*, the legal term used by the Roman Empire to describe the situation of Romans in recently conquered territory; being in a *colonia* meant, crucially, that such people remained Roman citizens, despite being surrounded by hostile people.[5] London was originally a Roman *colonia*—an island of civilization surrounded by, in Roman minds, savage people. New England fit the definition, too: a precarious settlement of English citizens surrounded by antagonistic people. Plymouth Plantation isn't often remembered as a garrison, but it essentially was, for it was surrounded by wooden palisades and had a watchtower. Indeed, many of the earliest male colonists in New England had military experience, many of the earliest towns had fortifications, and most of the earliest colonial households kept weapons.

Consider the list of "armes" purchased in England to be brought over to New England by the first Massachusetts Bay colonists. Among other things, the list included:

80 bastard musketts, with snaphances, 4 ffoote in the barrill, without rests;

06 longe ffowlinge peeces, with muskett boare, 6 foote longe, ½;

4 longe ffowlinge peeces, with bastard muskett boare, 5½ foote longe;

10 ffull musketts, 4 foote barrill, with matchcocks and rests;

90 bandeleeres, for the musketts, ech with a bullett bag;

10 horne fflaskes, for the longe fowling peeces, to hould a 1 a peece; & 100 swoordes x and belts;

60 cosletts, & 60 pikes; 20 halffe pikes;

12 blls powder, 8 barrills for the forte,

4 ffor small shott;

shott, 1lb to a bandeleere

8 peecs of land ordnance for the forte . . .

For great shott, a ffitt preportion to the ordnance.[6]

No colonists went hunting with "100 swoordes x and belts." Though the French, Dutch, and Spanish presented real concerns, Indians were the primary reason for such munitions and fortifications.

The very seal of the Massachusetts Bay Colony, designed in 1629, suggested how much the new arrivals had Native Americans on their minds. In it, an Indian stands, mostly naked, weapons pointed down, with *English* words coming out of his mouth: "Come Over and Help Us." The biggest assistance the English could offer, in their own minds at least, was the ultimate help: salvation in the form of Christianity. But it seems unlikely New England's Indians were calling for such help from across the ocean. Four centuries later, the seal seems naïve at best, a reflection perhaps of the loftiest hopes of some of the colony's proponents, and disingenuous at worst, a misdirection from the more realistic but less noble assessment that colonists had come to help themselves.

Contemporaries recognized the likelihood that colonization would cause the displacement of people. Francis Bacon, the prominent English philosopher, had written early in the seventeenth

The 1629 seal of the Massachusetts Bay Colony. *Courtesy of
the Office of the Secretary of the
Commonwealth of Massachusetts.*

century, "I like a *Plantation* in a pure Soil, that is, where People are
not *Displanted*, to the end, to *Plant* in others." Displanting (that is,
removing) people, he observed, could not be peaceful; doing so,
obviously, "is rather an Extirpation, then a *Plantation*."[7] Bacon's language serves as a reminder that the term "plantation," which later
came predominantly to signify large estates producing crops with
slave labor, in the seventeenth century predominantly meant settlement in a conquered country. That is, "plantation" was a synonym
for "colony," a prescient parallelism. When William Bradford, Mayflower Compact signatory and habitual Plymouth governor, titled
his journal of the colony's earliest days, he wrote "of plimoth plantation." When Captain John Smith offered his wisdom regarding
how "to erect a plantation," he suggested that he was writing for the
"planters of New England."

Thomas Hobbes, the great political theorist of the same century, had a more capacious definition of "plantation" than Bacon's,

explaining that *"Plantations, or Colonies,"* came about when "numbers of men [were] sent" from a land "to inhabit a Forraign Country, either formerly voyd of Inhabitants, or *made voyd then,* by warre."[8] Hobbes's plantation was Bacon's extirpation. Whether Bacon was realistic in hoping for planting without displanting or Hobbes was more accurate in assuming that the two went together, both were concerned with the question of displacement. John Smith, someone who had put actual boots on colonial ground, eschewed theory in favor of practical advice. He counseled New England colonists to make friends of the Indians rather than enemies, noting, "It is much better to helpe to plant a country than unplant it and then replant it."[9] But this time his advice was ignored: colonists who planted New England took the harder route.

The word "slave" derives from the Latin word for the Slavic people of eastern Europe, a fine reminder that "slave" and "African" were hardly synonyms in the early modern world, not least because many people enslaved throughout that world were not African.[10] In the Americas, huge numbers of slaves were in fact Indian. The question of whether Indians could and should be enslaved had been asked almost immediately after the Columbian encounter. Columbus himself did not need to ask it—he took its affirmative answer for granted—but many sixteenth-century observers expressed unease with Spanish colonization because of its enslavement of Indians. In 1550, Charles V convened fourteen theologians and officials of his realm to consider the matters of conquest, enslavement, and conversion of Native Americans. The Spanish philosopher Juan Ginés de Sepúlveda contended that some people of the world, including Indians, were what Aristotle called "natural slaves," since they showed clear signs of inherent barbarism. The Dominican priest Bartolomé de Las Casas argued the opposite, positing that "all men are alike in that which concerns their creation and all natural things, and no one is born enlightened." Las Casas contended, "The savage peoples of the earth may be compared to uncultivated soil that readily brings forth weeds and useless thorns, but has within itself such natural virtue that by labour and cultivation it may be made to yield sound and beneficial fruits."[11] He held that Indians could be saved and thus should not be enslaved. The official results of this great debate were inconclusive, and the tangible effects negligible. The treatment of Indians in Latin America continued to include enslavement (if not juridical, then actual).

The English colonization of North America came nearly a century after these debates. Even though the English hoped to do better than the Spanish, even though the initial colonial rhetoric of the English suggested that Indians held a special status, even though Indian salvation was, after all, one ostensible reason for colonization, there always remained a tension between words and deeds. On the one hand, colonizers described Indians as potential recipients of God's word; on the other, they arrived with swords and guns and garrisoned their towns.[12] To be sure, there were colonists like John Eliot, "the apostle to the Indians," who established fourteen "praying towns" in Massachusetts, in which by 1674 lived around 2,300 Indians, roughly 10 percent of the colony's estimated Indian population of 20,000 (colonists in *all* of New England at the time numbered roughly 60,000). Inhabitants of the praying towns were converts to Christianity, but this status did little to protect them in time of war or disruption.[13]

In any case, Eliot was an unusual man and his goals were similarly uncommon. Not many English colonists, after all, received the appellation of "apostle."[14] Eliot was born in 1604 in England and was a graduate of Cambridge. He apparently experienced his conversion to Puritanism sometime after graduation and decided to move to North America when the chafing, near-Catholicism of the archbishop of Canterbury William Laud drove so many Calvinists out of England. Eliot arrived one year after John Winthrop, on the same ship as Winthrop's eldest son and namesake, John Winthrop Jr. A man of learning and passion, Eliot brought with him more than twenty barrels of books on the voyage.[15] It is not hard to imagine him huddled on a damp ship, indifferent to the roiling waves and blowing wind, nose pressed to a book, fueled by a fierce urgency to honor God.

If his early life trajectory matched that of many other colonists to New England, his passion for missionary work soon distinguished him. He learned the Massachusetts language, lived among Massachusetts Indians, and eventually developed the idea of creating a single town in which all converted Indians could live in peace, under Christian guidance. In 1651, he achieved his goal, founding the first "praying town" of Natick on two thousand acres of land just outside the colonial settlement of Dedham, up the Charles River from Boston. But Eliot's zeal was not widely shared. Though the settlement was legal and approved, Dedham's inhabitants immediately resented its existence.[16] Their constant encroachments on Natick's allotment led John Eliot himself to complain to the General Court of Massachusetts, "Some [colonists] of Dedham do invade our line; upon one side, they forbid the Indians to plant, take away their rails which they have prepared to fence their grounds, and on another side have taken away their lands and sold them to others, to the trouble and wonderment of the Indians."[17] Even legitimate sales in the name of conversion frustrated colonists intent on expanding English control. Even *Christian* Indians were still in the way.

New England colonists had come to stay, and that was the problem. The general process called colonization has specific iterations that work differently depending on place and time. In some places, colonists establish what scholars have called "extractive colonies" or "colonies of exploitation." Such imperial endeavors are typified by "indirect control by colonial powers through a 'thin white line,' a relatively small, sojourning group of primarily male administrators, merchants, soldiers, and missionaries."[18] This sort of colonization was and is practiced in various parts around the globe—think of the initial Spanish conquest of Mexico, the Belgian Congo, the British occupation of Egypt or of South Africa. In general terms, such "extractive" colonies require indigenous labor to forward an empire's agenda. Through military or economic might, colonizers co-opt local peoples into working toward imperial goals, integrating indigenous labor into the larger colonial scheme. Though it is certainly disrup-

tive to local lives and culture, extractive colonialism prefers indigenous bodies to stay in place, as labor. Indeed, the success or failure of
these colonies turns on the question of whether they can successfully
harness such labor.

But there are other kinds of colonial endeavors, including a process that scholars have called "settler colonialism," in which the primary goal is to attain control of the territory, rather than to control
the labor of the people who live on the land.[19] In settler colonialism,
colonists arrive in larger numbers, focused on remaining permanently in the new territory. Such colonists don't want indigenous
labor to stay in place. Rather, under settler colonization, "a much
larger settler European population of both sexes for permanent settlement" arrives, mostly uninterested in using indigenous labor,
focused instead on the *land*.[20]

The North American English colonies clearly fit this model. While
the English would have been happy to harness indigenous labor for
their own purposes, and in some cases did so, using Native Americans
for labor was not central or crucial to their imperial goals. Instead,
the English above all wanted the land, for cultivation and habitation,
and to settle it according to their own terms. For that to happen, the
land had to be taken. But one never really *takes* land. Rather, the land
remains and its people have to go. In fact, the defining characteristic
of settler colonization is that at its base it is a "winner-take-all project whose dominant feature is not exploitation but *replacement*."[21]
Hobbes, Bacon, and John Smith had seen it coming.

Perhaps no word summarizes English colonization in North
America better than "replacement," because it was the removal or
subjugation, and then replacement, of some Native Americans with
other bodies that eventually defined the English strategy. Without a
general practice of removing Indians by killing them, exporting
them as slaves, and pushing many of the rest west or north or south
or simply *away*, African enslavement would have had no room to
grow in any American colony, an unpleasant example of Archime-
dean displacement.[22] Sugar production, dependent on African slave

labor, required Indian land both in the islands and in the regions that fed the islands. To cut enough trees to build the ships that carried Africans and goods throughout the Atlantic world, the English needed the land to be freed of hostile and powerful Indians. To grow the crops with which New England fed the West Indies, the land had to be cultivated the English way, free of Indian interference. To raise the livestock that would feed the Caribbean, that livestock had to be pastured and allowed to graze on land, unmolested. It was a problem to be solved that all this needed to happen on land that other peoples had long since claimed and used in very different ways.[23]

One solution, soon obvious to the colonists, to the problem of how to remove hostile Indians was the Atlantic slave trade: it offered the English a way to remove Indians from the region (for a profit) and then replace them with bodies who would work the land in a way meaningful to the colonizers. And in fact, enslaved Indians were overwhelmingly war captives, their enslavement a by-product of conflicts centrally about control of the land. Such incidental enslavement was an experience far from unique in history to New England Indians. The historian Robin Blackburn explained a different historical system of slavery: "One might say that many Roman slaves were sold because they had been captured, while many African slaves entering the Atlantic trade were captured so that they might be sold." His formulation might be paraphrased in this way: Indian slaves in New England were, mostly, sold because they had been captured in wars, whereas African slaves were captured in wars so that they might be sold.[24] The two sorts of enslavement were, however, related in the seventeenth century: the ridding of Indians invited the colonists' importation of African slaves. The Atlantic trade gave, and the trade took.

Sales of Indians into that Atlantic slave trade resulted from a variety of circumstances. Sometimes enslavement served as a punishment for a crime. In 1684, Thomas Wappatucke, an Indian, was found guilty of burglary and was sentenced to be "sold for a perpetuall servant," the proceeds of his sale to be distributed proportionally to those from whom he had stolen.[25] An Indian named Hoken, a "notoriouse theife," was sentenced in Plymouth to be "apprehended and sold or sent to Barbadoes, for to satisfy his debts and to free the collonie from soe ill a member."[26] Out of sight, into slavery, and, in view of Barbadian mortality rates in the seventeenth century, given a likely death sentence. This is another way the slave trade shaped the settlement of colonial New England. Even a seemingly local justice system explicitly incorporated the trade into its judgments—Hoken's judge *ordered* his sale to Barbados, and the profits from that sale into slavery soothed Hoken's damage to the society.

If crimes led to a trickle of enslaved Indians into the system, war brought a veritable flood. The Pequot War and King Philip's War, each occurring over only two calendar years, forty years apart, led to English control of huge swaths of new land, and large numbers of enslaved Indians. The Pequot War of 1636–38, fought between the Pequot Indians and colonists from Massachusetts and Plymouth, allied with Narragansetts and Mohegans, not only won new land for New England colonists but also led to the enslavement and commodification of hundreds of war captives, distributed among English and Indian victors alike.[27] After a series of deadly encounters, the war climaxed with an English attack on a Pequot settlement near the Mystic River in present-day Connecticut, an attack that killed at least four hundred Indians, mostly women, children, and old men. The colonial soldiers, recruited from Massachusetts and Connecticut, set the Pequot village's wooden walls on fire. Pequots who attempted to flee the flames were shot or stabbed by armed English soldiers and their native allies, as they emerged from the palisaded village. Most simply burned to death. The colonist Cotton Mather would later describe them as "terribly *Barbikew'd*."[28] The attack happened in May, 1637, only one year after the establishment of Connecticut Colony, seven years since the establishment of the Massachusetts Bay Colony, and seventeen since that of Plymouth Plantation. Any living hope of a gentle colonization surely died in the face of such a massacre.

More than two centuries later, when Herman Melville wrote

*Moby-Dick*, he named the monomaniacal Captain Ahab's ship, based in Nantucket, the *Pequod*. Ishmael, the enigmatic narrator, explained the name briefly: "*Pequod,* you will no doubt remember, was the name of a celebrated tribe of Massachusetts Indians, now extinct as the ancient Medes."[29] Of course, Melville was wrong about the extinction. Indians did not disappear from New England, and this is not a story of "vanishing Indians." Many remained, and fought, and survived, and some even thrived. Many migrated to other communities, and of course many died.[30] But Melville's intended parallel here is clear: like the tribe, the ship suffered from the consequences of single-minded acquisitiveness, and though Melville (or Ishmael) erred in his belief that the Pequots were made extinct by the war, he understood quite well how much suffering could derive from being in the way of fanaticism, spiritual or material. The final scene of *Moby-Dick* describes the *Pequod*'s sinking in the equatorial waters of the Pacific, the last part of it visible being the hand of Tashtego, an Indian harpooner from Martha's Vineyard, an island just south of Cape Cod. His drowning and the boat's destruction mirrored so many Indians' fate in the process of English colonization.

In fact, the Pequot War provided the colonists with a bounty of captives who faced a variety of grim fates like Tashtego's. From the more than one hundred prisoners seized from the swamp Ohomowauke by Israel Stoughton in July of 1637, a group of men was taken offshore on a ship and deliberately drowned. According to William Hubbard, "The men among them to the number of thirty were turned presently into Charons Ferry-boat, under the Command of Skipper Gallop, who dispatched them a little without [outside] the harbour."[31] Such brutal dispatch suggests a level of disdain for opponents that would not have been aimed at, say, European combatants.[32] Women and children were given away to allied Indian nations, "disposed of according to the will of the Conquerers, some being given to the *Narrhagansets,* and other Indians that assisted in the service."[33] Indeed, the 1638 Treaty of Hartford, which ended the war, assigned surviving Pequot men as captives to Indian allies of the English, explaining, neatly, "They shall no more be called Pequots but Narragansetts and Mohegans." Their new masters agreed to make yearly payments to the English in exchange for the captives. Here was another way bodies might be commodified, annual payments rather than lump sum purchases, but still the payment did not go to the laborer.[34] The treaty also, crucially, gave the English explicit ownership of the hard-won Pequot land, stipulating, "The Country that was formerly theirs . . . now is the English by Conqest."[35]

The English were, of course, as eager as their Indian allies to control captive bodies, and they quickly entertained ideas of capitalizing on their captures. Hugh Peter wrote from Salem to John Winthrop, "Wee have heard of a dividence of women and children in the bay and would bee glad of a share viz: a young woman or girle and a boy if you thinke good: I wrote to you for some boyes for Bermudas, which I thinke is considerable."[36] John Winthrop, still only seven years in the colony, wrote in a May 1637 letter, "The prisoners were devided, some to those of the river, and the rest to us." The boys, he explained, were sent "to Bermuda, by Mr. William Peirce, and the women and maid children are disposed aboute in the townes."[37] Winthrop had quickly acclimated to the ways of settler colonial life.

Other New Englanders wrote, as well, of boys sent to Bermuda, on the one hand, and women and girls kept in New England, distributed as slaves to colonial towns, on the other. But Winthrop recorded in his journal in June that Pierce had taken only "fifteen of the boys and two women" aboard the Desire, and that he had somehow missed Bermuda by a startlingly long shot, presumably owing to unfavorable winds, and had headed instead to Providence Island.[38] Where were all the other, undrowned men? What had happened to them? The sources are silent on their fate, perhaps underscoring just how venomous the Pequot War had been.[39] As for the English themselves, they certainly found their moral stature diminished by their actions. The Plymouth Colony governor William Bradford found that, after the Mystic massacre, the colonists' Narragansett allies mostly "forsooke" the colonists, perhaps because "they saw the English would make more profite of the victorie then they were willing they should."[40]

Only eight years later, John Winthrop's brother-in-law Emmanuel Downing, a lawyer of the Inner Temple in London, and a prominent member of his church, had profit on his mind when he wrote in 1645 to Winthrop to encourage war with the Narragansett Indians in order to eventually create profits in Barbados. Though the Narragansetts had been the New Englanders' allies in the Pequot War—the colonists had even rewarded them with Pequot captives—now times called for harsher relations. Downing suggested to Winthrop, almost wistfully, "If upon a Just warre the lord should deliver [the Indians] into our hands, wee might easily have men woemen and Children enough to exchange for Moores, which wilbe more gaynefull pilladge for us then wee conceive, for I doe not see how wee can thrive until wee gett into a stock of slaves suffitient to doe all our buisiness, for our Childrens Children will hardly see this great Continent filled with people."[41] His was a lenient just-war theory, and the profit he sought was precisely the sort that, according to Bradford's supposition, the Narragansetts had feared the New Englanders would pursue.

Downing added, almost as an afterthought, "I suppose you know verie well how we shall maynteyne 20 Moores cheaper then one Englishe servant."[42] By this he meant, of course, that slaves were cheaper to feed and clothe and house than any English servant, because more could be asked of them and much less given. Downing, then, saw in the Caribbean colonies an especially expedient way to rid New England of belligerent Indians, and he made the exchange's calculation polyvariable by estimating twenty "Moores" to be less of an investment than one English servant. That the exchange would be of goods for goods, not involving money, also seems worth noting. This might have been a market economy, but "money" as known today was scarce. It was far easier to exchange goods of equal value, or to deal in credit.[43] That is, if one had equivalent goods and credit to offer. If not, one could always hope for a just war to deliver them.

And indeed the Pequot War was not the last war that led to mass enslavement and exportation in seventeenth-century New England. Tensions between English and Indians over English encroachment on Indian land grew over the century, eventually exploding into King Philip's War. Wampanoags, eventully joined by Nipmucks, Pocumtucks, Narragansetts (English allies in the Pequot War), and Abenakis, fought against the English, loosely allied behind the leadership of the Wampanoag leader Metacom, who had been dubbed King Philip by the English. The war quickly involved slavery. In 1675, the first year of King Philip's War, the Quaker Rhode Island colonist and, at the time, deputy governor, John Easton, noted that "150 Indians came into a Plimouth Garrison volentarley" and that though these Indians had surrendered, the "Plimouth Authority sould all for Slaves (but about six of them) to be carried out of the Country." These, notably, were Indians who were persuaded to come under the protection of the English so that retaliation against them for the destruction of New Bedford could not be carried out. Their protection, in short, consisted of their being sold into slavery.[44]

One old man, though, was not sold: "he was decreped [and] could not go." He had been carried upon his son's back to the garrison, but when the son was sold away, he was left unprotected and immobile: useless to the English. The colonists debated how to dispose of the old man. Though "sum wold have had him devoured by Doges, but the Tendernes of sum of them prevailed," and instead of feeding him to their animals, they "cut off his Head."[45] Decapitation is a strange sort of tenderness, though when the spectrum of treatment includes being eaten by savage dogs, usual standards seem less applicable. Not only was this a sorry end for the old man, it perhaps implied that the colonists imagined a roughly comparable severity of treatment between chattel slavery and death: the younger captives would be worked to death, whereas the older man would reach his demise more swiftly. And this was when some were feeling tender. "Piety," said the great colonialist Perry Miller, "made sharp the edge of Puritan cruelty."[46] Perhaps more than any others, enslaved people lived on that knife's edge.

The notion of death as an act of mercy was widely held by the English. John Eliot, that dedicated Puritan missionary, had grave doubt about the righteousness of sales into slavery. "It seemeth to me," he said, "that to sell them away for slaves is to hinder the inlargment of [God's] kingdom." How can we, he asked, "cast away theire soules for whom christ hath, with an eminent hand provided an offer of the gospel?" Instead of enslavement, Eliot preferred execution. "To sell soules for money seemeth to me a dangerous merchandize," he argued. "If they deserve to dy, it is far better to be put to death under godly [rulers] who will take care if meanes may be used that they may die penitently."[47] To a man like Eliot, who took salvation seriously, it was an easy choice to prefer death among the saved to a life among the damned. The establishment of those fourteen "praying towns" in Massachusetts Bay between 1651 and 1674 was done to ensure that Indians would be kept surrounded by believers.[48] After all, as another colonist noted in the middle of the century, the Indians were enslaved in a worse way before the Europeans arrived, "poor captivated men (bondslaves to sin and Satan)."[49] We might notice, though the colonists seem to have missed what might have been a troubling parallel, that in such spiritual metaphors, Satan played the role of slave master.

It was Eliot, too, who wrote a letter after King Philip's War, remarking on the presence of Indians in Tangiers—perhaps the very same Indians about whom that startled Royal African Company agent had written to London. "A vessel carried away a great number of our surprised Indians," Eliot reported, "in the times of our wars, to sell them for slaves, but the nations whither she went, would not buy them." This was not unusual, for by the late seventeenth century Indians had a reputation for being unruly slaves. Thwarted in attempts to offload the captive cargo in the West Indies, the boat eventually, he said, "left them at Tangier; [and] there they be, so many as live or are born there." Eliot knew this because an Englishman had seen them and been given a message to take back to Boston for Eliot: "they desired I would use some means for their return home." The recipient of his letter was none other than Robert Boyle, a leading English intellectual and scientist. Eliot was writing to a sympathetic reader, but he still surely knew he stood little chance of success in this mission. New England authorities were unlikely to bring back home Indians who had been sold away during a war. Nonetheless, he dutifully passed on their request.[50]

Most sales of Indians to the West Indies occurred with the express approval of colonial legislatures: the merchants, supposedly more venal, were not merely acting alone. On August 16, 1676, as King Philip's War was slowly winding down, an act in the town of Providence declared the undersigners to have a "Right with Some others to a percell of Indians" recently arrived, to sell them, and to return to the town any who did not sell. The reverse side of the document authorized specific merchants and a captain to "transport the sayd Indians where they may be Sold, and to make Sale and Delivery thereof as fully, and as firmly, as if we were all personally present."[51] A similar decree from the authorities at Plymouth encouraged the sale of captive Indians into foreign lands. The decree stated that because some of the captives had fought *against* the English during the war, they could be "sold, and devoted unto servitude." Profits, authorities specified, would go to colonial coffers, and accordingly a treasurer was named to conduct sales on behalf of the colony.[52] Another war council from Plymouth considered the fate of a different group of captives, declared them also to be rebels, and agreed that the fifty-seven Indians should be "condemned unto perpetuall servitude" and sold by the colony "as oppertunity may present."[53] Opportunity of course presented itself—Plymouth was a port town on the Atlantic Ocean.

The stark results of enacting such laws can be found in colonial account books, in the form of prices assigned to Indian slaves. On December 29, 1676, colonists of the town of Providence recorded such accountings, in pounds, shillings, and pence, noting how much had been received as payment for more than twenty Indian captives. Some captives were paid for in currency or credit, while others were sold for goods of equal value.[54] Thus were prisoners turned into parcels, and then into profits.

This sort of entry was hardly an aberration in seventeenth-century records. The journal of the Boston merchant John Hull, who also trafficked in enslaved Africans, showed multiple sales of captive Indians. Some of the Indians, as in the Providence dealing, were sold individually to English households. Others were sold in groups so large they could have been intended only for the West Indian trade. The merchant Samuel Shrimpton, who had many ties to English colonies in the Caribbean, bought from Hull "4 Squawes, 3 girls, 2 infants" for thirty pounds, along with "1 old man, 3 squawes, and 2 for one returned by order" for nine pounds, and "1 man," who sold for two pounds, twelve shillings. The merchant Thomas Smith initially bought twenty-nine captives, including "10 Squawes, 8 papooses . . . 1 Woman, 4 little children" for the sum of forty-seven pounds, two shillings, and then purchased forty-one more captives, for eighty-two pounds. The colonist James Whitcomb bought thirteen captives, for almost fifteen pounds, presumably to sell later, at a profit. With prices so low, profits in the West Indies would have been impossible to miss.[55]

Commodified, Indian captives cheapened over time, their decreasing value reflecting their increased numbers. By the end of King Philip's War, it was a buyer's market. Consider the choosiness of James Noyes, a minister in Stonington, Connecticut, writing in 1676, the year the war ended. Writing to authorities, he requested a share of Indian captives, including four specifically: one girl of fourteen years of age, an "old squaw," a small child, and a young man. If one was available, Noyes also proposed having a boy of about sixteen years, on the cusp of adulthood. The minister had already returned an older man, who seemed "never used to work, & had bene sick & lame in his limbs." Noyes quickly realized after receiving the man that he "would doe me noe good."[56] Some years later, another English colonist would complain of a "negroe" whom he had purchased, that he had "bought him for a sound negroe but he proved lame," and he would therefore have to be disposed of as quickly as possible. [57] There was no point to owning an unserviceable slave.

A savvy consumer, Noyes wanted only certain kinds of laborers. But he was seeing, he noted with frustration, only a limited market because a large share of the captives had, regrettably for his purposes, been sent to Barbados, leaving mostly infirm men, women, and children. Taking such slaves was a dicey proposition—a buyer could end up supporting an unproductive laborer, exactly what he had avoided by returning the sickly older man—and he asked for assurances that if the captives proved "a pest to us," he could "sell them to English or some waye to rid our hands of them."[58] In other words, he wanted in writing an assurance that these captives were goods, not obligations, and that, as a consumer, he would have the option to exchange or return them if not satisfied. Indeed, a nineteenth-century New Orleans slave trader would hardly have paid more attention to the details of his chattel than did this colonial New England minister. Age, sex, health, and work ethic were all variables that merited evaluation. The frank tone, not to mention the reference to Barbados, makes evident as well that Noyes was familiar with the complex world of the slave market.

A large circle helped Noyes navigate the shoals of slave trading, and the last paragraph of his letter describes a cosmopolitan market for captive bodies. In it he explains that Catapazet, an Eastern Pequot leader, had asked him to "write about a girle, which her mother gave to him," after the girl's father and other relatives were "sent to Barbadoes." In receiving the girl from the English colonists, Catapazet thus became master to an enemy Indian girl. But he, like Noyes, found himself displeased with his captive, because she was troublesome and unhelpful. Rather than be stuck with a captive he did not want from a tribe he had fought, he sold her to "Ruth[,] Father Stantons Negro for two trucking cloth coats, and 5 yards of painted Calico." A captive's price could fall that far—sold to another person in bondage for some fabric.[59] Noyes's letter demonstrates how convoluted the processes of removal and colonization and enslavement could be. Some Indians clearly took advantage of the Atlantic slave trade, selling their enemies for a profit. That the buyer would be a "Negro"—and named Ruth, presumably a woman—only adds to the complications that ramified from colonial New England's role in the Atlantic slave trade.

A few New England colonists knew that such export trade was extreme. Some protested against the practice on moral grounds, though it may be that too much has been made of the few English voices of protest. Indian voices on the matter were louder. After the Pequot War, Roger Williams wrote from Providence to Governor John Winthrop, noting Narragansett objections to the enslavement of Pequot Indians, saying they "would be very gratefull to our neighbours [in Massachusetts] that such Pequots as fall to them be not enslaved, like those which are taken in warr." Instead, the Narragansetts preferred that captives taken into English hands be treated well and given shelter from the war.[60] But Williams himself did not really heed this plea in his own dealings with Indians. Only nine days after writing to John Winthrop to note that Indians objected to slavery, he wrote again to say, "It having againe pleased the most High to put into your hands another miserable drove of Adams degenerate seede, and our brethren by nature: I am bold (if I may not offend in it) to request the keeping and bringing up of one of the children." Williams had even identified his captive of choice. "I have fixed mine eye on this little one with the red about his neck," he wrote, but hastened to add that he would be happy with any captive Winthrop chose to send him.[61] Rhode Island colonists had not participated in the Pequot War, but were willing to help divide the spoils.

Williams was perhaps exactly the sort of Englishman who might have been expected to question the enslavement of Indians. Born circa 1603 to a gentry family, he, like John Winthrop, became a Puritan at some point in early adulthood, possibly while at Cambridge. But unlike John Winthrop, who played even his radicalism safely, Williams became a Separatist, someone who rejected entirely the authority and legitimacy of the Church of England. The North American colonies attracted him as a haven for nonconsenting Protestants, but he found even the Puritans of Massachusetts too close to the Church of England for his comfort. He refused an offer from that colony to pastor the First Church of Boston, preferring initially to reside among fellow Separatists in Plymouth. Even they, however, proved too welcoming to Church of England connections, and he returned to Massachusetts for a spell, until he was exiled for sedition: he had questioned too often and too abrasively the legitimacy of the colony's charter. No less a figure than John Eliot wrote a justification for his banishment. Still, despite the exile, Winthrop and others remained fond of Williams, for he could be kind and charming even in his stubbornness, and there was probably something appealing about his stalwart convictions in the face of repeated tests.[62]

So it was consequential that he considered the issue of Indian enslavement a grave one, and it carried weight when he seemingly embraced the dispersal of Indian captives into English servitude. When, one month later, Williams received the child he had asked for from John Winthrop, he wrote a thank-you note to explain why he had been interested in that particular captive, namely, that he had known the boy's parents. Indeed, the mother was still with Winthrop. But her claim on the boy seems to have been superseded by that of Williams, who mentioned that he intended to raise the boy well. He added that he would send someone to "fetch" the child, but before he did so, he requested one thing of Winthrop: "that you would please to give a name to him."[63] The child had a name already, but Winthrop was to give him a new one; he had a family, but now was to live with a colonist. This, though Williams had himself observed, in his *Key into the Language of America,* "Their [Indian] *affections,* especially to their children, are very strong; so that I have knowne a *Father* take so grievously the losse of his *childe,* that hee hath cut and stob'd himself with *griefe* and *rage.*"[64] The act of separating and renaming fits what some scholars have called the "intimacies of empire," the disruption and colonization of individual indigenous family relations that went on within the vast, sweeping process of colonizing of Indian land.[65]

Williams took this child with the red around his neck into his house, if not as a "slave," then as a servant of considerably debased status ("miserable drove of Adams degenerate seed" was hardly a compliment). The child was of value and was a war captive—so perhaps the term "slave" would have been appropriate. Regardless, such captivity and outright slavery were conditions that New Englanders thought about and made sense of in relation to each other. Williams himself came close to meditating on the distinction between captivity and chattel slavery, noting that on the issue of how captives might be treated, the Bible was somewhat vague.

> If they have deserved Death, tis Sinn to spare.
>
> If they have not deserved Death then what punishment? Whether perpetuall slaverie.
>
> I doubt not but the Enemie may lawfully be weakned and despoild of all comfort of wife and children etc.: but I beseech you well weigh if after a due time of trayning up to labour, and restraint, they ought not to be set free: yet so as without danger of adjoyning to the Enemie.[66]

Ultimately, Williams seems to have doubted that perpetual slavery for Indians was appropriate. But the difference between long indentures and perpetuity may have seemed a matter of semantics to a captive.

The keeping of Indian children in long-term servitude occurred throughout the seventeenth century. As early as 1647, the colonist Richard Morris wrote to complain about the loss of his "maid," who had been persuaded by her uncle to run away, to Morris's "gret dammeg, she being a Chilld of deth."[67] The phrase "child of death" meant that the girl had a death sentenced imposed upon her. When King Philip's son was caught after the war named for his father, colonists debated "whether Philip's son be a child of death." They eventually decided that children of traitors and rebels and murderers, especially leaders among those, could be found guilty for the actions of their parents and could be legitimately sentenced to death.[68] In this case, Morris didn't want the girl killed—indeed he claimed to be fond of her—but he did want her labor replaced either with another Indian or "onley let me have as much as woll purches mee a neger in hir room."[69] Another colonist, William Baulston, vouched for Morris's request to Winthrop. The girl was, he explained, a "Chilld of death delivered to [Morris] by the bay in the time of the pecod war." Her loss, ten years later, was a blow to Mistress Morris, who was old and infirm. But the loss could be smoothed, he also proposed, if not by the maid's return, then by enough "wampom as may purches eather an other Indean or blackmor."[70] It was the sort of equivalency Indians feared.

Indian children and Indian woman were the mostly likely to be kept in servitude. The 1676 will of Nicholas Easton, governor of Rhode Island and a Quaker, freed his "Indian Squa" and granted her child freedom upon turning twenty-five.[71] In this, it seems, he was following a new tradition. An act passed in Plymouth that same year suggested that children of surrendering Indians be dispersed among the English only until the children were twenty-four years old.[72] Evidence from one month later in Providence indicates that this policy of dispersing native children was not unique to Massachusetts or Plymouth. Appointed representatives of the town of Providence, including Roger Williams, decided how Indian children should be allotted, and for what amount of time:

> That all under 5 years old shall serve untill thirty
>
> All above 5 and under 10 shall serve till the 28 year of their Ag[e].
>
> All above 10 to 15 untill the 27 year of their age
>
> All above 15 to 20 untill the 26th year
>
> All from 20 to 30 shall serve 8 years
>
> All above 30–7 years: or as they can be sold.[73]

Passages like this provide a useful counterpoint with which to consider how Africans complicated understandings of race in early New England. As Roger Williams had struggled to understand whether and how Native Americans could be enslaved, he had also implicitly meditated on the underpinnings of the institution of slavery as a whole. It seems clear that Williams believed that Native Americans ranked above Africans in an English racial hierarchy. The former could be reduced to the status of the latter only in situations like the Pequot War, in which they had been captured as combatants fighting for a side deemed beyond redemption in a war against God's chosen people.

Throughout the century, hints of this sort of distinction between Indians and Africans appeared. In 1660, the Ipswich, Massachusetts, quarterly court explained, "The law is undeniable that the indian may have the same distribusion of Justice with our selves." In other words, the court held that Indians should be treated equally with English colonists by colonial laws, an idea that perhaps stemmed from an English perception that Indians were beginning to accept Christianity. As a result of their conversions, the court held, "the same argument" that applied to "the negroes" did not apply to Indians, "for the light of the gospel is begineing to appeare amongst them—that is the indians."[74] And yet, many "negroes" had also joined the church, as was well known. The problem with overcoming racially biased perceptions was that race was constructed by so many factors—ideology, religion, appearance, language, rank—and simply joining a church was never enough to erase all the other categories by which a body might be marked.

In any case, these distinctions never meant that English colonists forswore brutality when dealing with Native Americans. Indeed, they did not. The famous scholar of race and slavery David Brion Davis has correctly identified the reality that "although Africans and Indians for the most part *were* viewed differently, they received similar treatment, often were described with similar labels, and frequently were lumped together by law."[75] In Davis's observation lies an awkward historical truth: people's actions and their words too often diverge. English colonial ideology may have ranked Indians, as a group, somewhere above Africans, but that did not deter colonists from selling Indians into Caribbean slavery.[76] In fact, in New England's colonial racial hierarchy, the gap that mattered was not that between Indians and Africans but rather that which existed between both those groups and the English.

Even as Williams made his peace with certain acts of sale, the capturing and selling and buying excited comment and some unease among other colonists. The same year King Philip's War began, Rhode Island authorities took steps to make sure Indian slaves were not held in their colony, noting that the recent purchase by some colonists of captive Indians was upsetting and "apeares troublsome to most of the Inhabitants, and the Sufferinge Such Indians to abide amongs us may prove very prejuditiall." Accordingly, they ordered all such Indians sold out of the town.[77] It was simply too dangerous to keep such restless people enslaved so close to home, and perhaps strategically unwise, since it seemed to invite redemptive raids from the captives' nations (though selling them away also surely invited raids of a more preemptive or vengeful sort). African slaves proved a safer bet, since they were far from any kin or compatriots.

Colonists in the West Indies, too, eventually objected to the importation of New England Indians. Barbados authorities, for example, protested the trade from the north, worried about the ramifications of their island colonies becoming dumping grounds for Indians who had already proved themselves to be rebellious.[78] In a 1676 act, in the mist of the wartime boom, authorities on that island maintained, "Indians brought from New England, New Yorke, Roade Island, and the Collonyes adjacent are known to be notorious Villanyes." Such people had no place on Barbados, authorities declared, since their arrival introduced to the population "such obstinate Incorrigible Rogues and Cunning Thieves that from them greater mischiefe may happen to this Island then from any Negroes." The act requested the immediate removal of Indians from the island, and their return to New England, lest their cunning lead them to "contrive and carry on those dangerous designes which our Negroes of the[ir] Owne Nature are prone unto."[79] It is not clear how often such returns actually occurred.[80]

The King Philip's War–era importation of Algonquian Indians was no small matter for West Indian planters: one ship alone, the *Seaflower*, sailed from Boston harbor with roughly 180 Algonquians, "heathen Malefactors men women and children," arriving in Jamaica in November 1676. Those "captivated" Indians, a certificate accompanying them proclaimed, "had been sentenced and condemned to perpetuall servitude" for their "many notorious barbarous and execrable murthers villanies and outrages."[81] This sort of exportation happened despite an edict from the Massachusetts General Court two months earlier that the punishment for Indians who had killed English colonists should be execution, not exportation.[82] Perhaps the opportunity to profit from such prisoners outweighed the desire of English colonists in New England to see justice delivered. Colonists on Barbados, though, clearly resented being saddled with "notorious Villanyes."

Indeed, the specificity of the Barbados act's exclusion (New England Indians, but not those from, say, Suriname, South Carolina, or Virginia) speaks again to the tight connections New England had with the West Indies in general and with Barbados in particular. Yet if the Barbadian planters were becoming wary of New England's exports, other colonies, newer to sugar culture and thus perhaps with greater demand for labor, were more willing to receive New England Indians. John Taylor, an Englishman who visited Jamaica in the 1680s, described a varied pool of enslaved people. "Indians," he noted, "are of diverse nations brought hither as of Suranam, Florida, New England, etc., and are sold here for slaves," though he also observed that such slaves were not as desirable as Africans, because they tended either to escape or to kill themselves, "for they will not work." Taylor also listed differences between the treatment of Indians and of Africans. Nutrition for one, differed for Indian slaves; he claimed Indians were given the same meat rations as English servants, and were further permitted to hunt wild hogs and birds, allocations that stand in stark contrast to the food offered to enslaved Africans. Taylor calculated that one "faithfull Indian slave is as good as three Negro slaves," but asserted that Indians were less tractable than enslaved Africans, for "if you should use blowes to bring 'em therto, they would either runn away or murther themselves."[83]

And yet the exportation of slaves continued, perhaps because the fury of colonial wars overrode West Indian objections. In 1677, women of the Massachusetts fishing village Marblehead tore to pieces two living Indian captives held by sailors who came to port in the town. One of the sailors recounted that, upon its arrival in port, people "flocked" to the boat to gather news about the ship, its cargo, and other ships in the area. When they saw the Indian captives aboard, "they demanded why we kept them alive and why we had not killed them." The sailors answered that they hoped to receive some monetary reward for the Indians, but the colonists were not appeased by this answer, and "began to grow clamorous." Alarmed by the crowd, the sailors decided to take their captives to the town authorities; they carried the Indians to the town "with their hands bound behind them." An angry group of women soon gathered, taunting and insulting the captives. Then, one sailor remembered, the women surrounded the captives, took them away from the sailors, and "with stones, billets of wood, and what else they might, they made an end of these Indians." The sailors could not see what was happening to the captives until they were dead and the crowd apparently subsided. When calm, of a sort, had resumed, the sailors found the Indians dead, "with their heads off and gone, and their flesh in a manner pulled from their bones." And still, even in the face of the flayed corpses, the women were unrepentant. They explained that if they had allowed the sailors to take the captives to Boston, the prisoners would have been set free by colonial authorities. That was unacceptable: "said they, if there had been forty of the best Indians in the country here, they would have killed them all, though they should be hanged for it."[84]

This kind of hatred was endemic and undoubtedly facilitated the enslavement of Indians even in the face of familiarity. The origins of an African's enslavement remained invisible to most New England colonists, but the same could not be said for the origins of an Indian's, since most Indians enslaved in New England (though not all) were captured in a war. Indeed, at the point of sale into the Atlantic system, it was very likely that a merchant or a colonist could have said with certainty exactly where and how that Indian had been enslaved. The English colonists demonstrated in their documentation that they knew their names, and they knew their families. They sold people they knew into the West Indies, anyway.

Indians themselves were keenly aware of the English policy of exportation. One Nipmuck man explained why so many of his nation were against peace with the English. "Why," he asked, "shall wee have peace to bee made slaves, & either bee kild or sent away to sea to Barbadoes &c." Rather than that, he said, "let us live as long as wee can and die like men, and not live to bee enslaved."[85] That various Indian nations shared a loathing of the selling of captives into slavery is made clear by a brief mention in the colonist Quentin Stockwell's narrative of his own captivity during King Philip's War. At one point in his bondage, some women came to report that the English had captured "*Uncas* and all his Men, and sent them beyond the Seas." Upon hearing this, Stockwell's captors "were much enraged at this, and asked us if it were true." Though the English captives denied having exported anyone, their captors would not be appeased, and Stockwell remembered that, after the news, his captors "dealt worse by us for a season than before."[86] Sixty years after Squanto's enslavement by Thomas Hunt, Indians in New England remained furious at this sort of captivity and exportation; time could not heal these wounds, especially not when colonists in various ways kept ripping off the scabs.

James Quannapaquait, a Christian Indian from the praying town of Natick, captured during the same war, mentioned several times a fear of being sold away to Barbados. Indians preferred to be captured by native enemies, he said, "for if they came to the English they knew they shold bee sent to Deere Iland, as others were . . . and others feard they should bee sent away to Barbados, or other places."[87] Deer Island, a small mass of wooded land in the middle of Boston harbor, was owned by Samuel Shrimpton, one of the region's wealthiest merchants. With his grudging permission, and assurances from authorities that the Indians would not cut down any growing firewood, Shrimpton allowed the island to become a sort of seventeenth-century internment camp to which converted Indians from Natick were sent during King Philip's War. Their exile stemmed both from a fear on the part of the colonists that the Natick residents would turn on the English and from a fear on the part of people like John Eliot that vengeful colonists might fall upon the praying towns.

John Eliot traveled with the Natick Indians as they were transported to the island in late October of 1675, praying with them and encouraging them to keep their faith even amid their tribulations. Hundreds of Indians shipped out to the island at midnight, having waited for a favorable tide, shivering in the dark. When Eliot returned to the island in December of that same year, he found the Indians in horrid condition. Daniel Gookin, who accompanied Eliot, remembered, sadly, "The Island was bleak and cold, their wigwams poor and mean, their clothes few and thin."[88] Bereft of food and shelter, and left unattended in the New England winter, they suffered there from malnourishment and from diseases caused by squalid conditions; some died. Quannapaquait's fears, ranging from Deer Island to Barbados, mapped at least part of what has been called the red Atlantic, a corollary, just as tragic and coerced, to the more familiar black Atlantic.[89]

New England Indians' protests did not stem from an unfamiliarity with the idea of captivity. Indeed, an indigenous trade in captives existed in North America well before Europeans arrived, since Native Americans from across the continent practiced forms of what fell under the rubric of slavery. The Algonquian Indians who lived in what came to be called New England neighbored the southern- and eastern-most members of the Iroquois confederacy, people who practiced a form of captive taking that in some ways looked very like chattel slavery. But that Iroquoian practice of bondage differed in a key way from the model of slavery the English brought to the region, since Iroquoian raids took captives from neighboring tribes in hopes of assimilating them into Iroquoian culture. Whether that integration was successful or not is a matter of debate, but the adoption of captives to replace dead tribe members was its stated goal. This form of captivity thus offered myriad roads out of bondage; in general terms, though not always and not everywhere, Indian slavery, albeit forcefully, assimilated captives into their new culture, and the children of captives became fully part of the society.[90]

That is not to say that being the child of a captive in, for example, the Iroquois system carried no stigma—it often did—but that stigma generally lessened over time. In contrast, the English method of capturing people but then not engaging in any ritualistic ceremonies designed to assimilate them into their new culture—no dances, no ritual tortures (but plenty of nonritualistic tortures, to be sure), no adoption, and so on—intensified Indian fears about their fate after captivity.[91] And the children of enslaved people owned by the English also became slaves, permanently, barring some unusual legal intervention. That was a different sort of bondage.[92] A system that stole people from one culture, but did not apparently add them to another, was violently different from the captivity many Indians had known. As one scholar has noted, "in the Native view, as in many African societies, the opposite of slavery was not freedom: the opposite of slavery was kinship."[93] It may be that, from a New England Indian's perspective, the opposite of kinship would have been something like what happened on Barbados.

In fact, under the rough rules of the slavery system imported by the colonists, kinship could mean precisely slavery. By 1677, the selling of Indian children had become so prevalent that colonial courts attempted to regulate the process, forbidding colonists to buy the children of Indian captives without special permission from authorities.[94] But for many captives, such orders had little effect. In 1685, nearly a decade after the end of King Philip's War, an Indian named Peter, who along with his wife and children had been mistakenly "taken and made a slave," petitioned to have his daughter returned to him. The justification for his and his family's enslavement derived from Peter's having been classified as an enemy combatant during the war, yet Peter had actually volunteered his services to colonial forces in their war effort. Nonetheless, misidentified as the child of an alleged enemy, Peter's daughter had been "disposed" of to a colonist for "3 or 4 yeares service." Now, a decade later, she had still not been returned to her father.[95]

Tragically, the man's petition remained unresolved decades later. Peter Pratt, the "Queen's Attorney" (an appointed position charged with prosecuting criminal offenses), speaking to a court in 1705, found himself stumped by the conundrum of how to define the status of Peter's grandchildren, a third generation held in bondage three decades after the war. Vexed, Pratt put it to the court to decide whether these children should be considered "Slaves as [the] Negroes or as the Spanish or other Indians of the foreign nations Imported here from beyond the Seas" or whether they ought instead to be set free at a predetermined age. He asked the court, in other words, to distinguish between war captives and slaves, and to free the former.[96] That the distinction needed to be asked for, so many years after the war and about subsequent generations, suggests how uncomfortably vague the mechanisms for emancipation could be for Indian captives.

By the end of the seventeenth century, New England's Indian population had declined dramatically—though Native Americans still made up around 10 percent of the region's population, down from 25 percent before King Philip's War. One historian estimates that at least two thousand Indians from the region had fled west or north, while another one thousand "were captured and sold out of the country as slaves," a number that stands in rough equilibrium with the estimated numbers of enslaved Africans who were in the region at the turn of the seventeenth century.[97] The work of colonization had proceeded thus: Indians and Africans had replaced each other in ways orchestrated by settler colonists, for the purposes of profit and expansion. The Atlantic slave trade was a process, consisting of a series of moments in which people of diverse nations and cultures (African elites, European merchants, Indian adversaries) all agreed, at various times in different places, to capture and commodify other people. If enough had said no, the system might have faltered. But people predictably, tragically, said yes, in Europe, in Africa, in the West Indies, and in New England, and their individual moments of agreement helped facilitate, in the seventeenth century, a global trade. The eventual decision made by other people to say no, more than a century and a half later, would create a continental rupture.

If asked, could those early colonists have articulated the logic at work in the process? Could they have said, "We took this land for ourselves, driven in part by the chance to control more land to produce more products to sell to our customers in the West Indies, who are too busy to grow their own food because their sugar brings them such riches"? Perhaps English colonists in New England would have had trouble articulating that, exactly, but the records they themselves created and preserved suggest that they could and did see the neat math of replacement at the local scale. When Samuel Shrimpton or Thomas Smith bought dozens of Algonquian war captives, they did so with the profits and prices of the Atlantic slave trade in their heads. When colonial authorities authorized, time and again, the selling of Indian bodies for the good of the colony, they had in mind a market that centered on the West Indian trade, the slave trade. And when Indians objected vociferously and violently to the selling away of their family and friends and even enemies, when Nipmuck soldiers refused to surrender and declared they would rather "die like men" than be enslaved, they made clear they understood fully the logic of settler colonization.

# PART II

# LIKELY
## THAT OF
# NEW
# ENGLAND

This portrait of the Boston merchant Samuel Shrimpton shows, in the background, what may be an enslaved man. *Courtesy of the Massachusetts Historical Society.*

# CHAPTER 4

# Visible Slaves

What profit hath he that worketh in that wherein he laboureth?
—Ecclesiastes 3:9

O ne clear and substantive result of all the unplanting and replanting and movement and coercion and violence and separation was the growth of New England. Samuel Maverick later remembered that at the beginning of English colonization, the "place in which Boston (the Metropolis) is [now] seated," had been little more than a "Swamp and Pound." But by the first decades of the eighteenth century, another observer marveled, Boston's merchants had built a "Noble Peer, 1800 or 2000 Foot long," lined by a row of warehouses. At the Long Wharf, ships from around the world unloaded their goods, and from its head a person could walk straight to Boston's Town House, a building that housed merchant shops, government offices, and court chambers, and which was surrounded by bookshops selling the wares of the five printing presses in the town. Boston by the eighteenth century had ten churches. It was, said the onlooker, "the most flourishing Town for Trade and Commerce in the *English America*."[1]

The role of slave labor in the West Indies in fueling that tremendous growth is clear: enslaved people in the island colonies grew and harvested the crops that made profits for English colonists throughout the Atlantic world. The role of enslaved labor *in* New England in creating that wealth is, however, largely invisible, because enslaved people there did not do different work than their English counterparts; their slave labor was not distinguished from free labor.[2] The idea that some labor was the exclusive lot of enslaved people only developed over time, usually in places with sharply specialized work systems such as that required by sugar cultivation. Even the young and impetuous Henry Winthrop, who never fit anyone's image of the hardworking yeoman, had written from Barbados in 1627 that he and his laborers would "joine" in planting tobacco—the distinction he drew in that early moment was not in the labor but in the reward: the profits would be his alone.[3] Mostly, the precariousness of colonization's initial moment either required or facilitated an indifference to racialized labor regimes. While the land was still fiercely contested, and while the outcome of the colonial project was uncertain, there was little time to establish and enforce racial distinctions in labor and few reasons to do so. And in New England, where no cash crop ever developed, a racialized labor system took even longer to emerge. Similar situations existed during early colonization attempts in the Chesapeake and Carolinas and elsewhere in the Americas.[4] Seventeenth-century New England offers one window to how slavery functioned in a time and place where laborers were differentiated by race, even while their labor was not.[5]

That window also allows a glimpse of the varieties of experience that existed under the category of chattel slavery. Taken as a whole, the Atlantic slave system violently yoked disparate societies and regions, linking West Africa with Brazil with Barbados with New York with New England; the result was that people from any one of those regions might end up, however improbably, in any of the others, laboring in the way required by that specific locale.

Seen from above, the Atlantic system would have looked like something of a tempestuous spiral in constant flux and motion. At some point, though, the enslaved people who were transported thousands of miles in the grasp of that complicated trade, were released, permanently or momentarily, into the specific circumstances in which they lived their particular lives shaped in large part by the realities of the labor needs in the place they had landed. European colonists in the Americas were hardly passive recipients of a monolithic trade. Rather, time and again, colonists helped create an institution of chattel slavery specifically designed to suit the needs of their community. In doing so, they took the global and made it local. New England was no exception.

In 1679, an enslaved man called Wonn, owned by the colonist John Ingersoll, testified in a Salem witchcraft trial. This was slightly more than a decade before the famous trials of the same town, but witchcraft was endemic in New England and never limited to the Salem outbreak.[6] At the trial, Wonn told a gripping tale of his encounter with the occult. While he was going into the forest to gather wood, his horses were startled by something he did not see, and bolted, cartload of wood and all, into a nearby swamp. Only with great difficulty was he able eventually to extricate them from the bog. The problem lay not in the muck's depth but rather in the horses' adamant refusal to heed Wonn. Witnesses to the scene agreed that they had never seen horses behave that way. They believed the animals to have been bewitched.

That was only the beginning of Wonn's experience with the supernatural. A week later, as he went into the barn to get hay for the farm's animals, the shape of a woman appeared, standing on a beam and holding an egg in her hand. Wonn, startled, tried to strike the woman with a rake, but the vision disappeared. Fortunately, he had already recognized her: his neighbor "Goody Oliver."[7] Wonn did not take this apparition lightly. Terrified, and unable to strike the figure, presumably because she was only spirit and not substance, he ran into the house and told his master what he had seen. And still his troubles had not ended, for while at dinner that same night he saw two black cats, though the household had only one. On seeing the extra cat, Wonn exclaimed in surprise, "How came two black catts heare[?]" But before he could finish speaking, he "felt three sore gripes or pinches" that made him cry out.[8] Goody Oliver, Wonn's testimony suggested, wished the man to remain silent.

Despite what we can presume was his foreign origin, Wonn lived a New England life. He resided in his owner's household, approximately half a mile from the Oliver home, and so knew Goody Oliver by name and sight, such that he could recognize her wraith-like figure perched on a beam in his owner's barn.[9] He also probably understood local customs regarding witchcraft: the notions that horses could be bewitched, that black cats were related to witches, and that witches could hear words spoken at a distance and cause pain in response. Such notions may not have been unique to New England, but that Wonn testified to them in court suggests he knew that the English believed them.[10] He spoke English, and he ate dinner in the house, it seems with the family. He could harness a horse to an English sled, drive the conveyance, and then unharness that horse when, for example, it got stuck in a swamp while fleeing a witch. He could cut and stack wood, and he knew how to care for the domesticated animals, and generally to manage the property. He knew who owned what land around Salem and what various landmarks were called, and he was trusted to go into woods with horses, even though such a task offered a possible means of escape. And when he went into those woods, or anywhere else, he became visible to the larger community: we should remember that the colonists who testified to witnessing the bolting horses also witnessed an enslaved man laboring, and in such ways did familiarity with chattel slavery in early New England extend beyond slave-owning households.[11]

Wonn did, in short, the work of settler colonization: the clearing of forests, the raising of livestock, the planting of crops and the tilling of fields, and all the mundane tasks of building a society that resembled what the colonists had left behind in England. It was significant labor. Wonn was a valuable man to have around, valuable enough that his owner, John Ingersoll, continued to own human laborers until the end of his life; his will left to his daughter his "negro man by name Dick," valued at twenty pounds.[12]

A transoceanic trade system had brought Wonn to the Massachusetts Bay Colony, but once he was there, a local person bought him, and local people profited from the labor he performed according to local needs.[13] Because Wonn's encounter with the apparition of Goody Oliver occurred in early modern Salem, it included many of the key ingredients of the stereotypical colonial New England story—farming, witchcraft, and a woman titled "Goody." Yet in the middle of that tableau stood an enslaved man of African descent with a Spanish-sounding name. Wonn lived in the Salem of legend, its denizens fearful of the blackness of shadows and cats alike, quick to see witches, and to see in witches the most frightening manifestations of their subconciousness. But he also lived in the Salem of the Atlantic world, a bustling colonial port, a merchant's base looking outward to the Atlantic and to the West Indies.[14] This was the reality of seventeenth-century Salem: it was an idiosyncratic town in a specific colony, affected by and a constituent of a global trade. And what was true of Salem was true also, to some degree, of the rest of the region.

Labors like Wonn's played an obvious colonizing role in clearing the way for local planting, but their role in American colonization went much deeper—and wider—than that. Consider a tale about turpentine. In October 1695, John Pynchon, the Springfield merchant, signed a deed to free "Roco Negro" and his wife, Sue (they had been married eight years earlier), in exchange for twenty-five barrels of turpentine and twenty-one barrels of tar. Roco had two years to provide Pynchon with the stipulated goods; upon doing so, he and his wife would be free. Word of this agreement may have spread, because soon thereafter a man named Richard (Dick) Blackleech, possibly a freed slave, joined the contract, an addition that shortened by half Roco and his wife's term of servitude. Pynchon not only permitted this, he even added a preemptive clause insuring them against bad weather: if the summer proved too warm for a decent harvest of turpentine, he promised, they would get an additional year on the contract.[15] That one man of African descent would sign a contract to help others (who were enslaved) perhaps hints at a sense of community and solidarity among enslaved people in early New England. Whatever Richard Blackleech's motive, his undertaking such a considerable task certainly speaks to the imperative of freedom.

Such a story also shows the kind of labor enslaved people did in early New England. The agreement to provide eight hundred gallons of turpentine (at thirty-two gallons per barrel), plus twenty-one barrels of tar, was far from an easy task. The harvesting of turpentine and tar in colonial North America was done by "boxing" pine trees—a labor-intensive procedure that involved notching a tree's trunk with an ax and catching the sap in the notched area. The trees died after being boxed.[16] Such arduous work was not inherently dangerous, but the contested sovereignty of the forests of seventeenth-century New England made it so. Roco and Dick essentially contracted to go alone into unfamiliar forests inhabited by potentially unfriendly Indians to do onerous work, all in the hope of gaining Roco and his wife's freedom.[17]

It was perhaps ironic that both turpentine and tar were valuable primarily because they were used extensively in early modern shipbuilding, meaning that the labor of these men also helped build England's fleet.[18] That such work incidentally killed trees, thus clearing forests and making land available for English settlement, only underlines how the work of enslaved people was also the labor of a settler colonist. But in this case, the local implications of the work, the clearing of the forests for settlement, were just that, incidental. The economic aim of Roco and Dick's work for the merchant Pynchon was to convert sap in a New England forest into turpentine coating a Royal Navy hull.

Boxing trees was likely a new skill for these men, for though pine trees were found throughout the Northern Hemisphere in the seventeenth century, they did not grow in sub-Saharan Africa or in the Caribbean. Roco and Dick's ability to harvest these substances demonstrates skilled labor specific to New England. Furthermore, their extractive labors in the woods put in motion an entire industry, creating the need for a variety of work by other local skilled laborers. Another man of African descent who served Pynchon, Peter Swinck, made barrels for the resin that people like Roco and Dick gathered; he was, in other words, a New England cooper, though possibly enslaved.[19]

Though their labor and the knowledge it necessitated were peculiar to pine country, Roco and Dick's labor was nonetheless of a kind familiar across the Atlantic world of colonization: the labor of removal and replacement—this time not of people but of things. Brazilian rainforests, Jamaican forests, and New England woods all came down so that fences might go up. Already in 1612, a sort of marketing pamphlet described Virginia: "the company cut down wood, the Carpenters fell to squaring out, the Sawyers to sawing, the Souldier to fortifying."[20] A 1682 account of the province of Carolina noted that the hinterland of Charles Town was "pillaged of all its valuable Timber"; it calculated that "six men will in six weeks time, Fall, Clear, Fence in, and fit for Planting, six Acres of Land."[21] In New England, the Pequot War opened up the wooded interior just as the West Indies' timber shortage became acute, so industriously had the islands' forests been cleared.[22] Clearing the woods westward into Indian country, Roco and Dick's work nonetheless rooted New England in the east-facing Atlantic economy.[23] It was an additional unmentioned irony that, in many ways, the practice of clearing and then fencing New England land to exclude Indians mirrored the English process of enclosure that had forced countless English peasants to seek new opportunities in the Americas and elsewhere.[24]

Contracts like that signed by Roco and Dick to obtain freedom appear far less frequently than do documents meant to ensure the continued bondage of Indians and Africans. For the most part, New England colonists wanted to keep their slaves. Probate records, for example, inventories compiled after a person's death by supposedly neutral parties of some standing in the town, demonstrate that many colonists kept their slaves until their death and that the heirs of the estate, as well as the municipality, paid close attention to the dispersal of that human property.[25] Not only do the appraised prices permit a comparison of the relative worth of items within an estate—for instance, how colonists valued an enslaved African or Indian versus non-human property—but the existence of a probate record also presumes an appraisers' ability to assign slave values. The very act of valuation demonstrates, in other words, that even New Englanders who did not own slaves themselves could judge the fair price of a slave, and such records offer by far the clearest statements of the value of enslaved people in New England estates.

Enslaved people first appear in probate records roughly at mid-century. The 1661 Suffolk County, Massachusetts, probate record of John Stoughton lists the following possessions:

> 1 Stone horse, 1 Gelding Lame & Sickly
> one man Negro named John and & one Negro boy named Peter
> One beam Scales & 882 of Leaden waights
> Three bbs flower, 2 firkins of butter, bad[26]

Also mentioned among accounts owed to or by Stoughton were "old Cloaths for the Negro," worth fifty pounds of sugar. In such a short record is evidence that slaves were clothed with cast-off garments from colonists and that these two enslaved people had no surnames that mattered for the purposes of official records. The maker of the inventory thought it logical to include John and Peter in a list of possessions and to place them near livestock in that list. The probate record also hints at the kind of work John and Peter did for their owner: farming.

Wills and probate records make clear that New England households often owned only one or two enslaved people. The Salem merchant Theodore Price's modest estate included an unnamed "neager," valued at ten pounds, the same as a still. His house and land, in contrast, were worth one hundred sixty pounds.[27] The 1668 inventory of the estate of the much wealthier William Cottell of Newbury listed household furnishings, crockery, silver items, various debts, and "a neger maidservant." The 1664 inventory of Nicholas Davidson's Charlestown estate listed "Two Negroes Conugo and Marea" for twenty-eight pounds.[28] The 1673 inventory of the estate of Henry Short of Newbury amounted to nearly two thousand pounds and mentioned rooms, furnishings, and (finally) a single "negro man."[29] In Salem, the wealthy Thomas Savage's will, dated June 28, 1675, listed, among other things, sheets, a silver pitcher, and a "negro" woman.[30] The 1676 estate inventory of Salem's wealthy John Porter included "2 negro servants," worth forty pounds, and "3 Inglish servants," for thirty pounds.[31] At the end of the century, John Sanders of Salem left his two daughters "all [his] real estate, that is to say moneys, goods, household stuff, plate, and negro man Sambo, to be equally divided between them."[32] Where it had once taken Solomonic judgment to divide a person, now, thanks to his propertied status, Sambo could be sold and easily divided, financially.

The inventory of the estate of Benjamin Gibbs listed last "1 negro man named Hector," valued at thirty-five pounds, making Hector by far Gibbs' most valuable asset. The entire inventory was worth only one hundred thirty pounds. Hector's value thus represented more than a quarter of Benjamin Gibbs's worth.[33] At another point in his life, Gibbs, a self-described "Marriner," had in his possession "two Negro men called Ferdinando and Hector and one Negro woman called flora with one young Indian called Pegge," but he sold them to Joshua Scottow, along with most of Gibbs's land and possessions, including "two Cows," for almost two hundred pounds. The slaves were clearly an important part of the sale: the deed mentioned them three times, once by name and twice simply as the "negroes," each time in the same sentence as the "Indian Squaw," who may have been enslaved herself, and the "Cows."[34] Scottow was the author of a late century jeremiad, *Old Men's Tears for Their Own Declensions* (1691), in which he lamented the loss of a sense of mission among New England colonists.[35] (From this title, Perry Miller would take his valuable and much contested idea of a declension of piety among colonists during the seventeenth century.) Even sincerely pious people saw no contradiction between their religiosity and slavery.

There were some large-scale holdings in the seventeenth century, though even those were still far smaller than would be found centuries later on a cotton or rice plantation. Robert Cutt of Kittery, Maine, owned "Three Negro men 2 of them ould and decrepid," worth forty-five pounds, "Two Wimine Negros," worth thirty pounds, "Two Negro Wimine Children," worth twenty pounds, and "one Negro Lad," worth sixteen pounds.[36] The price rationale is clear: the highest-priced slave was either the "Negro Lad" or the nondecrepit "Negro man" (his exact price can't be determined from the records, but old and decrepit men certainly were valued at less than any other individual). Next were the adult women, presumably of reproductive age and thus potentially worth more. The least valuable were the girls and the old men; the former could probably not yet reproduce (but contained that possibility in their growing bodies), and the latter were beyond their productive work years. Owning eight slaves was unusual in early New England, but Cutt was a shipmaster and shipbuilder and had arrived in the region from Barbados. The enslaved Africans may have come along with him.[37]

If probate records testify to the larger community's assessment of a slave's value, wills attest to the individual owner's understanding of an enslaved person's worth. New England colonists wrote wills when they had an idea that death was approaching, and they wrote with at least one eye looking toward posterity. Their careful dispersal of their human property underscores how even a single slave could loom large in an owner's understanding of his or her own estate. George Clarke of Milford, Connecticut, wrote an early will on April 15, 1678, and took care to place slaves into his family's future, giving "two of my negroes, a man and a woman, to my son George Clarke, which he shall chuse," and "to my son Thomas Clark, one negro," and "another negro to my daughter Sarah."[38] The inheritance followed biblical injunction: Deuteronomy called for the eldest son to receive twice what his siblings inherited "by giving him a double portion of all that he hath: for he *is* the beginning of his strength; the right of the first-born *is* his."[39] A deacon, Clarke melded his scriptural knowledge with his knowledge of a key characteristic of the Atlantic system—that an enslaved man and an enslaved woman could reproduce enslaved children. While his eldest son received such a couple, Clarke's other children would have to make do with just one slave each, a legacy of only half the immediate value, and much less valuable once reproductive capacity was figured in.

Ten years later, though, the senior George Clarke wrote an addendum. In 1688, he declared "that besides the gift of a negro," he also gave to Sarah his "negro boy named Ishmail, desiring her to bring him up to reading, and to set him at liberty when he comes to the age of thirty-two years, or, if she please, a little sooner." That Clarke now owned this boy, not yet old enough to read, suggests that the enslaved couple may have reproduced in the interim ten years, giving Clarke yet more property to dispose of—Maverick's breeding comes to mind—but if that was the case, the young boy was being bequeathed away from his parents, to the sister of his current owner. It is also possible that Clarke bought the young boy, but, unlike the original slaves mentioned, the child seems to have aroused his active interest: Clarke knew and wrote his name (Ishmail) and desired that he be taught to read and be set free in his adulthood.[40] But this liberty was as yet, at best, a prospective freedom, for in the will Clarke noted that if his grandson "Jonathan Law should marry and need him more than she, I do give her liberty to dispose of him to the s[ai]d Jonathan."[41] These were decidedly conflicting liberties: the prospect of Ishmail to be "set . . . at liberty" by Sarah against "her liberty to dispose of him." The ways that one person's liberty might impede another's could hardly be more starkly shown.

The setting aside of enslaved children and adults for heirs, a sort of living futures contract, was not unique to Clarke. In his 1675 will, Newbury's Samuel Moodey, a surveyor, left to his oldest son his house with all adjoining lands, pastures scattered around the town, money, and his "Negro Boy"—all to be had when his son turned twenty-one.[42] Two years later, Daniel Peirce of Newbury left his namesake and oldest son his "housing lands goods and Chattels." A subsequent inventory of the substantial estate (with land valuing more than twelve hundred pounds) included, last among those goods, "Negros, 60li."[43] John Knight of Newbury had a sizable estate at his death. The farmer and merchant (he owned shares in a vessel that traded with Barbados) had done well in life. His three sons split the land and houses between them equally, his three daughters were each awarded eighty pounds, and his wife, Bathsheba, received everything else, including one "negar man" worth twenty-five pounds.[44]

The same awareness of value is demonstrated in wills that only reluctantly offer freedom to enslaved people who survived their owners. In the middle of the century, Atherton Hough, a colonist in Cambridge, willed freedom, albeit with ample caveats, to his slaves, "Francis Flascnoe my negro and his wife." Hough was careful to note that he "set them only at liberty after my son Samuells death, but if Frank [Francis] die before her then I do not set her at liberty."[45] The will of the colonist Antipas Boyse set his "negro servant, Janement . . . free for himself," provided Janement served Boyse's son faithfully for two years after the father's death.[46] Several years later, John Winslow ordered in his own will that his "negro girl Jane (after she hath served twenty years from the date hereof) shall be free."[47] Two decades of enslavement would see Jane well into her adult years. A Rhode Island colonist left his "negro Lango" to his wife, to be freed after her death.[48] And also in Rhode Island, Richard Smith bequeathed freedom to his slaves "Ceasar and his wife," after his death, and to his slave Ebedmelik, after Smith's wife's death. The couple's children, though, had to serve until they were thirty years old.[49] This sort of hedged freedom accentuated the value of enslaved people to their owners, even while acknowledging liberty as the desired condition for those people.

Indeed, that was the rub: implicit in these bequests of freedom was the recognition that enslaved people wanted their liberty. And yet, even people who believed themselves to be considerate masters, still owned slaves for long periods. In 1676, Elizear Barron bequeathed his "negro servant" to his wife, with the admonishment to "have a care of hime that he may suffer noe wronge." That care of him, apparently, included keeping the man, Shippio, enslaved for another nine years, because only in her own will of 1685 did Hannah Barron give to her "negro Shippio his time, chest, and clothing to performe the advice of my late husband." It seems clear, then, that the couple believed that enslavement itself would not cause the man to "suffer . . . wronge."[50] Their words of concern highlight just how slavery expanded in New England and elsewhere: not at the hands of self-styled sadists, but rather through the actions of ordinary people who considered themselves to be caring and responsible, who told themselves and believed that even if enslaved people longed for freedom, their own personal enactment of slaveholding was permitted, protective, and unproblematic.

And so it was that common people owned slaves and that the settling of their estates and the assessing of their property worked slavery into the legal regimes of the New England colonies more thoroughly than did any deliberative discussion of the institution. Rather, instance by instance, regulations regarding slavery emerged. In 1676, the mariner Paul White of Newbury complained of being overtaxed on his estate by too high an appraisal. His own appraisal of his holdings the prior year had included among his ratable estate "two heads, if a man of 84 years old and a Negro be ratable, 3s 4d."[51] His *if* allows us to infer what the records do not make explicit: that at some point in 1676 a group of Essex County authorities discussed and debated how enslaved people should be taxed, thus eventually codifying slavery without any direct debate on its legitimacy. By 1695, for example, a Rhode Island decree set firm tax rates for "negro servants and cattle," at one pound, eight pence, for an adult man, and one pound for an adult woman. In comparison, mature oxen were taxed at "three pence per head."[52] Twenty years earlier, in Massachusetts, there had been some confusion about taxation rates of chattel property, but now, at least in Rhode Island, clarity reigned. The implementation of such laws demonstrates how a legal system develops, step by step, in response to the mundane problems that crop up in its given society. Slaves themselves had been conscripts in the front line of colonization—lumbering woods, clearing land for planting, fencing enclosures—but the social rules regarding them were made up as part of the slow process of settling that followed.

Such laws demonstrated, too, how colonization and slavery were linked in formal ways. The ownership of slaves brought taxes to the colonial government in early New England—just as it did in other regions around the Atlantic world. And just as the payment of taxes irked owners elsewhere, the payment of taxes irked the likes of Newbury's Paul White. "Death and taxes," Daniel Defoe would write early in the eighteenth century, "are the certainties of life."[53] Not only were they themselves certainties for the colonists, but they carried with them questions and ambiguities that called for certainty. The case-by-case valuing of estates normalized slavery in the region as much as, if not more than, did the codification of any explicit slave laws, for these daily, particular interactions very probably affected colonists and their slaves more often than did sporadic issuances of new general codes.

The inclusion of enslaved people in documents like probate records and wills reflects the value of their labor in the New England colonies. But even though their work had worth, the labor they performed was prosaic and unremarkable. Many enslaved women, for example, provided domestic labor, because the feeding, cleaning, and clothing of people was a nonstop activity in New England throughout and after the process of colonization, and one for which help would always have been welcomed. Such domestic labor, though vitally important, was almost invisible in the records—and nearly always unwaged—whether the worker was enslaved or not.[54] Ironically, the worth of enslaved women's and girls' domestic labor was somewhat more visible than that of English servants and women within the house master's family, because though not wage labor, enslaved house servants' work nonetheless did have a market value in colonial New England, a value incorporated into the slave's own worth.

The worth of their labor can also be assumed from the simple reality that enslaved domestic workers were kept at all, for the maintenance of property, even of human property, cost money. People needed to be fed, clothed, and cured, and even if this was all done at bargain prices (think of the refuse fish, think of sick slaves being shipped down to Barbados to convalesce, think of inferior clothes), there were costs nevertheless. Andrew Sheppard of Boston owned "a negro girle," worth fifteen pounds when he died in 1676, but her duties likely related to Sheppard's wife, as evidenced by a list of debt's description of the girl as "Mrs. Sheppard's Negro."[55] Even though the young age of the Sheppards' "negro girle" probably explained the relative low worth assigned to her, still, she was worth money. But she also represented a cost, even a cause of debt, though perhaps a minimal one: upon his death, Sheppard owed ten shillings for the girl's clothing, two more shillings for unnamed "necessaryes for the Negro," and three pounds, eight shillings, for "seventeen weekes dyet for the negro at four shillings per weeke." Like her clothes, a slave's food was cheap, whether on Barbados or in Boston; an economy like that can be teased from the detail that food for "the negro" might be distinguished from that of the English. In such bills lies more evidence that even young slaves were profitable and helpful for a New

England colonist to own. Presumably, no shipwright would have held a young girl in slavery, paying—or at least owing—for her keep and clothing, unless she brought something of value to the household.

Sometimes that value derived not from specialized skill but simply from an ability to do the mind-numbing chores that no one else wanted to do. The New England colonist Ann Henchman's frustration with another colonist, voiced in a Suffolk County court in January 1672, spoke offhandedly to the mundanity of work during the cold months of the long New England winter. Complaining about her fellow colonist Joseph Rock's obstruction, she testified that he repeatedly sabotaged their attempts to get water, sometimes throwing away their pail, and sometimes damaging the pump, such that, "once our Negro [came] from the pump without water." In one English family's household, at least, a person of African descent was charged with the routine and tedious task of getting water from a well, someone whom Ann Henchman felt comfortable identifying with the possessive pronoun "our" and the generic term "Negro." The namelessness of the African in question hints at a status different from that of servants. (Though it is not clear from Henchman's comments whether "[her] Negro" was indeed enslaved, the nineteenth-century editor of the Suffolk County court records claimed, "Henchman and Rock conducted in partnership a store of general merchandise, and also owned cattle and negroes in common.")[56]

Quotidian tasks such as hauling water made up much of enslaved labor in seventeenth-century New England. True, some people performed the work directly tied to colonization, the extractive labors like Roco and Dick's forest-clearing and naval-fleet-building work in the woods. But that, too, could be and often was the daily task of a colonist as well. And just as many others did the daily tasks that went with running a colonial New England household, like fetching water from the well, ironing sheets, cooking dinner, tending the fireplace, darning socks, feeding the cows, and a thousand other chores that needed to be done whether a colonization campaign was underway or not.

This was, in fact, a paradox of New England slavery: while the Boston merchants and the Salem captains were providing the Atlantic slave trade with its fuel, investment capital, and were key players in pressing the Atlantic economy into the form of modern capitalism, the slavery practiced at home was not the forging of capitalism. Slavery in New England, at least when one got away from the docks, was often simply household labor in a household economy, even late into the century. New England slaves did not work in large-scale single-crop fields to harvest tobacco or sugar or anything else for export into the world market. Indeed, even elsewhere, most of the industrial agriculture that provided the longest-lasting images of slavery in the Americas came later. New England slavery was of its own time in early seventeenth-century America, while the West Indies, where the New England merchants did so much of their business, was ahead of it.

Though enslaved people never made up more than 5 or 10 percent of the population in New England's largest towns, and far less than that in rural areas, they nonetheless played a significant role in keeping the region's premodern economy functioning and growing. In urban situations, for example, some enslaved people handled the logistics of distribution and storage called for by a transport-based economy. In May 1680, a large and violent fire swept through much of Boston, laying "wast a Considerable parte of the Towne." This was no small setback; Boston at the time was the largest town in North America, bustling with some five thousand colonists, and growing monthly.[57] During and after the fire, some chaos prevailed, and some persons were "so wicked as to take the advantage of such occasions," by stealing what they pretended to be saving from various burning store-houses.[58] In addition, amid all the chaos and loss of records, some colonists claimed they had not picked up from warehouses before the fire goods they had ordered, and they demanded that their orders be filled again. One such man, Jonathan Dutch, asserted that he had never received a large order of ribbons and fabric but was caught in his lie by an enslaved man named Mingo who worked as the warehouse manager, and who was able to testify that the goods had in fact been delivered.[59] We might imagine Mingo, standing amid the bedlam of a burning colonial town, still attending to his duties, noting who received what merchandise, and when, from his warehouse at the port, stocked full of Atlantic goods.

Maritime duties were common for people of African descent, enslaved or not. In the fall of 1672, Alexander Wood, the master of a small fishing boat, sued John Chantry, master of the ketch *Truelove*, for a collision. The court decided, after hearing the evidence, to admonish the sailors on board the *Truelove* for recklessness; they included "the said master John Chantry John Mellons Junior Hugh Perins Henry James Joseph williams negro Joseph Wing Joseph Rawlings and Samuell Eaton marriners of the said ketch."[60] Here a "negro" is just one man in a long list of sailors whose careless sailing of their ketch into a smaller boat caused injuries and death to two men, though even the very word "negro" differentiated him from the rest of the crew. Presumably, the others were European-born or European-descended, but even that remains simply a presumption. Such fragmentary evidence requires speculation as well in even naming the "negro": the unsystematic grammar of the list leaves it unclear whether the "negro" was Joseph Williams or Joseph Wing or neither. If he was Williams or Wing, he had a last name, a relative rarity—but even that would be to presume that the list didn't simply mean, what seems most likely, to indicate "Joseph williams['s] negro."

That the "negro," whether Williams or Wing or Williams's, might be flagged "negro" and yet not be relegated to list's end perhaps implies the rough approximation of equality among crewmates. Shipboard relations could be strikingly more egalitarian than relations on land (compare the placement of the African man's name in this list with that of enslaved Africans' names in wills, next to the firkins of butter).[61] Whatever his social status, the evidence reveals that he labored side by side with at least seven other men aboard a large boat that one September evening sailed too swiftly and too close to the shore.

This mariner does not appear to have been found any more blameworthy than his mates, but an enslaved man in trouble with the law a decade later was not as fortunate. In May 1682, the Ipswich quarterly court heard charges against a young Englishman, Benedict Pulsipher Jr., charged with being aboard a boat with a "negro" and stealing wine, sugar, and food. For this crime, the younger Pulsipher was found guilty, ordered to pay a portion of the damages to the ship's owner, and sentenced to be whipped. Pulsipher's father appealed the verdict, blaming his son's actions on the influence of the "negro," who was an enslaved man. "By what I can learne," he lamented, "the said Negro did Intice my Child to commit that vileness." Pulsipher could rely on the court's sympathy, he thought, because the enslaved man's reputation long preceded him: "he . . . is very well known a wicked person."[62] But the judges might have thought of Proverbs 4:14: "Enter not into the path of the wicked, and go not in the way of evil men." They did not lessen the son's punishment.

Pulsipher's plea depended on vilifying the African man. He emphasized that the enslaved man had supposedly enticed his son on board the boat with the promise of alcohol, that the son had gone with the man because he knew that he worked on the ship, and that, once they were on board, it was the man who gave to his son the stolen goods, rather than the other way around. Furthermore, there were mitigating circumstances that the court needed to know: his "son was but of a very weak capacite (I pray God to give him more understanding) [and] Therefore might easily be Inticed by such a person as was the said Negro belonging to the said sloop." In other words, the father argued that his son was not smart enough to tell the difference between right and wrong. As evidence, he offered anecdotes of his son's repeated failures in school, and inability to learn basic life skills.[63] Pulsipher asked the court to consider his son not a thief but rather a naïve victim of a "Negro" with a bad reputation, which was not helped even though "his Master did often saverely correct him." Indeed, Pulsipher testified that even after this theft, the enslaved man continued his criminal ways, so "that his Master sold him for lesse than he would or might have done had he had been better."[64]

Pulsipher's short story offers many inroads into the life and labor of a slave in the region. It seems significant that the "Negro"— although "a person known to be so bad"—remained unnamed throughout Pulsipher's appeal, while the enslaved man's owner was named. The word "negro" apparently contained within it some sort of implicit indictment. Moreover, the man's reputation for wickedness was directly related to his status as a slave: Pulsipher knew to mention that the man's master had punished him, and that his bad reputation had lessened his value in the slave market. Proof of the man's immorality, in other words, was found in his purchase price. And yet, despite this reputation, the man was engaged in the management of a boat and was free while in port to walk around town and engage with English colonists who knew his reputation.

If the senior Pulsipher's narrative can be trusted, the unnamed "negro" could size up well the intellectual capacities of Pulsipher Jr., and could say the right words to reel him in. Language ability is one benefit of a forced cultural immersion, and the ability to speak a mutual language offers the opportunity to persuade and manipulate. Whether or not the enslaved man played Pulsipher Jr. as deftly as the father insisted, his actions do provide an example of the opportunities for social engagement afforded an enslaved man removed from the plantation societies that dominated the West Indian colonies. Loneliness and isolation, along with increased surveillance, could be characteristics of such a life. But the cultural immersion forced upon an isolated slave might also have fostered an increased ability to understand and negotiate the enslaving society. And slaves who dwelled and worked in more urban settings, like port towns, sometimes found greater mobility and opportunity for independence, none more so than one who, like this man, moved about at ease in the maritime world.

One sign of the cultural knowledge gained from immersion is the use by enslaved people in New England of individual legal agreements to earn their manumission through additional labor, as Roco and Sue had done with the aid of Richard Blackleech. An enslaved man named Angola parleyed a deal with Anna Keayne, the wife of the prominent Boston merchant Robert Keayne, to essentially buy his freedom.[65] Angola first appeared in the records in Robert Keayne's 1653 will:

> Item I give and bequeath to my Three Negars if they be live-ing with me at the time of my death, namely to Angola, Negar, forty shillings & to Richard my Negar fforty shillings & to his wife Grace Negar twenty shillings to be payd to them in some young Heifers to rayse a stock for them two yeares after my decease, yea though they should be disposed of to any other place before by my executors & if they should be still kept or imployed at my ffarme or in the service of my son or wife I hope they wilbe as dilligent & carefull in there busines & as serviceable to them as they have beene to me while I lived.
>
> Item I give Richard Negars Legacy to his daughter Zipora if she be alive at my death.[66]

Three years later, when Robert Keayne died, his appraisers included in his estate "2 Negros and a child Negro." Angola was one of those two adults.

Later the same year, a free man of African descent called Sebastian Kane contracted with Keayne's widow to buy Angola's labor for a set time, after which Angola would gain his freedom.[67] The contract bound "Bostian Ken Commonly called Bus Bus Negro of Dorchester in New England" to pay Anna Keayne eighteen pounds, in installments. Sixteen pounds would come in the form of wheat, peas, or barley, and the final two pounds would come from Angola himself, his legacy from Robert Keayne. Furthermore, as security, Sebastian Kane bound his house and land and the year's wheat harvest to Keayne's widow, and the end of the contract stated that, as a result of the agreement, "Angulos time of freedome" would begin that month. Various colonists signed the deal, while Sebastian Kane made his mark.[68] Kane himself was a man of some substance: a 1663 deed of sale lists "Sabastin Kine negro," who was "Comonly Called Buss," as the owner of a third of the ship *Hopewell*.[69] Kane later sold his estate, which contained, along with the ship, a barrel of liquor, another of sugar, and two of fish—all products of Atlantic trade.[70]

Angola was, according to all evidence, a good member of the colony. Being allowed to buy his own freedom attests to this, as does Sebastian Kane's willingness to put so much at stake to help him do so. In freedom, too, Angola inspired New Englanders' admiration. Richard Bellingham, thrice governor of the Massachusetts Bay Colony, seems to have told many the story of when Angola had once rescued him when the governor's boat sank in a river. Angola came out, laid hold of Bellingham, and got him into his boat. In doing so, Bellingham recalled, Angola "saved my life, which kindese of him I remember." Bellingham further said, according to witnesses, "Besides my giving him fifty foot square of my land to him and his I shall See hee shall not want whilst I live."[71] Angola had risen during his life in New England, from slave to free man to man of property, thanks to his basic human decency and, perhaps more importantly, his skill with a boat.

The governor's offered parcel was small—fifty square feet of land was not much then or now. Still, it was a memorable gift to some. "Memeno Negro aged about 60 years" remembered the act of giving, which occurred while he and Angola were carrying wood into the governor's yard. Bellingham stopped them, gave them a cup of wine and then, while "stroakeing Angola on the head," said, "I have given you a peice of Land of fivety foot square Now I am in a good mood goe and take itt."[72] It was an act of gratitude by the governor, and yet any semiotician would find much of interest in the governor's words and actions. Angola was a husband, a father, a free man, and yet the governor felt free to stroke him on the head and almost paternalistically offer land to the man he was stroking: "Now I am in a good mood." Did the governor stroke English colonists on the head? It seems unlikely. Did Angola enjoy being stroked? Worse things could happen to a person, to be sure, but we might wonder how it felt to an adult man to be petted, however kindly the caress was intended, however much land and a home might have been desired.[73]

The contract Angola and Sebastian Kane put to Anna Keayne gave a name to Angola's release: "freedome." In New England, in 1656, the opposite of slavery was freedom, which meant that New England colonists, even as they enslaved Indians and Africans, understood the converse as well. The intricate relationship between slavery and freedom was always fraught with fine distinctions in the American colonies, but all of the contradictions and hypocrisies derived from the immanent truth that "slavery" was in effect an antonym for "freedom," and that "freedom" meant to not be a slave.[74] And for all the metaphysics of Protestant theology about slavery as a natural state of being, the more practical document of the legal contract recognized that slavery was an earthly imposition, undone as easily as a business partnership, and far more easily than, say, a marriage. The contract imagined freedom, and thus slavery, as historicism, as subject to change with time, and it invested itself with the authority to produce that change, as when it looked into the future and lyrically described it as "Angulos time of freedome."

There were, after all, free people of African descent in New England, as there were elsewhere in the Americas. One, Dorcas, "the blackmore," had joined Dorchester's first church in 1641 (Samuel Maverick's father, John Maverick, was the first minister of the church). Her joining the congregation was noteworthy to John Winthrop, who included in his journal the fact that "a negro maid, servant to Mr. Stoughton of Dorchester, being well approved by divers years' experience, for sound knowledge and true godliness, was received into the church and baptized." In 1653, the church authorities in Dorchester voted on whether or not "Dorcas was to be Redeemed" from slavery. The vote was affirmative, the congregation members having decided that they would somehow, whether "from the whole church by Contribution or otherwayes," jointly raise the funds to buy her freedom.[75] Richard Mather, father to Increase Mather, and grandfather to Cotton Mather, presided over the vote. And that too was significant; Richard Mather held a prominent place in Massachusetts society. That he personally interacted with slavery, even if only to redeem a woman from its grasp, demonstrates the broad reach of the institution.

This vote had momentous import in Dorcas's life, no doubt, since she was granted legal freedom. But the vote also highlights that "free" status was not a prerequisite for acceptance into a church in early New England, nor did church membership automatically confer freedom. One could be enslaved and still be a member of the First Church of Dorchester, as Dorcas was for many years. Years later Cotton Mather himself weighed in on this point, posing the rhetorical question "What *Law* is it, that Sets the *Baptised Slave* at *Liberty*?" and answering, "Not the *Law of Christianity*," which clearly "allows of *Slavery*."[76] A complicated man—Nathaniel Hawthorne later famously characterized him as embodying "all the hateful features of his time," and Perry Miller called him a "most nauseous human being"—Cotton Mather owned slaves himself. Dorcas may have been lucky to encounter the grandfather rather than the grandson.[77] In any case, in 1677, more than two decades after her legal redemption, and three decades after her spiritual one, Dorcas joined the First Church at Boston, still free, still churched.[78]

Hers was a remarkable story, but it was probably the exception rather than the rule. A 1643 promotional tract, *New Englands First*

*Fruits,* recounted with admiration the story of Dorcas, a "black-more maid, that hath long lived at *Dorchester,*" noting her theological knowledge, her awareness of "experience of a saving work of grace in her heart, and a sweet savour of Christ breathing in her." She underwent both a private "trial" before the church elders and a public confession of her conversion—in this way mirroring the trials of faith as endured by English colonists—and was accepted into the congregation. But even the promotional tract noted that she was unusual, observing that "her friends and Kindred [were] still in their sinnes."[79] Dorcas joined the Dorchester church only four years after Samuel Maverick's attempt to breed another "negro woman," which means that Dorcas's "long" stay at Dorchester already before her admission to the church made the two women contemporaries, albeit with startlingly different experiences. Even as slavery became more embedded into New England's culture, freedom remained always a possibility—though it also always remained only one possibility of many.[80]

Indeed, the question of freedom was no idle topic for seventeenth-century New Englanders. Rather, it obsessed them. That the early New Englanders imagined their cherished liberty in direct opposition to loathsome bondage speaks to how acutely slavery was on the New England mind. After John Winthrop had defeated his political opposition in a 1645 Massachusetts Bay Colony court, he proceeded to offer "a little speech" on the limits of liberty, a gratuity that Perry Miller described as "nothing less than the final twist of an inquisitorial thumb-screw."[81] But beyond gloating, Winthrop's words amounted to a treatise of covenant-based, or rather contractual, political theory. "The great Questions that have troubled the Countrye," he observed, "are about the Authoritye of the magistrates & the Libertye of the people." Winthrop sought to reformulate these two not as at odds with each other but rather with the latter dependent on the former: he insisted that civil liberty "cannot subsist withoute" subjection to authority. To do so, he put forth an example of a "womans owne choise" to marry a husband and freely choose "to be subjecte to him, yet in a waye of Libertye, not of bondage."[82] Winthrop's imagery suggested much about the social universe of the New England Puritans, and perhaps that of other colonists too. The ideal of civil liberty depended upon political subjection to government authority—a subjection well understood as a woman's subjugation to her husband, which in turn ought to be understood in opposition to bondage—the subjection of a slave or serf.[83]

The examples of Dorcas and Angola imbue Winthrop's words with immediate social significance. Like marriage, slavery was an institution familiar to colonial New Englanders, more visible than saints, more visible than God, certainly more visible than the unseen covenant that Winthrop hoped and trusted his government held with his Lord. The ready examples all around of people bought and sold and owned made Calvinist metaphors about bondage and servitude even more powerful and complicated, because freedom was clearly understood to be the preferable state.

People's actions made this clear, as when William Stitson, a deacon in Charlestown, declared in his 1688 will, "Six months after my decease my negro Sambo shall have his freedom."[84] Stitson's words imagine the dilemma slightly differently than the "time of freedom" conceptualized in Angola's contract: here a freedom awaits Sambo already, but only after Stitson's death may Sambo have it. Stitson's words didn't suggest slavery as Sambo's proper or natural station— indeed, there is an intimation that slavery was an unnatural imposition in the phrasing "shall have *his* freedom," with the pronoun somehow hinting that the liberty was Sambo's to begin with.

Similarly, Sarah Rundell in 1694 left to her daughter Rebecca Raynsford, wife of John Raynsford, "Marriner," one hundred pounds and her "negro woman Ruth" for an eighteen-month term of service, after which Ruth was to receive "her absolute freedom from all manner of servitude." (Rundell's other daughter received no slaves, but did stand to inherit from her mother all monies that might come from "debts as due and owing to me in Barbados.")[85] Presumably, Raynsford could not sell Ruth, and presumably, she could not rescind her mother's promise of eventual freedom. These terms, practically speaking, made her mother's gift more like a loan than an inheritance. Lending slaves was common in New England, as was the renting out of slaves, though neither usually led then to freedom. Also common was the renting out of indentured servants, but while the renting out of indentured servants technically required the permission of the indentured person, slaves could be lent at the master's will.[86] Ruth's circumstances, then, were muddled: Rundell hadn't precisely turned her into an indentured servant, and Ruth was offered no say about going to Raynsford's household, but neither was Ruth to be truly Raynsford's slave. Ruth, rather, was to remain a dead woman's slave for eighteen months, ordered to serve a living heir who did not own her. What sort of duties would Ruth have felt obligated to perform in the meantime? What liberties—what freedoms—would she have felt entitled to that another slave would not? What sort of punishments could she have faced for any insubordination? Perhaps she considered that the most prudent course of action was to keep her head down and work for eighteen months, and so gain the "absolute freedom" prescribed in the bequest.

Absolute freedom. Sarah Rundell's declarative phrasing implied degrees of servitude and of liberty, and hinted that she did on some level recognize a partial freedom already enacted before the eighteen months ended. Time did peculiar things to slavery, and it also played tricks with Ruth's "freedom," just as it had for the boy Ishmail whom George Clarke had intended, perhaps, to be set one day at "liberty." Liberty and freedom—such revolutionary language here was accumulating meaning and significance, used to define human chattel in the mid-seventeenth century.

But arresting as the phrase "absolute freedom" may be, it was not particularly indicative of the social relations enjoyed by even an unenslaved African or Indian person in New England. As John

Winthrop's "little speech" suggested, to be free in New England was still to remain enveloped in a thick web of social hierarchy. The governor's petting the head of Angola offers only one tangible example of how English colonists felt free to treat people of African or Indian descent differently. In another instance, two fifteen-year-old Bostonians testified in 1694 that while gathered on "Forthill," they had met "a Negroman," who fell into conversation with them and offered to buy one of the boys' earrings; to show that he could do so, the man flourished some silver coins and a piece of gold. The boys, surprised to see the man with so much money, queried him on its provenance. He boasted, foolishly it turns out, that he had even more gold, that he had got the money "a privaterring," and that he worked on an English ship operated by the Royal Navy.[87] Soon after the man left, another colonist came and asked the boys "whether they saw any negro thereabout." They answered that "there was one just parted from them . . . [and they] informed him that said negro had gold about him and that they would go and catch him."[88]

Together, the three English colonists went after the first man and, upon finding him, ordered the "negro" to strip, and then searched for the gold and the pieces of eight, found by unbuttoning the knees of the man's breeches, which had been folded up and served as a sort of pocket. The Englishman confiscated the gold and silver and "went away commanding the s[ai]d negro to go with him." One of the boys testified additionally that the man had flaunted gold to the boy's father and some other men earlier in the day.[89]

This too happened in early New England: African mariners, probably impressed into the Royal Navy, wandered through port towns, boasting and admitting of privateering (though perhaps the age of his audience had something to do with how he fashioned that tale). The man spoke English, wore English-style breeches with knee buttons, moved freely about Boston (until he didn't), spoke openly with colonists, and carried foreign coinage. And still, even if the man was free, he did not act as the equal of any of the English colonists he encountered: he obeyed orders to strip from a man unknown to him, and the boys felt free to "catch him," a phrase and action they might not have applied to an Englishman. In such ways could race make even freedom less than absolute.

In parts of the Chesapeake and South Carolina, large populations of enslaved people labored on plantations far from English colonists. That separation, along with the large-scale importations of more enslaved Africans, allowed and fostered the creation of cultures distinct from that of English colonists. It was a kind of isolation that allowed, for example, the emergence of languages like Gullah.[90] By contrast, in seventeenth-century New England, laborers were deeply enmeshed in the larger society. Even while strands of a slave culture could be glimpsed in occasional acts of solidarity, and while enslaved people of color took part too in a somewhat distinct popular culture of the region's lower ranks, it remained true that the small holdings of seventeenth-century New England permitted less cultural autonomy.

If it was not a distinct slave culture or a working-class culture, the culture that enslaved Africans participated in could look distinctly plebeian—probably more rough-and-tumble than the culture of New England's elite merchants and leading ministers. In the midst of a 1672 trial of three men accused of stealing wine from a Mr. Hubbard, in Ipswich, one of the accused testified that he had carried a gallon of wine stolen from his house to the house of another colonist, and that there the alcohol had been drunk by several other men, including "Nath. Emerson, Arthur Abbot and a negro."[91] As so often happened, the "negro" was granted no name, but we might also notice that he was an accepted mate of this group of English servants, a drinking companion if not a peer in other social spheres.

Enslaved people navigated many social situations, and if sometimes they drank stolen wine in their leisure, more often they remained on call in the worlds of their masters; most often, in other words, it was the master who was drinking. That was the case in a 1680 incident in which an enslaved man intervened to protect William Fanning's wife from her drunken husband's abuses. Indeed, Mrs. Fanning had been drinking, too, and, along with her husband was charged with the misdemeanor crime of intoxication. Additionally, William was charged for subjecting his wife to violence while swearing and cursing. A witness named Jonathan Clarke said "that in the house Fanning threw things at his wife, kicked her, and swore he would cripple her and she showed the marks of her husband beating her, as she did to others, and said if the negro had not taken him off, he would have killed her."[92]

The text begs the reader to consider what the "negro," so casually referenced, thought of these affairs. Had he witnessed the continual violence that left marks on his mistress's body? Did he often have to intervene? Did his presence in the household mean that Fanning could beat his wife with more impunity, knowing that another man was there to restrain him? How did the man understand the relationship between Fanning and his wife, and between the Fannings and himself? Witness, as he was, to intimate domestic disputes, he was at once privy to confidences otherwise kept within a family and yet was distanced from the family by race. And part of the service he provided was to prevent his mistress from being murdered. Given the oppressiveness of chattel slavery, it can be startling to read of enslaved New Englanders doing such good deeds, coming to the aid of English colonists even when other English would not. And yet they did. When the colonist Richard Cordin allegedly attempted to rape Mary Roffe in a stable and when Roffe cried out for help, a woman in the house stayed put, but "sent out the negro" to rectify the wrong even while embodying another.[93]

Such horrifying stories make clear that enslaved Africans and Indians in early New England, like all inhabitants of an early modern English household, saw many things that might now be considered intimate, secret, in the course of their daily duties. In the early modern world, privacy was still a thing of the future, and the small-holdings of New England slavery meant close proximity to the lives of masters, which could get slaves into sticky predicaments. In 1677, James Black, an enslaved man of African descent, caught the colonist George Major in the act of stealing meat from the house early one morning, when Black's master was away in Boston. Major immediately predicted the obvious: that Black's master would first accuse the enslaved man. Major told Black that if he said nothing about the strange occurrence, Major would give him a reward.[94] Black's presence in the house meant that he could catch Major in the act, but his status as an enslaved man meant that he was likely to be the first accused of the crime.

We get a fairly clear picture of James Black's everyday life from this story. James Black knew Major well enough to go to his house subsequently, and Major knew him, too: later Black admitted that Major had previously asked him to steal wool and powder and meat.[95] Black knew that Major should not have had the meat, and knew his master's travel plans (that he had gone to Boston and so there should not have been any noise in the house). He slept upstairs, probably in the attic, because he came "down" to investigate the noise. He had his own trousers and shoes, but he slept at least partially unclothed. He understood his job to include protecting the house when strange noises arose—he did not go to awaken his mistress or anyone else. He had many jobs, then, but none of them were marked by his race or by his status; he was an enslaved person in an English household, doing unremarkable labor.[96]

The need for such labor was a primary reason English colonists owned enslaved Africans and Indians. But slaves are social capital, too, and their ownership could both instantiate and substantiate a colonist's social rank and identity. The sociologist of race Orlando Patterson has pointed out that "in a great many slave-holding societies masters were not interested in what their slaves produced," but rather sought "the strong sense of honor the experience of mastership generated." The historian Walter Johnson has further argued that nineteenth-century slaveholders "imagined who they could be by thinking about whom they could buy."[97] For New England's wealthiest colonists, many of whom were merchants rather than farmers, the ownership of enslaved people who were *not* needed for physical labor could be a sign of prosperity and prominence, perhaps particularly so in a town like Boston, where the close proximity of neighbors meant that the display of slave ownership could carry extra weight.

Such a display was described in the spring of 1691, when witnesses came to Boston's county court to give testimony regarding a brutal knife attack on an enslaved "negro" man called Dick, owned by Samuel Shrimpton, the prominent New England merchant. At the time of the attack, Shrimpton was, one historian estimates, "the richest man in Boston," at the very center of New England's thriving economy.[98] He was a dandy of a man, with long flowing hair, and carefully trimmed bangs. A late seventeenth-century portrait of Shrimpton has in the background an enslaved man, perhaps the only extant image of an enslaved person in seventeenth-century New England. Indeed, it is possible that the portrait depicted Dick, the unfortunate slave who formed part of Shrimpton's entourage one night when a drunken colonist named Robert Watson approached, verbally accosted Shrimpton, and then lunged at Dick with a knife, slicing the man's throat halfway across his neck.

The affair seemed to puzzle witnesses. Shrimpton himself professed utter ignorance regarding Watson's motives. He was walking home from dinner at a friend's house, when he stopped in the street to speak with another colonist. It was then, he said, that Robert Watson came by, "a person altogether unknown unto me." The man seemed, Shrimpton said, "to be in drinke" and he "railed exceedingly against me and called me rogue and sonne of a whore and whore-master." Shrimpton's father and mother, Henry and Elinor, had in fact been neither, but then as now the insults of a drunken man were best ignored. Shrimpton was blunt: "Perceiving [Watson] to be a stranger and in drinke as I thought I tooke little notis of him."[99]

The prerogative to take little notice of the man certainly accrued to Shrimpton by virtue of his wealth; his social standing likely protected him from having to respond to the inebriate. This was Shrimpton's good fortune, all the more so since he may have had a bad temper in moments of conflict. Some five years earlier, after a heated exchange, Shrimpton had begrudgingly apologized for having spoken "with too Loud a voice, and in too violent, A manner, for which I am hartily Sorry and humbly Crave your pardon."[100] But that incident had been a complicated case of insulting an equal.[101] Robert Watson, instead, was beneath Shrimpton's notice, perhaps precisely because the merchant had subordinates such as Dick standing nearby whose implicit obligation was to respond to such insults. One of the greatest prerogatives of the wealthy is surely the privilege of having proxies fight their battles.

And so it happened: while Shrimpton claimed to take "little notis" of Watson, Dick's enslaved status required him to respond to the insults to his master.[102] Shrimpton testified, "My negro . . . asked Watson if he knew me and what made him give me such language." Dick's intervention turned out to be unlucky. Watson answered Dick, "You Rogue doo you belong to him," and then drew his knife and slashed Dick "from his ears into his jaw through his cheek into his gums a gash about five inches square and had sertainly suddanly cut the negroes throat, had not some people coming prevented him." Do you *belong* to him? The answer to that question provided the enraged drunk man with an outlet for his fury. Rather than an assault on Shrimpton's person, the attack became destruction of Samuel Shrimpton's enslaved property.

Shrimpton's son also witnessed the attack, and remembered that after Watson had sliced Dick's throat, the man swore, "God damee I will Marke the master of this House as I have done the negro," and further threatened, "I will marke the House too," thus perhaps referring ominously to Shrimpton family members.[103] But he did neither; his fury was spent on Dick. When the son asked Watson why he had attacked Dick so terribly, Watson only "answered he was sorry he did not cut his throat," and went on to "utter many oaths & curses in the street." Another colonist, Harry Gonny, testified that he had run after Watson and warned him that he would have to face the town council for justice, to which Watson "answered God Dame the Council they are all a piell of Cheating Rogues."[104]

The action continued in the wake of the street attack. After cutting Dick, according to Samuel Shrimpton, Watson "followed another negroe of mine up to my house and when I came home I found him in my house quarreling with my kinsman." (This makes at least two slaves in the entourage that escorted Shrimpton to dinner.) Shrimpton, who had a cane with him, told Watson to leave the house, and "caned him" him when the man dawdled. Watson finally left, "swearing and Cursing and threatening." Shrimpton professed himself to be as confused by the events as anyone else. "The man," he said, "I never saw in my life nor heard of him," though Shrimpton admitted that he had "since been informed that I was no friend unto his [illegible] or his wife."[105]

A variety of characteristics made Shrimpton no ordinary Bostonian. Certainly his wealth set him apart.[106] And after his wealth, contemporaries remarked on his arrogance. His fellow colonist Samuel Sewall, no fan of impropriety, noted many of Shrimpton's shortcomings, all of which stemmed from the man's propensity to enjoy life just a little too much. "Mr. Shrimpton, Capt. Lidget, and others," Sewall indignantly reported to his diary, "come in a Coach from Roxbury from 9. aclock or past, singing as they come, being inflamed with Drink." Sewall noted with disdain that the group stopped nearby to "drink Healths, curse, swear, talk profanely and baudily to the great disturbance of the Town and grief of good people." The old Puritan, who frowned on riotousness and profanity, could barely stomach the scene: "Such high-handed wickedness has hardly been heard of before in Boston."[107] But he may have been understating the case. Perry Miller once remarked that "the more one studies the history of Puritan New England, the more astonished he becomes at the amount of reeling and staggering in it."[108]

It was perhaps this sort of behavior by Shrimpton, and just this sort of arrogance, that triggered Robert Watson. But Dick paid the price. His presence in the region originated in the grasp of a global trade, but he had his throat slit in the midst of the most homegrown of disputes—so local, so petty, that his owner did not even know what the fuss was about.

Deposition of John How. *Courtesy of the Connecticut State Library.*

# CHAPTER 5

# Intimate Slavery

Woe to him *that is* alone when he falleth; for *he hath* not another to help him up.
Again, if two lie together, then they have heat:
but how can one be warm *alone*?

—Ecclesiastes 4:10–11

In 1669, an enslaved African woman in Massachusetts called Hagar became pregnant and was required by authorities to reveal the name of the father. Under examination, Hagar accused her owner's son, the colonist John Manning, of having impregnated her, explaining that he "had often fellowship with her." But she also admitted that she and Daniel Warro, "Negro servant to Capt. Gookin," had a relationship as well. Warro had come, she explained, "one night and knockt at the doore and shee went out with him into the streete and had the use of her body." This pairing was not repeated, she insisted, and furthermore she swore that "no other man have had to do with her in that kind since shee came to New England."[1] Her emphasis on having had only two sexual partners presumably gave her identification of her child's father more heft.

Though authorities had indicted her for fornication, Hagar had her own accusations to level. She took advantage of being in front of a magistrate to voice her grief and indignation about being in New England. She asserted her authority as a "married woman" who had "a husband living in Angola, by whome shee had a child, about three years since." Hagar explained that "shee ws stoalen away from her husband and child which sucked on her breast, and was brought away to the Barbados, from whence shee was in short time shipped for New England."[2] By the letter of Puritan law, this made her slavery illegal, because slaves could not legally be taken by kidnapping—it was this very sort of event, man-stealing, that had once occasioned John Winthrop to convene a court, in the case of the *Rainbow*. But now, twenty-five years later, it seems that Hagar's grief aroused little interest.[3]

Certainly the magistrate who heard the case, Thomas Danforth, took no action to investigate her illegal bondage. The rules of property seem to have trumped Hagar's grief over another child, another pregnancy, another mate, and another life. Possibly Danforth was not an ideal judge for a woman pleading illegal slavery: both he and his daughter owned slaves.[4] But perhaps he was affected by the woman's story. A pious Puritan, he may have thought of a tragic question posed in Isaiah, "Can a woman forget her sucking child, that she should not have compassion on the son of her womb?"[5] And in fact, Thomas Danforth knew something about lost children himself. Of his own twelve offspring, all of his seven sons died before he did.[6] Nonetheless, Hagar's story was beyond his remit.

Still, the court's apparent lack of interest need not be our own. We might consider what Hagar felt about the possibility of bearing the child of her owner's son, given her already tragic past. Indeed, we might wonder whether a relationship between John Manning and Hagar could have been welcome or consensual on her part. Whatever their relationship, he was never convicted of fornication with Hagar. In fact, during her labor, according to Englishwomen in attendance, Hagar rescinded her identification of Manning as the father and instead pointed to Daniel Warro.[7] We might further notice that she had kept count of the years since she had seen her nursing infant, and that she continued to insist on the primacy of her marriage and her family across the Atlantic, reminding us again that not all people in New England considered themselves *of* the region, that some people sat in New England homes only reluctantly, dreaming of other people and other places.

The embrace of chattel slavery in the region meant, by definition, that New England's colonists violated time and again the personal relations of the people they owned. Like enslaved people throughout the Atlantic world, enslaved people in New England, both men and women, Indian and African, knew that their fates and those of their loved ones were almost wholly controlled by their owners. The fact that New England's slaveholding households generally owned only one or two slaves at a time has been used to suggest these enslaved people were integrated into English homes in a way plantation society did not facilitate.[8] But in truth, their presence in a colonial home happened only because at some point they had been removed from their own communities and families elsewhere. To be the only slave in a seventeenth-century New England household did not mean that you were treated as one of the English family. Rather, it meant primarily that you were missing, like Hagar, from your own family, whether your family had lived in Gambia or Massachusetts, and that you had been purchased or awarded, and placed as property in a home that was not your own. Perhaps you were treated relatively well, perhaps not; perhaps you acclimated, perhaps not. But your English owners only had the opportunity to treat you mildly or badly, and you could only adjust or not, after you had been taken from your children, your parents, your siblings.

Such separation was certainly true for the first generation of enslaved Africans in North America, "saltwater slaves," who had crossed the Atlantic Ocean against their will. And it was true also for enslaved Indians, those who had been sent away from the region, and those imported into New England, saltwater slaves not from Africa. Experience Mayhew, a missionary to Indians on Martha's Vineyard, described the life of James Spaniard, a *"Spanish Indian"* who had been "brought from some part of the *Spanish Indies* when he was a Boy, and sold in New England." Spaniard, Mayhew said, remained long "discontented" in New England, because "he laid much to Heart the unkind Treatment he had met whital, in being separated from all his Friends and Relations, and brought out of his Country into a strange Land, from where he never expected to return again."[9] Eventually, Spaniard gained his freedom, married, and had a son, but only after his long discontentment.

This threat of partition remained true even for subsequent generations of enslaved people, since a defining feature of chattel slavery continued to be separation of kin according to the vagaries of the market. At the heart of the experience of chattel slavery in the Americas, in other words, was not differentiated, raced productive labor, but differentiated, raced reproductive labor: the reality that the children born to enslaved people might not remain with their parents, and that enslaved people themselves had been taken from their own natal families.[10] In this way, too, New England matched other English colonies. In 1662, Virginia's General Assembly codified what was apt to be by then a fairly common practice: that children inherited the status of their mother—*partus sequitur ventrem.* The assembly legislated that "all children borne in this country shalbe held bond or free only according to the condition of the mother," and that "any christian" who committed "fornication with a negro man or woman" would pay double the fines that would have been imposed had their partner been English.[11] But such customs were by no means limited to Virginia; twenty-four years earlier, Samuel Maverick had relied on the idea of an inheritable slave status when he ordered one of his slaves to rape another in hopes of breeding them.

There were, then, many versions of a "New England family." One version adheres closely to the model laid out in classic histories: the patriarchally governed family of English colonists.[12] An English family, wrote William Gouge in 1622, "is a little Church, and a little commonwealth . . . it is as a schoole wherein the first principles and grounds of government and subjection are learned."[13] This ideal family consisted of a married couple at the center of a household, with dependents arranged in appropriate levels of deference below; it formed the foundation of the culture.[14] Indeed, this hierarchical family arrangement, as the scholar Edmund Morgan described it, mirrored the larger "social order," whose "essence . . . lay in the superiority of husband over wife, parents over children, and master over servants in the family, minister and elders over congregation in the church, rulers over subjects in the state."[15]

Without these little commonwealths, colonists feared the society would falter; the family unit was essential to the stability of that larger culture. William Bradford described its essentiality well in explaining why the Pilgrims of Plymouth Plantation abandoned communal property, the colony's original approach. "This community" he later wrote of those first years, "was found to breed much confusion and discontent and retard much employment that would have been to their benefit and comfort." The younger men disliked working for other "men's wives and children," while their wives, "commanded to do service for other men, as dressing their meat, washing their clothes, etc., they deemed it a kind of slavery."[16] And so Bradford, even in explaining something as basic as community service, relied on an understanding of bondage to make his case, by emphasizing a crucial distinction: the English were not slaves, did not do forced labor, and did not owe their labor outside their families. Bradford did not view slave labor as distinct work. Rather, the distinction that he thought mattered lay in whom one was working for: household labor outside the family could mean slavery. In theory, and in one version of reality, enslaved people were dependent members of the English *household*. But they were not part of the colonial English *family*.

Surely it was more complicated to form a family as an enslaved person, in large part because the biological family was so fragile in a chattel system. Whereas the English family was patriarchal, we might see enslaved families as matrilineal because the status of the mother so often determined the children's fate, and because, as the historian James Sweet has argued, "masters were not bound to recognize the paternal claims of African men whose children were born outside of Christian wedlock," leaving mothers to raise, nurture, and educate their children, as far as possible.[17] Whereas the English version of the New England family had stability at its core, the enslaved version was fraught with a tenuousness that could threaten family ties at any moment.[18] The English family model relied on coherence with a goal of perpetuity through things like inheritable estates, while the enslaved New England family formed part of those actual inheritable estates and as a result experienced nearly constant incoherence, in its literal sense, through the separation by sale and commodification of kin.

Such a scattering of families, through capture, kidnapping, or sale, was central to the early modern Atlantic market, with its emphasis on slaves as individual commodities.[19] West Indian trade, even with New England, was made on the backs of broken families. In 1670, the colonist William Hollingworth sued the colonist Michael Powell Jr. "for several goods left with said Powell in Barbadus and Verginea, and money in New England." The lawsuit was settled amicably, but its conclusion involved the return of a "little negro boy" of Powell's, "known by the name of Seaser now in the hands of Mr. William Hollinworth."[20] However it was that the various properties had been commingled, the resolution of the conflict entailed making sure that Seaser ended up with his rightful owner, not with his parents.

Twelve years later, in November 1682, the Massachusetts colonist John Keene brought suit against Thomas Bligh, for keeping from Keene and his wife "a Negroe boy by name James." That the court awarded Keene the munificent sum of thirty pounds (roughly the market price of an enslaved African) *and* James suggests that it took the case very seriously and regarded the loss to Keene's wife as a significant financial blow.[21] Here, muted by the impersonal nature of the court record, is evidence of another enslaved family torn asunder. Where was the mother or the parents of James? And what rights had they to sue for the return of their son? The answers bear repeating: the court did not concern itself with them.

This sort of casual severing of kin made personal relations fraught with sorrow for enslaved people all over the Atlantic world, including in colonial New England, an area with a widely dispersed slave population, where enslaved people might live miles from one another. Captive Indians from the region, but not those who had been imported, potentially had the consolation of family in the immediate vicinity, though that consolation existed only so long as they were not sold into slavery in the West Indies or Bermuda or North Africa. But even a small separation can seem quite far when the people separated are parents and children, and when someone else owns, literally, their time. And many enslaved Africans in the region must not have lived near any kin at all. While people of African descent who lived in port towns might have seen other Africans every day, those farther inland might have had such sightings only sporadically, if ever. And yet, even as Atlantic enslavement divided natal relationships in aggressive and generally permanent ways, it also inevitably, produced new families, as enslaved people reproduced in their new, unchosen settings. That enslaved people also contributed to the colonial population was at once ironic, unavoidable, and somehow, in some instances, an act of creation in a world of destruction.[22]

How does family begin? Is it with sex, with conception? With a child's birth? With the profession of commitment between lovers? For the Puritans, it began with marriage. But contracts of servitude often expressly forbade servants to marry—"he shall not commit Fornication, nor contract Matrimony within the said term," dictated one 1692 model indenture contract—and it went without saying that the enslaved also could not freely marry.[23] There were exceptions, of course. English servants sometimes did marry, and so, sometimes, did slaves.[24] But even a recognized marriage might not protect an enslaved person from the cruelty of separation from his or her partner. Even as solemnized marriages among enslaved people increased later in the seventeenth century, the possibility of sale remained very real. "Puritan love of money proved stronger than respect for domestic ties," argued the historian Lorenzo Greene, who noted various reasons that enslaved families who had been legitimated by colonial authorities might be dissolved: the death of a master, or sheer profit motive.[25]

Or revenge. When Hannah, an enslaved and married woman, was accused and convicted of stealing silver medical instruments, she was sentenced to a fine and a whipping, but the colonist from whom she had allegedly stolen asked for still more. He reminded the court that the whipping had served the colony's interest by publicly reminding people of the dangers of criminality, but that he had personally received little from her punishment. He asked the court to remember that it had long been custom "in this Countrey, & approved by Authority to sell servants to satisfy Judgments of this nature, when their Masters have refused to satisfy the same." In other words, he asked the court to remember that Hannah had value in her very body, married or not, and that selling her might produce a profit that could go toward his loss.[26]

Whether because of legal proscription or enslaved people's own choices, it seems that such condoned marriages were relatively rare. After all, how could a servant be a patriarch? How could a mother properly be a maid? The problem of family for the enslaved and indentured of New England, then, began with the problem of their regulated status: colonists had criminalized the act of making a family, as they understood it, for servants and slaves. And yet, servants and slaves, legally refused the statuses of father and mother, nonetheless fathered babies and mothered them. Thanks to the documentation of punishments meted out as part of the authorities' attempts to prevent such behavior, we have evidence of the activity that begat both the babies and the penalties that resulted. To read of the punishments for the fornication of those without marriage rights is to read about the varieties of slave families in early New England, and of the attempts of authorities to deny them.

Whether because of their shared restriction from marriage or because of the isolation they shared, some enslaved people and servants found fellowship with each other. Social hierarchies placed slaves at the lowest rung of society's ladder, but English servants stood on a rung only just above slaves, and they too could be far from home, if they even had a home to be away from. One historian has pointed out that in Essex County, Massachusetts, "the great majority of farm servants whose names entered the court records . . . possessed no local kin of any kind."[27] That depth of isolation surely contributed on occasion to a willingness to enter into cross-cultural relationships.

Such relationships were far from rare. At midcentury, an enslaved woman in Salem called Katherine was ordered to pay forty shillings or be whipped, for birthing a child out of wedlock. Her owner, Daniel Rumball, promised to pay the fine, apparently thus preventing the whipping. It was common practice in New England, where authorities had no interest in raising unsupported children, to require the father be named, but in this case, perhaps because the mother was enslaved, no man was implicated.[28] But when Katherine became pregnant again three years later, a colonist was implicated. In Salem, in 1653, authorities fined James Thomas for fornication with a "negar servant of Danyell Rumball," and ordered him to pay weekly maintenance for the child.[29] In November of that year, presumably after this second child had been born, Katherine was again accused of fornication, and received again the option of being fined, this time twenty shillings, or being whipped.[30] The introduction of a new child undoubtedly complicated household matters. Would a "negar servant" be able to fulfill her duties with a child to raise? Would the child be Rumball's property (was Katherine?), or would it be free, given its paternity? Would Rumball have seen the child as a mouth needing food and a back needing clothing, or would he have seen hands that would eventually do valuable work? He doubtless saw the child differently than did Katherine.

James Thomas was himself a servant, though English, and good behavior was not one of his more notable attributes. In July 1644, he had been whipped as punishment for disobeying his master; four years later, he was fined for being publicly drunk. Shortly after that, he was caught stealing codfish and further found guilty of lying.[31] It was the following year that Katherine had her first child, and two years later that she had her second child, of which Thomas was proclaimed the father. Paternity does not seem to have mellowed him, for he was soon back in court. In June 1653, he was again fined for inebriation, and again in December 1654, by then father to at least one but perhaps two children.[32] Katherine had partnered with a disreputable man. But given her straitened circumstances, it's no certainty that falling in with a more reputable man, had one been available, would have improved her lot in any tangible ways.

Such interracial couplings continued throughout the century. In 1660, Jugg, "Capt. White's negro," was convicted of fornication (having birthed a child) and sentenced to be whipped.[33] She later identified the English colonist Walter Tayler as the father. When Tayler denied it and threatened to sue her owner for defamation, the court slapped him with a fine of forty shillings for "commencing a vexatious suit." Apparently enough eyewitnesses had testified to the relationship that denial was implausible.[34] In the fall of 1672, Christopher Mason, an English servant, was "convict of getting Mr. Rock's Negroe maide Bess with Childe." Mason admitted his guilt to the court, which sentenced him to be whipped with twenty stripes, to pay court fees, and to put up a bond of twenty pounds in order to ensure his future good behavior. Three months later, Bess was also sentenced to be whipped twenty times and to pay court fees.[35] In 1677, the Ipswich quarterly court ordered "Joss, merchant Wainwright's negro," whipped for fornication, and "to pay to Sarah Gowin or her father 2s. per week every week or 8s. per month or to be distrained for it by the marshal."[36] Gowin was English; Joss, African. Presumably Gowin had given birth to Joss's child. Born in North America to a European mother and African father, this was a new world's child, one of many.[37]

Of course, Englishwomen and Englishmen, too, were also con-victed of fornication and could also be lashed and fined. But an Englishwoman found pregnant out of wedlock could hope to retain her child, could aspire for that child to overcome the burden of bas-tardy. An enslaved woman who found herself pregnant could never expect anything so benign—because her child was property. More-over, for all the apparently consensual couplings made visible by these fornication cases, we might consider just how many noncon-sensual relations must have occurred, if New England's version of chattel slavery was anything like that in the rest of the Atlantic world.

And still, the evidence nonetheless makes apparent that some enslaved men and women in New England managed to create rela-tionships that they valued, including some cross-racial ones, and that they understood the relationships to be valid. Toney, a "Negro Servant" to Samuell Clarke of Milford, Connecticut, was charged in 1688 with impregnating Sarah Smith, another of Clarke's ser-vants, but English. Both parties confessed, Smith testifying that she "never had to doe with any other man." Smith's words say so much, including that she did not think of herself, no matter what the court thought, as promiscuous, but rather as essentially monogamous. Most importantly, her testimony explicitly says that she saw Toney as a *man*. He was, of course—not even slavery could obviate the obvi-ous. The court sentenced Toney to pay eighteen pence a week and to be lashed on his bare body twenty times. Smith avoided immediate whipping because the childbirth had left her weak, though she was handed a hefty fine of twenty shillings cash or forty shillings worth of goods, with the threat that if she could not pay, a whipping awaited her when she regained her health.[38] One scholar has seen this case as indicative of a shift away from the whipping of English colonists as punishment, thus emphasizing the increasingly stark social dis-tinction between people of African descent and people of Euro-pean ancestry.[39] Moreover, as fines and penalties became steeper, it may be that some enslaved people grew less willing to accept them. Already in 1680, a Marblehead indictment of a "negro servant of

Richard Rowland" for fornication came to little use: the constable of Marblehead reported the man was not to be found.[40]

Though "negros" and Indians sometimes partnered with English persons, and sometimes with each other, records suggest that they tended more often to form consensual partnerships with a member of their own group, when possible.[41] In 1673, George, a "Negroe servant" in Newport, in the colony of Rhode Island, was sentenced to be whipped fifteen stripes for fornication with Maria, another "negro servant." She was whipped, too.[42] In 1678, the Salem quarterly court sentenced "David, Mr. Pilgrims neager man, and Judeth, Capt More's neager," to be whipped for fornication. David received ten lashes, and Judith received the option of five lashes or a fine. Though no baby was born from this union, two eyewitnesses swore to the relationship; one testified that he had often seen David visiting Judith, and Judith's owner stated that he had several times warned David to stay away. The warnings did not work, not on that couple and not on others.[43] Two years later, Hager, a "neager" woman belonging to a colonist named Rucke, and her partner Tony, another "neager," belonging to a colonist named Batter, were found guilty of fornication and were sentenced to be whipped or pay a fine.[44] These cases were far from rare; people inevitably found each other, as they always have. In the middle of a spring night in 1682, an African man snuck away from the Charlestown household of Solomon and Mary Phipps and into the garret of another house for an assignation with the maid, an African woman, "like he hath done," it came out when he was caught, "at severall other times before."[45]

Regardless of the risks, enslaved women had sex with men and predictably then sometimes had children. "Mr. Warrens Indian" Jasper confessed to and was convicted of fornication in 1672, with "Mr. Warren's Negro" Joan. She was convicted of the same offense, eventually producing evidence of their guilt in the form of an illegitimate infant.[46] Here an Indian man and a woman of African descent were in servitude in the same house. In 1674, Juniper, "John Hales' negro," was presented for fornication and sentenced to be fined or whipped; the same year, Marea, "Negro Servant to mr. Simon Lynde," was "convict by her own confession in Court of committing Fornication and having a bastard Childe."[47] In 1677, "Grace William Colemans Negro" was convicted of fornication and birthing a child out of wedlock, and was sentenced by a Suffolk County court to twenty stripes.[48] Shortly thereafter, again in Suffolk County, Kathalina, a "Negro Servant," accused another (probably Irish) servant of being the father of the "Bastard Childe born of her body about a month agone." The man denied his part in parentage, and fate rendered the fact of his complicity in the conception sadly moot; the baby died soon after birth. The imputed father was dismissed with a fine. But Kathalina, like women throughout history, was not able to deny parentage—the child had come out of her own body. She confessed to and was convicted of fornication and of having birthed a child out of wedlock. The court sentenced her to be whipped fifteen stripes, or to pay a fine of forty shillings, a fine later reduced, by the mercy of the court, by half.[49]

Pregnancies were the usual telltale evidence of criminalized love. In June 1674 in Salem, "Richard Dole's negro called Grace" drew an indictment for fornication, apparently because she was visibly pregnant. The indictment did not name her partner. Five months later, in November, the sentence came down: she was to be whipped or fined. Presumably the court had waited until the baby was born before passing judgment, for New England courts do not appear often to have whipped visibly pregnant women, even those who were enslaved. The following year saw Grace again indicted for having another child out of wedlock, and four months later, again after recovering from the birth, she was sentenced to a whipping or a fine. This time, Grace accused "Mingo, Rich. Dole's negro," of having fathered her child, and the court accordingly ordered him to pay both maintenance for the child and the cost of the trial.[50]

It seems remarkable that no one else accused Mingo of having fathered Grace's children, since the two slaves lived in the same household. Grace in particular surely knew who could have impregnated her, so her silence until after the birth is curious. She may have been protective of Mingo, or she may have been afraid of the reactions of a different father if she spoke; after all, in other places at other times, as many would have known, an enslaved woman's owner would have been a likely candidate for an unowned pregnancy. Maybe the easiest explanation for her silence is that authorities simply did not press the case of an enslaved woman giving birth if the master did not insist. Whatever the particular rationale may have been for her initial silence, it opens up inner worlds of interests and ideas to think of that silence as a social strategy.

And owners may have had strategies, too. The same month that Grace finally named Mingo as her children's father, Dinah, Benjamin Roff's "negro-woman, of Newbury," was also charged with fornication and sentenced to a whipping. The father of her child was Tom, another slave owned by Mingo's master, Richard Dole.[51] Was Dole encouraging his slaves to breed? Certainly he deemed them to be of value: he owned them for a long time and viewed them as property worth bequeathing. More than two decades after Grace had borne a child, she was given her freedom in Dole's will, "if she will accept of it," while his "negro servant Betty" was given her freedom after two more years of service. As for the children of these fornication cases, they remained enslaved. Dole willed his "negro boy Tom" (presumably the child of Dinah and Tom) to one of his sons; the "negro boy Mingo" (presumably the child of Grace and Mingo) he bequeathed to another son.[52]

And so it went. New England antifornication codes failed spectacularly to legislate sexual behavior among enslaved people. There is something touching in that failure, something perhaps admirable about the determination of people to have liaisons, to form connections in a world determined to deny them. But, of course, not all people can or do fight restrictions, and some spectacular harm must have been done to people's lives in the administration of punishment. The threatened and real whippings and humiliations almost certainly did prevent other enslaved and indentured New Englanders from stealing away to the meadow or climbing through an open chamber window. All of them, those who stole away and those who did not, were thus kept from settling into something more stable, into what might well be thought of as family life. But even that recognition falls short of comprehending the rank tragedy that resulted from enslavement—the root problem was not that restrictions were put on making a family, but rather that those enslaved in seventeenth-century New England had already been rent from any family they had. The problem was that they were in English homes at all.

It was no doubt a heavy burden, physically and emotionally, to carry a child destined for enslavement. No extant sources record how it felt for a woman to carry a pregnancy that would produce a child over whom she would have no control; what it meant to feel your body thicken, belly swell, breasts engorge, all the while knowing that your child could be taken from you at your owner's whim. Some women may not have been willing to give their children up to that fate; over the years, several enslaved women stood accused of infanticide, at least two of whom were alleged to have disposed of their liveborn infants in outhouses.[53]

Similarly, in 1674, "Anna Negro servant to Mrs. Rebeckah Lynde," a widow from Charleston, was charged with birthing a "Bastard" and then murdering it. The jury apparently could not agree whether or not Anna had borne a live child, but it did find Anna guilty of birthing a child while unmarried and then disposing of the body. As punishment, she was ordered to stand tied to the gallows by a rope around her neck for one hour, and then to be tied to a cart and paraded to the prison while being whipped thirty times. After that, provided that her owner paid the legal costs and prison charges, she could be discharged from custody.[54] The public shaming and the elaborate punishment speak both to the severity of the crime in English eyes and to the court's, and probably her owner's, desire to keep her alive.[55] Anna's own understanding of the crime (if in fact she believed she had committed a crime at all) remains obscured.

Indeed, personal motivations are always hard to ferret out. On January 8, 1664, an order was issued to take into custody "a negro woman" named Zipporah, for having fornicated with a "negro man," for having borne a child as a result of the relationship, and for having then killed the child and stealthily buried its corpse. The alleged crime came to light when a colonist found a decapitated infant body.[56] Surprisingly, there was some confusion over whether the corpse found without its head was the same as the body that Zipporah had buried, not because there were so many decapitated bodies of children in the Massachusetts Bay Colony but rather because the found infant appeared to be "whitish," whereas Zipporah and witnesses argued that the infant born of her body was "blackish."[57]

During Zipporah's trial, various witnesses came to the court to describe their knowledge of her pregnancy. Elizabeth Mellows, a servant, testified that "she was in the house but not in the roome" when the "negroes child" was born, and that soon after the birth, her mistress came down "and bid her take up Coales[,] for her negro was delivered of a dead child." Mellows acknowledged that she saw the child, "but did not well observe it," and noted that it was "of a darkish Coulor the thighs and leggs." She further reported that three English women—her own mistress, "Mrs Parker," Zipporah's owner, "Mrs. Manning," and another woman, "Mrs. Sands"—told her to keep the event secret, because the child was "deadborne." She questioned this advice, saying that "she never heard that such a thing was kept secret." The women reassured her on this point, and Zipporah's owner cryptically explained that "she meant to send the negro to the Barbadoes."[58] The threat of the West Indies, a Dantean hell, always lingered over the heads of New England's African inhabitants, even those who had just endured a stillbirth.

Mrs. Sands also testified. She said that she had first known of Zipporah's pregnancy when "Besse the Negro" came into her shop and informed her that "Mrs. Mannings negro looks very bigg and that she should doe well to tell hir mistress of it." Sands promised to look into it and asked Mrs. Manning about the issue, but was told that Zipporah was not pregnant—that her apparently obvious extra weight was instead merely "fatte." Manning went on to say that Zipporah had recently menstruated ("had the Custom of women upon her"). This seems to have alleviated doubt, and Sands went away satisfied, until she was later summoned when Zipporah began to labor ("the wench being in payne"). She was initially reluctant to come, but ultimately did assist the birth and felt, she reported, "the head Come to the birth and at the next [labor] payne the child Came into her hands the head limber and the child dead." She further testified that she had viewed the child and seen "the face and head and the breast" and that it was "black as a negro."[59]

The colonial authorities wanted to know whether Zipporah had birthed and thus killed a live child, but the secrecy with which the body was disposed of made answering their questions difficult. Zipporah herself testified "she knew not she was with child till she was quicke [in labor]." After giving birth, she further said that "Mrs. Parker bid hir goe & bury the child & that she went and made a hole nere the sand where the water was," and buried it there. It was surely no small feat to rise from childbirth and bury a recently born, dead infant, but all of the witnesses agreed that Zipporah had done so. Mrs. Parker, when asked directly whether she had asked Zipporah to bury the body, answered simply, "She did." Though she did not spare Zipporah this task, Parker did testify that she "tooke the child & putt it in a Ragg" and then "bid [Zipporah] to get a Negro woman to her."[60] Sympathy and comfort, evidently, were best left to those of the same race.

It seems a terrible story of loneliness, of childbirth and pain and death, in a house far from home. And yet, it need not have been, for even if the Englishwomen present were unwilling to offer comfort, a community of other "negroes" was nearby. The most notable absence was, of course, that of the purported father of the infant, who was apparently never called during Zipporah's labor to wait for the birth, and was never called afterwards, to testify. But other "negroes" were nearby, too. There was, for example, Besse, who had first told Sands that Zipporah was pregnant. And another woman, "Mary negro the wife of Franck Negro," apparently attempted to visit Zipporah. She later said that upon "hearing her Country woman Zipporah was ill abed," she went to see her the next morning, but was intercepted by Mrs. Manning. Mary explained that she had come to "see her Countrywoman that she heard was ill abed." But Manning said, "No[,] she [Zipporah] was well on her leggs."[61] The term "country woman" suggests a relationship understood to derive from a common point of origin. But while that relationship bound Mary to Zipporah, it distanced both, whether they were free or enslaved, from the English-women who surrounded them.[62]

It demands reflection, this separation in the face of proximity, the way that perceptions of ethnicity or skin color or religion or all of them combined into something now called race could thwart solidarity and sympathy in what otherwise might have seemed a fundamentally human moment. In September of that year, Ann Parker and Ann Manning were publicly admonished before the congregation of the First Church of Boston "for Concealing the sin of fornication in their negro servant."[63] Zipporah's thoughts on their sins might have run a different course. It seems worth underscoring, too, that had the child lived, Zipporah's story might have read as simply one more case of an enslaved woman accused of fornication, and the terse lines of her indictment and punishment would have rendered invisible the solitary labor, the hostile household, and the isolation she suffered.

There could be a vast emotional gulf between master and slave, even in close quarters. Nearly twenty-five years later, a "Spanish Indian" woman enslaved in the town of Weymouth, in the Massachusetts Bay Colony, left the English home of Stephen and Hannah French, where she served, and gave birth in the home of a local Indian sachem called (by the English) Charles. He appeared at the French house a day later, announcing that the "squa" had "lost her piganiny

[baby] yesterday a little before sunsett."[64] What was certainly a tragedy quickly also became a melodrama when the colonist John Vining spread the rumor that the child was born alive "and that it was throwed out to the hogges and they had eat some of it and the child['s body] lay by the wigwam Dore."[65] Again, as with Zipporah's case, the interest of the court lay in whether the woman had committed infanticide, a supposition based entirely on Vining's testimony. Hannah French, the woman's mistress, did not think there had been a murder, because she did not think the fetus had been healthy. She testified that the pregnancy had been painful and that the woman had "for severall weeks [exhibited] a most violent distemper," and that she had seen "issue of water and clots of blood running out" of the woman's body, a hint of the terrors and pain that pregnancy could hold for women in the seventeenth century.

Ultimately the enslaved woman was acquitted of the charge of infanticide, possibly because no body could be found, and possibly because Hannah French's testimony was compelling. But surely the woman could not have escaped unscathed, for her owner's testimony demonstrates that she for some weeks endured a painful pregnancy among people she served but whom she did not trust to help her during her labor. Hannah French testified that the Indian woman "would often cry out her belly was a fire and that shee should go into the Ground," possibly a non-native English speaker's way of indicating that she felt like dying. French was not indifferent to the situation, and further testified that she consulted "severall women of good experience," all of whom agreed that the woman's condition would prevent her from "bring[ing] forth a living Child for that which should have nourished the Child was continually issuing from her."[66] And yet, it seems that the Indian woman did not perceive this attention from the English women as helpful. Though the term "Spanish Indian" almost certainly meant she was neither local to the region nor related to the Native Americans in the area, she fled her owner's English home to that of an Indian family when her labor became too much to bear, seeking help from a household of her own choosing.

The story of Silvanus Warro, an enslaved man owned by Daniel Gookin, demonstrates how kinship ties and community could also bind. Gookin was a man of some authority in New England, a "Puritan of the Puritans," one biographer called him.[67] A soldier and merchant, he served on the governing council in Massachusetts for several decades. He came to New England in 1644, after living in both Maryland and Virginia. In Massachusetts, he settled first in Boston and then in Cambridge, and he owned property in Massachusetts and Maryland. After spending time in Cromwell's England, from where he had encouraged New Englanders to migrate to Jamaica, Gookin returned to New England in 1660 after the restoration of the English monarchy under Charles II.[68]

He was, through most of this, a slave owner. Gookin's move to New England in 1644 was followed at some point by that of the brothers Silvanus and Daniel Warro, two enslaved boys who had been "borne, bred & educated" in Gookin's house, the children of two enslaved parents: Jacob and Maria Warro. (In 1655, Indians in Maryland killed Jacob—countercolonial violence affected even enslaved colonists.)[69] Daniel Warro was the man whom the enslaved woman Hagar, under duress and in the throes of childbirth, had finally accused of fathering her child.

New England's paternity and fornication laws also ensnared Silvanus, his brother. Silvanus Warro lived with Gookin (except when Gookin went to England) as a slave, in New England until 1667, when Gookin sold him for eight years (perhaps a rental more than a sale) to the colonist William Parke of Roxbury.[70] In March 1672, while working in Parke's household, Warro was sent to prison in Boston, "for his Comitting fornication with Elizabeth Parker & begitting her with chyld, & for his disobedience & night walkeing."[71] Elizabeth Parker was an English servant of Parke's, indentured to him most likely because her own family was impoverished. In April 1672, just after being released from Boston's prison, the Suffolk County court convicted Warro of "Stealing mony from his master Deacon William Parks [and] having a false Key to his Box." Under interrogation, Warro confessed to the theft and was sentenced to pay Parks twenty pounds "in Mony" and to be whipped twenty lashes.[72] The whipping presented one sort of difficulty, but the twenty pounds in money was an impossibility. It would have been a substantial fine for most colonists and unimaginable for an enslaved man.

But the punishment only got worse. The court had not forgotten Warro's child with Elizabeth Parker, and it ordered that Warro pay weekly support toward the baby's maintenance. Just as the fine was out of his reach, so was such a weekly dunning. Warro could hardly hope to come up with that kind of money, with or without the key to his master's money box, a limitation the court anticipated. It had a contingency plan ready: in case Warro could not pay, the court decreed, Silvanus should be sold for the equivalent value.[73] In this way, both the enslaved man and his master would be punished, for the former would be uprooted while the latter would have to turn over the profits from the sale of his slave to the town to pay for the child's maintenance. Authorities perhaps intended such punishment to remind slave owners that they should control their slaves. For Warro, fornication, stealing, and running away turned out to have dire consequences, for he faced a complete separation from his family.

Precisely because Warro had kin, his transgressions affected many people, including especially his son. The infant's mother, Elizabeth Parker, was from Lancaster and had returned there after the birth, but that town did not want the responsibility of raising an illegitimate child, and her family was in no position to provide much help. Her father was poor and lived in a house that was, authorities insisted, "soe mean that when it Raines there is noe drie plac in it and many times [he has been] forced to goe to other houses for shelter and for lodging." Besides these deplorable material conditions in the household, Lancaster authorities reported grave spiritual lapses in the family, including that Edmund Parker's son, Elizabeth's brother, had neither education nor religion. He had not attended church services in more than a year and, when admonished for this lapse, had been "full of forward and peevish and provoking language." They wondered, pointedly, whether a father who had raised such a son could really be "fit to take more young ones into his family."[74]

After some deliberation, those authorities decided that he was not. But neither was the child returned to his own father, who was, after all, enslaved and still liable himself for the fines he had accrued through his thefts. Roxbury authorities decided instead that Silvanus Warro Jr. be taken from his grandfather's house and then, when able, put out to service for thirty years, "for the defraying those necessary charges hee [Parke] hath expended about the keeping thereof."[75] History repeated itself, for again a Warro son was separated from his parents. Though the child was half English, and free by virtue of his mother's status, he was effectively indentured for a huge portion of his adult life, removed from the protection of his parents.

The older Warro, enslaved and imprisoned, received a different offer. Knowing that the punishment for stealing from Parke still hung over Warro's head, Gookin offered the man a choice: be sold out of the colony to pay his debts, or be sold to Jonathan Wade, a local colonist and slave owner. Gookin warned Warro that if he chose to remain local, the trouble would have to end, and he would have "to be content to live with Mr. Wade for else he must be sold out of ye Country to satisfy the Court's sentence." Warro opted to stay with Wade. Strangely, Gookin attempted to sweeten the deal by playing matchmaker. He pointed out that Wade already owned some African slaves and that Warro "might fall in with Mr. Wade's Negro Wench and live well."[76] His gist was obvious: better by far that Warro should partner with another enslaved African.

The final sale of Warro to Wade included payment to Parke for almost five years of "unfaithfull Service," scathing wording to be sure, and for part of the stolen money. In all, Parke received slightly more than twenty-six pounds from Wade in exchange for Warro's service for the rest of his life.[77] Gookin apparently felt some guilt over his part in this transaction, because in a 1682 letter to the court he sought to undo the deal. Gookin argued that: "If any have right to him tis myself who Bred him from a child [and] his parents were my vassals [and] his Brother is now my servant [and] this poore negro now in his old age is willing and desirous to end his days in my service." Gookin sought the court's pity, noting that even though Warro was old and thus unlikely to be of much use as a laborer, Gookin still found himself unable "to withdraw [his] naturall affection to him."

As an argument it seems convoluted to modern eyes; to Gookin it made perfect sense. He felt an obligation to Silvanus Warro because of nearly feudal obligations—his father had been Gookin's vassal. That vassalage rather than enslavement was the framework that Gookin used is both unusual and striking. But it seems somehow undercut by talk of having "bred" Silvanus and of his "having a right to him."[78] If it seems obvious now that the initial enslavement of Warro's parents, their child's separation from his family, and the conditions of chattel slavery had done harm to Silvanus as much as any later sale, it was not so clear at the time. Gookin was a sincere man, and a principled one who saw no contradictions between his actions and his words regarding Warro. Ultimately, the court remained unswayed, ruling that Wade had paid enough to have Warro serve him forever, and that Gookin had no say in the matter.[79] He had sold Warro, and that transaction mattered.

The child of Silvanus Warro and Elizabeth Parker had a difficult life himself. In 1707, "Silvanus Warrow [Jr.] a Mollato man," was brought before the selectmen of Boston for residing in that bustling town without permission. They described the man as a "Lame Cripple," resident in town since the preceding November, after having finished his apprenticeship with "Mr. Budge of New Bristoll." Boston authorities had little interest in supporting the disabled man, who had presumably now completed his assigned thirty-year indenture, and they sternly "warn[ed] him to depart out of this Town."[80] Used, perhaps abused to the point of lameness, and then discarded: the life of Silvanus Warro's son demonstrated that long-term indentures could be fearsome in their own way.

In fact, for those who had lived lives of servitude away from family, old age could be truly fearsome. Because slavery was, at its core, an institution of labor, its effects on those past prime laboring age were most pernicious. Scholars have discussed how slavery as an institution changed over the course of American history, but it of course also changed over the life of an individual enslaved person. At some point, an investment in human property became, in financial terms, a liability rather than an asset, and slaveowners had to account for the care of aging people who had been taken from the family that might naturally have sheltered them in their dotage. Slave owners eventually thought about this; in 1702, the colony of Connecticut passed a law requiring owners to support older slaves. Noting a tendency among colonists to free their slaves only after those slaves "had spent the principall part of their time and strength in their masters service," leaving those newly freed people without any support or shelter in their last years, the colony mandated that former owners be liable for the support of any indigent freed people found within colony borders.[81]

Enslaved people also considered the problem of how to support themselves in their maturity; survival was a real and pressing concern for a person extracted from kin relations, although certainly most of the terror of that situation went unrecorded by colonists. Only sometimes do the records catch the strategies used by enslaved people to ameliorate the cold reality that they were depreciating and thus less appreciated. One example of this is a late-century court case in the Connecticut Colony, with the following accusations at its heart: that an elderly slave of the late governor Theophilus Eaton of the former New Haven Colony had illegally sold some of the governor's land and had then left the colony for New York with the proceeds of the sale. He had been the slave of an important colonist. Contemporaries described Eaton, the founding father of the New Haven Colony, as a pillar of righteousness; Cotton Mather, never one to understate an issue, later memorialized Eaton as "the Guide of the *Blind,* the Staff of the *Lame*, the Helper of the *Widow* and the *Orphan*, and all the Distressed." Eaton was, according to Mather, "Prudent, Serious, Happy to a Wonder," as well as pious.[82] He was also a well-traveled man: he had lived in Denmark for at least three years before coming to New Haven, and he was extensively involved in the Baltic trade, of goods, not people, through the East-Land company, a prosperous group of merchants. By the time he came to New England, in 1637, Eaton had amassed a considerable fortune.[83]

He and others immigrated first to Massachusetts, but moved on relatively quickly, perhaps because that colony was in the midst of a painful theological dispute, now known as the antinomian controversy, or perhaps because they saw better opportunities for trade farther south. Indeed, New Haven's deep harbor made it ideally situated to take advantage of both inland trade via the Connecticut River and Atlantic trade. It also benefited from its close proximity to New Amsterdam, nestled at the mouth of the majestic Hudson River. Several influential early New Haven colonists, like Isaac Allerton and John Davenport, spoke Dutch and traveled there frequently.[84]

By the time that Governor Eaton's elderly enslaved man, John Whan, headed there, perhaps in 1667, New Amsterdam had been rechristened New York, after the Dutch surrendered Fort Amsterdam to the English in 1664 (the same year New Haven Colony reluctantly accepted its merger into Connecticut). Slaves had been there since at least 1625, if not before; more than a decade earlier than in New England. Many of New Amsterdam's enslaved people were Angolan in the early years, when the Portuguese dominated the slave trade. John Whan's unusual name, had it been spelled Juan, might have indicated previous experience with people from the Iberian Pennisula, though no surviving testimony about him speaks of such origins. By 1630, at least sixty African slaves lived in New Amsterdam, some held privately and others owned by the Dutch West India Company.[85] In place in New Amsterdam was a sort of half slavery, in which it was not unusual to be granted freedom in adulthood, in exchange for, say, an "an annual payment of a portion of [a slave's] crops . . . and one fat hog, upon penalty of return to bondage." By 1650, people of African origin had spread across Manhattan Island, and this notion of half freedom became commonplace. In no other place in early North America was legal freedom so available, and certainly no other similarly large and established community of Africans was anywhere close to New Haven.[86]

Eaton owned a minimum of three people of African descent. By 1644, one named Anthony testified in a court case brought against Eaton's wife, Anne, after she had accused him of bewitching "the beer because it would not run when mashed."[87] By midcentury, Eaton also owned John Whan and his wife, who eventually created more tangible problems. During Theophilus Eaton's lifetime, according to the testimony of his daughter, Hannah Jones (she had married William Jones), he had "two Negro servants bought with his many servants for ever or during his pleasure according to Leviticus, chapter 25, verses 45–46."[88] Hannah Jones repeatedly emphasized their chattel status: "These wear," she said, "a part of my honored fathers estate, personell estate as well as his land real estate." That the two "Negroes" were slaves, not servants, was a distinction that would matter immensely to her case. The slaves served, she emphasized, "for ever or during [Theophilus Eaton's] pleasure"—a time span to be determined, in other words, by their owner. One man's pleasure could mean another man's enslavement. And yet, Eaton seems to have been as kind as a master could be.

His daughter attested to his generosity—a largesse invariably circumscribed, to be sure, by the slave system in which it operated. John Whan and his wife, she testified, "being stricken in years, [and] not like to have any posterity, [and] allso being maryed lawfully with my fathers consent, [and] being *both* his servants or slaves," apparently began to think about their future. This concern was made more serious by the wife's evident senility. As Jones put it, "the woman growing both old and very crazy" asked Eaton to "build them a littill house on some bit of ground being past labour promising she would serve him as far as she was able." Eaton apparently had agreed to this.

Perhaps he was familiar with the Dutch model of slavery, in which elderly slaves were set free to care for themselves, or perhaps he had sympathy for the old couple, or perhaps he more pragmatically found this suggestion a good way to stop feeding two extra mouths.

Jones testified that her father built the couple a house at the end of his land, not too far from the meeting house because the slave woman was not able to walk far, with the understanding that the slave woman would still work a bit for the Eaton family, spinning and doing small jobs. John Whan was further required to work three days a week for the governor, though he was allowed three days of his own time to provide for his own maintenance and that of his wife. They were allowed to plant crops in the land surrounding the house, and generally they lived independently. All of this, according to Hannah Jones, was done with the understanding that both Whan and his wife remained slaves of Theophilus Eaton, living in a house built on his orders and still owned, like them, by him. She testified that although they lived apart from the family, "still they were both servants to him and a part of his estate and [her father] might at his own pleasure have taken them off his lot or sold them to another master."[89]

New Haven in the seventeenth century was an orderly and pious colony, famously organized into nine squares, the center square containing a marketplace and green. Eaton's land was on the northeast corner of the green, a substantial property. Whan's parcel would have been well-placed by most standards, no matter where it was located in Eaton's holdings. And just as he would have been well positioned to observe the goings-on of the town, the townspeople would have quickly become familiar with the sight of the governor's slaves.

But things must have changed after the death of Governor Eaton in 1658; neither his will nor his probate inventory mentions the Whans, an interesting omission, but not proof that they were free.[90] After Eaton's death, his widow became executrix of the property, and she allowed John Whan and his wife to stay in the "littell house."

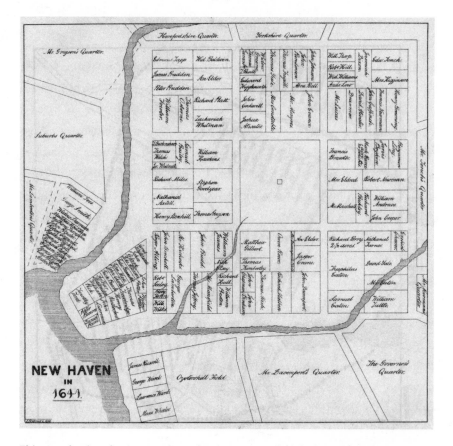

This reproduction of a 1641 map shows the nine squares of original New Haven. Reproduction of Brockett's Map of New Haven in 1641. *Courtesy of the Yale University Art Gallery.* Gift of the Reverend Anson Phelps Stokes, B.A. 1896, M.A. (Hon.) 1900, L.L.D. 1921.

But some time thereafter, she also died, leaving that portion of the estate to Hannah Jones and her husband. And soon after that, John Whan's wife also died. Three deaths in such quick succession probably seemed very dislocating to John Whan, particularly that of his wife. But, in losing Eaton, who had been kind enough to give him, in some manner, a house and land, Whan had lost a prominent benefactor, albeit in the form of a master.

Such a loss had immediate repercussions. Not long after those three people intimately connected to his life died, Whan was called into court to answer a complaint that he had harbored a stranger in his house. An apparently baffled Whan asked for clarification of the code, which was read to him. When the illiterate Whan protested that he had not known of the rule, "he was told that the law was printed, wch although he could not read himself, yet It had beene his duty to have used means to have informed himself." Whan, perhaps seeing the futility of more argument, promised to inform himself better in the future, and he was not punished.[91] This visitor may help explain Whan's eventual departure. Perhaps his unnamed visitor was from New Amsterdam and encouraged Whan to remove himself there. Or perhaps he had had enough of being held accountable to laws he could not read in a place he did not want to live.

One other event described in the records may shed light on his departure from New Haven. In 1661, John Lambert was brought before the court of New Haven, charged by Hannah Jones's husband, William. Lambert stood charged of slander, specifically, of having accused Williams Jones of writing two contracts that differed substantially in substance regarding Whan's status and labor requirements. The contract given to Whan for his signature stated that "he was engaged to help Mr. Jones, to help him to plow his land, and to mowe or reape his corne, to mowe his grasse and to help him home with the hay, to cutt his winter wood and to doe anything else which Mr. Jones should require him to doe," without any mention of pay.[92] It was a contract for a return to slave labor, essentially. Lambert was at William Jones's house when the contract was delivered, and Whan then told him that the paper should state that he was "freed from all worke." After hearing that, Lambert read the contract and "told John Wan that he was engaged to worke, to which he answered that then Mr. Jones had cuzzened him, and done no right."[93] To be cozened was to be "cheated, beguiled," an English phrase Whan had possibly learned through experience. This odd series of events ended with Lambert's apologizing for having slandered Jones, saying that though he had once considered Whan "as greatly wronged . . . he now saw his error." Was Whan convinced, too, or did he see Jones's actions as a betrayal, and pocket his grievance until he could make his escape?

Certainly it was neither a hasty nor an entirely secretive departure, for six years after the contract dispute Whan approached William Jones and offered to sell the land. Jones refused the offer, but agreed that Whan could still live in the house, pointing out that Whan "was an old man and he would not have him negleckt his soule and go not whither least he ruened himself." Hannah Jones said she did not hear about this, Whan's first attempt to sell the land, until much later; she found it astonishing. She eventually decided that Whan had simply wanted a gift of money or goods from William Jones, and that this was his indirect way of asking for it. She considered this likely because, in her opinion, Whan knew "we shuld have bin unwilling to turn this old Negro out of dores, nor be less kind according to ability than my father was." What Hannah Jones read as indirect supplication, later readers might see as a defiant assertion of his autonomy.

Hannah Jones's testimony offers details about Whan's life, such as that he spoke English, since he spoke quite clearly to William Jones, apparently without a translator. This passage also suggests that Whan considered himself to be free and to be the owner of the land, since it seems very foolish indeed to try to sell land illegally to the person from whom it was stolen. As Whan surveyed the terrain of New England, he saw room in it for free Africans, for he apparently did not expect his skin color to keep him from achieving freedom. Or it may be that something in his past led him to expect manumission rather than perpetual servitude. One detects a sense of legitimate entitlement, too, in his wife's alleged insistence that they be given a little house to live in. Again, the connections to New Amsterdam, with its tradition of half slavery for older people, seem relevant. Also interesting is that John Whan was familiar with English notions of business. His attempt to sell the land first to William Jones suggests that he grasped which buyers would be most interested: those with land adjoining his property. And lastly, though Hannah Jones was the daughter of Theophilus Eaton, and thus the daughter of his presumed master, John Whan opted not to deal with her in selling the land but with her husband—so he also understood English gender rules regarding business and property transactions—he may in fact have understood coverture, the idea that a woman's legal rights were controlled by her husband.

He was persistent. John How, a neighbor, testified that Whan next came to his house and tried to sell the land to How's father, because "he was going to New York to his countrymen." The puzzled father, believing the land to belong to William Jones, sought to clarify what Whan meant. "My father said I suppose you can not sel it," How testified. But "Whan said yes he cold for his life be sure." Having addressed legal considerations, How's father became pragmatic. He tried to dissuade Whan from leaving by pointing out his age: "my father said that is unsartan for hoe knows how short that [your life] may be: your an old man and had therefore beter stay and injoy it as long as you live." But given the distrust between the Jones family and himself, John Whan knew there would be no enjoyment or security if he remained in New Haven. He responded with the starkly poignant retort that "if he should be sicke no body would comfort him and therefore he wold sell it and goe to his country folks."⁹⁴

"If he should be sick, no body would comfort him"—the pain and loneliness conveyed in the simple statement is devastating. Whan's was such a human desire, and one so heartbreakingly akin to the grief felt by many other uprooted people who found themselves marooned in strange environments, surrounded by strange people. Inked onto an irregularly shaped piece of parchment, transcribed into oddly spelled phrases, Whan's words, mediated, but somehow still immediate, have survived over the centuries to speak to the reality of chattel slavery in such an isolated place: that there was no succor in a marketplace, no safety net of kin and love. An old man by then, at least according to John How's father, the lonely Whan looked around New Haven and saw no community. He wanted, he said, to go to "his country folks."

Was this idea of a community in New York simply a mirage imagined by an old man? Likely not. It seems Whan knew that a community of Africans was living in New York, as already noted—perhaps he had even spent time in New Amsterdam prior to his arrival in New Haven. But his going there also implies that Whan knew he did not belong in New England. He knew, despite the protestations from his paternalistic owners, that they were not his country folk. Instead, Whan's words provide an apt definition of how some enslaved people came to view family: people who would comfort you when you are sick, a definition that recalls the enslaved Indian woman fleeing her owner's home while in the throes of labor to give birth among people she too might have considered more akin and thus more kin and so hopefully more kind.

In the end, Mr. How's reluctance to buy the land did not dissuade Whan. He eventually sold it to Thomas Mix (sometimes called Meeks), a neighboring colonist, and then he did indeed apparently leave and go to New York. After the sale, he disappears from New England documents. Hannah Jones realized that the land had been sold only after the fact, and it was then that the legal wrangling ensued. She insisted (though her husband did not) that Whan had never been freed or ever become the legal owner of the land. A 1692 petition to the General Court at Hartford shows her still trying to reclaim the land. Ironically, Whan appears to have won over public opinion even as she insisted he had lost: in the petition, Jones called the land "two acres of land called Whans lot."[95] New Haven colonists, familiar with the lawsuit and the trouble, had taken to calling the land by the name of the enslaved man who had once lived there.

It was in some ways a pyrrhic victory, for this achievement on the part of an enslaved man was also inescapably a colonial achievement: the land here called "Whans lot" had once been controlled by Quinnipiac Indians. Indeed, English settlement in the area began only in the wake of the Pequot War, parts of which were fought in what would become New Haven. Here, then, is one glimpse of what happened after the replacement of Indians by colonists (and enslaved Africans) had occurred.[96] But colonial complicity aside, it was a small victory, and one Whan probably never heard about. One of the last witnesses in the case, the New Haven colonist Thomas Trowbridge, testified that he had visited New York and "inquired of one of the Bow[e]ry for John Whann, and he told me he was dead."[97] Against the odds, at least one New England slave had succeeded in dying in a place and among people of his choosing.

# RULES
## For the Society of
# NEGROES. 1693.

WE the Miserable Children of *Adam*, and of *Noah*, thankfully Admiring and Accepting the Free-Grace of GOD, that Offers to Save us from our Miseries, by the Lord Jesus Christ, freely Resolve, with His Help, to become the Servants of that Glorious LORD.

And that we may be Assisted in the Service of our *Heavenly Master*, we now Join together in a SOCIETY, wherein the following RULES are to be observed.

I. It shall be our Endeavour, to Meet in the *Evening* after the *Sabbath*; and *Pray* together by Turns, one to Begin, and another to Conclude the Meeting; And between the two *Prayers*, a *Psalm* shall be Sung, and a *Sermon* Repeated.

II. Our coming to the Meeting, shall never be without the *Leave* of such as have Power over us: And we will be Careful, that our Meeting may Begin and Conclude between the Hours of *Seven* and *Nine*; and that we may not be *unseasonably Absent* from the Families whereto we pertain.

III. As we will, with the Help of God, at all Times avoid all *Wicked Company*, so we will Receive none into our Meeting, but such as have sensibly *Reformed* their Lives from all manner of Wickedness. And therefore, None shall be Admitted, without the Knowledge and Consent of the *Minister* of God in this Place; unto whom we will also carry every Person, that seeks for *Admission* among us; to be by Him Examined, Instructed and Exhorted.

IV. We will, as often as may be, Obtain some *Wise and Good Man*, of the *English* in the Neighbourhood, and especially the Officers of the Church, to look in upon us, and by their Presence and Counsil, do what they think fitting for us.

V. If any of our Number, fall into the Sin of *Drunkenness*, or *Swearing*, or *Cursing*, or *Lying*, or *Stealing*, or notorious *Disobedience* or *Unfaithfulness* unto their Masters, we will *Admonish* him of his Miscarriage, and Forbid his coming to the Meeting, for at least *one Fortnight*; And except he then come with great Signs and Hopes of his *Repentance*, we will utterly Exclude him, with Blotting his *Name* out of our List.

VI. If any of our Society Defile himself with *Fornication*, we will give him our *Admonition*; and so, debar him from the Meeting, at least *half a Year*: Nor shall he Return to it, ever any more, without Exemplary Testimonies of his becoming a *New Creature*.

VII. We will, as we have Opportunity, set our selves to do all the Good we can, to the other *Negro-Servants* in the Town: And if any of them should, at unfit Hours, be *Abroad*, much more, if any of them should *Run away* from their Masters, we will afford them *no Shelter*: But we will do what in us lies, that they may be discovered, and punished. And if any *of us*, are found Faulty, in this Matter, they shall be no longer *of us*.

VIII. None of our Society shall be *Absent* from our Meeting, without giving a *Reason* of the Absence; And if it be found, that any have pretended unto their *Owners*, that they came unto the *Meeting*, when they were otherwise and elsewhere Employ'd, we will faithfully *Inform* their Owners, and also do what we can to Reclaim such Person from all such Evil Courses for the Future.

IX. It shall be expected from every one in the Society, that he learn the *Catechism*; And therefore, it shall be one of our usual Exercises, for one of us, to ask the *Questions*, and for all the rest in their Order, to say the *Answers* in the *Catechism*; Either, The *New-English* Catechism, or the *Assemblies* Catechism, or the Catechism in the *Negro Christianized*.

Cotton Mather, "Rules for the Society of Negroes." *Courtesy of the American Antiquarian Society.*

# CHAPTER 6

# The Law of the Land

If thou seest the oppression of the poor,
and violent perverting of judgment and justice in a province,
marvel not at the matter.

—Ecclesiastes 5:8

C hoosing where and how to die was a grim but effective way for
an enslaved person to express autonomy, but not all enslaved
people were able to do so as cleanly as did John Whan. In 1661,
a jury of inquest in the Massachusetts Bay Colony presented its find-
ings in the matter of the unexplained death of a slave, John, a "negro
of Mr. Henry Bartholomew." The jury members had investigated the
place "wheare the neagroe was found lying and a gun lying by him."
They had also heard the testimony of various witnesses from the
scene, and then viewed the corpse, observing that a "shot went in to
his body being about or Just beneath his short ribs one his leaft side,
and came partly through about his shoulder blad behind." The angle
of the bullet led the jurors to agree "that [John] did willingly contrive
& was the only acter in his owne death by the shooting of the sayd
Gun into his own body."[1] In other words, the man had stood the butt

of the gun on the ground, put the muzzle against the bottom of his ribs, and pulled the trigger.

It can't have been easy to view such a scene. Colonial muskets, notoriously inaccurate from a distance, could at close range make a shredded mess of a human chest. Regular colonists or their servants would have cleaned the body, since medical professionals barely existed in the seventeenth century. And really, there was no need for them, since most denizens of the early modern world were intimately familiar with injury and death—it would take an industrial revolution to distance people from the evident gore of life. Still, that John's death resulted from suicide certainly made the scene more ominous, more solemn, and also more depraved to any English colonists who viewed the corpse. Someone, or many, had carried the body from the scene of the shooting to a more serene and protected place. Someone, or many, rolled John's body over and pulled up his clothing to show the jury his bloody chest and back. Everyone present had to deal with the horror of the suicide, an act that Puritans regarded as a grave sin, an affront to God's plan, a defiant unwillingness to see divine ideas fulfilled.

Or maybe, when the victim was a slave, the suicide's sinfulness mattered less? Some years later, Wait Winthrop, grandson of John Winthrop and a veteran of King Philip's War, wrote to his brother Fitz-John about "black Tom," an enslaved African he had apparently been given or lent, who was of "little servis." Wait noted caustically that the enslaved man "used to make a show of hanging himselfe before folkes, but I beleive he is not very nimble about it when he is alone." This is a different view of Wait Winthrop, who was, after all, a magistrate, joking casually about a mock hanging enacted by an enslaved man. And it is an odd view of colonial New England, a place where an enslaved man might repeatedly shock or amuse or bore colonists by pretending to kill himself. In any case, the mock gallows were of less interest to Wait than the man's ineffectiveness as a laborer. Wait pragmatically counseled his brother that if he found the man of little use, he should "eyther sell him or send him to Virginia or the West Indies before winter."[2]

Massachusetts law held that any person guilty of "self-murther" should be "denied the priviledge of being Buried in the Common Burying place of Christians." Instead, the corpse should be buried along "some Common High-Way" and a "Cart-load of Stones laid upon the Grave as a Brand of Infamy, and as a warning to others to beware of the like Damnable practices."[3] But slavery complicates that stark legislation. In seventeenth-century New England, a community burial ground was not always available to enslaved Africans or Indians, only some of whom were Christian, a fact that underscores that Calvinism did not offer the place's only way of understanding the suicide. If John was not Christian, it is also entirely possible that he intended his suicide to send his soul not to a Christian heaven but back to Africa, or somewhere of his own choice. For John, this might have been a redemptive rather than damnable act.[4]

John's owner, Henry Bartholomew, was a well-respected and successful Salem merchant. Like most prominent New England merchants' lives, Bartholomew's was well documented. He arrived in Massachusetts early in the colonial period, and he thrived. Though he began his life in Salem with a mere half acre of land, he had a talent for acquiring property and eventually became a considerable landowner—one historian suggests that Bartholomew and his fellow Salem merchants pursued land grants so vigorously for the status and social power granted by such readily visible property; a similar logic may have governed his choice to acquire human property.[5] Bartholomew married Elizabeth Scudder, daughter of another leading family, and together they had ten children, the last of whom was born just three years before the 1661 suicide. One of those children married a man who was eventually "killed . . . by a negro, while on a trading voyage" in Maryland, in 1675. Henry himself died in 1692, outliving his slave by thirty-one years.[6]

About John the records say only that in the fall of 1661 he was an enslaved man in a coastal town in New England who took his fate into his own hands.[7] But his act must have reminded slave owners and slaves who heard of the death of the ultimate way an enslaved person could say no.[8] When John found himself with a gun and took the opportunity to end his life, he also destroyed Henry Bartholomew's property and investment. Whether John's was an act of grief over a dead loved one, a protest against the treatment life had given him, an act of an unstable man, or something else entirely, his act *did*, indubitably, mean that New England authorities had to incorporate understandings of enslaved status into their construction of their colonial state. By encountering and responding to particular acts, New England colonists incorporated slavery into their society and into their institutions, as on the chilly fall day in Salem when some English colonists stood in a wind-swept field and examined the dead, half-naked body of an enslaved man of African descent, to determine why he had shot himself through the heart. In such moments, those colonists were forced to use their legal system to confront the reality of slavery. Throughout the Americas, the slow accrual of such moments, instances that required the state's adjudication, created slave regimes.

It wasn't unheard of for slaves to have guns, but New England authorities were wary of the practice. In 1652, all "Scotsmen, Negers and Indians inhabiting with or servants to the English, from the age of sixteene to sixty yeares," had been ordered to undergo military training. But only four years later, the laws changed to forbid "negroes or Indians, although servants to the English," from training, whereas "no other person shalbe exempted from trayning but such as some law doth priviledge."[9] In other words, Africans and Indians, and only Africans and Indians, should no longer be trained in the use of firearms. What had the authorities observed in the preceding four years to change their minds about "Negroes and Indians" with guns? It seems clear why colonists might not have wanted Indians, in the context of settler colonization, to have guns. The threat from enslaved "negroes" is less obvious, but surely stemmed from several realities, among them the possibility that, like John, they might destroy themselves, and the truth that all enslaved people were also, inherently, potential rebels, as colonists in Virginia and the Carolinas and on Barbados and Providence Island learned at various moments.

Fear of slave conspiracy was real even in the first century of English settlement in New England. In 1690, a man named Isaac Morrill was arrested for allegedly enticing "negroes" to follow him to Canada, join an invading force, and then return to New England as joint conquerors with the French, saving "none but only the Negro and Indian Servants." Allegedly involved in organizing this plot were James, a "negro slave," and Joseph, an "Indian slave."[10] Unsurprisingly, given these sporadic panics, the law against arming slaves stayed in effect. In 1693, Massachusetts again exempted "indians and negro's" from militia training.[11]

Such alarms notwithstanding, the most likely threat from a "negro" with a gun was that he or she might wield it to avenge an individual grievance. But seventeenth-century guns, again, were slow and inaccurate. Reloading after a shot could take as long as twenty seconds, the process occupying both hands, a procedure complicated enough to allow any targeted people to flee or retaliate. It may be that the risk of giving a gun to even an aggrieved individual enslaved person was not that much greater than the risk of handing him or her a spade or a scythe.[12] Which is not to say that guns were not a threat, but rather that, in the context of the chattel slave system of the Americas, farm tools might also be.

In fact, the unreliability of a gun as a weapon meant that crimes committed with it could be explained away as accidents. When "Robert Trayes, negro," was tried for a shooting incident in 1684 in Scituate, a coastal town in the Plymouth Colony, he received a light sentence even though his actions caused the death of a colonist. The court ruled that not having "the feare of God before youer eyes, and being instigated by the diviel," made Trayes "felonuously, willfully, and presumtrously fire of a gun att the dore of Richard Standlake."

Trayes missed the door, but badly wounded the leg of Daniel Stand-lake, necessitating its amputation, an operation from which Stand-lake died. The jury found Trayes guilty of the death of Standlake but cleared him of murder charges and released him with the "admoni-tion to lay it much to hart that one should lose his life by him." He was fined three pounds and sentenced to be whipped, with the option to pay his way out of the corporal punishment.[13]

This sentence's relative lightness can most easily be explained by the court's understanding that the act was unintentional ("Throw misadventure"), that Trayes had intended to shoot a door, not a per-son. Also, Robert Trayes had a first and last name and so was per-haps a free man, another reason to understand the light sentence: the actions of a free man were not a challenge to the slave system. A similar case involved "Robin Negro Servant of Andrew Gardner of Muddy River," who was indicted for killing an English colonist in Cambridge, with a blow over the head with a stick. Robin pleaded not guilty, and the jury seems to have found his case compelling, find-ing him guilty only of manslaughter. Again, though the leniency of his sentence suggests he might have been free, it also highlights that, even in 1689, justice was not decided on racial terms alone. A man of African descent could be innocent of a crime.[14]

Certainly punishments could be much more severe. Only six years earlier, "Nicholas Negro" had been charged with "presenting a gun at his Master John Roy of Charlestown Loaden with two Iron Sluggs and wounding him with a knife." (Note here again the inef-ficiency of a gun as a weapon; the man had a loaded gun but used a blade for the attack.) As punishment, the court sentenced Nicholas to twenty-nine stripes of a whip, and a fine. But worse, as often hap-pened with violent slaves, the man was also ordered to remain in jail at his owner's expense until "hee dispose of him out of the Coun-try."[15] In other words, for his action, he was banished. The rule that an owner pay for a misbehaved slave's stay in prison served at least three purposes: it saved the county the costs of feeding and keeping the prisoner, it heightened an owner's desire to sell the slave, and it punished the owner for failing to keep the slave in appropriate behavior. Selling an unruly slave out of the colony also had multiple advantages: it made her or him someone else's problem, served as a lesson to those left behind, and profited the owner, provided the owner could find a buyer quickly enough to keep the costs of maintaining the slave in jail from increasing. One imagines that this incentive did spur plenty of owners to initiate quick sales, perhaps at discounted prices. Thus a local crime had an imperial solution, making use of a transcolonial trade in its local punishments and codes. Thus, again, through local crimes of all sorts did New England pull itself into that larger Atlantic slave world organized around slavery.

In all, records involving gun violence are relatively rare among New England's enslaved population. Guns were hard to hide, hard to steal, and thus difficult for slaves to use. Other weapons were more readily available. Fire was an obvious option: as a weapon it could be wielded by strong and weak alike, and it was readily available in almost every home. English colonists knew of its applicability as a weapon long before they crossed the Atlantic. Before the development of slate mining in the nineteenth century, thatch (dry vegetation like straw or reed or rushes) was the preferred roofing material, and it burned wonderfully, making it a prime target for aggrieved workers, frantic lovers, and anyone else with incendiary intentions wanting to inflict maximum damage for minimum exposure.[16] Even accidental conflagrations were difficult to control. In 1641, John Winthrop recorded that "upon the Lord's day at Concord two children were left at home alone, one lying in a cradle, the other having burned a cloth, and fearing its mother should see it, thrust it into a hay stack by the door." The cloth was still smoldering, and the ensuing fire burned not only the hay and house but also the infant. That same month, Winthrop reported that "two houses were burned at Sudbury."[17] "That fearfull sound of fire and fire," wrote the poet Anne Bradstreet after her house burned, "layd my goods now in the dust . . . My pleasant things in ashes lye / And them behold no more shall I."[18]

Uncontrolled fire drove fear into the hearts of colonists because it was nearly unstoppable. In fact, the ease, versatility, and effectiveness of arson could not be ignored, and it proved ubiquitous in warfare. The 1637 massacre at Mystic was only the most notorious example of fire's military efficacy. John Underhill, a soldier in that expedition, recounted later that he set one side of the Pequot fort aflame with gunpowder, while another soldier entered from another direction with a lit torch, and that their fires met in the center and "burnt all in the space of halfe an houre." The fire defeated even the most determined of fighters. Many brave soldiers, Underhill noted, "were unwilling to come out, and fought most desperately through the Palisadoes, so as they were scorched and burnt with the very flame, and were deprived of their armes, in regard the fire burnt their very bowstrings, and so perished valiantly."

Another advantage of fire for combatants was its volatility, which meant that aggressors didn't have to discriminate among targets: they could set the flames loose and then stand back, their hands now washed. Fire dispensed, in other words, with traditional conventions of war. Underhill noted that though "mercy they did deserve for their valour, could we have had opportunitie to have bestowed it; many were burned in the Fort, both men, women, and children."[19] Having set fire to both entrances, the attackers were able to slaughter at will those who finally ventured out to escape the flames. William Bradford, the first governor of the famed Plymouth Colony, noted in his diary, "It was a fearful sight to see [the Indians] thus frying in the fire and the streams of blood quenching the same, and horrible was the stink and scent thereof." That is, blood streaming from fresh corpses extinguished the fires that had forced the victims to their death. Bradford, who was not present at the massacre, noted that "the victory seemed a sweet sacrifice, and [the victors] gave the praise thereof to God, who had wrought so wonderfully for them."[20] Fire, in this rendering, was a gift from God.

It could also seem a tool of the devil. At dawn on February 10, 1676, in the middle of King Philip's War, a confederation of Nipmuck,

Narragansett, and Wampanoag Indians attacked the small town of Lancaster in the interior of the Massachusetts Bay Colony, setting fire to the houses, killing twelve inhabitants and wounding many more. This attack was probably retaliation for a preemptive assault by united colonial militia from Plymouth, Massachusetts, and Connecticut two months earlier on a Narragansett fort hidden in a "horrid *Swamp*" in Rhode Island. That surprise attack on Indians who had been allied with the English, but who were now rumored to be plotting against them, had killed more than seven hundred Indian combatants, plus, according to Cotton Mather, "Old Men, Women, [and] Children, *Sans* number."[21] Called the Great Swamp Fight, it was one of the more decisive battles in the long and bloody King Phillip's War. The stealth of it angered Narragansetts, and the assault on Lancaster was in large part retribution.

Among the residents of Lancaster was Mary Rowlandson, wife of an influential Puritan minister. She later wrote of the event, "Quickly it was the dolefullest day that ever mine eyes saw." She and others longed to stay inside their house, sheltered from the violence, but the burning walls soon forced them out.[22] Less than two months previously, colonists had torched Narragansett wigwams in the Great Swamp in Rhode Island.[23] Now Rowlandson was presented with a choice of burning to death or venturing out into the arms of the attackers, precisely the choice offered to Indian victims at Mystic in 1637 and the Great Swamp in December 1675. She did stir out and was captured and forcibly marched far from her home; her children were taken from her (some were killed, brutally), and she served a family against her will until her redemption from bondage nearly three months later.[24]

Were English captives, like Mary Rowlandson, enslaved? It's a question worth pondering. For a time, Rowlandson had no control over her food, her safety, her children. She was denied her own religion, she was traded from family to family, forced to live and work in a culture not hers marked by a language she did not speak. She called her captors "Master" and "Mistress," though some servants did so as well. Her condition proved to be temporary, but at the time of her captivity, she could have only hoped that would be the case. But here is one clear matter of distinction: the point of her most evident commodification, ironically, came at the moment of her redemption. Once purchased for twenty pounds, she was free. For Africans and Indians captured into Atlantic slavery, in contrast, the moment of their commodification was most often the moment that sealed their bondage. It was either ironic or predictable that the Rowlandsons stayed in the house of the colonist James Whitcomb after being redeemed from captivity and before being reunited with her surviving family. Whitcomb had received and sold many New England Indians captured in King Philip's War into West Indian slavery.[25] Mary Rowlandson's first stop on her road back to freedom was thus at the house of someone who traded in captive bodies.

Just as combatants on all sides in colonial wars noted its providential effectiveness, enslaved, captured, and colonized people of all sorts could hardly have avoided seeing fire's usefulness as a weapon in individual circumstances. In 1646, unhappy colonists complained to authorities that "some Indian or Indians had wilfully and malitiously burned some quantities of Pitch and tar of theirs togeither with beddinge, a Cart, and its furniture with heaps of Candlewood, tooles, and work."[26] By 1652, Massachusetts had already passed a law dealing specifically with arson. With good reason, New Englanders were always fearful of the enemy within. "If any person," the law warned, was found guilty of having "set on fire any *Dwelling House, Meeting House,* [or] *Store House,*" the penalty would be death.[27] Despite the warning, arson continued throughout the colonies. A decade later, a colonist named Elinor Howell petitioned the town of Hartford for money to pay for damages caused by "Indians and Negroes" in burning her property. She received twelve pounds.[28] Roughly contemporaneously, Increase Mather, the famous Boston minister (and, at least at his life's end, slave owner), noted with some alarm in his diary that slaves had attempted to set fire to "several . . . houses in town but all discovered."[29]

Because fire was widely available, and essential to early modern life, it could not be kept from slaves. In 1641, John Winthrop wrote in his journal that "a godly woman of the church of Boston, dwelling sometimes in London, brought with her a parcel of very fine linen of great value." This woman, Bridget Pierce, prized the linen too much, according to Winthrop, and had accordingly "been at charge to have it all newly washed, and curiously folded and pressed, and so left it in press in her parlor over night."[30] *Pride goeth before destruction*, of course; New Englanders learned Proverbs in their cradles.[31] Winthrop's narrative does not initially make clear who did all this washing and folding and pressing, but we might infer whose task it was from the linen's fate. Pierce, it turns out, "had a negro maid [who] went into the room very late, and let fall some snuff of the candle upon the linen, so as by the morning all the linen was burned to tinder, and the boards underneath, and some stools and part of the wainscot burned, and never perceived by any in the house, though some lodged in the chamber over head, and no ceiling between."[32]

John Winthrop, true to form, found a lesson in the story: "It pleased God," he noted, "that the loss of this linen did her [Pierce] much good, both in taking off her heart from worldly comforts, and in preparing her for a far greater affliction by the untimely death of her husband, who was slain not long after at Isle of Providence."[33] Not everyone would find the loss of linen adequate preparation for a spouse's death, but Winthrop was a man who could see salvation in every sorrow. Besides, Winthrop had four wives in his lifetime. He had learned to find consolation in the widowed state.

Bridget Pierce's husband was none other than Captain William Pierce of the ship *Desire*. Surely his slaves knew what sort of cargo Pierce carried (perhaps he had brought this same inattentive "negro maid" to New England in his own ship) along with linen, and that alone might have been reason enough for a frustrated woman to take easy revenge on her vain mistress by burning her "very fine linen." Indeed, the detailed description of the linen's maintenance—the laborious and particular washing, folding, and pressing it required—makes it very likely that such a chore was not done by the mistress but rather by the "negro maid." After all, it was for just such purposes that wealthy wives of merchant captains had slaves. It takes no stretch of the imagination to read the burning not only as an act of protest but also as a pragmatic time-saver: no special linen, no extra work. A casual act of dropping burnt wick onto linen, "very late at night," might have saved the enslaved woman hours of labor. And who was most likely to have slept above the linen, with "no ceiling between" and yet not have noticed or smelt the burning of linen, and some stools, and part of the walls? Servants and slaves. One observer of contemporary English life, the antimonarchical millenarian John Brayne, noted of arson that the "Burning of houses, and such like effects of unnatural envy," would continue until "oppression and ignorance of the law of God were removed from the shoulders of the poore."[34]

Brayne's suggestion that incendiaries might simply be unfamiliar with God's law seems implausible, but his point that arson derived from oppression is well taken. The maid's deed, intentional or not, illuminated the early New England social hierarchy as surely as it illuminated Bridget Pierce's linen. Seen by this light, the New England household had its own internal dangers, sometimes born of careless accident, and sometimes of a servant's or a slave's envy—whether that envy was unnatural, as Brayne would have it, or not. In any household, servants' and slaves' quarters were naturally dens of resentment and grievance. In a thriving trading town, household masters and their wives were apt to have their vanities and to import too much value in objects—Winthrop's "worldly comforts." And when a maid burned something of value to tinder, it would only be natural that anxiety, suspicion, and mutual distrust lingered in the household long after the fire was quenched.

As Brayne suggested, arson could be used to destroy more than linen. In 1681, a Boston grand jury indicted "Maria Negro servant to Joshua Lambe of Roxbury" for arson. On one July night, Maria allegedly burned two houses in Roxbury: that of Joshua Lamb, and that of Thomas Swan, a local doctor. The indictment noted that, according to her confession, Maria first burned down the house of Swan by taking "a Coale from under a still and carried it into another Roome and laid it on floore neere the doore." Leaving a smoldering coal on a wooden floor eventually set the floor on fire, and placing it near a door presumably blocked at least one exit (doors were few and far between in seventeenth-century houses). The strategy seemed designed to allow Maria both time for and a means of safely exiting the house before fire consumed the structure. After placing the coal in Swann's house, Maria returned to Lamb's house. There, the indictment alleged, Maria entered through a hole near the back door, presumably because at night the door was shut tight, and set that house on fire as well. Maria confessed, perhaps under duress, that she had set the fire with a hot coal held carefully between two pieces of wood, which she had placed on the floor in a bedchamber. For this act of arson, she was sentenced to be to be taken "to the place of Execution and there be burnt."[35]

The vague wording of the execution order has allowed debate about whether Maria was to be burned to death, or whether she was instead to be executed first in a different manner, her corpse then incinerated. Increase Mather claimed in his diary that Maria was burned alive. He noted that on September 22, 1681, there had been three executions in Boston, "An Englishman for a Rape. A negro man for burning a house at Northampton and a negro woman who burnt 2 houses at Roxbury July 12—in one of which a child was burnt to death." Mather further noted that "*the Negro woman was burned to death*—the 1st that has suffered such a death in N.E. [New England]"[36] In contrast to her gruesome auto-da-fé, the court ordered that the "negro servant" named Jack be hanged until dead and his corpse then taken down from the gallows and "burnt to Ashes in the fier with Maria negro."[37]

If Increase Mather was correct in suggesting that Maria was burned alive, he was apparently also correct in asserting that hers was the first public execution by fire in New England, a dubious distinction. There were Caribbean examples of precisely such torturous deaths, but evidence of earlier examples in New England does not exist.[38] At a local level, the fact that Maria's punishment for a crime involving fire was to be killed by fire suggests that *lex talionis*, the law of retaliation, might have been applied. But such retaliation was officially disfavored in early New England, since no less a person than Christ himself had preached against it.[39] And yet examples of people turning the other cheek to their enslaved property are rare.

Maria's crime, the killing of her master, could also have fallen under the category of "petit treason" in seventeenth-century English law; the punishment, for women who committed such a crime was burning to death, while men who did so might be drawn and quartered or otherwise tortured, the public in both cases able to enjoy the spectacle.[40] The difference stemmed, the prominent jurist William Blackstone explained more than a century later, from a desire to maintain the modesty of a woman's body, which might be disrobed by the effects of other sorts of torture. Even if modesty was maintained, the punishment remained horrible, as Blackstone knew. He observed that being burned alive "is to the full as terrible to sense as the other [being drawn and quartered]."[41] Indeed, there are few good ways to be killed.

Was Maria burned to death because she was a woman? The sex-specific punishments for "petit treason" suggest it is conceivable. The "negro man" in Northampton whom Mather mentioned, who burned a house as well, was not burned to death. The intersection of her race and her gender might explain why she was, according to Mather, the only person to receive this punishment in New England. Maria's motivations for her alleged nocturnal crimes were not discussed in court.[42] The court was far more interested in what she had done: left her home in the dark of the night to set her owner's house and the home of her owner's sister and brother-in-law on fire. In punishing her, however, it could be that the court was guided more by her status—enslaved, a woman, African—than by her deed.[43]

Seventeenth-century New England, like the entire early modern world, was dark at night in a way citizens of the age of electricity can no longer fathom. Night was a time for most colonists in early New England to withdraw inside a shelter, to close and lock the doors, to stay close to family. Wandering about was dangerous. But since enslaved people in New England often had no family with them to draw close, they might have had a further sense of the night as a time when owners would not be about and when they would not be called to labor. Though the New England colonists were undoubtedly sincere in their imaginative fears of haunted nightscapes, one wonders how much of their elaborate cosmology was meant, or at least became used, as a policing method to scare potential mischief makers— earthly ones—so that they might remain in bed.[44] Conversely, for Maria and other captive people, the colonial New England night meant free time and unmonitored space, an invisible world of opportunity counterposing daylight's subordination and scrutiny. Indeed, by 1690, Connecticut had passed a curfew, a law forbidding "negroes" from being away from "the place to which they doe belong" without a written pass from their owner. The law authorized "any" English inhabitant to apprehend such "negroes," effectively deputizing the free citizenry while reinforcing racial hierarchies.[45]

A few years later, Cotton Mather would include in his list of rules for "Negros" a prohibition against wandering at night.[46] Even such a luminary as Mather, the scion of Massachusetts's most famous family (save, perhaps, the ubiquitous Winthrops), was concerned about nocturnal wanderings. Such rules and laws seem well advised, at least from the viewpoint of slave owners, though they must have been ineffective. No lights illuminated Roxbury's roads, and still Maria proved able to sneak into two houses. In this, she showed her aptitude at what the historian Stephanie Camp has called "mobility in the face of constraint," a key challenge to overcome for enslaved people. Successful illicit slave movement undermined slave owners' control of their human property. Maria's nocturnal movement, unsupervised and presumably unapproved, led to just the sort of act Mather and masters feared from unsanctioned slave mobility.[47]

But probably not every nighttime roam began with such a willful intention, and wakefulness was not always a choice. Mary Rowlandson had found that rest came less easily for those held in bondage, even after redemption. *"I can remember the time,"* wrote Rowlandson after her own horrific captivity, *"when I used to sleep quietly without workings in my thoughts, whole nights together, but now it is other wayes with me."*[48] The nightmares of bondage were ferocious and surely not limited to English captives. Some enslaved people must have relived, in the silence of the night, the separation, and the violence that defined their condition. Surely for some, a walk in the night air, whatever devils lurked there, offered the possibility of escaping the demons in their heads as they lay in their beds: a heartbreaking long-ago last glimpse of a child, a murderous fury at a cruel world, a worry about friends left behind, or a terror yet to come. Who could sleep soundly in a world governed by horrors, no matter how many small joys might accumulate during the day?

Whatever her personal reasons for night walking, Maria was not alone that night. Her confession named two other slaves as accomplices. Strikingly, they were not local. Roxbury, a "faire and handsome Countrey-towne" of about 120 houses, populated by inhabitants who "were all very rich," according to one midcentury observer, was an appendage to the larger town of Boston.[49] And apparently the enslaved communities of the two towns communicated, for two enslaved men from Boston were accused of joining Maria in her alleged crimes. The first, "Mr. Walkers Negro Man," was called Cheffaleer.[50] The other, "Mr. pemerton's Negro Man," was called Coffee. While the latter stayed behind, perhaps acting as lookout, Maria claimed that Cheffaleer went with her to set Swann's house on fire. Two English witnesses also testified that Cheffaleer had acted strangely on the night in question. One, a colonist named Hannah Foster, said that on that evening she was visiting the Walker house and heard, as she supposed, "a negro Grumble to himself, which lay Just over [her] head." Alarmed by the grumbling, Hannah said, she stayed awake for a long spell, during which time she "heard him with his feet on the floor, and the reason [she] could not sleep was because was something [*sic*] afraid of him, not being used to such." But despite hearing what she thought were footsteps apparently leaving, and despite her feeling that he was a frightening man doing frightening things, she could not prove that he had ever left the house.[51]

Susannah Walker, mistress of that house, remembered that the evening of the fire, she had been visiting her neighbors. While she was there, she remembered, one of her children arrived to tell her, "[Tha]t our negro was come home and that he had been a drinking and she did not care to stay at home & desired me to goe home." By the time Walker arrived home, Cheffaleer had already gone to bed. Making the story more complicated, Walker on arriving found a "Cumbustion or quarrilling with the Indians before our doore." The entire household rose to investigate this affair. Even Cheffaleer poked his head out from the attic (where he apparently slept), for Walker "saw the Negro looke out at the garrett window and call out & ask what the matter was with the Indians." The scuffle seems to have died down. Walker entered the house and later, she testified, she "hard him [Cheffaleer] come doune," presumably the same moment that Foster heard his feet on the floor. Unfortunately for the court's purposes, neither woman could definitively state that she had seen him leave the house, and thus neither he nor Coffee was convicted, spared from a death sentence. But they were somehow not exonerated. The two men were still ordered to be "sent out of the country," a sentence that seems to highlight the existence of another, paralegal system for slaves in New England.[52]

The arson had a lasting effect. The Mathers, at least, were still talking about it years later. In *Pillars of Salt*, Cotton Mather's history of "some criminals executed in this land, for capital crimes," published at the century's end, he described a man brought to be executed who "came to the Gallowes, and saw *Death* (and a Picture of *Hell* too, in a *Negro* then *Burnt* to *Death* at the Stake, for *Burning* her Masters House, with some that were in it,) before his Face."[53] But Mather can't have been the only colonist unsettled and perturbed by the event. That an enslaved woman allegedly crept about the town at night, using everyday coal to set fire to houses must have shaken the small community. To argue otherwise is to miss the precariousness of English settlements in the region and to ignore how threatening it would feel to know that this time the threat came not from the well-known danger of an Indian attack but from within the town itself. If the severity of Maria's sentence, burning alive at a stake, was any indication, the English sought to terrify anyone who might consider copying Maria's act—evidence that her crime was seen as something larger than an individual action. In the autumn of 1681, the conflagrations of King Philip's War were no distant memory. Nor did two major uprisings coincident with that war—a servants' rebellion in Virginia and a slaves' rebellion on Barbados—seem distant to New Englanders. The generalized fear of vast conspiracies could enhance the severity of the punishment of unfortunate individuals.

Such acts of individuals also inevitably increased fears of vast conspiracies. The first evidence of heightened vigilance came just three days later, when another slave in another town in the colony committed arson. The fugitive slave, Jack, burned a house to the ground in Northampton, while looking for food to eat. Jack was one of the two other criminals whose execution Increase Mather had recorded in his diary, given the specific sentence of hanging, his corpse to be "burnt to ashes in the fier with Maria negro."[54] It took fifteen days to fetch Jack from Northampton to Boston for the execution, and cost the county more than two pounds in transportation fees (Joseph Hawley went via Springfield and charged for horse hire, "ferridge," and feed, along with accommodation costs).[55] Given how long this trip took, it seems unlikely that news of Maria's arson made it from Boston to Northampton, so as to inspire Jack's crime, in a mere three days. But colonial authorities may have seen some connection, since they ordered the two executed together. Sheer expediency may also have linked them; efficiency demanded the use of a single pyre for three bodies, and the holding of one, joint execution day. Regardless, even though Africans made up only a small minority of the New England population, nonetheless two of the three people executed in Boston on September 22, 1681, were enslaved Africans.

There are more clues regarding Jack's motivations for his crimes. When questioned about his reasons, Jack explained that he "came from Wethersfield and is Run away from Mr. Samuell Wolcot because he always beates him sometimes with 100 blows so that he hath told his master that he would sometime or other hang himself."[56] Samuel Wolcott was a merchant with connections to the West Indies. That, along with Wethersfield's position along the Connecticut River, might help explain how Jack came to be enslaved so far inland.

More difficult to explain is Wolcott's alleged brutality. One hundred blows was an extreme punishment, seemingly more typical of the West Indies than New England. Jack might have been exaggerating, but it may also be that Samuel Wolcott was a cruel master, one worth fleeing. Jack told the court that he had been on the run for "one weeke and halfe since" and that he had "stole a Gun at the next Towne viz Southfeild and hath left it in the woods he laid it downe in a Path because it had noe flint in it."[57] Even in this brief testimony, some details of Jack's life appear: he knew guns well enough to understand that without a flint to strike the spark, it would not fire. He also knew that would be a difficult part to find, which probably explains his decision to leave the heavy gun (all seventeenth-century guns were heavy) in the woods, rather than lug it along in vain hopes of finding what he needed.

Jack first made his way to the house of Anthony Dorchester, a good choice for a fugitive since Dorchester, a miller, also ran a ferry across the river that John needed to cross to elude pursuers.

But Dorchester was hardly a provincial miller; accounts relating to him show him selling wheat "ground for Barbados."[58] Jack came to Dorchester's house around noon and asked for a "Pipe of Tobacco." Dorchester told him there was some on the table, which Jack took, along with a knife lying beside it. He then apparently tried to draw a sword on Dorchester, but did it so awkwardly that the sixty-year-old Dorchester was able to capture and bind him, "with the help of [his] wife and daughter." Even bound, Jack was dangerous. When the man went "scrabling in his Pocket," Dorchester related, "I suspected he might have a knife and searching found my knife," which Jack had stolen from the table.[59] Dorchester, in his role as ferry owner, surely encountered strangers often. Still, he seemed remarkably unfazed by the arrival of a "negro" at his door, suggesting that he encountered "negroes" often enough to find them unremarkable. It was some sort of irony that Jack asked for tobacco, an American crop by then increasingly harvested by enslaved people, who were not immune to its lure.

A Springfield court sentenced Jack to prison, but he seems to have escaped. Thirteen days after his sentencing, he "wittingly and felloniously sett on fier" a house in Northampton, "by taking a brand of fier from the hearth and swinging it up and doune for to find victualls." His arson could be understood as unintentional, since he sparked the fire while moving a torch to look for food in a strange larder, but the court chose to see it as a deliberate act—perhaps in the wake of Maria's arson, slaves had lost the benefit of the doubt, or perhaps they had never had it.[60] Jack was caught and sentenced to death by hanging, and then to be "burnt to ashes in the fier with Maria Negro."[61] No charges were placed against Samuel Wolcott, despite Jack's testimony against the man. If Jack's flight tells us that he was willing to contest his slavery, his punishment tells us that authorities brooked little resistance. But Jack's punishment had begun before his resistance. Wolcott's hundred blows had provoked his flight; even before he fled, Jack had threatened to hang himself. Colonial authorities made good on his threat.

Not all crimes committed by enslaved people in New England were violent or frightening. Some were hardly noteworthy at all: a Boston court record in 1642 merely notes that "Mincarry, the blackmore was admonished, and dismissed," without specifying his infraction.[62] Inebration was a common petty complaint (remember Cheffaleer's drunken state) brought before authorities. A 1680 warrant named Joseph Gray for "absence from the ordinances, Matthew Nixon, for drunkenness, [and] Joseph, the mulatto, for excessive drinking and making a disturbance in the street."[63] In that word "mulatto" lies evidence of a growing awareness of complicated racial categories.

Measuring the social impact of such infractions remains difficult. Drunkenness might have meant relatively little to either the authorities or the slave, so long as it stopped there. It might also have been a push against boundaries by a man testing limits (and it does seem to have been men, be they English, Indian, or African, who did the drinking). Regardless of their individual motivations, these kinds of actions had larger consequences, such as the eventual development of racialized intoxication legislation. In 1652, a Massachusetts law regarding public drunkenness stipulated that "everie person" found incapacitated by drink would be fined ten shillings. By the end of the century, legislation existed that specifically targeted Indians and people of African descent. In 1695, the Massachusetts legislature observed that "diverse ill disposed and indigent persons" had begun to sell "strong Beere, ale, Cider, Wine, Rhum, or other strong liquors, or drinks, and to keep common tipling houses, therein harbouring and entertaining Apprentices, Indians, Negroes & other idle and dissolute persons, tending . . . to all impropriety & debaucheries."[64] To stem this tide, legislators forbade the selling of liquor to such customers. Once a vice of all—"everie person"—drunkenness had become a problem associated with people of color, along with apprentices and "dissolute persons," and legislated in that vein.

Inebration was one kind of crime; theft threatened propriety and property far more grievously. A 1698 special court in New Haven

County brought charges against "Cush a Negro Man" for stealing a horse from a colonist named William Barker. Two English accomplices were charged with him, William Collins and his wife. Testimony led the court to believe that Cush had committed the crime and that he had then "conveyed the horse to Goodman Collins," who apparently was going to sell the animal or keep it for his own. This was thwarted by Barker's setting dogs on the scent of the horse. When Cush "heard the dogs bark he said in the hearing of said Collins that he was Catcht." Hunting dogs were in use in New England for various purposes: the flushing out of game, protection, the hunting and killing of wolves, and also, apparently, the chasing of thieves. Colonists used mastiffs, ferocious animals that could tear an animal or man to pieces. Cush thus did well to take shelter.[65] By the nineteenth century, dogs were common tools for the catching and killing of slaves; it turns out that in late seventeenth-century New England, they were common enough, as well, that Barker knew to send out the dogs and that Cush knew they meant his capture.[66] Eventually, Cush and the horse were both found on the Collins property, and Cush confessed to the crime. As punishment, he received twenty lashes while the Collinses received a fine.[67]

Acting with an English accomplice may have provided some cover for an enslaved person. Will, a "negro," testified that as he returned home late one night, he encountered "a short man with a wigg that lives near the millbridge met him and askt him where he was going." Will obligingly told the man that he was returning home, and the man asked him to help remove some items from a nearby house. Will complied, and once at the house, the man removed "all his clothing to his shirt and went into a little window in the backside of Captains Banks house and handed out to [Will] a silver tankard, three spoons, & two forks," and some additional silver items. That night, they divided the loot, with the man promising to come pick up what he had left with Will the following week. Will buried some items, but "gave the spoon to Capt. Banks Negro man to keep till he called for it."[68]

Not surprisingly, this story of a mysterious man who instigated the crime and then disappeared, did not hold up well in court, and Will was convicted. Still, even a weak defense like this illuminates the life of one slave in New England. His own words testify to a fair amount of mobility. Will was allowed to be out alone at night, and he knew where a house was with silver for the taking. He knew by name the owner of the house he robbed, he knew that Captain Banks also owned a slave, and he apparently knew the slave (the spoon given to the other slave may have been a bribe in exchange for silence; or perhaps Will had no place to hide it). Will testified in English, meaning he had lived among English colonists long enough to have learned the language. And we can assume that he also knew that pulling silver items out of a window in the middle of the night was not approved behavior, and that it might be best to cast blame on a (probably invented) colonial accomplice. It was probably crimes like this that led Massachusetts early in the eighteenth century to prohibit "any free person" from buying *any* goods from "any Indian servant, or negro or molatto servant, or slave," without the permission of their master, lest the buyer be liable for as much as triple the stolen goods' value.[69]

Theft was a very common crime. "John Negro," the "slave of Capt John Williams of Sittuate," was convicted (after confessing) in 1686 of burglary "in breaking his said Masters house in the night and stealing mony, writings, and divers good and carying the same away from thence." Accordingly, the court sentenced John to pay various court costs and "to stand on the Gallows one hour and be burnt in the hand with the letter B and pay charge of prosecution, Imprisonment, and Court fees."[70] Note that John had to break into Williams's house during the night. Where slaves slept in New England is not always clear, but in this case John did not sleep in the house.[71] It appears that the house was locked against his entry, that he had to "break" into it. Was this a sign that the man was not trusted, or simply one example of a slave in New England sleeping in a barn or other outbuilding?

Also curious is the fact that he stole "writings." Was the man literate? Were the writings valuable? Money and goods seem understandable, but it is harder to imagine what good "writings" could do for a burglar, except irrefutably link him to a crime scene. On the other hand, if John wanted to harm his owner more than he wanted to help himself, stealing "writings" in the form of a journal, an account book, or letters could be devastating to a colonist.[72] As for his punishment, the branding seems to have been prescribed often for burglary: a General Quarter Session of the Peace held at Boston on January 1, 1695, sentenced the "Negro ceasar" to be "branded with the letter B and to pay 3 s being treble damage."[73] Branding marked the man, to be sure, but it also penalized the master, who then owned visibly unyielding human property. It reminded all that here was a servant not adequately controlled, hence here was an incompetent master.[74]

Similarly, in October 1698, a court at Hartford heard the case of "a Negro named Abraham," charged with "breaking upon several houses and that on the Sabbath day and committing severall robberies and breaking prison at Fairfield." For that list of crimes (and after Abraham's confession), the court sentenced "him to be severely whipt and branded on the forehead with the letter B." Abraham was enslaved and thus his owner was legally responsible for the fine (some thirteen pounds) appended to these physical punishments. "If his master shall refuse to satisye for the damages that he hath done and to pay the charges of his apprehending and conveying to prison and keeping there," the court warned, then the enslaved man could "be sold for money to pay the said damages and charges." In other words, if his owner, who lived on Long Island, refused to pay the county of Hartford a fine amounting to almost half the purchase price of an adult male slave, Abraham faced being sold, presumably out of the area (since known thieves were unlikely to be welcomed locally).[75] This punishment was tailor-made for an African already enslaved and commodified.

The next year in Hartford, "James a Negro Servant" of John Pantry Jr., a wealthy merchant, was convicted of breaking into a shop and, once inside, "Stealing of bisket upon the Sabbath day." A repeat offender, James received no mercy. Because this was the second time that the man had been found guilty of such a crime, he was sentenced to thirty lashes "upon the naked body and to be branded on the forehead with the letter B."[76] Punishment here meant to suffer physical pain, and to suffer humiliation at the same time. Recall that James had stolen food ("bisket") twice, a paltry thing to steal, although he was owned by a wealthy man in what was largely considered the land of plenty. Given that he risked branding to obtain the food, it seems fair to wonder whether or not the man had enough to eat.[77] Again, the choice of the "Sabbath day" for the theft, a day when shops would be closed and proprietors away, seems quite pragmatic. Abraham had also chosen the Sabbath as his time of crime—though the breaking of Sabbath was considered an added offense—perhaps because this was the point in the week when slaves were subject to the least surveillance.

Enslaved people stole food frequently. A theft of grain from a mill by Tony, a "Neagor servant" in Lynn, may have been premeditated—he used a bag "hee brought," seemingly for the purpose of the theft.[78] Tony, like James, was caught, and the miller complained that this was not the first time Tony had stolen from him. And in 1692, "Servis Negro," was accused of "stealing and threatening to steal Mr. Astwoods Negro Girls and being Convict of stealing some tomato goods out of Mr. Pombrookes House of about 5s value." For these threats and actual thefts, the court ordered Servis fined twenty-five shillings, or that "he be severely and publiquely whipt," admonishing him that his next offense would receive a more severe punishment.[79] The relatively trifling theft of five shillings' worth of tomatoes seems somehow out of place amid the other accusations.

The recurrence of food as the target of slaves' theft prompts questions about the treatment of slaves, and of servants too, in New England. It is startling to think of hunger where there was no dearth, and the courts gave no indication of considering starvation a mitigating factor in any of these cases. But, then, as the French Revolution historian Richard Cobb observed, "hunger is an embarrassing topic for a regime the rulers of which eat unusually well."[80] Leaving aside the first years of England settlement, New England colonists as a rule ate unusually well. But the lowly could go hungry. A Massachusetts apprentice reported in 1657 that it took him some time to switch to eating "his master's food, viz. meate and mik, or drink beer, saying that he did not know that it was good, because he was not used to eate such victualls, but to eate bread and water porridge and to drinke water."[81] If this was the experience of an English apprentice, what was that of a slave?

Indeed, Tony's and James's acts of petty theft in the face of such severe punishments may speak forcefully to their need for food, food unavailable to them not because of any famine but only because they were slaves. Their attempts to remedy slavery-induced hunger in some ways were resistance to a particularly corporeal part of their slavery. Of course, colonists in New England had long understood that food could be racially categorized; remember the refuse fish sold to West Indian colonies. But enslaved people may have rejected such distinctions. Faced with the choice between obedience and hunger on the one hand and defiance and sustenance—and the possibility of punishment—on the other, they chose to feed themselves and pay the consequences.[82]

The most valuable property an enslaved person could steal, of course, was himself or herself, and enslaved people in New England did run away.[83] A 1697 broadside advertised for the return of an Indian servant, proclaiming, "Ran way the 13th of this Instant June, from his Master, William Tilly of Boston, Rope maker, a *Carolina* Indian Man-servant, named *Tom*, about Two and Twenty Years of Age." The advertisement, anticipating the notorious runaway slave notices of the eighteenth and nineteenth centuries, went into great detail about

Tom.[84] He spoke English well, it announced, and is "a well-set Fellow: He hath on a new black Hat, a new light coloured cloth Coat with pewter Buttons, lin'd with yellow, canvas Breeches buttoned at the Knees with pewter buttons, yarn Stockings Tarred, Leather Heel'd Shoes." If Tilly's description of this "well-set Fellow" was any guide, Tom set out in some fine apparel. One can well imagine Tom considering himself dressed for freedom, canvas breeches buttoned smartly at the knees, the buttons' pewter matching that of his cloth coat—new, like his hat.[85] That Tom was a Carolina Indian again highlights the existence of an intercolonial slave trade not limited to Africans; not all Indians were local. It also suggests he had more confidence in places to run to. If not a native of the region, he was, it seems, at least a native of the continent, and perhaps he even knew or imagined he knew of friendly ways and means to return home.

That same year, a merchant in New York wrote a letter asking for help from sea captains who traveled frequently to New England, explaining that almost four years ago "a mollatto by name Jack or John . . . ran away from my Plantation att the upper mills." Jack or John proved an able fugitive, and remained at large despite years of searching. His frustrated owner "could never track him farther than Stradford in Connecticut: so that I judge he gott to Road Island, and perhaps is gon from there with some of the Pryvateers that fitted out there for the Gulph of Portya." "If hee bee [on a ship]," his owner admitted, "its not unlikely but he is or has been at st. mary's or Maddagascar." Years later this man still wanted his human property back. "Pleaese (when you come there)," he asked, "make a strickt Inquiery after him." The slave seems to have struck his owner's particular fancy: "Hee is a remarkable fellow, looks extreem squint, speaks verry good English and Dutch and is of stature verry tall." It would be a remarkable success if any captain was able to find the man from such a sparse description, but his erstwhile owner remained optimistic and determinedly masterful: "If you should meet with him," he commanded, "take him up, [I am] hereby Impowering you so to doe."[86] But the trail was three years cold and the oceans were big; this owner's deputizing of captains seemed the desperate act of an unexpectedly powerless man.

Here is yet another way to envision late seventeenth-century New England: as an entrepôt for runaway slaves looking to board ships to freedom. John was a runaway slave from New York, who had possibly headed to New England (he had been traced to Stratford in the Connecticut Colony), from whence his owner believed he had boarded a ship headed to the Persian Gulf ("Gulph of Portia"), a term often used in the seventeenth century to refer generally to the Indian Ocean. For some reason, Jack's owner surmised the man had knowledge of, or a relation to, two specific locations in that area: St. Mary's, a set of islands off the coast of India, and Madagascar. The owner also knew that the man spoke both Dutch and English, strongly suggesting a relationship to the Dutch East India Company, which had connections and outposts throughout the Indian Ocean region. But his Dutch background is muted in this case; his life appears here courtesy of records involving New England, specifically Rhode Island, which, Jack's owner believed, was well known for the existence of privateers who outfitted there for journeys all the way to the Indian Ocean.[87]

Most runaway slaves could not plan an escape that spanned two oceans and half the globe, but Jack's owner's assessment of his slave's capabilities cautions us not to underestimate what was possible in the early modern Atlantic world. Water escapes happened; in 1649, a stowaway Indian woman was found on board a ship headed *to* New England from Bermuda. The "Indian Squa a servant to a poore man there [in Bermuda]" had somehow made her way aboard the ship "and hidd her selfe." She was not discovered until the ship arrived in Boston, whereupon she was "committed to a keeper" until she could be sent back to Bermuda. But the woman escaped, once more, from that keeper and could not be found in time to be "sent Againe to the Bermodes."[88] The "Againe" suggests she was familiar to New Englanders and indeed implies that she was originally from the region. She had, against the odds, stolen herself and returned home. Her escape reminds us that the enslaved human cargo shipped around the Atlantic world paid close attention to the circuits of trade, so that they might find their way back home.

Enslaved people of African descent, though, whether first generation or later, seldom had such proximity to their homes, and when they ran away, their destinations must have mostly been uncertain. New England's isolation could be deadly to a runaway slave. George March's "negro" left his owner's house in October of 1680 and was found a week later, dead. The inquest into his death found no indication of violence upon the corpse, and the jury decided he had died of exposure, possibly a runaway slave with nowhere to run.[89] An enslaved person fleeing a plantation in eighteenth-century Saint Domingue or Jamaica or Brazil could hope to find shelter in a maroon community in the mountains, where their combined numbers afforded some protection. But an enslaved man in early New England, especially one of African descent, marked apart by appearance, language, and general culture, surrounded by few peers, could find little refuge outside his master's home.[90]

Moreover, enslaved people of African descent who ran away risked encountering hostile native forces, for it was never clear that Indians differentiated between English colonists and their enslaved African laborers, save in noticing their different skin color.[91] (Some evidence suggests that some New England Indians esteemed black as the color of beauty; but what was seen as black is a matter of debate.)[92] A Huguenot traveler to Boston in 1687 assured his readers that their slaves would not run away, "for the Moment one is missing from the Town, you have only to notify the Savages, who provided you promise them Something, and describe the Man to them, he is right soon found."[93] A story from King Philip's War, told by a young Nathaniel Saltonstall, noted that Indian attackers had ambushed a town where they "took much Cattel from young Mr. Harris, and killed a Negro Servant of his; and having done this Mischief, returned Home with their Booty."[94] In a 1690 Schenectady raid, Native Americans killed eleven African slaves and took prisoner only five, despite possibly knowing that such slaves were worth money to their English owners.[95]

Indeed, in the famous Deerfield massacre, among the first to die were enslaved Africans The morning of February 29, 1704, more than 200 French, Abenaki, Huron, Mohawk, Iroquois, and Indians of assorted other groups descended on Deerfield, Massachuetts, killing 50 inhabitants and capturing 112. One of the captives, John Williams, later recorded his memories of the attack, in which "some [attackers] were so cruel and barbarous as to take and carry to the door, Two of my Children, and Murder them, as also a Negro Woman."[96] That unnamed "negro woman" was John Williams's African slave Parthena. Later that same day, after a forced march away from Deerfield and the group's arrival at their first night's campsite, Williams recounted, "Some of the Enemy who brought drink with them from the Town, fell to Drinking, and in their Drunken fit they kill'd my Negro man, the only dead Person, I either saw at the Town or in the Way."[97] The dead "negro man" was Williams's other African slave, Frank.[98] The allied Indian attackers, it seemed, made no distinction between English colonists and their enslaved servants, coerced colonists.

Yet despite the difficulties of escape and the dangers all around, runaway slaves did become a problem in New England. In 1690, Connecticut authorities passed a law regarding runaway "negroes," enslaved and free. The law required all "negroes" away from their homes to carry passes; it also essentially deputized all English colonists by authorizing them to question any such whom they encountered. Furthermore, ferry operators were forbidden to transport any "negroe" without a pass. Such new restrictions were necessary, the act stated, because so many persons had "purchase[d] negroe servants" who had then fled.[99] Massachusetts passed a law in 1680 declaring it unlawful for any large ship to depart the colony with "negroes aboard," a law that was only partially enforced because it was not really enforceable.[100] Ships carrying Africans and Indians came and went from the New England colonies. And the enslaved people on board watched and learned and bided their time, just as did enslaved people elsewhere in the Americas. God, Saint Paul wrote to the Corinthians, "will not suffer you to be tempted above that ye are able." Rather, "with the temptation [He will] also make a way to escape, that ye may be able to bear *it*."[101] One wonders whether any enslaved people in New England, sitting upright on balcony benches in stifling meetinghouses, had ever heard Paul's letter discussed, and one imagines that they did not need to.

# PART III

# BACKING
## INTO
# MODERNITY

[ 1 ]

## The Selling
### OF
# JOSEPH
## A Memorial.

FORASMUCH *as Liberty is in real value next unto* Life: *None ought to part with it themselves, or deprive others of it, but upon most mature Consideration.*

The Numerousness of Slaves at this day in the Province, and the Uneasiness of them under their Slavery, hath put many upon thinking whether the Foundation of it be firmly and well laid; so as to sustain the Vast Weight that is built upon it. It is most certain that all Men, as they are the Sons of *Adam*, are Coheirs; and have equal Right unto Liberty, and all other outward Comforts of Life. GOD *hath given the Earth* [ *with all its Commodities* ] *unto the Sons of* Adam, P*sal* 115. 16. *And hath made of One Blood, all Nations of Men, for to dwell on all the face of the Earth, and hath determined the Times before appointed, and the bounds of their habitation : That they should seek the Lord.* Forasmuch then as *we are the Offspring of* GOD &c. *Act* 17.26,27,29. Now although the Title given by the last ADAM, doth infinitely better Mens Estates, respecting GOD and themselves; and grants them a most beneficial and inviolable Lease under the Broad Seal of Heaven, who were before only Tenants at Will : Yet through the Indulgence of GOD to our First Parents after the Fall, the outward Estate of all and every of their Children, remains the same, as to one another. So that Originally, and Naturally, there is no such thing as Slavery. *Joseph* was rightfully no more a Slave to his Brethren, than they were to him : and they had no more Authority to *Sell* him, than they had to *Slay* him. And if *they* had nothing to do to *Sell* him; the *Ishmaelites* bargaining with them, and paying down Twenty pieces of Silver, could not make a Title. Neither could *Potiphar* have any better Interest in him than the *Ishmaelites* had. *Gen.* 37. 20, 27, 28. For he that shall in this case plead *Alteration of Property*, seems to have forfeited a great part of his own claim to Humanity. There is no proportion between Twenty Pieces of Silver, and LIBERTY. The Commodity it self is the Claimer. If *Arabian* Gold be imported in any quantities, most are afraid to meddle with it, though they might have it at easy rates; lest it it should have been wrongfully taken from the Owners, it should kindle a fire to the Consumption of their whole Estate. 'Tis pity there should be more Caution used in buying a Horse, or a little lifeless dust; than there is in purchasing Men and Women : Whenas they are the Offspring of GOD, and their Liberty is,

——— *Auro pretiosior Omni.*

And seeing GOD hath said, *He that Stealeth a Man and Selleth him, or if he be found in his hand, he shall surely be put to Death.* Exod. 21. 16. This Law being of Everlasting Equity, wherein Man Stealing is ranked amongst the most atrocious of Capital Crimes : What louder Cry can there be made of that Celebrated Warning,

*Caveat Emptor !*

And

# CHAPTER 7

# The Selling of Adam

Also take no heed unto all words that are spoken;
lest thou hear thy servant curse thee.

—Ecclesiastes 7:21

S amuel Sewall came to New England in 1661, when he was only nine years old. By 1700, he was nearly fifty, newly appointed as a justice of the Massachusetts Colony Superior Court, and living comfortably off the profits of his business as a Boston-based merchant involved in global trade; in just one transparent sign of his wealth, the combined windows of his house had more than 480 panes.[1] He was also a colonist with a reputation for reflection and contemplation. Three years earlier, he had become the only judge in the Salem witch trials ever to apologize for his participation in the trials, an experience of humiliation and repentance that greatly affected him.[2] Unlike many of the new merchant class, Sewall still took seriously the mission of New England. Surrounded by what he saw as a new permissiveness smuggled in amid New England's prosperity, he remained faithful to the old ideals. In this way, he was typical of a generation that was only reluctantly "backing into modernity," as Perry Miller put it.[3] Sewall had given up neither the idea of a city on a hill nor the ruthless soul-searching that inhabiting such a place required. As his witchcraft apology revealed, he mixed self-examination with the rare capacity humbly to admit having been wrong.

In 1700, Sewall wrote *The Selling of Joseph: A Memorial*, a three-page pamphlet focused on the problem of enslaved Africans (but not Indians) in New England, and the first writing from New England to call for slavery's abolition. Reflecting on the current condition of the Massachusetts Bay Colony and more specifically that of his longtime hometown of Boston, he noted, "The *Numerousness* of Slaves at this day in the Province, and the Uneasiness of them under their Slavery, hath put many upon thinking whether the Foundation of it be firmly and well laid; so as to sustain the Vast Weight that is built upon it." His thoughts led him to conclude that the foundation had rotted, and he lamented that people should pay more attention to their purchases of livestock or gold than to their transactions involving human chattel. Remember, he told his readers, those slaves "are the Offspring of GOD, and their Liberty is, . . . *Auro pretiosior Omni*"— more precious than all gold. If God made the world, he reasoned, then "all Men, as they are the Sons of *Adam*, are Coheirs; and have equal Right unto Liberty, and all other outward Comforts of Life."[4] It was the first unabashed antislavery statement by a New England colonist.

By the end of the seventeenth century, certain fundamental questions about English colonization in New England had been answered, at least in the minds of colonists. Would the colonies in the region survive? Almost certainly yes. Would they be Puritan? Of a sort: Protestant, still, but perhaps less ardent than some of the first generation. One historian has suggested they were on a "redefined errand," less isolated from English intellectual currents.[5] Would the Indian nations in the region be able, either separately or allied, to repel the

European invaders? Most likely not. Their numbers were diminished enough, the remainder subjugated enough, the English powerful enough, that the northeastern seaboard at least seemed momentarily stabilized in an uneasy peace, controlled mostly by the new English occupants, the violence of settler colonization having done its work and now largely moved away from the coast. Nearly a century of fighting had settled the land and these questions.

Unsurprisingly, slavery had settled too—by now, its substance had been worked thoroughly into the new society. To be sure, a certain few colonists, like Samuel Sewall, started to examine the growth of New England slavery, to question both its roots and its flowering. But people like Sewall were few. Indeed, he was not even so much like the founding generations he idealized. Sewall spoke in the name of a past that had never really happened; he dreamed that the city on the hill truly had shined upon the world and that only now, suddenly impelled by the articles of commerce, the children of great men had dimmed its light. But, of course, the brighter the light, the darker the shadows. Slavery had always been there, at the center of the trade that had helped New England grow and flourish.

Still, Sewall was not alone among the English in questioning the practice of enslavement. By the end of the seventeenth century, English critics of West Indian planters and their practices had already appeared. Morgan Godwyn's 1680 *The Negro's & Indians Advocate* had relied on Christian sentiments to bolster its criticisms of slavery. Godwyn, an Anglican preacher, a graduate of Christ Church College, Oxford, and a sometime resident of both Virginia and the West Indies, argued that Africans and Indians had as much right as Europeans to attain a knowledge of Christianity and that masters who kept their slaves in ignorance of that religion were sinners themselves.[6] In a supplement to the *Advocate,* he critiqued the treatment of slaves by supposedly Christian owners, including "their frequent Emasculating, Amputations of Leggs, cropping off of *Ears* (and of *Heads* too), *scant Allowance for Food* and *Cloaths,* and (often) no less *working*, than *starving* them to *Death*, and their *unmerciful Correction* of them." He questioned the motives behind any refusal to preach to slaves, wondering whether owners preferred to leave slaves unsaved so that they might more easily and legitimately be mistreated.[7] In 1685, he took the pulpit in Westminster Abbey to preach, his text for the day an ominous biblical verse from Jeremiah: "Also in thy skirts is found the blood of the souls of the poor innocents." He used the authority of Westminster to call slave owners "mammonists," greedy to earn money at the expense of their slaves' souls, along with their own.[8]

In 1684, another Englishman, the vegetarian hatter Thomas Tryon, published a treatise of more than two hundred pages, entitled *Friendly Advcie* [sic] *to the Gentlemen-Planters of the East and West Indies*. Though its argument was less explicitly antislavery than that of Sewall's tract, Tryon's writing described in stark detail the brutal treatment of West Indian slaves by their English owners, including the whipping and overworking of pregnant women, the abuse of children, the sundering of families, and the pettiness of owners. The entire piece rested on the assumption that the tenets of Christianity prohibited, if not slavery itself, then the harsh treatment of slaves that it produced in practice.[9]

Even in North America, antislavery sentiment among colonists began slowly percolating, and some groups were expressing unease with slavery by the end of the seventeenth century. In 1688, a Quaker meeting in Germantown, Pennsylvania, protested the growing slave trade, asking, "Is there any [among you] that would be done or handled at this manner?" The authors invoked the Golden Rule—"there is a saying, that we shall doe to all men like as we will be done ourselves; making no difference of what generation, descent or colour they are."[10] And five years later, the Monthly Meeting of Friends in Philadelphia published a tract that began by acknowledging that Christ's message of salvation was "preached unto all, without Exception, and that *Negroes, Blacks,* and *Tannies* are a real part of Mankind." Given this, the pamphlet recommended "to all our Friends and Brethren, Not to buy any Negroes, unless it were on purpose to set them free." The authors ended by outlining the worst depredations of the slave trade, stressing the cruelty of separating "the Husband from the Wife, and the Children from the Parents," and also the sadistic tortures inflicted on slaves in the name of punishment. This all led, they concluded, to a "great Reproach of the *Christian Profession*."[11]

This sort of ferment was in the Atlantic air, but there were also specific reasons for Sewall's antislavery polemic. His own explanation emphasized his personal unease. On June 19, 1700, he recorded in his diary, "Having been *long* and much dissatisfied with the Trade of fetching Negroes from Guinea at last I had a strong Inclination to Write something about it; but it wore off." But the discomfort continued, he wrote, and "at last reading Bayne, Ephes. about servants, who mentions Blackamoors; I began to be uneasy that I had *so long* neglected doing any thing."[12] The English Puritan Paul Bayne, in his 1617 commentary on Paul's Epistle to the Ephesians, had mentioned "Blackmores," but he did so to *differentiate* between perpetual slavery of "Blackmores" and the ephemeral subservience of those then called to higher stations.[13] With the early seventeenth-century Puritans as his intellectual source, Sewall ran his ideas in a radically different, grounded course.

His attention was finally brought to focus on the matter by a petition delivered to his house. Soon after Sewall finished reading Bayne, he explained to his diary, a flurry of coincidental activity kept antislavery sentiment before his mind. First, a friend showed Sewall a petition for "freeing a Negro and his wife, who were unjustly held in Bondage." Next, Sewall noted that a local committee was attempting to pass a law that would tax imported slaves at forty shillings per person, so as "to discourage the bringing of them." Finally and perhaps most importantly, "Mr. C. Mather resolves to publish a sheet to exhort Masters to labour their [the slaves'] Conversion." All this,

Sewall noted, brought him to believe he had been "call'd of God to Write this Apology."[14]

Sewall's own explanation for authoring *The Selling of Joseph* makes explicit that the problem had been *long* on his mind—*so long*, in fact, that he had had time to consider writing a tract, dismiss the idea, and come back to it, prompted by friends and circumstances. Nor was he alone in his mental unease. Some Boston authorities wanted to tax slave traders to limit the trade, and no less a colonist than Cotton Mather was uncomfortable with leaving "Negros" in an unconverted state. Sewall turned to his pen in response to a slowly simmering concern for the ways of the world he lived in, a world that had long been filled with captive African (and Indian) slaves.[15]

Sewall knew slavery well. His diary contains an entry regarding an African slave named Jethro among its first pages. In 1676, during King Philip's War, Sewall related the story of a summer attack by Narragansett Indians on English colonists, observing that one unfortunate colonist had been killed near his house, stripped, and decapitated and that "Jethro, [a] Niger," had been taken captive and then redeemed. Jethro took part in his own escape—from war captivity, back into slavery—when he seized an opportunity to flee his captors and join English forces. Once returned, Jethro provided tactical intelligence about the Narragansett forces.[16] As a reward for his help, he was even, eventually, granted his freedom by Plymouth authorities.

Sewall's diary is full of other interactions with enslaved and free Africans and Indians, local and foreign. He paid attention to events relating to Caribbean slavery, reporting, *"Friday, January 29th* [1686] . . . It seems there's a discourse that the K[ing] should motion to have all the Negroes at Jamaica baptized."[17] He also knew about Caribbean slave resistance, inscribing, *"Thorsday, September 17* [1685]. News comes to Town of the rising of the Negroes at Jamaica."[18] This was less than two months after the August revolt had broken out on several plantations in St. Catherine Parish, Jamaica, leading to murderous violence between slave rebels and colonial troops that stretched into the neighboring parish of St. Mary's. In the thirty years since the English had captured the island from the Spanish, Jamaica had experienced a series of slave revolts, violent paroxysms that would be followed by an even larger revolt exactly five years after the July 31, 1685, uprising.[19] In all likelihood there were few in Boston, when news of the revolt came to town, who wished they had taken up Cromwell's proposal to leave New England for Jamaica.[20]

Sewall also encountered slavery closer to home, among neighbors. He hired slaves, knew slaves, and had family members who owned slaves. Less than three months after he noted the Jamaican slave revolt, he wrote, "Several [colonists] have had the Small Pocks; buried a Negro."[21] Years later, he sadly remarked, *"March 9, 1693 . . . One of Mr. Holyoke's Twins falls into the Well and is drownd, no body but a Negro being at home; was a very lovely Boy of about 4 years old."*[22] More prosaically, enslaved Africans served him: *"Thorsday, Oct 6* [1687] *. . . In the Even[ing] Captain Prentice's Negro brings my Horse."*[23]

Slaveholding occurred even in his family. His wife was the daughter of John Hull, a wealthy Boston merchant who sold enslaved Indians into the West Indies.[24] And like his father-in-law, Sewall was a successful merchant who took advantage of the Atlantic market. In February 1688, he shipped to Barbados more than twenty barrels of fish, along with sundry goods. The same day he exported thirty barrels of mackerel on board the *Hopewell*. Onto the *Adventure*, bound for Jamaica, went forty barrels of pork. Another thirty barrels of mackerel went to Antigua. Indeed, his business records from his letterbook show that his top four exports were, in order, mackerel, fish oil, cod and other fish, and pork. His second- and fourth-biggest imports were, unsurprisingly, sugar and molasses (cotton and "hair sieve-bottoms," used to construct nets, were first and third, respectively). Sewall traded with places as disparate as London, Bristol, Barbados, the Bermudas, St. Christopher's, Tortugas, Jamaica, the

Leeward Islands, and Antigua.[25] His exported fish and pork fed slaves, who produced the sugar and molasses that he imported, along with the nets that would allow New England's colonists (mostly English, but some enslaved) to catch more fish to keep the cycle going. He was in this way one more embodiment of John Smith's earliest predictions for New England.

It was, then, from a position of knowledge that Sewall penned his polemic against slavery. *The Selling of Joseph* took its title from a biblical story: Joseph, the child born in his father's "old age," was favored by his father, and this aroused the jealousy of his brothers. After Joseph had what his brothers took to be a particularly impudent dream predicting they would someday bow before him, some of them plotted to kill him. Another brother intervened, and the complicitous brothers, instead of murdering Joseph, stripped him and sold him to passing merchants, who then sold him to the king of Egypt; he became a valued adviser to the king. In a neat ironic turn, some years later famine led Joseph's brothers to journey to the court to plead in prostration for grain, thus fulfilling Joseph's dream.[26]

This story, which hinges on the unlawful sale of Joseph by his brothers, provided the cornerstone to Sewall's argument in *The Selling of Joseph*. "Originally and Naturally," Sewall declared in the pamphlet, "There is no such thing as Slavery." As evidence, he cited the example of Joseph's illegitimate captivity, denying that Joseph was rightfully enslaved or sold. Since the brothers had no right to sell him, Sewall argued, the buyers had no right to purchase him, and the sale was illegal; with this move he put the burden of guilt on the buyer, finding them complicit in the purchase. "There is," he held, "no proportion between Twenty Pieces of Silvers, and LIBERTY."[27] Because no amount of money could be a fair price for freedom, Sewall concluded that all enslavement was illegal and immoral. Indeed, he reminded his readers that God himself had ordered, *"He that Stealeth a Man and Selleth him, or if he be found in his hand, he shall surely be put to Death.*" And such a punishment was fair, Sewall thought, considering the gravity of the crime, which he placed among the "most atrocious of Capital Crimes." Indeed, he asked, "what louder Cry can there be made of the Celebrated Warning, *Caveat Emptor!*"[28]

Let the buyer beware! As in his choice of title, Sewall seized here on the act of sale. This he deemed the weak link of slavery's chain of defense. Whereas Tryon and Godwyn had emphasized the ill treatment of slave hands by their masters, Sewall held out for especial opprobrium not incidents of torture but the moment of commodification. It was evidence both of a New England mind at work and of Sewall's awareness of New England's role in the Atlantic slave trade. Perceiving New England backsliding into a moral abyss, Sewall found no better proof of his fellow colonists' sinful embrace of commerce than in their part in facilitating the slave market.

It was an incisive claim. But not all of his authorial moves were so deft. In arguing that all slavery was illegitimate, and in using biblical citations to bolster his point, Sewall set himself up for failure because, by the terms of his society, he was wrong. English colonists in New England knew that God had in fact allowed slavery, just as he had allowed servitude of other sorts, just as he had allowed mastery and ownership. Their world rested on just such an understanding. In that regard, nothing had changed since Winthrop had founded the city on a hill, because nothing needed to. Only four years earlier, Cotton Mather wrote that by natural design "there must be a *Superiority* and an *Inferiority*; there must be some who are to *Command*, and there must be some who are to *Obey*." Mather went on to explain that among those who were to obey, there were two kinds: servants for terms, and slaves for life. "Some of you are under the *Yoke* of Servitude by a perpetual *Vassalage*, to those who have by Sword or Price purchased a Dominion over you," Mather noted. "Others of you are under the *Yoke* of Servitude by a Temporary *Agreement*, which you have made with some, to be subject unto them for a while upon such and such Considerations."[29] Regardless of how the bondage came to be, he declared both to be permitted. Mather knew that slaves, held in "perpetual vassalage" by violence, were legitimate. His neighbor Sewall knew the opposite.

Samuel Sewall and Cotton Mather were contemporaries, peers, friends, and even distantly related, though Mather's two grand-fathers—John Cotton on one side and Richard Mather on the other—made his lineage far more exalted than Sewall's in New England society. Both Richard Mather and John Cotton were, as one biogra-pher noted, "Moses-like figures" in New England. Richard Mather was, moreover, the father of Increase Mather, Cotton's father and himself a man of formidable learning and experience, who preached at the age of twenty-two from the pulpit of his father's Dorchester church, the very same church that had voted to redeem Dorcas. John Cotton was, of course, the same Puritan minister who had offered a sermon to John Winthrop's ship before it sailed for New England. Eventually, Richard Mather married John Cotton's widow, meaning that Increase Mather's marriage to Maria Cotton (John Cotton's daughter) was a legal marriage to his stepsister. From this tangled web, New England's version of royalty, emerged Cotton Mather, named first and last for New England's premier families. No less a person than John Eliot, "the apostle to the Indians," participated in Cotton Mather's ordination to the ministry; Eliot was roughly eighty years old at the time.[30]

Sewall's heritage was far less prominent, though in wealth and status and probably intelligence, he was Mather's peer, and he was Mather's close and lifelong friend. They moved in the same circles, shared companions, dined together, commiserated over politics. Sewall attended Boston's Third (South) Church, Mather attended and preached at the Second (North) Church. Nearly three decades into the eighteenth century, and well into their dotage, they both had their portraits painted. In his, an aged Sewall looks down with a twinkle in his eye, pudgy, avuncular, gray curls peeking out from under his sober black cap, worn to keep warm his balding head.[31]

Samuel Sewall. *Courtesy of the Massachu-setts Historical Society.*

Cotton Mather. *Courtesy of the American Antiquarian Society.*

Mather sat for his portrait within a year of Sewall's, and though eleven years younger, managed somehow to look older, certainly sterner. Whereas Sewall sported his natural locks, Mather chose a remarkable periwig that only accentuated his prominent nose and stark eyebrows.[32] Their diaries demonstrate both to have been pious and introspective, but Sewall seemed less tortured by life, less haunted by family. Mather never quite lived up to the goals he set for himself, never quite forgave himself for not having been in that first generation of mythical immigrants.

Like Sewall, Mather lived and worked in the upper levels of colonial society, and like Sewall, he thought deeply about the issue of slavery. Sometimes that was made evident only obliquely, as when Cotton Mather mentioned in the middle of a 1689 political tract that, as a result of recent legislation, "the people in *New-England* were all *Slaves* and the only difference between them and *Slaves* is their not being bought and sold."[33] The metaphor depended on the audience's knowing how slaves were treated, and its rhetorical power derived from the reader's understanding that such a fate would be anathema for the New Englanders in question, as it evidently was for Cotton Mather.

But the prolific Puritan also thought and wrote about slavery directly, and if publication dates are any guide, chattel slavery had been troubling Mather even longer than it troubled Sewall. In 1693, for example, Mather wrote the "Rules for the Society of Negroes," and he meant an actual society, a formal organization. It was Mather's brainchild for the weekly religious instruction of Africans in New England, both enslaved and free. His idea was that converted Africans might teach others about Christianity, much in the model of John Eliot's "Praying Indians." (Like Eliot's experiment, the society would not enjoy enduring success.) Mather claimed that a group of Africans asked him for help in setting up such a group. "A company of poor *Negroes*," he recounted, "of their own Accord, addressed mee, for my Countenance, to a Design which they had, of erecting such a *Meeting* for the Welfare of their miserable Nation that were Servants among us."[34] Despite Mather's enthusiasm for the project, his rules suggest that he could not help seeing New England's African inhabitants as potential makers of trouble. Thus, rule number two demonstrates his concern about the control of bodies:

> II. Our [members of the society] coming to the Meeting, shall never be without the *Leave* of such as have Power over us: And we will be Careful, that our Meeting may Begin and Conclude between the Hours of *Seven* and *Nine*; and that we may not be *unseasonably Absent* from the Families whereto we pertain.

Rule number seven makes explicit the fears implicit in the second:

> VII. We will, as we have Opportunity, set our selves to do all the Good we can, to the other *Negro-servants* in the Town; And if any of them should, at unfit Hours, be *Abroad*, much more, if any of them should *Run away* from their Masters, we will

afford them *no Shelter*: But we will do what in us lies, that they may be discovered and punished. And if any *of us,* are found Faulty, in this Matter, they shall be no longer *of us.*

And again concerned about control, rule number eight:

VIII. None of our Society shall be *Absent* from our Meeting, without giving a *Reason* of the Absence; And if it be found, that any have pretended unto their *Owners,* that they came unto the *Meeting,* when they were otherwise and elsewhere Employ'd, we will faithfully *Inform* their Owners, and also do what we can to Reclaim such Person from all such Evil Courses for the Future.[35]

The many rules reveal much about Mather's larger world. First, the ownership of bodies was commonplace enough to warrant the creation of a common, weekly meeting. Second, those numerous slaves had somehow shown the potential or the willingness to be unruly. And third, and perhaps worst of all, there had been hints they might enact that unruliness in groups. Locally, this was only one year after the Salem witch trials, where Cotton Mather had been so prosecutorially active—his obsession with control had recently been terribly breached. There was a wider context as well: remember the inclusion in Samuel Sewall's diary of slave revolts in Jamaica. Such revolts struck a fearful note for New England ears. Clearly, Mather in 1693 was worried about the same sort of things that Sewall would mention seven years later, when he referred to unrest of slaves chafing against their bonds. Sewall pointed out that the slaves' "continual aspiring after their forbidden Liberty, renders them Unwilling Servants."[36] Mather's rules aimed to prevent that from happening.

Mather himself had recently and obliquely made the same connection between aspirations of liberty and unfaithful service, but he drew a different conclusion. In *A Pastoral Letter to the English Captives in Africa,* written and published in 1698, Mather intended to let

English captives in North Africa know that they had not been forgotten and that, no matter how hard their burden, New England's colonists would remember their own. Mather could not offer consolation without including some admonishments. Above all, he argued, the important thing was to remain Christian, whatever trials came the captives' way, for the results of doing otherwise would be hellish. God would punish such lapses, he warned with italicized menace, "with the *Vengeance of Eternal Fire in the World to come, where the Smoke of your Torments will Ascend for ever and ever.*" Mather was certain his advice would save their eternal souls, as he compared being unsaved to the "worst sort of *Slavery*" and insisted that becoming a Christian was the only redemption that mattered.[37]

When Sewall found hypocrisy in colonists' lamenting the treatment of their friends and family in North Africa, even while refusing to consider their own enslavement of Africans, he was almost certainly speaking at least partly to Mather. But they disagreed. Like Mather, Sewall was concerned about the burden upon the soul, but his calculations left the New Englanders in arrears. He doubted "whether all the Benefit received by *Negro* Slaves, will balance the Accompt of Cash laid out upon them; and for the Redemption of our own enslaved Friends out of Africa." Sewall's own answer was clear: the slave trade was too wrong to make up for any spiritual rewards Africans might derive from being in New England.[38]

In many ways, then, Sewall intended his pamphlet to speak both to Mather and to the long-standing situation in the colony, rather than to any specific case. But authorial intentions rarely determine a reader's response, and general critiques too often pique specific individuals. Sewall's writing sparked a debate he might not have anticipated. John Saffin, a colonist, merchant, and slaveholder, took *The Selling of Joseph* personally and then took Sewall to task, penning a direct reply. Saffin was a prominent citizen in his own right—no Samuel Sewall or Cotton Mather, to be sure, but also no servant. He was born, like Sewall, in England and had immigrated as a child to New England, settling in Scituate, in the Plymouth Colony, by 1643. Aside from a short residence in Virginia (1654–57), he stayed in New England, eventually moving to Boston, where he was long a member of the First Church.[39] He was also a prosperous merchant, one of the wealthiest men in Massachusetts, and more than seventy years old when *The Selling of Joseph* was published. He buried eight sons in their childhoods; he outlived two wives.[40]

Saffin had long-standing ties to the slave trade and slavery. He, for example, knew Jethro, the enslaved man briefly captured by Narragansett Indians during King Philip's War. Saffin, as the executor of Jethro's late owner's estate, was involved in the case regarding his eventual reward of freedom. The court, apparently on Saffin's advice, even supplied clothing and food for Jethro.[41] But Jethro's freedom was an unusual reward. Saffin remained involved with the slave trade over the next decades. One 1681 letter shows him concerned about a shipment of slaves he had invested in, despite the Royal African Company's legal control of the market.[42] He also wrote an elegy for John Hull, Sewall's merchant father-in-law.

> But tis a woefull and a Gloomy-Day,
> When Righteous men are taken thus away;
> Heaven Speaks aloud to Mortalls, reads ther Doom
> Such are Removed from Dire ills to Come;
> O may not this, this sad Catastrophe
> Fore run the loss of our Dear Liberty.[43]

Hull, symbol to Saffin of dear liberty, had been, among other things, a slave owner.

It is not clear that Saffin personally owned many slaves, but he did eventually own a man named Adam. In 1694, Saffin leased Adam along with some land and some animals to a man named Thomas Shepherd, promising Adam his freedom if he served Shepherd faithfully for seven years. Yet Adam did not serve faithfully, at least not in Saffin's discriminating opinion, and at the end of the seven years, he attempted to rent Adam again to another man. Adam disagreed that Saffin still owned him, claimed that he had fulfilled the terms of the contract, refused to go to work for the new owner, and then ran away. He eventually ended up in Sewall's offices, asking for help and thus involving the judge personally in the matter. Sewall took Adam's side, and this seems to have angered Saffin no end, his anger apparent when he penned *A Brief and Candid Answer*.[44]

From the general perspective of his time, Sewall's arguments seemed actually quite weak, which Saffin did not fail to observe.[45] At Sewall's claim that all men had equal claims to liberty, Saffin scoffed and invoked what was truly common sense at the time. Suggesting such an equality, he said, "seems to invert the Order that God hath set in the World," an order that placed some people to be "Low and Despicable; some to be Monarchs, Kings, Princes and Governours" and, crucially, some "to be born Slaves, and so to remain during their lives." Without these critical stratifications, Saffin pointed out, "there would be a meer parity among men," a situation that would be contrary to God's will. His argument could have come word for word from Mather's earlier sermon on the duties of servitude. Few Christians in seventeenth-century North America, the odd Quaker aside, would have questioned that the world was built in a hierarchical manner, governed by one God, and organized into myriad crucial levels of status and responsibility.[46]

Saffin rejected Sewall's argument that the Bible did not permit slavery, by emphasizing what was commonly understood to be the legitimizing factor for enslaving Africans: that they were foreign.[47] Sewall had also argued that enslaved Africans took the place of English servants, who might otherwise have added rather than detracted to the general tone of society. Saffin agreed that "white"servants would be far preferable to "black Servants." "Who doubts that?" he asked, curtly, but he still failed to see how that meant slavery was wrong.

Freeing slaves, Saffin argued, would punish owners who had bought them legally and would lose money they had invested.[48] And, he continued, even if Sewall could persuade the General Assembly to pass a law freeing all the slaves, *and* to reimburse their owners with public funds, *and* abolish the trade—it would still never pass a vote, because somehow someone would have to pay to send the freed people out of the country, "or else the remedy would be worse than the Disease."[49] By this Saffin meant that Massachusetts would have to deal with a population of freed people, something Sewall himself had acknowledged as a problem: "There is such a disparity in their Conditions, Colour, and Hair, that they can never embody with us, and grow up into orderly Families, to the Peopling of the Land: but still remain in our Body Politick as a kind of extravasat Blood."[50] "Extravasate" blood is blood outside of its normal vessel, and thus constituting a serious problem. Even Sewall had trouble imagining a commingling of Africans with English; like so many white nineteenth-century abolitionists, his antislavery sentiment did not imply an inclusionary worldview.

Sewall had objected to arguments in favor of continuing the trade so that the Africans might be converted to Christianity, explaining, "Evil must not be done, that good may come of it."[51] This contention that saving souls was not of paramount interest was nearly heretical (it was, after all, a legitimating reason for the colonies), and Saffin took little time to dismiss the argument, retorting that it was hardly a bad thing to bring such souls and such bodies out of heathen states into Christian lives.[52] Like nineteenth-century arguments for keeping Africans enslaved in order to save them, Saffin's piety rings false to present-day ears, but to most of his English contemporaries he was simply stating an obvious and long-standing fact.

Finally, Sewall had critiqued the idea that slavery was legitimate in the region because colonists had purchased lawful captives taken in foreign wars. He observed that "every war is upon one side Unjust" and that thus "an unlawful War can't make lawful captives." Even if

Africans did have wars with each other, he said, that gave the English no right to buy captured combatants from either side. After all, it would not be acceptable to do so with Englishmen. For example, Sewall maintained that if a group of Englishmen should go fishing and another group of Englishmen "should Surprise them, and Sell them for Slaves to a Ship outward bound: they would think themselves unjustly dealt with; both by Sellers and Buyers." And yet, he pointed out, "we have no other kind of Title to our *Nigers*."[53] Saffin's response to this might best be described as dismissive. "If we must stay while both parties Warring are in the right," he bristled, "there would be no lawful Captives at all to be Bought; which seems to be ridiculous to imagine."[54] Saffin was simply unable to imagine a world without commodified captives, or at least he could not do so without ridiculing the notion.

Saffin ended the first part of his tract with a short piece of verse (the scholar Albert Von Frank has called him "one of the important minor poets of seventeenth-century Massachusetts," parsed praise, to be sure), titled "The Negroes Character." It was hardly a positive depiction of "Negroes," and the last line sneered at Sewall's audacity at comparing such people to the biblical Joseph.

> Cowardly and cruel are those *Blacks* Innate,
> Prone to Revenge, Imp of inveterate hate,
> He that exasperates them, soon espies
> Mischief and Murder in their very eyes.
> Libidinous, Deceitful, False, and Rude,
> The spume Issue of Ingratitude.
> The Premises consider'd, all may tell,
> How near good *Joseph* they are parallel.[55]

The poetry ended what had been an abstract discussion of the legality and righteousness of slavery. The second part of Saffin's *Response*, at once more personal and less persuasive, told his side of the specific troubles he had with Adam, in the process offering another glimpse of a life of an enslaved person in the region, filtered through the refracted light of a master's gaze. Saffin began by describing his reasons for sending Adam to Thomas Shepherd, Saffin's tenant on land he owned in Bristol. The loan of the man, he said, had been for Adam's own good. "Knowing the said Negro to be of a proud, insolent, and domineering spirit, yet had a cunning serpentine Genious," he began, with words reminiscent of his doggerel, he felt the work would be "for his [Adam's] own benefit (if it were possible)," in that having a new master, even if only temporarily, would "oblige him to obedience, and [encourage him] to go on cheerfully, quietly, and industriously in his Busines, for the mutual benefit of both Landlord and Tenant."[56]

But objections to these stated reasons came up later in the court cases. If Adam was so unpleasant, people wondered, why did Saffin not simply sell him? Why the concern for his spirit? Why, if he was known to be unruly, would Saffin lend him to a friend? Indeed, Thomas Shepherd, the very friend to whom Adam was originally lent, might have wondered the same thing. He testified at length about the problems he had encountered with his hired slave, declaring that Adam had been a "disobedient Turbulent outrageous and unruly Servant in all respects," who had failed to fulfill the terms of his contract.[57]

But Saffin himself seemed to blame both men to some degree for Adam's behavior, claiming that Shepherd was too lenient with his slave. For one thing, Saffin complained, he had allowed Adam to have some land of his own on which to plant tobacco, a situation that allowed Adam to earn "about *Three Pounds* a year, besides his own use." As if this leniency and financial independence was not bad enough, Shepherd allowed unsettling equality at the dinner table. "His said Master," Saffin continued, "also set him at his Table to eat with himself, his Wife & Children, (for which indeed I have blam'd him.)"[58] A few years later, the Boston colonist Sarah Kemble Knight would comment with some asperity on similar laxity of slave ownership in Connecticut. There, she noted, masters allowed "slaves to sit at Table and eat with then, (as they say to save time,) and into the dish goes the black hoof as freely as the white hand."[59] Chattel slavery required distance, she and Saffin knew, rather than familiarity.

Shepherd seemed, in both his own testimony and that of Saffin, to be a man ill equipped to handle racial slavery. Indeed, long before his contracted time with Adam was completed, Saffin remembered, Shepherd "did earnestly intreat me to take the said Negro away." The reason, Shepherd explained, was that Adam was "so proud and surlie" that Shepherd was unable to control him. He told Saffin that he was afraid to reprimand the slave, let alone strike him, "for fear he should do him or his Children some mischief." It appears that Shepherd knew how slave mastery *should* work, that he understood that violence was allowed and was often called for, but he had no heart for it, a reluctance made only greater by his very real fear that Adam would wreak nasty revenge upon Shepherd's family in response to any beating. Such moments, such human hesitation, such fear, lay bare the effort it took to solidify mastery; some people simply could not do it.[60]

In the absence of an owner fully versed in the ways of slave punishment and coercion, and in the presence of a slave savvy enough to take advantage of that absence, the slave system broke down, for its functioning depended on a willingness to resort to violence. When Shepherd could not or would not use force to subdue impertinence, Adam learned that his own resistance was not useless. From the viewpoint of a master, it was among the most dangerous lessons a slave could learn. It was at least partly to prevent slaves from learning this lesson that societies created slave laws, removing the onus of slave control from individuals and ensuring, moreover, that individual slave owners could not undermine the system through their particular weaknesses. This odd case, involving an owner's reproach of a lessee's management of an enslaved person makes visible what must mostly have been hidden: the violence expected and required of the chattel slave system.

Saffin finally relented and took Adam away from Shepherd, one year before his term of service was set to expire. But the man did not reform after returning with Saffin to Boston, though according to his owner he was treated well, had only light work duties, and received the same food as English servants. Despite this kind treatment, Saffin said, "he was so quarrelsome and contentious, calling the Maids vile names, and threatening them (as they said) that they were sometimes afraid to be in the Room with him; and both my Wife and my Sister *George*, have often desired me to turn him the said Negro out of the house, for they could not endure his pertinacy."[61]

It fell to the courts to decide Adam's status. An early jury found against Adam, but his advocates immediately protested that the case was corrupted. John Saffin, it turned out, was one of the judges sitting on the case in the Superior Court, and he had not recused himself. For that reason, and some other irregularities, including accusations that Saffin had tampered with the jury, the case was appealed.[62] Justice was a drawn-out process in early New England, just as it can be today, and this case was no exception. The retrial was delayed at least once by Adam's having contracted smallpox.[63] Sewall grew hugely impatient with the delays, even finding himself inspired, after hearing that a new trial had been ordered, to write some of his own poetry about Saffin's apparent obsession with the case. The insults in the poem are made only harsher by Sewall's intense hatred of wigs, a fashion that Saffin had apparently adopted.

> Superannuated Sqiuer, wigg'd and powder'd with pretence,
> Much beguiles the just Assembly by his lying Impudence.
> None being by, his bold Attorneys push it on with might and main
> By which means poor simple Adam sinks to slavery again.[64]

Sewall's poetry was on a par with Saffin's—a touch too reliant on alliteration—but the insults still must have stung. Regardless, the case dragged on for roughly three years. While the appeals wended their way through the courts, Saffin was granted the right to lend Adam once more, this time to Captain Timothy Clarke. Again trouble ensued, as the frustrated Adam, who strongly believed he should be free, was less than civil to Clarke. The latter attempted to discipline Adam by striking him with a stick, sparking a fight.[65] Soon thereafter, despite possibly being a slave, Adam sued Saffin.

Adam's lawsuit essentially charged Saffin with harassment. Adam explained that he was a "freeman" and able "to prove his liberty." Given that, he argued that Saffin's attempt to claim "him as his slave, doth unjustly vex him." He asked for one hundred pounds in damages. In response, Saffin threatened to sell Adam out of the colony, a move that was blocked by a decree from the courts. Saffin next petitioned the governor and the legislature to help him circumvent the courts, explaining that the situation had gone through various courts for more than two years and still had no resolution. He asked for pity, claiming he had become, against nature, a "meer Vassall to his slave," as he was still responsible for paying for his maintenance, including clothes and food and even medical care when Adam came down with smallpox. But the legislature was no more moved by his arguments than the courts had been.

The final verdict in the case appeared in November 1703, when the Superior Court of Judicature declared once and for all that "Adam and his heirs be at peace and quiet and free with all their Chattles . . . for Ever."[66] But even such a generous ruling turned out to offer Adam only a limited liberty, for Massachusetts authorities were concerned about the abundance of freed people in their midst. In 1707, an act was passed to prohibit "Free negroes" from hosting in their homes "negro or molatto servants without the leave and consent of their respective masters or mistresses." It also required all "free male negro's or molatto's" at least sixteen years old to provide military service; it furthermore obliged all such able-bodied men in every town to provide work in repairing roads and any other service asked of them, at the discretion of the authorities. Failure to fulfill any of these requirements resulted in a fine, while failure to pay the fine condemned the evader to prison.[67]

Adam was nonetheless a fully diligent freed man. His name appears nearly every year after the law's passage, doing his assigned portion of the legislated corvée labor. In 1708, he was assigned eight days of road work; in 1710, he worked for four days; he worked three days in 1711, 1712, and 1713. In 1714, he worked two days, and in 1715 he was assigned only one.[68] The gradually shortened assignments possibly reflected the reality that Adam was getting older. Indeed, by 1710, he had outlived his former owner. But he could not have forgotten John Saffin, since he bore his name. On all the records, he was always listed as "Adam Saffin." One wonders who might have been more displeased with this instance of renaming: the freed man who bore his owner's name, or the man who had given it. John Saffin cared about names, we know—he wrote a "brief elegy" for his son who had died, who carried "that name of mine."[69] But Adam Saffin had lived.

One also wonders how Samuel Sewall came to write such radical sentiments in *The Selling of Joseph*. Sewall had a close relationship with one slave in particular: Bastian. He married Bastian and his wife, and he later baptized their children.[70] It could be that such personal experience altered his views on a harsh institution. But Sewall's own words suggest he himself had complicated views on people of African descent—remember his doubts about whether people of such "extravasat blood" should ever mingle with English colonists. In any case, personal relationships could never be counted on to soften views on slavery. Mather and Saffin and others knew slaves more intimately than did Sewall, and yet they experienced no such softening.

Was it perhaps, then, his experience with the Salem witchcraft trials? Some years later, Sewall publicly recanted his participation in the events. Standing in front of the congregation, Sewall heard read aloud his statement that he desired to "take the Blame and Shame" of the tragedy upon his shoulders, and he asked for both the congregation's forgiveness and God's pardon for his role in the trials.[71] Does having to issue a public apology like this make a person more inclined to question the workings of the world? Did having made one major mistake leave Sewall more inclined to be on guard against making more? Did having once doubted the validity of the legal system make him more skeptical of other laws and other courts? He was mute on the topic of how his apology made him feel and how it reverberated through the rest of his life's frequent encounters with enslaved people.

But perhaps what he thought about his apology is moot. His pamphlet fell into oblivion until reprinted by the Massachusetts Historical Society in 1864, in the middle of a bloody war about slavery in which New England understood itself to be the cradle of liberty, still the righteous beacon to the land. On his own contemporaries, however, the pamphlet had little effect. Despite Sewall's protestations as the seventeenth century closed, slavery grew steadily in eighteenth-century New England. Few if any of Sewall's fellow colonists were persuaded by his arguments. His was one in a long line of what one scholar has called the "long history of sincere but inconsequential protest."[72]

The Mathers, periwigged and pious, certainly were not persuaded. In 1723, Increase Mather died a slave owner, but forbade his heirs to sell "his Negro servant," bequeathing the man "his liberty let him then be esteemed a Free Negro."[73] And decades earlier Cotton Mather had recorded in his diary a "surprising Thing." Some congregation members who knew he wanted a servant at a reasonable price bought him "a very likely *Slave*; a young Man, who is a *Negro* of a promising Aspect and Temper." Mather wasted no time in exercising the rights of any master. Though the enslaved man was an adult and had a name already, Mather renamed him Onesimus, Greek for "useful."[74] What's in a name? Mastery.

But Cotton Mather, even by the standards of colonial New England, was always an obstinate man. Perhaps more tellingly, Sewall failed to convince others even closer to home. Fourteen years after the publication of *The Selling of Joseph*, his own son and namesake, Samuel Sewall Jr., placed the following ad in the *Boston News Letter* to announce a sale: "several Irish *Maid* Servants time, most of them for Five years, one Irish *Man* Servant, who is a good Barber and Wiggmaker, also Four or Five likely Negro Boys."[75] The first antislavery tract written in North America went unheeded even among the author's own family.

Portrait of John Potter and his family, ca. 1740. *Courtesy of the Newport Historical Society.*

# A Thousand Such Fellows

Lo, this only have I found, that God hath made man upright;
but they have sought out many inventions.

—Ecclesiastes 7:29

In October of 1704, an intrepid English colonist named Sarah Kemble Knight traveled alone, overland, from Boston to New York and back. Beset at various points by floods, by unfriendly tavern keepers, by lumpy bedding, by cold, and by fatigue, Knight nonetheless managed to keep a lively journal of her travels. One week into her trip, she arrived in New Haven, "where [she] was received with all Possible Respects and civility." Exhausted, she rested there awhile before continuing to New York. During her stay, for her amusement, her hosts told her a "pleasant" story of a recent court case in the town.

"A negro Slave," she recounted, "belonging to a man in the Town, stole a hogs head [a cask of liquor] from his master, and gave or sold it to an Indian, native of the place." That Indian man then sold the stolen cask to someone in the town, an act that somehow revealed the theft. "The Heathen was Seized" and taken summarily to the local magistrate's house for questioning. But the justice was away from his home, working in his fields harvesting "pompions" (pumpkins) with a colleague. The accused thief was accordingly hurried out to the fields himself and brought before the two judges. In the absence of a bench, one was made of pumpkins, and the trial began.

"You Indian why did You steal from this man?" one judge asked. "You sho'dnt's do so—it's a Grandy wicked thing to steal."

Upon hearing this, the other justice objected to the style of the question. "Hol't Hol't," the observer cried. "You speak negro to him. I'le ask him. You sirrah, why did You steal this man's Hoggshead? Hoggshead? (replys the Indian,) me no stomany [understand]." To clarify his meaning, the justice pulled off his hat and "patted his own head with his hand," saying, "Tatapa—You, Tatapa—you; all one this. Hoggshead all one this."

"Hah!" replied the Indian man, somewhat cryptically. In further response to the judge's pantomime explanation, the man said, "now me stomany that." Upon hearing this, "the Company fell into a great fitt of Laughter, even to Roreing," such that the justice could not restore order.[1]

Knight's story provokes more puzzlement than laughter today, for the joke is obscure and the casual slang is incomprehensible.[2] But as a description of colonial New England at the beginning of the eighteenth century, the story succeeds. Consider what her tale reveals: a small New England town, provincial enough that two prominent colonists who held the title of justice still worked in their own fields to gather their crops on a fall day. This was a rural world in which people in positions of great authority might (how ridiculous!) sit on pumpkins to render judgments. To that relatively urbane and sophisticated Bostonian, Sarah Kemble Knight, of course, this all seemed even funnier, country mice performing for her town mouse eyes.

We might notice something else: that this was also, even in the small town of New Haven, a strangely, dangerously, cosmopolitan world. We might see first that the instigator of the entire affair was a "negro slave," who stole alcohol. We might observe that this slave knew an Indian willing to receive stolen goods and fence them. And we might further note that even though that Indian was a "native of the place," English colonists understood it to be well within their purview to seize him and try him according to English laws, in English courts. These same English colonists were indeed so familiar with Africans and Indians that they understood each group to speak differently. "Grandy wicked," the observers knew, was how a "negro" talked. When speaking to Indians, a colonist should instead use other words and phrases.

And this wasn't just local knowledge. Knight, a woman from another colony, followed the jokes, including those not in English—the terms and humor seem to have been transcolonial. Indeed, it was a connected world in other ways: Knight's eventual entry into New York occurred in the company of her relative Thomas Trowbridge of New Haven, the same man who had finally confirmed through questioning in the Bowery that John Whan, the enslaved man from New Haven, had successfully fled New England and had died among his country folk, in New York.[3]

By the opening of the eighteenth century, slavery was embedded in the New England colonies, an accepted and familiar part of the society. Where Samuel Shrimpton had once placed his slave in the background of his portrait, now some wealthy families had their portraits painted with their slaves foregrounded as props, property signifying prosperity. Indeed, the institution of chattel slavery grew steadily over the next decades, peaking at roughly midcentury, and dying only very slowly as the nineteenth century approached.[4] The reasons for that slow death are many and convoluted. To be sure, the soaring rhetoric of the American Revolution resonated strongly with New England colonists, and certainly the institution had never been the mainstay of the regime's local labor force. But much of the impulse toward freeing the area's slaves came from the agitation of freed and enslaved people in the region, some of whom were by now fifth-, sixth-, and seventh-generation New Englanders.

In Massachusetts, legal bondage ended almost with a whimper, when a decision in the 1783 Quock Walker case declared slavery unconstitutional in the state (though the practice did continue after the case).[5] In 1783, Rhode Island and Connecticut both enacted "gradual emancipation" laws: children born to enslaved mothers after March of 1784 would not be enslaved for life, but rather could count on receiving their legal freedom at some point. In Connecticut, that point came after twenty-five years of enslavement; in Rhode Island, it initially came at twenty-one years for male children, or eighteen years of age for female children, though the legislature quickly removed that age difference and required all children of enslaved mothers to serve for twenty-one years.[6] Such emancipations were the very definition of gradual, for a scattering of slaves were legally held in New England through the 1840s.[7]

And for the vast multitudes, the history of the region's earliest relationship to slavery was quickly forgotten. In 1838, Nathaniel Hawthorne, the great, somber fabulist of colonial New England, traveled to Williams College's commencement, where he took in the scene with his usual keen eye: the students, the onlookers, the peddlers and gingerbread sellers, the drunks, the farmers, and "a good many blacks among the crowd." Hawthorne spent some time observing these "blacks," among whom he especially noted an old man, now freed, who spoke with a "strange kind of pathos, about the whippings he used to get, while he was a slave—a queer thing of mere feeling, with some glimmerings of sense." There were others, too, who drew the author's attention: a "gray old negro . . . of a different stamp, politic, sage, cautious, yet with boldness enough, talking about the rights of his race, yet so as not to provoke his audience, discoursing of the advantages of living under laws." Then there was a "drunken negro," who inspired the disdain of "three or four well dressed and decent negro wenches." Presumably there were even more freed people in the crowd, watching the commencement and the merriment, along with whites and perhaps Indians—though if there were any of the latter, they did not draw Hawthorne's attention. "On the whole," the quintessential chronicler and intellectual of New England concluded cryptically, "I find myself rather more of an abolitionist in feeling than in principle."[8]

Williams, then and now, was located in a rural corner of Massachusetts, close to Vermont and New York, hidden among the Berkshires. It was not, it seems, a place Hawthorne associated with slavery or African Americans, and he struggled to explain to himself their presence. "I suppose," he finally decided, "they used to emigrate across the border, while New-York was a slave state."

Later that same year, in a tavern in Hartford, Hawthorne was surprised again to encounter "a negro respectably dressed, and well-mounted on horseback, travelling on his own hook, calling for oats and drinking a glass of brandy and water at the bar—like any other Christian." Hawthorne was not alone in appraising the man's qualities. Sitting near him was a fellow traveler from Wisconsin who said, upon observing the same scene, "I wish I had a thousand such fellows in Alabama." Hawthorne was struck by this comment. "It made a queer impression on me," he wrote, "the negro was really so human—and to talk of owning a thousand like him."[9]

Hawthorne's astonishment at seeing people of African descent in a New England crowd and in a New England tavern, underscored just how effectively the importance of slavery to the region's development had been erased from memory. The realities of New England's colonization, the memory of violence and Indian removal and replacement had faded, at least among Anglo-Americans. What mattered to Hawthorne was where slaves were now: in the America South, growing cotton. There had been more than a thousand enslaved Africans, and perhaps even more enslaved Indians, in the seventeenth-century New England about which he would write so perceptively and tragically, and even more in the eighteenth century, but Hawthorne had forgotten them or perhaps had never known they were there. It was a startling oversight in a man known for piercing vision.

Twenty-four years later he was still placing slavery exclusively in the South. Writing in *The Atlantic*, in the middle of the Civil War, he commented on an odd kinship between New Englanders and enslaved people in the Chesapeake:

> There is an historical circumstance, known to few, that connects the children of the Puritans with these Africans of Virginia, in a very singular way. They are our brethren, as being lineal descendants from the Mayflower, the fated womb of which, in her first voyage, sent forth a brood of Pilgrims upon Plymouth Rock, and, in a subsequent one, spawned slaves upon the Southern soil,—a monstrous birth, but with which we have an instinctive sense of kindred, and so are stirred by an irresistible impulse to attempt their rescue, even at the cost of blood and ruin. The character of our sacred ship, I fear, may suffer a little by this revelation; but we must let her white progeny offset her dark one,—and two such portents never sprang from an identical source before.[10]

Several ships named *Mayflower* set sail from England's ports in the seventeenth century, and one of them took slaves to the Caribbean. It was not that of the famed Pilgrims, which was already on its last legs when it arrived at Plymouth. Hawthorne was mistaken in thinking they were actually the same ship. But in metaphorical terms, of course, he was absolutely right.

# Acknowledgments

Many people and institutions helped me write this book, and I am happy to have the opportunity to thank them. None are responsible for any errors of fact or reasoning that may remain in the text.

From start to finish, this project received funding from a variety of sources. They include Yale's Center for International and Area Studies, now the MacMillan Center, which offered funding for Caribbean research. The Yale History Department gave me the A. Bartlett Giamatti Fellowship, and Yale University offered a John F. Ender Summer Research Fellowship. I owe thanks to the J. William Fulbright Fellowship Program and to my friendly cohort of fellows in the West Indies. Thank you to the New England Regional Fellowship Consortium Grant Program, which made possible research at the Boston Athenaeum, the Massachusetts Historical Society, and the New England Historic Genealogical Society. I was honored to be a Barbara S. Mosbacher Fellow at the John Carter Brown Research Library, and a Peterson Fellow at the American Antiquarian Society, and a W. M. Keck Foundation Fellow at the Huntington Library. The Gilder Lehrman Institute funded research at the New-York Historical Society. I am indebted to the talented librarians and archivists at all of those institutions. Thanks also to the Broadbent Junior Research Fellowship in American History at Christ Church College, Oxford University. I was particularly pleased to receive a Mrs. Giles Whiting Foundation Dissertation Fellowship in the Humanities from Yale University. Later on, Yale's Gilder Lehrman Center provided substantial funding for me to return to New Haven during a research leave, and Princeton's faculty funding provided the rest.

I would never have become a historian without the strong base provided by Elizabeth Colwill and William Cheek, both then at San Diego State University. I am grateful to them (and to Aimee Lee Cheek) for helping me understand what questions matter. Long before that, Eileen Razarri Elrod made me an early Americanist, and Susan Frisbie taught me how to really *read*.

This project started as a dissertation for the Department of History at Yale University, and my stalwart committee deserves praise for shepherding a unwieldy project to completion. Stuart Schwartz taught me to think broadly and comparatively, lessons that fundamentally changed this book for the better. David Blight provided nineteenth-century counterpoints, and a humanist perspective. Jon Butler taught the seminar in which I wrote what became my first published history piece, and has been a loyal mentor ever since, whether in Connecticut or in his beloved Minnesota. And finally, John Demos remains a model scholar and writer, and honorary member of our family. My children love to visit him at the "farm," to help him stack firewood, and try out all of his precious old tools and instruments. I thank him here for all that, but mostly for his unswerving friendship.

For community in New Haven during graduate school and after, I thank Theodore Anderson, Adam Arenson, Shary Barnes, Jennifer Bryan, Gerry Cadava, Allegra di Bonaventura, Kate Cooney, Alejandra Dubcovsky, Caitlin Fitz, Paul Grant-Costa, Tammy Ingram, Charles Keith, Sophia Lee, Jake Lundberg, Dodie McDow, Bob Morrissey, Alison Norris, Lindsay O'Neill, Angela Pulley-Hudson, Johanna Ransmeier, Jake Ruddiman, Ed Rugemer, Aaron Sachs, Camilla Schofield, Tatiana Seijas, David Spatz, Helen Veit, and Owen Williams.

I finished my dissertation while a junior research fellow in Oxford, and I thank the members of the Christ Church College Senior Common Room for their collegiality. My appreciation also goes to the scholars at the Rothemere Center for American History, particularly Richard Carwadine, Gareth Davies, Jay Sexton, and Peter Thompson, for their warm welcome to a bewildered American. For Sunday roasts, Isis walks, and much more, I thank David Gilks, William Pettigrew, Alison Price, Gemma Shore, Julie Wood, and Mara Keire.

Various seminars and conferences heard and read excerpts from this book. Excerpts and drafts of chapter 1 were presented at the Ohio Seminar, where John Brooke and Margaret Newell offered helpful ideas; to the Columbia Seminar on Early American History, where Zara Anishanslin, Evan Haefeli, and others braved a snowstorm to discuss my work; and to the Washington Seminar during which Rick Bell, Holly Brewer, Clare Lyons, James Henretta, and other participants helped me hone my ideas and my text. Versions of chapter 2 were presented first to the Omohundro Conference in New Paltz, where Paul Mapp and Peter Silver, along with the insightful audience, asked helpful questions, and later to the NYU Atlantic Studies Seminar, where Patricia Bonomi, Karen Kupperman, and many others offered sage advice. A smart audience at the Omohundro Conference in Halifax, Nova Scotia, heard excerpts from chapter 3, and I give special thanks to Alan Gallay for his comments there; participants in the Colonial Americas Workshop at Princeton also read the chapter. Excerpts from an early version of chapter 6 were presented at the McNeil Center for Early American Studies, (which also saw my first presentation on the earliest iteration of this project), and to the Yale Early American Historians. Fellows at the Gilder Lerhman Center at Yale University heard a presentation on the entire book, as did the American Studies Workshop at Princeton University.

More than a few extremely generous people read this entire manuscript for me. In particular, I need to thank John Demos, Caitlin Fitz, Joseph Fronczak, Jane Kamensky, and James Merrell for their comments, insights, and encouragement. Vincent Brown, Paul Grant-Costa (paleographer extraordinaire), and Jennifer Morgan each read parts of this book and made crucial interventions, for which I am grateful.

The Department of History at Princeton University has provided me with a welcoming and intellectually challenging workplace. Colleagues not mentioned already who also read and commented on parts or all of this work include Jeremy Adelman, Alec Dun, Katja Guenther, Dirk Hartog, Alison Isenberg, Rob Karl, Matt Karp, Emmanuel Kreike, Jon Levy, Beth Lew-Williams, Rosina Lozano, Erika Milam, Dan Rodgers, Marni Sandweiss, Keith Wailoo, and Sean Wilentz. My heartfelt thanks go to Bill Jordan for steadfast support and wise advice. I am indebted also to Judy Hanson (Princeton) and the late Florence Thomas (Yale) for administrative support at various stages of this project. Katlyn Carter provided able research assistance, and I am beyond grateful to Andrew Ferris for indefatigable fact-checking and more.

I feel an immense amount of gratitude to Bob Weil, a genuine editor, who believed in this project from the moment he read my proposal, and then improved it with every heavy stroke of his thick blue pen. For the cover, my appreciation goes to Steve Attardo; for his meticulous copyediting, I thank Otto Sonntag; for skilled production, Anna Oler, Nancy Palmquist, Don Rifkin, and Rebecca Homiski; for assistance in matters big and small, Will Menaker. My appreciation to Wendy Strothman for guiding me through the process.

I would be remiss if I did not acknowledge some regulations that allowed this book to become what it is: the generous Parental Support and Relief Policy of the Graduate School of Yale University, the United Kingdom's Statutory Maternity Leave, and Princeton University's Family Friendly leave policies. Many people (mostly feminists) fought long and hard to achieve these kinds of policies, and I am very grateful to have benefited from their victories. These statutes did not make writing this book *easy*, but they surely made it possible.

My parents and brother live in California, where I grew up and where much of my heart remains. I miss them all. No words could fully convey to my parents my gratitude for all they did and do. Nonetheless, I thank them here, in irrevocable print, for their love of me and mine, especially of their three beloved grandchildren.

Those children are very young as I write these words, too young to read this (or care), and they surely do not understand how much the fact of their existence changed the tenor of this project. But I am indebted to them anyway, for offering me daily a beautiful counterpoint to the cruelty I study. The Puritan poet Anne Bradstreet once wrote to her own children, "I happy am, if well with you." My sentiments, exactly.

Finally, I thank Joseph, for everything.

# *Notes*

## Abbreviations

CCHS      *Collections of the Connecticut Historical Society* (Hartford, CT: The Society, 1860–1967)

CCR      J. H. Trumbull and C. J. Hoadly, eds., *The Public Records of the Colony of Connecticut* (Hartford: Brown & Parsons, 1850–90)

CSMP      *Publications of the Colonial Society of Massachusetts* (Boston: The Society, 1892–1924)

EAS      *Early American Studies: An Interdisciplinary Journal*

ECCR      George Francis Dow, ed., *Records and Files of the Quarterly Courts of Essex County, Massachusetts* (Salem, MA: Essex Institute, 1911–21)

JAH      *Journal of American History*

JJW      Richard Dunn, James Savage, and Laetitia Yeandle, eds., *The Journal of John Winthrop* (Cambridge, MA: Belknap Press of Harvard Univ. Press, 1996)

MAC      Massachusetts Archives Collection, Massachusetts State Archives, Columbia Point, MA

Mass. Arch.      Massachusetts State Archives, Columbia Point, MA

MBCA      John Noble, ed., *Records of the Court of Assistants of the Colony of the Massachusetts Bay* (Boston: County of Suffolk, 1901–28)

MCR      Nathaniel B. Shurtleff, ed., *Records of the Governor and Company of the Massachusetts Bay in New England* (Boston: W. White, 1853–54)

MHS      Massachusetts Historical Society, Boston

MHSC      *Collections of the Massachusetts Historical Society,* all series (Boston: The Society, 1863–)

MHSP      *Proceedings of the Massachusetts Historical Society* (Boston: Massachusetts Historical Society, 1879–1998)

NEHGR      *New England Historical and Genealogical Register* (Boston: New England Historic Genealogical Society, 1847–)

NEHGS      New England Historic Genealogical Society, Boston

NEQ      *New England Quarterly*

PCR      David Pulsifer, ed., *Records of the Colony of New Plymouth in New England* (Boston: William White, 1854–61)

PREC      George Francis Dow, ed. *The Probate Records of Essex County, Massachusetts* (Salem, MA: Essex Institute, 1916–20)

PRO      The National Archives (formerly Public Records Office), London

RICR      John Russell Bartlett, ed., *Records of the Colony of Rhode Island and Providence Plantations in New England* (Providence: A. C. Greene, 1856–65)

SD      M. Halsey Thomas, *The Diary of Samuel Sewall* (New York: Farrar, Straus and Giroux, 1973)

WMQ      *The William and Mary Quarterly*, 3d ser.

WP      *Winthrop Papers* (Boston: Massachusetts Historical Society, 1929–)

YIPP      Yale Indian Papers Project, Yale University

### Note on Sources

1 New England colonists' biblical preferences, and the transition from the Geneva Bible to the King James Bible, are discussed in Harry S. Stout, "Word and Order in Colonial New England," in *The Bible in America: Essays in Cultural History*, ed. Nathan O. Hatch and Mark A. Noll (New York: Oxford Univ. Press, 1982), 19–38.

2 John Cotton, *A Briefe Exposition with Practicall Observations upon the Whole Book of Ecclesiastes* (London, 1654), 160. Perry Miller and Thomas H. Johnson, editors of a collection of Puritan writings, observed of Ecclesiastes that it "more than any other book of the Bible is concerned with what might be called secular issues, [and thus Cotton's] work is a mine of information on Puritan attitudes that are seldom discussed in the more strictly theological writings." Miller and Johnson, *The Puritans: A Sourcebook of Their Writings* (New York: American Book Company, 1938), 799.

### Introduction: The Cause of Her Grief

1 For the latest estimates of the Atlantic slave trade, see "Assessing the Slave Trade Estimates Table," in *Voyages: The Trans-Atlantic Slave Trade Database*, http://slavevoyages.org/tast/assessment/estimates.faces (accessed Dec. 18, 2014). For the Indian enslaved population, see Brett Rushforth, *Bonds of Alliance: Indigenous and Atlantic Slaveries in New France* (Chapel Hill: Univ. of North Carolina Press, 2012), 9.

2 Richard S. Dunn has noted that the various people who came to be called Puritans "were in much firmer agreement about what was wrong with the ritualistic Church of England than about what sort of church should replace it in New England." Dunn, "An Odd Couple: John Winthrop and William Penn," *MHSP* 99 (1987): 21. For a discussion on the limitations of "Puritan-

ism" as a category, see Michael Winship's "Were There Any Puritans in New England?," *NEQ* 74, no. 1 (2001): 118–38. On Puritanism in general, see Patrick Collinson, *The Elizabethan Puritan Movement* (New York: Oxford Univ. Press, 1990); idem, *The Religion of Protestants: The Church in English Society, 1559–1625* (New York: Oxford Univ. Press, 1984); Peter Lake, *Moderate Puritans and the Elizabethan Church* (New York: Cambridge Univ. Press, 1982); and the very useful anthology *The Cambridge Companion to Puritanism*, ed. John Coffey and Paul C. H. Lim (Cambridge: Cambridge Univ. Press, 2008).

3 Harry S. Stout, *The New England Soul: Preaching and Religious Culture in Colonial New England* (New York: Oxford Univ. Press, 1986), 50. The literature on Puritanism and Puritan New England is, to say the least, vast. A selection of work on the entity we might call "Puritan New England" includes Francis Bremer, *The Puritan Experiment: New England Society from Bradford to Edwards* (Hanover, NH: Univ. Press of New England, 1995); John Demos, *A Little Commonwealth: Family Life in Plymouth Colony* (New York: Oxford Univ. Press, 2000); idem, *Entertaining Satan: Witchcraft and the Culture of Early New England* (New York: Oxford Univ. Press, 1982); idem, *The Unredeemed Captive: A Family Story from Early America* (New York: Vintage, 1994); Stephen Foster, *The Long Argument: English Puritanism and the Shaping of New England Culture, 1570–1700* (Chapel Hill: Univ. of North Carolina Press, 1991); David D. Hall, *Worlds of Wonder, Days of Judgment: Popular Religious Belief in Early New England* (New York: Alfred A. Knopf, 1989); idem, *The Faithful Shepherd: A History of the New England Ministry in the Seventeenth Century* (Chapel Hill: Univ. of North Carolina Press, 1972); idem, *A Reforming People: Puritanism and the Transformation of Public Life in New England* (New York: Alfred A. Knopf, 2011); Jane Kamensky, *Governing the Tongue: The Politics of Speech in Early New England* (New York: Oxford Univ. Press, 1997); Carole Karlsen, *Devil in the Shape of a Woman: Witchcraft in Colonial New England* (New York: W. W. Norton, 1987); Kenneth A. Lockridge; *A New England Town: The First Hundred Years: Dedham, Massachusetts, 1636–1736*, rev. ed. (New York: W. W. Norton, 1985); Perry Miller, *The New England Mind: The Seventeenth Century* (New York: Macmillan, 1939); idem, *The New England Mind: From Colony to Province* (Cambridge, MA: Harvard Univ. Press, 1953); Edmund S. Morgan, *The Puritan Dilemma: The Story of John Winthrop* (Boston: Little, Brown, 1958); idem, *Visible Saints: The History of a Puritan Idea* (Ithaca, NY: Cornell Univ. Press, 1968); idem, *The Puritan Family: Essays on Religion and Domestic Relations in Seventeenth-Century New England* (Boston: Trustees of the Public Library, 1944); Mary Beth Norton, *In the Devil's Snare: The Salem Witchcraft Crisis of 1692* (New York: Alfred A. Knopf, 2002); Mark A. Peterson, *The Price of Redemption: The Spiritual Economy of Puritan New England* (Stanford, CA: Stanford Univ. Press, 1997); Laurel Thatcher Ulrich, *Good Wives: Image and Reality in the Lives of Women in Northern New England, 1650–1750* (New York: Alfred A. Knopf, 1982); Mark Valeri, *Heavenly Merchandize: How Religion Shaped Commerce in Puritan America* (Princeton, NJ: Princeton Univ. Press, 2010); and Michael P. Win-

ship, *Godly Republicanism: Puritans, Pilgrims, and a City on a Hill* (Cambridge, MA: Harvard Univ. Press, 2012). A recent succinct and cogent summary of the place of New England in colonial North American historiography is Mark Peterson, "Why They Mattered: The Return of Politics to Puritan New England," *Modern Intellectual History* 10, no. 3 (2013): 683–96.

4  For scholarship that downplays the Puritan nature of New England in favor of economic or other frameworks, see, among others, Bernard Bailyn, *The New England Merchants in the Seventeenth Century* (Cambridge, MA: Harvard Univ. Press, 1955); William Cronon, *Changes in the Land: Indians, Colonists, and the Ecology of New England* (New York: Hill and Wang, 1983); Christine Heyrman, *Commerce and Culture: The Maritime Communities of Colonial Massachusetts, 1690–1750* (New York: W. W. Norton, 1984); Stephen Innes, *Creating the Commonwealth: The Economic Culture of Puritan New England* (New York: W. W. Norton, 1995); Daniel Vickers, *Farmers and Fishermen: Two Centuries of Work in Essex County, Massachusetts, 1630–1850* (Chapel Hill: Univ. of North Carolina Press, 1994). Scholarship on the region that emphasizes Native American and English encounters includes Katherine Grandjean, *American Passage: The Communications Frontier in Early New England* (Cambridge, MA: Harvard Univ. Press, 2015); Francis Jennings, *The Invasion of America: Indians, Colonialism, and the Cant of Conquest* (New York: W. W. Norton, 1975); Richard W. Cogley, *John Eliot's Mission to the Indians before King Philip's War* (Cambridge, MA: Harvard Univ. Press, 1999); Jill Lepore, *The Name of War: King Philip's War and the Origins of American Identity* (New York: Alfred A. Knopf, 1998); Ann Marie Plane, *Colonial Intimacies: Indian Marriage in Early New England* (Ithaca, NY: Cornell Univ. Press, 2000); Ann M. Little, *Abraham in Arms: War and Gender in Colonial New England* (Philadelphia: Univ. of Pennsylvania Press, 2007); Jenny Hale Pulsipher, *Subjects unto the Same King: Indians, English, and the Contest for Authority in Colonial New England* (Philadelphia: Univ. of Pennsylvania Press, 2005); David J. Silverman, *Faith and Boundaries: Colonists, Christianity, and Community among the Wampanoag Indians of Martha's Vineyard, 1600–1871* (New York: Cambridge Univ. Press, 2005); and Alden T. Vaughan, *New England Frontier: Puritans and Indians, 1620–1675* (Norman: Univ. of Oklahoma Press, 1995).

5  The looming exception to this is Lorenzo Greene's groundbreaking *The Negro in Colonial New England, 1620–1776* (New York: Columbia Univ. Press, 1942), now out of print for more than thirty years. Greene's papers, now held at the Library of Congress, include his personal reflections on how he came to write his book; he was given an unwanted assignment in a seminar: "The Abolition of Slavery in New England, 1775–1800." Greene, a black New Englander, recalled thinking in protest that "slavery never existed in New England." Lorenzo Greene Papers, box 92, folder 6, Library of Congress. An earlier, but fascinating, discussion of the topic comes in George Henry Moore's *Notes on the History of Slavery in Massachusetts* (New York: Appleton, 1866). Several scholars have attempted to explain why early New England's relationship to

slavery has been so neglected. See Joanne Pope Melish, *Disowning Slavery: Gradual Emancipation and "Race" in New England, 1780–1860* (Ithaca, NY: Cornell Univ. Press, 1998); Margot Minardi, *Making Slavery History: Abolitionism and the Politics of Memory in Massachusetts* (New York: Oxford Univ. Press, 2010); and Robert K. Fitts, *Inventing New England's Slave Paradise: Master/Slave Relations in Eighteenth-Century Narragansett, Rhode Island* (New York: Garland, 1998), for their respective explanations of how the topic of slavery in New England was, to use Fitts's term, "sanitized" (p. 3). In 1974, Peter Wood observed, "Traditionally, colonial historians have given the most attention to the northern settlements, where Negro presence was slightest. . . . Scholars of black history, on the other hand, while paying great attention to the southern region, have concentrated for the most part on the national period." Wood, *Black Majority: Negroes in Colonial South Carolina from 1670 through the Stono Rebellion* (New York: Alfred A. Knopf, 1974), xiii. Since then things have changed, with both African and Indian slavery gaining new attention: Peter Benes and Jane Montague Benes, eds., *Slavery/Antislavery in New England*, Dublin Seminar for New England Folklife Annual Proceedings (Boston: Boston Univ., 2005); and John Wood Sweet, *Bodies Politic: Negotiating Race in the American North, 1730–1830* (Baltimore: Johns Hopkins Univ. Press, 2003). See also Allegra di Bonaventura, *For Adam's Sake: A Family Saga in Colonial New England* (New York: W. W. Norton, 2014); C. S. Manegold, *Ten Hills Farm: The Forgotten History of Slavery in the North* (Princeton, NJ: Princeton Univ. Press, 2010); Anne Farrow, Joel Lang, and Jenifer Frank, *Complicity: How the North Promoted, Prolonged, and Profited from Slavery* (New York: Ballantine, 2005); and Catherine Adams and Elizabeth H. Pleck, *Love of Freedom: Black Women in Colonial and Revolutionary New England* (New York: Oxford Univ. Press, 2010).

6  Once neglected, the topic of Indian slavery has received more attention in recent years. On the general topic of Indian slavery in North America, see Juliana Barr, *Peace Came in the Form of a Woman: Indians and Spaniards in the Texas Borderlands* (Chapel Hill: Univ. of North Carolina Press, 2007); James Brooks, *Captives and Cousins: Slavery, Kinship, and Community in the Southwest Borderlands* (Chapel Hill: Univ. of North Carolina Press, 2002); Robbie Etheridge and Sheri M. Shuck-Hall, *Mapping the Mississippian Shatter Zone: The Colonial Indian Slave Trade and Regional Instability in the American South* (Lincoln: Univ. of Nebraska Press, 2007); Almon Wheeler Lauber, *Indian Slavery in Colonial Times within the Present Limits of the United States* (New York: Columbia Univ. Press, 1913); Christina Snyder, *Slavery in Indian Country: The Changing Face of Captivity in Early America* (Cambridge MA: Harvard Univ. Press, 2010); Rushforth, *Bonds of Alliance*; and Alan Gallay, *The Indian Slave Trade: The Rise of the English Empire in the American South, 1670–1717* (New Haven, CT: Yale Univ. Press, 2002). On New England specifically, see Margaret Newell, "The Changing Nature of Indian Slavery in New England, 1670–1720," in *Reinterpreting New England Indians and the Colonial Experience*, ed. Colin Calloway and Neil Salisbury (Boston: Colonial Society

of Massachussetts, 2003). Pulsipher's *Subjects unto the Same King*, though not specifically about Indian slavery, spends considerable time on the topic, especially regarding the aftermath of King Philip's War. Alan Gallay explains the long-standing tendency to overlook Indian slavery as a teleological mistake, encapsulated in the following question: "African slavery became the prevalent form of labor in the United States, so how important could Indian slavery have been?" Gallay, ed., *Indian Slavery in Colonial America* (Lincoln: Univ. of Nebraska Press, 2009), 2.

7  Smith had also, perhaps less famously, even before that, been captured in Transylvania and sold into Turkish slavery. His master stripped him naked, "shave[d] his head and beard so bare as his hand," and ordered "a great ring of iron, with a long stalke bowed like a sickle, rivetted about his necke." Smith's position was dire: "slaves of slaves to them all," though he admitted that among slaves there was really very little distinction, "for the best [enslavement] was so bad, a dog could hardly have lived to endure." John Smith, *The True Travels, Adventures, and Observations of Captain John Smith in Europe, Asia, Affrica, and America from Anno Domini 1593 to 1629* (London, 1630), 24.

8  John Smith, "The Generall Historie of Virginia, New-England, and the Summer Isles," in *Captain John Smith: Writings with Other Narratives of Roanoake, Jamestown, and the First English Settlement of America*, ed. James Horn (New York: Library of America, 2007), 591. For a discussion of an even earlier captivity of a much less famous Wampanoag named Epenow, who was kidnapped in 1611 from New England, taken on a forced tour of sorts of Europe, and then also returned through luck and skill to the region, see Silverman, *Faith and Boundaries*, 1–5.

9  Ferdinando Gorges (the elder), "A Briefe Relation of the Discovery and Plantation of New England and of Sundry Accidents therein Occurring . . . ," in *Sir Ferdinando Gorges and His Province of Maine*, ed. James Phinney Baxter, vol. 1 (Boston: Prince Society, 1890), 209–10.

10  Ibid., 210.

11  On Squanto and Slaney, see Jace Weaver, *Red Atlantic: American Indigenes and the Making of the Modern World, 1000–1927* (Chapel Hill: Univ. of North Carolina Press, 2014), 58–60. The Newfoundland Company had ties to Spain. It was run by "prominent merchants" who "already had experience of the fishery and of trade to the Iberian peninsula, the major market for Newfoundland cod." Gillian T. Cell, "The Newfoundland Company: A Study of Subscribers to a Colonizing Venture," *WMQ* 22, no.4 (1965): 613. The professional biography of John Slany was typical of such people; he was a ship owner, a successful merchant, and an investor in both the Newfoundland Company and the East India Company. His brother had an even more cosmopolitan career. Humphrey Slany traded with Spain, the Barbary Coast, the Atlantic Islands, and even Guinea, thus tying slavery through kinship to the Newfoundland Company before Squanto was kidnapped. Ibid., 615.

12  William Bradford, *Of Plymouth Plantation* (New York: Modern Library, 1981), 87–89.

13  Edward Winslow, *Mourt's Relation: A Journal of the Pilgrims at Plymouth* (Boston: John Kimball Wiggin, 1865), 114.

14  "Bill of Sale, 1648" [in John Winthrop's handwriting], *WP*, 5:196–97.

15  *JJW*, 246.

16  On the cutting of wood on harbor islands, see William Wood, *New Englands Prospect* (London, 1634), 19.

17  Paul J. Lindholdt, ed., *John Josselyn, Colonial Traveler: A Critical Edition of Two Voyages to New-England* (Hanover, NH: Univ. Press of New England, 1988), 24.

18  For a longer discussion of this case, and the silences surrounding it, see Wendy Anne Warren, "'The Cause of Her Grief': The Rape of a Slave in Early New England," *JAH* 93, no. 4 (2007): 1031–49.

19  Samuel Sewall, *The Selling of Joseph: A Memorial* (Boston, 1700), 1. On Tituba, see Elaine G. Breslaw, "Tituba's Confession: The Multicultural Dimensions of the 1692 Salem Witch-Hunt," *Ethnohistory* 44, no. 3 (1997): 535–56; Chadwick Hansen, "The Metamorphosis of Tituba, or Why American Intellectuals Can't Tell an Indian Witch from a Negro," *NEQ* 47, no. 1 (1974): 3–12; Bernard Rosenthal, "Tituba's Story" *NEQ* 71, no. 2 (1998): 190–203; Veta Smith Tucker, "Purloined Identity: The Racial Metamorphosis of Tituba of Salem Village," *Journal of Black Studies* 30, no. 4 (2000): 624–34. The two enslaved Africans were Mary Black and Candy. Paul Boyer and Stephen Nissenbaum, eds., *The Salem Witchcraft Papers*, vol. 1 (New York: De Capo Press, 1977), 113–14, 179–81.

20  "Narrative of a French Protestant Refugee in Boston in 1687," *The Historical Magazine and Note and Queries, Concerning the Antiquities, History and Biography of America*, 2d ser., vol. 1 (Morrisania, NY: Henry B. Dawson, 1867), 296.

21  At the time of the attack, Deerfield was a town of "about 50 families and about 260 to 270 inhabitants," an "inbred and inward-looking community" with an economy based on "traditional, subsistence farming." And yet, African slavery was a part of its economy, and African slaves were a part of its community. Evan Haefeli and Kevin Sweeney, *Captors and Captives: The 1704 French and Indian Raid on Deerfield* (Amherst: Univ. of Massachusetts Press, 2003), 115, 126.

22  While scholars agree on the population of English inhabitants of the New England colonies, it is more difficult to count the population of enslaved people in this fledgling colonial world that was not yet securely regulated and tabulated. Lorenzo Greene estimated that at the end of the seventeenth century there were probably 1,000 enslaved people of African descent in the combined New England colonies. Greene, *Negro in Colonial New England*, 73. The reigning economic synthesis of colonial North America estimates the population of enslaved Africans to have been much larger: around 1,700 people. John J. McCusker and Russell R. Menard, *The Economy of British America, 1607–1789* (Chapel Hill: Univ. of North Carolina Press, 1985), 103. The authors rely on statistics from the U.S. Bureau of the Census's *Historical Statistics of the United States, Colonial Times*. The latest scholar to wrestle

with the problem has come up with similar numbers, estimating the population of enslaved Africans in New England to have been somewhere around 1,600 in 1700. Tomlins, *Freedom Bound: Law, Labor, and Civic Identity in Colonizing English America, 1580–1865* (New York: Cambridge Univ. Press, 2010), 426. It is almost impossible to figure out when those enslaved Africans arrived, and from where, and how many had died in or were traded away from the region before the century ended. An additional problem is that none of these authorities attempted to count enslaved Indians, a group whose status was less obvious and whose presence was less discussed. Scholars believe that hundreds and possibly thousands of enslaved Indians were shipped out of the region. How many Indians were held in slavery *in* the region is even more obscure, because the status of Indians within the region is difficult to determine. Some were in wage servitude, some were in indentured servitude, some were in something perhaps very much like chattel slavery, and some were in situations that perhaps blurred the distinctions between those categories. Margaret Newell has estimated that New England authorities enslaved over 1,300 Indians in the seventeenth century. Newell, "Indian Slavery in Colonial New England," in *Indian Slavery in Colonial America*, ed. Gallay, 33. Almon Wheeler Lauber, the earliest authority on Indian slavery in colonial North America, described the situation in stark terms: "To arrive at any knowledge of the exact number of Indian slaves in any of the English colonies is impossible." Lauber, *Indian Slavery in Colonial Times within the Present Limits of the United States* (New York: Columbia Univ., 1913), 105. Given those limitations, at *most* it seems safe to say enslaved Indians and Africans made up 10 percent of the total population within the borders claimed by English colonists.

23 Among these are Richard S. Dunn, *A Tale of Two Plantations: Slave Life and Labor in Jamaica and Virginia* (Cambridge, MA: Harvard Univ. Press, 2014); Rushforth, *Bonds of Alliance*; Gallay, *Indian Slave Trade*; Wood, *Black Majority*; Jennifer Morgan, *Laboring Women: Reproduction and Gender in New World Slavery* (Philadelphia: Univ. of Pennsylvania Press, 2004); Snyder, *Slavery in Indian Country*; Smallwood, *Saltwater Slavery*; Philip Morgan, *Slave Counterpoint: Black Culture in the Eighteenth-Century Chesapeake and Lowcountry* (Chapel Hill: Univ. of North Carolina Press, 1998); Ira Berlin, *Many Thousands Gone: The First Two Centuries of Slavery in North America* (Cambridge, MA: Belknap Press of Harvard Univ. Press, 1998); James Brooks, *Captives and Cousins*; and Vincent Brown, *The Reaper's Garden: Death and Power in the World of Atlantic Slavery* (Cambridge, MA: Harvard Univ. Press, 2008).

24 Peter Silver, "The Older South?," *Reviews in American History* 31, no. 2 (2003): 200. Sven Beckert has recently called this period in global history a time of "war capitalism," preceding the development of stable capitalism. Beckert, *Empire of Cotton: A Global History* (New York: Alfred A. Knopf, 2014), 31–39.

25 Christopher Tomlins points out that "in 1640, the Virginia colony had no more than 150 blacks in a population of more than 10,000; in 1660, fewer than 1,000 in 26,000," while "the Massachusetts Bay Colony actually had more

need at an early point in its development for a clear legal definition of enslavement than Virginia, given that only eight years after the arrival of the English
and directly in the wake of the Pequot War of 1637, the colony's government
had begun shipping Indians taken captive during the war to the Caribbean."
In short, "during the 1640s and 1650s, there were more slaves in New England
and the mid-Atlantic region together than in the Chesapeake." Tomlins,
*Freedom Bound*, 425–26. Regarding numbers, Moses Finley, the great historian of ancient slavery, had relevant words: "What difference did it make . . .
whether Athens had 100,000, 200,000 or 400,000 slaves? Was the evil less
if there were only 100,000? I see no validity in an ethical system that holds
such a question to be meaningful. . . . I should say that there was no action or
belief or institution in Graeco-Roman antiquity that was not one way or other
affected by the possibility that someone involved *might* be a slave." Finley,
*Ancient Slavery and Modern Ideology* (New York: Viking 1980), 64–65. See
also Stephanie Smallwood, *Saltwater Slavery: A Middle Passage from Africa
to American Diaspora* (Cambridge, MA: Harvard Univ. Press, 2007), 3: "The
comparative weight of numbers should by no means be seen to establish a
hierarchy of relevance."

26  Winthrop D. Jordan, "The Influence of the West Indies on the Origins of New
England Slavery," *WMQ* 18, no. 2 (1961): 243.

27  Richard S. Dunn, *Sugar and Slaves: The Rise of the Planter Class in the English
West Indies, 1624–1713* (Chapel Hill: Univ. of North Carolina Press, 1972), 336.

28  Michel-Rolph Trouillot, *Silencing the Past: Power and the Production of
History* (Boston: Beacon Press, 1995), 18. A scholar of slave advertisements in
eighteenth-century New England notes that "though slavery never flourished anywhere in New England to the extent that it did in Britain's southern
and island plantation colonies, relativism and static observations about its
marginality obscure the ways in which New Englanders at certain times, in
certain places, and under certain conditions made the institution work. Too
great a focus on slavery's negligibility in Massachusetts has perpetuated the
New England studies tradition of exceptionalism by masking ways in which
developments and trends in New England dovetailed with broader currents
of slavery and political economy." Robert E. Desrochers, "Slave-for-Sale
Advertisements and Slavery in Massachusetts, 1704–1781," *WMQ* 59, no. 3
(2002): 624.

29  John Winthrop, "A Modell of Christian Charity," *MHSC*, 3d ser., 7:46–47.

30  One of the greatest examinations of Winthrop's words remains Perry Miller's
essay "Errand into the Wilderness," in *Errand into the Wilderness* (Cambridge, MA: Belknap Press of Harvard Univ. Press, 1956), esp. 4–6.

31  This is reminiscent of Orlando Patterson's observation that "without slavery
there would have been no freedmen." Patterson, *Slavery and Social Death: A
Comparative Study* (Cambridge, MA: Harvard Univ. Press, 1982), 342.

32  Morgan, *The Puritan Dilemma*, 203.

33  Ecclesiastes 1:15.

### Chapter 1: Beginning

1 John Smith, *A Description of New England*, in *The Complete Works of Captain John Smith (1580–1631)*, vol. 1, ed. Philip L. Barbour (Chapel Hill: Univ. of North Carolina Press, 1986), 323; Elizabeth Mancke, "Negotiating an Empire: Britain and Its Overseas Peripheries, c. 1550–1780," in *Negotiated Empires: Centers and Peripheries in the Americas, 1500–1820*, ed. Christine Daniels and Michael V. Kennedy (New York: Routledge, 2002), 243; Alison Games, *Web of Empire: English Cosmopolitans in an Age of Expansion: 1560–1660* (New York: Oxford Univ. Press, 2008), 50.

2 Smith, *Description of New England*, 309, 319.

3 *Romeo and Juliet*, in *The Riverside Shakespeare*, ed. G. Blakemore Evans (Boston: Houghton Mifflin, 1997), II, ii, 43.

4 J. B. Trend, *The Civilization of Spain* (London: Oxford Univ. Press, 1944), 88, cited in Lewis Hanke, *Aristotle and the American Indians: A Study in Race Prejudice in the Modern World* (Bloomington: Indiana Univ. Press, 1959), 8, 127n31.

5 [Thomas Shepard? John Eliot? John Wilson?], *The Day-Breaking If Not the Sun-Rising of the Gospell with the Indians in New-England* (London, 1647), 18. Roger Williams made a similar observation: "Two sorts of *names* they had, and have amongst *themselves*. First, *generall*, belonging to all Natives, as Nínnuock, Ninnimissinnôwock, Eniskeetompaûwog, which signifies *Men, Folke*, or *People*. Secondly, particular *names*, peculiar to severall *Nations*, of them amongst *themselves*. . . . They have often asked mee, why wee call them *Indians Natives*, &c. And understanding the reason, they will call themselves *Indians*, in opposition to *English*, &c." Williams, *A Key into the Language of America* (London, 1643), To the Reader. On naming throughout the colonial Americas, see J. H. Elliot, *Empires of the Atlantic World: Britain and Spain in America, 1492–1830* (New Haven, CT: Yale Univ. Press, 2006), 32–35.

6 Smith, *Description of New England*, 327.

7 Ibid., 330–31.

8 Richard Frethorne, "Letter to his father and mother, March 20, April 2 and 3, 1623," ed. Susan Myra Kingsbury, *The Records of the Virginia Company of London*, vol. 4 (Washington, DC: GPO, 1935), 59.

9 Karen Ordahl Kupperman, "Apathy and Death in Early Jamestown," *JAH* 66, no. 1 (1979): 24. The classic description of Jamestown mayhem remains Edmund S. Morgan, *American Slavery, American Freedom* (New York: W. W. Norton, 1975), 44–91.

10 Smith, *Description of New England*, 330.

11 Adam Smith wrote in 1776, "To found a great empire for the sole purpose of raising up a people of customers, may at first sight appear a project fit only for a nation of shopkeepers. It is, however, a project altogether unfit for a nation of shopkeepers; but extremely fit for a nation whose government is influenced by shopkeepers." Smith, *The Wealth of Nations* (New York: Bantam Classic, 2003), 779–80.

12 Smith, *Description of New England*, 310.

13 "Dead flies cause the ointment of the apothecary to send forth a stinking savour" (Eccles. 10:1).

14 Transatlantic voyages took roughly ten weeks on average. David Cressy, "The Fast and Furious Ocean: The Passage to Puritan New England," *NEQ* 57, no. 4 (1984): 520; James Boswell, *The Life of Samuel Johnson* (New York: Penguin, 2008), 86.

15 Edward Ward, *A Trip to New England* (London, 1699), in *Boston in 1682 and 1699*, ed. George Parker Winship (Providence, RI: Club for Colonial Reprints, 1905), 35.

16 Samuel Danforth, *A Brief Recognition of New England's Errand into the Wilderness* (1670).

17 Edward Winslow, *Good Newes from New-England* (London, 1624), the Epistle Dedicatory.

18 Edwin Mead, "Pilgrim Ports in Old England," *New England Magazine* 25 (1901): 395–412.

19 John Cotton, *God's Promise to His Plantation* (London, 1630), 8–9.

20 Cotton especially noted Matt. 13:45–46: "Again, the kingdom of heaven is like unto a merchant man, seeking goodly pearls: Who, when he had found one pearl of great price, went and sold all that he had, and bought it."

21 For this justification, Cotton turned to Acts 16:12: "And from thence to Philippi, which is the chief city of that part of Macedonia, *and* a colony: and we were in that city abiding certain days."

22 John Cotton, *God's Promise,* 9–10.

23 Perry Miller, *The New England Mind: The Seventeenth Century* (Cambridge, MA: Harvard Univ. Press, 1983), 35. Mark Peterson argues that this tendency to see early New England as a place hostile to profits and capitalism is in marked contrast to British historiography, which tends to see Puritanism as a driving force toward capitalism. He argues that this discrepancy derives from a nationalist impulse on the part of scholars who want a "pre-capitalist moment in the American past, or for a yardstick against which to measure America's soulless materialism. . . ." Peterson, *The Price of Redemption: The Spiritual Economy of Puritan New England* (Stanford, CA: Stanford Univ. Press, 1997), 16–17.

24 Barbour, *Works of John Smith,* 1:346.

25 William Wood, *New Englands Prospect* (London, 1634), 77.

26 "Elizabeth I letter to Lord Mayor of London," PC 2/21, f 304 (11 July 1596), PRO.

27 On the treatment of indentured servants, see John Donoghue, "Out of the Land of Bondage: The English Revolution and the Atlantic Origins of Abolition," *American Historical Review* 115, no. 4 (2010): 943–74; and Simon P. Newman, *A New World of Labor: The Development of Plantation Slavery in the British Atlantic* (Philadelphia: Univ. of Pennsylvania Press, 2013), 71–136.

28 E. W. Bovill, *The Golden Trade of the Moors: West African Kingdoms in the Fourteenth Century,* 2nd ed. rev. and with additional materials by Robin Hallet (Princeton, NJ: Markus Weiner, 1995), 107.

29 Herbert S. Klein, *African Slavery in Latin American and the Caribbean* (New

York: Oxford Univ. Press, 1986), 10–13. For an excellent study of early African caravan routes and Islamic trade, see Bovill's classic *Golden Trade of the Moors*. Also see Carl N. Degler, "Slavery and the Genesis of America Race Prejudice," *Comparative Studies in Society and History*, no. 1 (1959): 49–66, esp. 62.

30  James Lockhart and Stuart Schwartz, *Early Latin America: A History of Colonial Spanish America and Brazil* (New York: Cambridge Univ. Press, 1983), 17–19, 24–27.

31  Klein, *African Slavery in Latin America*, 12–20.

32  Robin Blackburn, *The Making of New World Slavery: From the Baroque to the Modern, 1492–1800* (New York: Verso, 1997), 106–19.

33  Robert Harms, *The Diligent: A Voyage through the Worlds of the Slave Trade* (New York: Basic Books, 2002), xv.

34  On the transition from Portuguese to Dutch to English slave traders, see David Brion Davis, *The Problem of Slavery in Western Culture* (Ithaca, NY: Cornell Univ. Press, 1966), 129–34, quotation on p. 46.

35  Blackburn, *Making of New World Slavery*, 220. For a discussion of early Spanish colonization, see Daniel K. Richter, *Before the Revolution: America's Ancient Pasts* (Cambridge, MA: Harvard Univ. Press, 2011), esp, 67–87.

36  Blackburn, *Making of New World Slavery*, 219–21.

37  John Hawkins, "The Second Voyage of Sir John Hawkins," in *The Hawkins' Voyages during the Reigns of Henry VII, Queen Elizabeth, and James I*, ed. Clements R. Markham (New York: Burt Franklin, 1970), 70–72.

38  Ibid., 21.

39  John Hawkins, "The Third Voyage of Sir John Hawkins," in *The Hawkins' Voyages*, ed. Markham, 70–72.

40  Harry Kelsey, *Sir John Hawkins: Queen Elizabeth's Slave Trader* (New Haven, CT: Yale Univ. Press, 2003), 32–33. Karen Kupperman notes that Queen Elizabeth granted to Sir Francis Drake, yet another pirate turned merchant, "a sumptuous locket with her portrait in miniature on one side and on the reverse a cameo showing an African head in classical profile superimposed on a European head," just one more example of English familiarity with Africans. Kupperman, *The Jamestown Project* (Cambridge, MA: Belknap Press of Harvard Univ. Press, 2007), 127.

41  "William Towerson's First Voyage to Guinea, 1555–6," "William Towerson's Second Voyage to Guinea, 1556–7," and "William Towerson's Third Voyage to Guinea, 1558," in *Europeans in West Africa, 1450–1560*, ed. John William Blake, vol. 2 (London:Hakluyt Society, 1942), 360–410, 410–30. For a general discussion, see K. G. Davies, *The Royal African Company* (New York: Longmans, Green, 1957), 38–40.

42  Richard Hakluyt, *Hakluyt's Voyages: The Principal Navigations, Voyages, Traffiques and Discoveries of the English Nation*, ed. Irwin R. Blacker (New York: Viking, 1965).

43  E. G. R. Taylor, "Samuel Purchas," *Geographical Journal* 75, no. 6 (1930): 537–38.

44 Blackburn, *Making of New World Slavery*, 220–21.

45 Thomas Herbert, *Some Yeares Travels into Divers Parts of Asia and Afrique* (London, 1638), 9.

46 David Eltis, *The Rise of African Slavery in the Americas* (Cambridge: Cambridge Univ. Press, 2000), 118–21. See also Davies, *Royal African Company*, 97–101; and William Pettigrew, *Freedom's Debt: The Royal African Company and the Politics of the Atlantic Slave Trade, 1672–1752* (Chapel Hill: Univ. of North Carolina Press, 2013), 22–25.

47 "A List of Ships Freighted by the Royall African Company Since January 1673/4," Colonial Office Papers 1/31, fol. # 32, PRO; George Frederick Zook, *The Company of Royal Adventurers Trading into Africa* (Lancaster, PA: New Era Printing, 1919), 4–5; David Galenson, *Traders, Planters, and Slaves: Market Behavior in Early English America* (New York: Cambridge Univ. Press, 1986), 14–15, 146.

48 John Carter, Whiddah, to Royal African Company, Jan. 6, 1687, in *Further Correspondence of the Royal African Company of England Relating to the "Slave Coast," 1681–1699* (Madison: Univ. of Wisconsin Press, 1992), 44.

49 Paul Bayne[s], *An Entire Commentary upon the Whole Epistle of the Apostle Paul to the Ephesians: Wherein the Text Is Learnedly and Fruitfully Opened, with a Logicall Analysis, Spirituall and Holy Observations, Confutation of Arminianisms and Popery, and Found Edification for the Diligent Reader* (London, 1643), 694–95 (emphasis added).

50 For a similar observation, see Degler, "Slavery and the Genesis of American Race Prejudice," 54–55; and Margaret Newell, "Indian Slavery in Colonial New England," in *Indian Slavery in Colonial America*, ed. Alan Gallay (Lincoln: Univ. of Nebraska Press, 2009), 34: "'Slavery' and 'servitude' were poorly defined terms in British America for much of the seventeenth century." Edmund Morgan observed that "in the seventeenth century ['servant'] meant anyone who worked for another in whatever capacity, in industry, commerce, or agriculture, as well as in what we now call domestic economy," and that "Negro and Indians slaves were also known as servants, and so were apprentices." Morgan, *The Puritan Family: Religion and Domestic Relations in Seventeenth-Century New England* (New York: Harper and Row, 1966), 109. See also Linda M. Heywood and John K. Thornton, "'Canniball Negroes,' Atlantic Creoles, and the Identity of New England's Charter Generation," *African Diaspora* 4, no. 1 (2011): 79–80.

51 Morgan Godwyn, *The Negro's and Indians Advocate* (London, 1680), 36.

52 Michael Walzer, *The Revolution of the Saints: A Study in the Origins of Radical Politics* (Cambridge, MA: Harvard Univ. Press, 1965), 169; Bayne, *Commentary*, 5.

53 William Hubbard, *The Happiness of a People in the Wisdome of Their Rulers* (Boston, 1676), 9–10.

54 Deut. 15:12–17.

55 Lev. 25:44–46. New Testament verses also supported the institution. In his First Letter to the Corinthians, Paul offered what must have seemed like poor

solace to slaves: "For he that is called in the Lord, *being* a servant, is the Lord's freeman: likewise also he that is called, *being* free, is Christ's servant." He further warned, since redemption was at hand, "Let every man, wherein he is called, therein abide with God." 1 Cor. 7:21–24.

56 Karen Ordahl Kupperman, *Providence Island, 1630–1641: The Other Puritan Colony* (New York: Cambridge Univ. Press, 1993), 26, 325–35. Kupperman notes that Providence Island colonists overcame Puritan unease over slavery through hubristic reasoning: an "inward-turned logic allowed the company dedicated to Providence to assume that God had provided perfectly acclimated heathens to work in tropical fields. If God had not intended their use, why did he make Europeans ill-suited to such labor conditions, while Africans worked so well under the hot sun?" Ibid., 178. Parts of this description of Providence Island in the context of Maverick's breeding experiment were first published in Wendy Anne Warren, "'The Cause of Her Grief': The Rape of a Slave in Early New England," *JAH* 93, no. 4 (2007): 1041.

57 Karen O. Kupperman, "Errand to the Indies: Puritan Colonization from Providence Island through the Western Design," *WMQ* 45, no. 1 (1988): 75–81; idem, *Providence Island*, 170–72. For the quotation from Gov. Nathaniel Butler of Providence Island, see ibid., 172.

58 *The Laws and Liberties of Massachusetts: Reprinted from the Unique Copy of the 1648 Edition in the Henry E. Huntington Library* (San Marino, CA: Huntington Library, 1998), 4; Elizabeth Donnan, ed., *Documents Illustrative of the History of the Slave Trade to America*, 4 vols. (Washington, DC: Carnegie Institution, 1930–35), 3:4n2. The words "and such strangers" were removed from the law in its later iterations, presumably to facilitate the enslavement of Indians who were no longer strangers, having by then lived with the English for decades. Christopher L. Tomlins, *Freedom Bound: Law, Labor, and Civic Identity in Colonizing English America, 1580–1865* (New York: Cambridge Univ. Press, 2010), 424–25.

59 George Henry Moore, *Notes on the History of Slavery in Massachusetts* (New York: D. Appleton, 1866), 11, 18; Morris L. Cohen, "Legal Literature in Colonial Massachusetts," in *Law in Colonial Massachusetts, 1630–1800*, ed. Daniel R. Coquillette (Boston: Colonial Society of Massachusetts, 1984), 250.

60 Tomlins, *Freedom Bound*, 424–26. He notes that this is "at odds with the usual chronology [of Anglo-American slavery] in which mainland slavery has its beginning in Virginia in 1619."

61 This law actually became applicable to most of the colonies, which were at the time of its writing joined in a political entity called "The United Colonies of New England," sometimes known as the New England Confederation, a mostly military union that generally mattered most during times of war. See Harry Ward, *The United Colonies of New England, 1643–90* (New York: Vantage, 1961). See also *PCR*, 9:69–71.

62 *CCR*, 1:532.

63 Tomlins, *Freedom Bound*, 416–17.

64 For a fascinating and complementary article about the evolution of slavery in seventeenth-century Virignia, see John C. Coombs, "The Phases of Conver-

sion: A New Chronology for the Rise of Slavery in Early Virginia," *WMQ* 6, no. 3 (2011): 332–60.

65  See, e.g., "List of Goods from New England," Admiralty Court Records, 106/ 314, #230, PRO. See also William A. Pettigrew, "Free to Enslave: Politics and the Escalation of Britain's Transatlantic Slave Trade, 1688–1714," *WMQ* 64, no. 1 (2007): 3–38.

66  *JJW*, 573 (emphasis added).

67  Ibid., 602–3.

68  Robert E. Moody, ed., *The Saltonstall Papers, 1607–1815*, vol. 1 (Boston: MHS, 1972), 138–39.

69  *JJW*, 604.

70  *MCR*, 2:136.

71  Jeremy Belknap, *History of New-Hampshire* (Philadelphia, 1784), 1:23; William Hubbard, *A General History of New England* (Cambridge, MA: MHS, 1815), 219–20.

72  *MCR*, 2:168, 176.

73  *JJW*, 604. Keysar and Smith's business disagreements were settled quickly, *MCR*, 2:129.

74  Donnan, *History of the Slave Trade to America*, 3:8n8.1. Edmund Morgan noted that Virginia's colonists also distinguished between buying slaves and actually enslaving them. "Virginians," he observed, "had only to buy men who were already enslaved, after the initial risks of the transformation had been sustained by others elsewhere. They converted to slavery simply by buying slaves instead of servants." Morgan, *American Slavery, American Freedom*, 297.

75  Lorenzo Greene, *The Negro in Colonial New England, 1620–1776* (New York: Columbia Univ. Press, 1942), 67–68.

76  Richard Jobson, *The Golden Trade; or, A Discovery of the River Gambra, and the Golden Trade of the Aethiopians* (London, 1623), 88–89.

77  John 3:19.

78  Donnan, *History of the Slave Trade to America*, 3:9n9.2.

79  Ibid., 9.

80  Ibid., 10.

81  Ibid., 12–13.

82  "Acts and Orders made at the Generall Court of Election held at Warwick," *RICR*, 1:243 (emphasis added), cited in Donnan, *History of the Slave Trade to America*, 3:108n81.1.

83  See Winthrop Jordan, "The Influence of the West Indies on the Origins of New England Slavery," *WMQ* 18, no. 2 (1961): 245n8.

84  Donnan, *History of the Slave Trade to America*, 3:15.

85  "Letter from John Saffin, John Usher, and others to William Welstead, 12 June, 1681," Jeffries Family Papers, MHS. See also Donnan, *History of the Slave Trade to America*, 3:15–16. For another analysis of this trip, see Albert Von Frank, "John Saffin: Slavery and Racism in Colonial Massachusetts," *Early American Literature* 29, no. 3 (1994): 256.

86  *MAC*, 449a–b.

87 *MAC*, 61:449b.

88 This estimate is based on Donnan's collection; the slave voyages database lists only fourteen.

89 Donnan, *History of the Slave Trade to America*, 3:14–15.

90 Will of Simon Bradstreet, *Suffolk County Probate Records*, 11:276–82, NEHGS.

91 One historian who has recently analyzed in great detail the intercolonial slave trade estimates that at least fifty enslaved Africans arrived per year from the Caribbean between 1641 and 1700, with direct imports from Africa accounting for some additional number. This number would double most current estimates of New England's enslaved African population in 1700. Gregory E. O'Malley, "Beyond the Middle Passage: Slave Migration from the Caribbean to North America, 1619–1807," *WMQ* 66, no. 1 (2009): 163.

92 "Governor Cranston to the Council and Trade of Plantations, December 5, 1708," in Cecil Headlam, ed., *Calendar of State Papers. Colonial Series. America and West Indies: June, 1708–1709* (London: His Majesty's Stationery Office, 1922), 171.

## Chapter 2: The Key of the Indies

1 *JJW*, 692.

2 Virginia DeJohn Anderson, *New England's Generation: The Great Migration and the Formation of Society and Culture in the Seventeenth Century* (New York: Cambridge Univ. Press, 1991), 17–19.

3 Bernard Bailyn, *The New England Merchants in the Seventeenth Century* (Cambridge, MA: Harvard Univ. Press, 1955), 46.

4 *JJW*, 692–93.

5 Ibid.

6 John Winthrop's statement has not gone unnoticed. More than fifty years ago, Bernard Bailyn wrote, "In the first half of the seventeenth century, particularly from 1620–1650, the leading mercantile nations of Europe flung their commercial frontiers westward to the American continent and made of the whole Atlantic basin a single great trading area." He described an English Atlantic economy shaped like a "polygon formed by lines drawn between port towns in the British Isles, Newfoundland, the American mainland, the West Indies, the Wine Islands, and the continent of Europe," and noted that "New England merchants became important agents in maintaining the efficiency of this mechanism." Bailyn, *New England Merchants*, 86. More recently, he asserted that "New England, not more than 5 percent of whose population was African, was dependent on the African slave trade for its economic survival since the major markets for its agricultural products were the West Indian slave plantations." Bailyn, *Atlantic History: Concept and Contours* (Cambridge, MA: Harvard Univ. Press, 2005), 84. An early discussion of the links between the West Indies and New England can be found in Vincent Harlow, *A History of Barbados, 1625–1685* (Oxford: Clarendon Press, 1926), 268–91.

7 Ira Berlin, *Many Thousands Gone: The First Two Centuries of Slavery in North

*America* (Cambridge, MA: Belknap Press of Harvard Univ. Press, 1998), 8, 47.
Here Berlin draws on the work of Moses Finley, *Ancient Slavery and Modern
Ideology* (New York: Viking, 1980), 79–80. Christopher L.Tomlins usefully
complicates Berlin's categories, suggesting a third option: *"societies with
slavery."* By this he means that there is a step between societies with slaves
and slave societies, a step in which "slavery is consciously instantiated as an
institution to the perpetuation of which the society is committed." But that,
he points out, "does not mean the society has or necessarily ever will become
a slave society." Tomlins, *Freedom Bound: Law, Labor, and Civic Identity in
Colonizing English America, 1580–1865* (New York: Cambridge Univ. Press,
2010), 417n58.

8  Fernand Braudel elucidated a similar problem in his classic history of the
Mediterranean world; in arguing for what he called a *"global* Mediterranean,"
he acknowledged having to disregard "conventional boundaries." But the
rewards were greater than the risks, Braudel felt. To tell the whole story of
the Mediterranean, he needed to "imagine a hundred frontiers, not one, some
political, some economic, and some cultural." Braudel, *The Mediterranean
and the Mediterranean World in the Age of Philip II*, vol. 1, trans. Siân Reynolds
(Berkeley: Univ. of California Press, 1995), 168–71. Braudel's influence on the
writing of history can hardly be overstated, and the history of early America
has shown its own version in the form of an approach now called "Atlantic
history." Practitioners of Atlantic history generally insist on broader borders
in their recounting of the early modern empires and colonies. The Atlantic
World literature is long and growing. Some sample books include Alison
Games, *Migration and the Origins of the English Atlantic World* (Cambridge,
MA: Harvard Univ. Press, 1999); David Armitage and Michael J. Braddick,
eds., *The British Atlantic World*, 1500–1800 (New York: Palgrave, 2002); Nich-
olas Canny and Anthony Pagden, eds., *Colonial Identity in the Atlantic World,
1500–1800* (Princeton, NJ: Princeton Univ. Press, 1987); April Lee Hatfield,
*Atlantic Virginia: Intercolonial Relations in the Seventeenth Century* (Philadelphia: University of Pennsylvania Press, 2004); Karen Ordahl Kupperman,
*The Atlantic in World History* (New York: Oxford Univ. Press, 2012); Jack P.
Greene and Philip D. Morgan, eds., *Atlantic History: A Critical Appraisal* (New
York: Oxford Univ. Press, 2009); and John K. Thornton, *A Cultural History of
the Atlantic World, 1250–1820* (New York: Cambridge Univ. Press, 2012). I am
aware of and chastened by Bernard Bailyn's observation that Atlantic history
did not develop "in imitation of Fernand Braudel's concept of Mediterranean
history," nor is "it simply an expansion of the venerable tradition of 'imperial
history, either British, Spanish, Portuguese, or Dutch." Bailyn, *Atlantic History*, 4–5. Immanuel Wallerstein's concept of a "world-economy" is applicable
here; he defines a "world system" as one "larger than any juridically-defined
political unit . . . [where] the basic linkage between the parts of the system
is economic." This stands in contrast to an empire, which is a political unit.
Wallerstein, *The Modern World-System I: Capitalist Agriculture and the Origins of the European World-Economy in the Sixteenth Century* (Los Angeles:

Univ. of California Press, 2011), 15. See also his discussion of "the boundaries of an entity" (301). More recently, Eliga Gould has proposed the useful notion of "entangled histories," which "examined interconnected societies," that somehow mutually constitute each other. Gould, "Entangled Histories, Entangled Worlds: The English-Speaking Atlantic as a Spanish Periphery," *The American Historical Review* 112, no. :3 (2007): 766.

9 Daniel Vickers, *Farmers and Fishermen: Two Centuries of Work in Essex County, Massachusetts, 1630–1850* (Chapel Hill: Univ. of North Carolina Press, 1994), 47; Stephen Innes, *Labor in a New Land: Economy and Society in Seventeenth-Century Springfield* (Princeton, NJ: Princeton Univ. Press, 1983). Innes postulated the existence of three distinct zones of English settlement: "an urbanized coastal region, typified by Boston and Salem; a subsistence farming region comprised of towns like Dedham and Andover; and an area of highly commercialized agriculture, such as the towns of the colony's breadbasket—the Connecticut River Valley" (p. xvi).

10 Recently, more historians have begun to question what one has called "Atlanto-myopia," a failure to see the Atlantic and the Indian Oceans as "one single British commercial and communication system." H. V. Bowen, "Britain in the Indian Ocean Region and Beyond: Contours, Connections, and the Creation of a Global Maritime Empire," in *Britain's Oceanic Empire: Atlantic and Indian Ocean Worlds, c. 1550–1850*, ed. H. V. Bowen, Elizabeth Mancke, and John G. Reid (Cambridge: Cambridge Univ. Press, 2012), 45–65, esp. 46–47. Alison Games notes that while "historians have approached English expansion as a story largely understood within the context of separate ocean basins," what she calls a "global perspective" better explains the process. Games, *The Web of Empire: English Cosmopolitans in an Age of Expansion, 1560–1660* (New York: Oxford Univ. Press, 2008), 14.

11 Cited in Richard S. Dunn, *Sugar and Slaves: The Rise of the Planter Class in the English West Indies, 1624–1713* (Chapel Hill: Univ. of North Carolina Press, 1972), 236; and Winthrop Jordan, "The Influence of the West Indies on the Origins of New England Slavery," *WMQ* 18, no. 2 (1961): 248.

12 Dunn, *Sugar and Slaves*, 314.

13 Alan Gallay notes that "New England, indeed, succeeded without slavery as its primary labor source, but the region's economic success owed to its participation in an Atlantic-world economy that hinged on slave-produced goods. New Englanders actively engaged in the international slave trade, processed slaved-produced sugar into rum, and supplied slave colonies with food and lumber." Gallay, "Introduction," in *Indian Slavery in Colonial America*, ed. Alan Gallay (Lincoln: Univ. of Nebraska Press, 2009), 14.

14 Barbara Solow, "Introduction," in *Slavery and the Rise of the Atlantic System*, ed. Barbara Solow (New York: Cambridge Univ. Press, 1991), 1.

15 John Doggett Sr., to John Winthrop Jr., 1652, Win/1, folder "1652," Win/1, Winthrop Papers [transcriptions], unpublished collections, MHS.

16 Jordan, "Influence of the West Indies," 247.

17 John J. McCusker and Russell R. Menard, *The Economy of British America,*

*1607–1789* (Chapel Hill: Univ. of North Carolina Press, 1985), 47. "Mercantilism," a contested term, can most generally be described as the "shared perception among those who controlled northern and western Europe from the sixteenth to the eighteenth century that foreign trade could be made to serve the interests of government—and vice versa." Ibid., 35. As importantly, "mercantilists believed that they lived in a world of scarcity . . . in which economic life was necessarily one of vicious competition . . . [because] trade was a zero-sum game." Steve Pincus, "Rethinking Mercantilism: Political Economy, the British Empire, and the Atlantic World in the Seventeenth and Eighteenth Centuries," *WMQ* 69, no. 1 (2012): 12. Pincus's piece is the centerpiece of a fascinating forum on the usefulness of the term "mercantilism," a concept that stands in some contrast to "capitalism," also a contested term, but defined by one scholar as a profit-seeking economic system that usually operates "within an arena larger than that which any political entity can totally control." Wallerstein, *Modern World-System I*, 348.

18  On the Navigation Acts, see Menard and McCusker, *Economy*, 46–47; Bernard Capp, *Cromwell's Navy: The Fleet and the English Revolution, 1648–1660* (New York: Oxford Univ. Press, 1989), 73–105; J. E. Farnell, "The Navigation Act of 1651, the First Dutch War, and the London Merchant Community," *Economic History Review* 16, no. 3 (1964): 439–54; Simon Groenveld, "The English Civil Wars as a Cause of the First Anglo-Dutch War, 1640–1652," *Historical Journal* 30, no. 3 (1987): 560–65; J. R. Jones, *The Anglo-Dutch Wars of the Seventeenth Century* (New York: Longman, 1996); and C. H. Wilson, *Profit and Power: A Study of England and the Dutch Wars* (New York: Longmans, Green, 1957).

19  On Cromwell's Western Design, see Dunn, *Sugar and Slaves*, 20–23; Nicole Greenspan, "News and the Politics of Information in the Mid Seventeenth Century: The Western Design and the Conquest of Jamaica," *History Workshop Journal*, no. 69 (2010): 1–26; Stanley Arthur Goodwin Taylor, *The Western Design: An Account of Cromwell's Expedition to the Caribbean* (Kingston, Jamaica, 1965); and Carla Gardina Pestana, "English Character and the Fiasco of the Western Design," *EAS* 3, no. 1 (2005): 1–31.

20  Daniel Gookin, "To all Persons whom it may Concern," May 25, 1656 (Cambridge, MA), Broadside, Early American Imprints, ser. 1, Evans, 39168, Bodleian Library, Oxford Univ.

21  Richard Vines to John Winthrop, July 19, 1647, *WP*, 5:172. Vine himself was diving into the business enthusiastically, having bought two adjoining plantations, for a combined total of fifty acres, and an unnamed number of "negros." The combination of these two purchases, he hoped, would begin making a profit of tobacco in as little as six months; but his real plans involved planting sugar for the next year's harvest.

22  Though the historiographical tendency was once to dismiss Barbados as a marginal outpost until sugar took off well into the century, recent scholarship has questioned this emphasis on a "sugar revolution." Russell Menard argues that "contrary to the argument of advocates of a sugar revolution, the planters of Barbados had been quite prosperous in the immediate pre-sugar

era and their prosperity had played an important role in financing the rise of sugar." He also found evidence that "plantation agriculture and African slavery had preceded sugar to the island." Menard, *Sweet Negotiations: Sugar, Slavery, and Plantation Agriculture in Early Barbados* (Charlottesville: Univ. of Virginia Press, 2006), xii.

23  Vickers, *Farmers and Fishermen*, 99.

24  "Report of His Majesties Commissioners concerning the MASSACHUSETTS, 1665," carton 36, folder 47, Endicott Family Papers, MHS.

25  "Samuel Maverick to the Earl of Clarendon," "The Clarendon Papers," in *Collections of the New-York Historical Society for the Year 1869* (New York: New-York Historical Society, 1869), 20.

26  Edward Johnson, *Wonder-Working Providence of Sions Savior in New England* (Andover, MA: W. F. Draper, 1867), 43.

27  Consul Maynard to Lord Arlington, April 18, 1671, SP 89/11, fol. 107, State Papers, PRO. See ADM 106/314, #230, PRO, for an 1675 example of a shipping contract of New England goods.

28  "Captain Bredon's Relation of the State of Affaires in New England at his coming from thence in 1660," carton 36, folder 41, Endicott Family Papers, MHS. See also "Clarendon Papers," 16–19.

29  On a similar point, see Christian J. Koot, "A 'Dangerous Principle': Free Trade Discourses in Barbados and the English Leeward Islands, 1650–1689," *EAS* 5, no. 1 (2007): 132–63. Joyce Appleby usefully emphasized the contingent nature of the development of capitalism in "The Vexed Story of Capitalism Told by American Historians," *Journal of the Early Republic* 21, no. 1 (2001): 14.

30  "Captain Bredon's Relation of the State of Affaires in New England at his coming from thence in 1660," carton 36, folder 41, Endicott Family Papers, MHS (emphasis added). See also "Clarendon Papers," 16–19. For more on royal commissioners, including Bredon and Maverick, see Jenny Hale Pulsipher, *Subjects unto the Same King: Indians, English, and the Contest for Authority in Colonial New England* (Philadelphia: Univ. of Pennsylvania Press, 2005), 37–69.

31  On family economy, see Louise A. Tilly and Joan W. Scott, *Women, Work, and Family* (New York: Holt, Rinehart and Winston, 1978); also Jan de Vries, *The Industrious Revolution: Consumer Behavior and the Household Economy, 1650 to the Present* (New York: Cambridge Univ. Press, 2008). Capitalism proceeded with the help of family networks through the nineteenth century. Naomi R. Lamoreaux notes that, even in the late eighteenth and the nineteenth centuries, "merchants and manufacturers hired members of their own kinship groups as apprentices, employees, and clerks, gave them priority in business dealings, and took them in as partners after they gained experience. More important, they seem to have felt bound to give preference to family members even when doing so contravened their own interests. In overseas trade, for example, merchants often put their own agents, or supercargoes, on ships to oversee the commercial aspects of a voyage." She further observes,

"Despite the damage wrought by incompetent relatives, it was difficult for merchants of this period to bypass kin and transact with people outside the family." Lamoreaux, "Rethinking the Transition to Capitalism in the Early American Northeast," *JAH* 90, no. 2 (2003): 446.

32  Edmund S. Morgan, *The Puritan Dilemma: The Story of John Winthrop* (New York: Little, Brown, 1958), 1–45.

33  For a concise discussion of John Winthrop Jr., see Richard S. Dunn, "John Winthrop, Jr., and the Narragansett Country," *WMQ* 13, no. 1 (1956): 68–86. See also Frederick John Kingsbury, "John Winthrop, Junior," *Proceedings of the American Antiquarian Society* 12 (1897): 295–306.

34  John Winthrop Jr. to John Winthrop, 1629, in J. Savage, ed., *The History of New England from 1630 to 1649 by John Winthrop*, 2 vols. (Boston: Phelps and Farnham, 1825), 1:360–61.

35  Lawrence Shaw Mayo, *The Winthrop Family in America* (Boston: MHS, 1948), 81–110.

36  Larry Gragg, "A Puritan in the West Indies: The Career of Samuel Winthrop," *WMQ* 50, no. 4 (1993): 768–86.

37  "Forth Winthrop to John Winthrop, Jr.," Dec. 1626, *WP*, 1:338.

38  "Henry Winthrop to Emmanuel Downing (?)," Aug. 22, 1627, *WP*, 1:356–57.

39  "Papers relating to the Early History of Barbados and St. Kitts," ed. N. Darnell Davis, *Timehri: The Journal of the Royal Agricultural and Commerical Society of British Guiana*, new ser., 6 (1892): 329.

40  Richard Ligon Gent., *A True & Exact History of the Island of Barbados; Illustrated with a Mapp of the Island, as Also the Principall Trees and Plants There, Setforth in Their Due Proportions and Shapes, Drawne Out by Their Severall and Respective Scales* (London, 1657), 55.

41  David Brion Davis, *The Problem of Slavery in Western Culture* (Ithaca, NY: Cornell Univ. Press, 1966), 12.

42  Winthrop to John Winthrop, Oct. 15, 1627, *WP*, 1:362.

43  Thomas Fones to John Winthrop, April 2, 1629, *WP*, 2:78–79. It probably did not help that John Winthrop Jr. had married Elizabeth's sister, properly and with his uncle's blessing.

44  "Early History of Barbados," *Timehri*, 345–46, also cited (with different page numbers) in Dunn, *Sugar and Slaves*, 59.

45  John Winthrop to Henry Winthrop, Jan. 20, 1629, *WP*, 2:66–68.

46  Karen Ordahl Kupperman, "Introduction to Richard Ligon," in *A True and Exact History of the Island of Barbados*, ed. Kupperman (Indianapolis, IN: Hackett, 2011), 14. Thanks to Karen Kupperman for pointing out this fact when I presented portions of this chapter at the NYU Atlantic Seminar. Another participant observed that Winthrop's confusion just underlined that when it came to a market economy, "no one was in charge and no one knew what they were doing."

47  John Winthrop to Henry Winthrop, Jan. 20. 1629, *WP*, 2:66–68.

48  John Winthrop, June 1630, *WP*, 2:265, 265n2. Elizabeth Fones went on to marry twice more and in total had eight children. Her second husband aban-

doned her and disappeared, and her third marriage created a minor scandal because many believed her to still be married. She left New England and eventually settled in New York.

49 *WP*, 2:302; *JJW*, 38.

50 "William Berkeley to John Winthrop, Jr.," June 25, 1648, *WP*, 5:232.

51 "William Berkeley to John Winthrop, Jr.," June 12, 1648, *WP*, 5:229.

52 "Sir George Downing to John Winthrop, Jr.," Aug. 26, 1645, *WP*, 5:43–44. For a brief discussion of the younger John Winthrop, see Innes, *Labor in a New Land*, 173–74.

53 "Extracts from Henry Whistler's Journal of the West India Expedition," in C. H. Firth, ed., *The Narrative of General Venables, with an Appendix of Papers relating to the Expedition to the West Indies and the Conquest of Jamaica, 1654–1655* (New York: Longmans, Green, 1900), 146.

54 Winthrop Paper Transcripts, June 4, 1666, Unpublished [WIN/4], MHS.

55 *SD*, 1:95.

56 Joshua Micah Marshall, "A Melancholy People: Anglo-Indian Relations in Early Warwick, Rhode Island, 1642–1675," in *New England Encounters: Indians and Euroamericans, ca. 1600–1850*, ed. Alden T. Vaughan (Boston: Northeastern Univ. Press, 1999), 95. Bailyn, *New England Merchants*, 88–90; Peleg Sanford, *The Letter Book of Peleg Sanford of Newport* (Providence: Rhode Island Historical Society, 1928), iv–v, and passim.

57 For Thomas Savage's will, see Robert Charles Anderson, *The Great Migration: Immigrants to New England, 1634–35*, 7 vols. (Boston: NEHGS, 1999–2011), 6:18182; and J. A. Vinton, *The Symmes Memorial: A Biographical Sketch of Rev. Zechariah Symmes* (Boston: David Clapp and Son, 1873), 24.

58 Will of William Brenton of Newport, Feb. 9, 1674, microfilm 3:1:143–45, *Plymouth Colony Probate Records*, NEHGS.

59 Bailyn, *New England Merchants*, 135.

60 For a similar discussion of merchant networks, see Mark Valeri, *Heavenly Merchandize: How Religion Shaped Commerce in Puritan America* (Princeton, NJ: Princeton Univ. Press, 2010), 40.

61 East Boston Separates (microfilm collection), 2, 3, 4, 7, 11, Shrimpton Family Papers, MHS.

62 Ledger Page, Shrimpton Family Papers, reel 1, MHS; Sale to Samuel Shrimpton, 1687, Greenough Papers, 1680–96, MHS.

63 Payment to Edward Beartles, 1698, Greenough Papers, MHS.

64 John Helden to Samuel Shrimpton, March 16, 1699, Greenough Papers, 1699–1700, MHS.

65 Inventory of the Estate of Samuel Shrimpton, Shrimpton Family Papers, reel 1, MHS.

66 Bailyn, *New England Merchants*, 83.

67 *Suffolk Deeds*, ed. William Blake Trask et al., 14 vols. (Boston: Rockwell and Churchill, 1880–1906), 1:262.

68 G. Andrews Moriarty, "Genealogical Notes on Rev. Samuel Parris of Salem Village," *The Essex Institute Historical Collections*, vol. 49 (Salem, MA:

Essex Institute, 1913), 354–55; G. Andrews Moriarty Jr., "Barbadian Notes," *NEHGR* 67 (1913): 365–66.

69  Ibid., 352, 352n46.

70  On Gurdon Saltonstall and his son, see K. J. Winter, "Jeffrey Brace in Barbados: Slavery, Interracial Relationships, and the Emergence of a Global Economy," *Nineteenth-Century Worlds: Global Formations Past and Present*, ed. Keith Hanley and Greg Kucich (London: Routledge, 2008), 46.

71  Will of Simon Bradstreet, Suffolk County Probate Records, 11:276–82, NEHGS.

72  Anne Bradstreet, "In Reference to Her Children," *Several Poems Compiled with Great Variety of Wit and Learning* (Boston, 1678), 245.

73  MAC, 61:212.

74  Thanks to Jane Kamensky for pointing out the notion of the West Indies as New England's graveyard.

75  See Sidney Mintz and Richard Price, *The Birth of African-American Culture: An Anthropological Perspective* (Boston: Beacon Press, 1976), 42–43; Richard Ligon, *A True and Exact History of the Island of Barbados* (London, 1673), 46.

76  "Richard Simsons Voyage to the Straits of Magellan and S. Seas in the Year 1689," Sloane 86, British Library, f. 57, cited in Marcus Rediker, *The Slave Ship: A Human History* (New York: Penguin, 2007), 277.

77  A version of the following paragraphs was first published in Wendy Anne Warren, "'The Cause of Her Grief': The Rape of a Slave in Early New England," *JAH* 93, no. 4 (2007): 1031–49. A discussion of shipboard community is found in Rediker, *Slave Ship*, 276–84.

78  It is difficult to estimate slaves' shipboard mortality in the early seventeenth century, since the slave trade was not professionalized until the later decades of the century. For a one-in-three estimate for 1663–1713, see David Eltis, *The Rise of African Slavery in the Americas* (Cambridge: Cambridge Univ. Press, 2000), 185. Stephanie Smallwood estimates that "twenty percent of the Africans carried into the Atlantic in the seventeenth century died at sea, and 40 percent of cargoes experienced mortality levels above that benchmark." Smallwood, *Saltwater Slavery: A Middle Passage from Africa to American Diaspora* (Cambridge, MA: Harvard Univ. Press, 2007), 150.

79  On the unknown nature of the crossing for enslaved Africans, and ways of escaping it, see Smallwood, *Saltwater Slavery*, 132–45, and Rediker, *Slave Ship*, 284–301.

80  Daniel Mannix, *Black Cargoes: A History of the Atlantic Slave Trade, 1515–1865* (New York: Viking, 1962), 128–29.

81  Sir Henry Colt, "The Voyage of Sir Henry Colt," in *Colonising Expeditions to the West Indies and Guiana, 1623–1667*, ed. V. T. Harlow (London: Hakluyt Society, 1925), 63, 65.

82  Richard Ligon, *A True and Exact History of the Island of Barbados* (London, 1673), 46.

83  John Norton, "The Epistle Dedicatory," in *The Orthodox Evangelist; or, A Treatise wherein Many Great Evangelical Truths Are Briefly Discussed, Cleared, and Confirmed* (London, 1657), 6 (unpaginated).

84 Miscellaneous, box 2, folder 12, 1659, Robert Gibbs, Misc. Collection, American Antiquarian Society, Worcester, MA.

85 "Negros for the Account of Mr. John Usher, 1681," Miscellaneous Bound Manuscripts, vol. 1679–1687, MHS.

86 Dated Oct. 30, 1697, MAC, 61:357.

87 MAC, 9:137.

88 *Suffolk Deeds*, 9:336.

89 "A True Inventory of the Moneys Goods Cattle & Chattles Belonging & Appertaineing to the Estate of Major Nicho: Shapleigh," *York Deeds*, vol. 5, ed. William M. Sargent (Portland, ME: Brown Thurston, 1889), fols. 15–16.

90 For a similar discussion of gentry slave owners in early colonial Virginia, see John C. Coombs, "The Phases of Conversion: A New Chronology for the Rise of Slavery in Early Virginia," *WMQ* 68, no. 3 (2011): 350–53.

91 On "gentry," see Darett Rutman, *Winthrop's Boston: Portrait of a Puritan Town, 1630–1649* (Chapel Hill: Univ. of North Carolina Press, 1965), 72–77. The historian Stephen Innes cannily observed that these men, whom he called "merchant-entrepreneurs," served as buffers for their entire regions, "absorbing price variations and carrying charges in inventories of foodstuffs and soft goods to provide an economic cocoon for the townsfolk." Innes, *Labor in a New Land*, 175.

92 Bailyn, *New England Merchants*, 96.

93 Innes, *Labor in a New Land*, xix, 16.

94 See *Suffolk Deeds*, 11:334; "Peter Swinck," *The First Century of the History of Springfield: The Official Records from 1636 to 1736*, 2 vols. (Springfield, MA: H. M. Burt, 1898–99), 2:643.

95 Bernard Bailyn cautioned against generalizing about the isolation of inland merchants, pointing out that it is not true "to say that these essentially rural districts had no trade except to Boston and Manhattan. On the contrary, there were men in the Connecticut River towns and along the Sound and Narragansett Bay who managed a considerable exchange of goods; but their dealings were different from those of the Bostonians. They dealt in a secondary orbit of trade, sending a small but steady flow of local produce to the southern colonies or occasionally to the West Indies. They had fallen completely out of contact with the European sources of manufactures." Bailyn, *New England Merchants*, 95.

96 For an in-depth discussion of Pynchon's trade networks, see Innes, *Labor in a New Land*, 32–40. For a similar point in a different place, see Hatfield, *Atlantic Virginia*, 37–38.

97 Thomas Pynchon, *Mason & Dixon* (New York: Henry Holt, 1997), 615–16.

98 "Estate of Obadiah Antrum of Salem," *PREC*, 2:13.

99 "Estate of Henry Ball of Salem, 1678," *PREC*, 3:313.

100 "William Painter of Barbados," *Middlesex County in the Colony of the Massachusetts Bay in New England: Records of Probate and Administration; March 1660/1–December 1670*, ed. Robert H. Rodgers (Boston: NEHGS, 2001), 321–22.

101 *Suffolk Deeds*, 5:180–82.

102 Probate Inventory of Sir William Phip[p]s, PROB 5/743, PRO. Phips eventually moved back to England. Kenneth Silverman, *Life and Times of Cotton Mather* (New York: Harper and Row, 1984), 138–39.

103 Abstracts of Early Wills, 1665, NEHGS.

104 Stephen J. Hornsby, "Geographies of the British Atlantic World," in *Britain's Oceanic Empire*, ed. Bowen, Mancke, and Reid, 31–32.

105 Account of a Boston Merchant, 1688, MHS.

106 "Estate of Paul White of Newbury," 1679, *PREC*, 3:331.

107 "Estate of Nathaniel Mighill," 1677, *PREC*, 3:173.

108 "Estate of John Jones of Newbury," 1677, *PREC*, 3:193–94.

109 "Estate of William Pearce," 1678, *PREC*, 3:241.

110 "Estate of William Robinson of Salem," 1677, *PREC*, 3:285–86.

111 *ECCR*, 4:389.

112 Ibid., 389–90.

113 Ibid., 2:173–74.

114 *Records of the Suffolk County Court, CSMP*, 29:45–48.

115 Ibid., 40–52.

116 Craig Muldrew, *The Economy of Obligation: The Culture of Credit and Social Relations in Early Modern England* (New York: St. Martin's Press, 1998), 101.

117 Peter Mathias discusses kinship networks and relative risk in "Risk, Credit and Kinship in Early Modern Enterprise," in *The Early Modern Atlantic Economy*, ed. John J. McCusker and Kenneth Morgan (New York: Cambridge Univ. Press, 2000), 15–35.

118 On transcolonial financial affairs, see David Cressy, *Coming Over: Migration and Communication between England and New England in the Seventeenth Century* (New York: Cambridge Univ. Press, 1987), 184–90.

119 *Suffolk Deeds*, 2:223. Hagborne self-identified as a "shoomaker," ibid., 3:253.

120 On this point, Bailyn notes that family networks could take merchants only so far in Atlantic trade, and that at some point traders became "obliged to make fresh acquaintances among the merchants and planters in [the West Indies]. Two methods were most commonly used. Since most of the trade to the south was conducted in small vessels with small cargoes, a merchant would send his shipmaster to the markets he had selected with instructions to use his own discretion in selecting men to deal with. Over a period of time some of these transient contacts became firm commercial bonds which formed the framework of a lifetime of trade. But, for those who had capital to start with and some knowledge of the distant markets, the best method was to send a letter of credit to someone of good reputation and in this way to found an agency that could be relied on for advice on new opportunities or dangers to avoid." Bailyn, *New England Merchants*, 87–88.

121 "Richard Lord's Discharge to Samuel Wyllys," July 20, 1685, *CCHS*, 21:282.

122 "John Lucas' Bond," July 23, 1685, *CCHS*, 21:282.

123 "Arbitrators Award About Cabbage Tree Plantation," Aug. 15, 1685, *CCHS*, 21:283–85.

124 On the Puritans' plain style, from John Cotton to Anne Bradstreet, see Perry Miller, *The New England Mind: The Seventeenth Century* (Cambridge, MA: Harvard Univ. Press, 1954), 331–62.

## Chapter 3: Unplanting and Replanting

1 Thomas Hamilton to [London], 1675, ADM 106/311, fol. 167, Records of the Navy Board and the Board of Admirality, PRO.

2 Figures for pre-European contact Native American populations are always contested; this figure comes from Neal Salisbury, *Manitou and Providence: Indians, Europeans, and the Making of New England, 1500–1643* (New York: Oxford Univ. Press, 1982), 24–30. Some estimates are lower. Kathleen Bragdon, *The Columbia Guide to American Indians of the Northeast* (New York: Columbia Univ. Press, 2005), 7, suggests somewhere roughly between 70,000 and 150,000 people lived in the region before European contact. Bert Salwen, "Indians of Southern New England and Long Island: Early Period," in *Handbook of North American Indians*, vol. 15, *Northeast*, ed. William C. Sturtevant (Washington, DC: Smithsonian Institution, 1978), 160–68.

3 Daniel Gookin, *Historical Collections of the Indians in New England* (Boston, 1792), 7. For Gookin's role, see David Silverman, *Faith and Boundaries: Colonists, Christianity, and Community among the Wampanoag Indians of Martha's Vineyard, 1600–1871* (New York: Cambridge Univ. Press, 2005), 63.

4 Salwen, "Indians of Southern New England and Long Island," 160–68.

5 *Oxford English Dictionary Online*, s.v. "colony, n.," accessed March 2015. For more discussion of the etymology of "colony," see V. Y. Mudimbe, *The Invention of Africa: Gnosis, Philosophy, and the Order of Knowledge* (Bloomington: Indiana Univ. Press, 1988), 1–3.

6 "Armes for 100 men," 1628, *MCR*, 1:26.

7 Francis Bacon, "Of Plantations," in *The Essays; or, Counsels, Civil and Moral* (London, 1663), 192–93.

8 Thomas Hobbes, *Leviathan* (London, 1651 "Head Edition"), 131.

9 John Smith, "Advertisements for the Unexperienced Planters of New England, or Any Where," *The Complete Works of Captain John Smith (1580–1631)*, vol. 3 (Chapel Hill: Univ. of North Carolina Press, 1986), 294.

10 David Brion Davis, *Inhuman Bondage: The Rise and Fall of Slavery in the New World* (New York: Oxford Univ. Press, 2006), 49. See also Robin Blackburn, *The Making of New World Slavery: From the Baroque to the Modern, 1492–1800* (New York: Verso, 1997), 54; and Alan Gallay, "Introduction," in *Indian Slavery in Colonial America*, ed. Alan Gallay (Lincoln: Univ. of Nebraska Press, 2009), 11. Of course, sometimes people did use the terms synonymously. Though English colonists and merchants often used "African" or "Moore" or "Negroe" to mean a slave without even needing to clarify, they also had occasion to describe Indians explicitly as slaves. In the New England mind, to be an African was almost always to be a slave, but to be a slave was not always to be an African.

11 The reigning authority on this topic is still Lewis Hanke, *Aristotle and the*

*American Indians: A Study in Race Prejudice in the Modern World* (London: Hollis and Carter, 1959), esp. 28–61. For the Las Casas quotation, see *Apologética historia,* cited and translated ibid., 112.

12 Jorge Canizares-Esguerra, *Puritan Conquistadors: Iberianizing the Atlantic, 1550–1700* (Stanford, CA: Stanford University Press, 2006), suggests we should see similarities in the colonizing models of New England and Spanish America.

13 These numbers are from Daniel K. Richter, *Facing East from Indian Country: A Native History of Early America* (Cambridge, MA: Harvard Univ. Press, 2001), 95–96; for slightly different population numbers, see Jenny Hale Pulsipher, *Subjects unto the Same King: Indians, English, and the Contest for Authority in Colonial New England* (Philadelphia: Univ. of Pennsylvania Press, 2005), 74–75. One nineteenth-century historian argued that John Eliot himself learned to speak "an Indian language" from an enslaved Indian man, taken during the Pequot War: cited in Francis Jennings, "Goals and Functions of Puritan Missions to the Indians," *Ethnohistory* 18, no. 3 (1971): 201.

14 On John Eliot, see Richard W. Cogley, *John Eliot's Mission to the Indians before King Philip's War* (Cambridge, MA: Harvard Univ. Press, 1999). For an early use of the appellation, see Increase Mather, "A Letter concerning the Success of the Gospel amongst the Indians in New England," in Matthew Mayhew, *The Conquests and Triumphs of Grace: Being a Brief Narrative of the Success Which the Gospel Hath Had among the Indians of Martha's Vineyard* (London, 1695).

15 Cogley, *John Eliot's Mission,* 45–46.

16 Ibid., 106–11.

17 "The humble petition of John Eliot," 1669, *Early Records of the Town of Dedham, Massachusetts, 1659–1673,* ed. Don Gleason Hill (Dedham, MA, 1894), 4:279, cited in Pulsipher, *Subjects unto the Same King,* 76.

18 Daiva Stasiulis and Nira Yuval-Davis, "Introduction: Beyond Dichotomies— Gender, Race, Ethnicity and Class in Settler Societies," in *Unsettling Settler Societies: Articulations of Gender, Race, Ethnicity and Class,* ed. Daiva Stasiulis and Nira Yuval-Davis (Thousand Oaks, CA: Sage, 1995), 3; also cited in Margaret D. Jacobs, *White Mother to a Dark Race: Settler Colonialism, Maternalism, and the Removal of Indigenous Children in the American West and Australia, 1880–1940* (Lincoln: Univ. of Nebraska Press, 2009), 2–3.

19 Patrick Wolfe, *Settler Colonialism and the Transformation of Anthropology: The Politics and Poetics of an Ethnographic Event* (New York: Cassell, 1999), 163.

20 Stasiulis and Yuval-Davis, "Introduction," *Unsettling Settler Societies,* 3. Frederick Hoxie has argued for the usefulness of the term "settler colonialism," pointing out that it "allows scholars to present indigenous populations in other than solely cultural terms . . . [and thus avoid] narratives rooted in the 'clash of cultures'" paradigm. Hoxie, "Retrieving the Red Continent: Settler Colonialism and the History of American Indians in the US," *Ethnic and Racial Studies* 31, no. 6 (2008): 1158–59. A summary of the evolution of "settler

colonialism" as an idea is Lorenzo Veracini, "'Settler Colonialism': Career of a Concept," *Journal of Imperial and Commonwealth History* 41, no. 2 (2013): 313–33.

21  Emphasis added. Wolfe, *Settler Colonialism*, 163. See also Patrick Wolfe, "Settler Colonialism and the Elimination of the Native," *Journal of Genocide Research* 8, no. 4 (2006): 387–409. A critique of this theoretical framework as potentially implying an inevitability to the process (and thus again silencing the colonized) is articulated in Alissa Macoun and Elizabeth Strakosch, "The Ethical Demands of Settler Colonial Theory," *Settler Colonial Studies* 3, nos. 3–4 (2013): 426–43. James H. Merrell has taken exception to the use of the term "settler" in work on colonization, since it implies the land was unsettled before the arrival of colonists. Merrell, "Second Thoughts on Colonial Historians and American Indians," *WMQ* 69, no. 3 (2012): 451–512.

22  This is an obvious connection, but one often overlooked—a part of the larger problem of not seeing the "colonial" period as a process of colonization. The editor of Roger Williams's letters, for example, notes of King Philip's War that "for all its deleterious effects, the war had produced an unanticipated benefit: it had wiped out or driven away the last of the Indian occupants in the western territory, leaving the disputed acreage open for expansion and settlement." "Climax of the Pawtuxet Controversy: Editorial Note," in *The Correspondence of Roger Williams*, ed. Glenn W. LaFantasie, 2 vols. (Hanover, NH: Brown Univ. Press/Univ. Press of New England, 1988), 2:733. But, of course, this was the very point of the war rather than an unanticipated benefit.

23  The historian Neal Salisbury argued in *Manitou and Providence*, 166, that "by 1633, commercial exchange around Massachusetts Bay had shifted from portable commodities, principally furs, to the land itself." Settler colonialism as a process was hardly limited to Anglophone areas. Daniel H. Usner has described a similar removal through sale to the Caribbean of Indians by French colonists in colonial Louisiana, in *Indians, Settlers, & Slaves in a Frontier Exchange Economy: The Lower Mississippi Valley before 1783* (Chapel Hill: Univ. of North Carolina Press, 1992), 25. Brett Rushforth describes colonial New France's experiments with sending Iroquois captives into Mediterranean slavery, in *Bonds of Alliance: Indigenous and Atlantic Slaveries in New France* (Chapel Hill: Univ. of North Carolina Press, 2012), esp. 135–53.

24  Blackburn, *Making of New World Slavery*, 10. Michael Guasco has argued that enslavement was "arguably not nearly as desirable to most colonists as simply eliminating Indians." Guasco, *Slaves and Englishmen: Human Bondage in the Early Modern Atlantic World* (Philadelphia: Univ. of Pennsylvania Press, 2014), 193.

25  "Thomas Wappatucke, Indian," Court Records, *PCR*, 6:153.

26  "Hoken Court Record," *PCR*, 5:151–52. Richard S. Dunn notes the existence of Indian slaves in Jamaica, very likely captives in King Philip's War. Dunn, *Sugar and Slaves: The Rise of the Planter Class in the English West Indies, 1624–1713* (Chapel Hill: Univ. of North Carolina Press, 1972), 269–70.

27  The most comprehensive discussion of the Pequot War is Alfred A. Cave, *The*

*Pequot War* (Amherst: Univ. of Massachusetts Press, 1996). See also Ronald Dale Karr, "'Why Should You Be So Furious?': The Violence of the Pequot War," *JAH* 85, no. 3 (1998): 876–909.

28 William Bradford, *Of Plymouth Plantation, 1620–1647* (New York: Modern Library, 1981), 331–32; Bernard Bailyn, *The Barbarous Years: The Peopling of British North America: The Conflict of Civilizations, 1600–1675* (New York: Alfred A. Knopf, 2012), 446–47; Cotton Mather, *Magnalia Christi Americana; or, The Ecclesiastical History of New-England* (London, 1702), bk. 7, p. 43.

29 Herman Meville, *Moby-Dick* (New York: W. W. Norton, 2002), 69.

30 The problem of erasure of Indians from North American history is immense. On New England's history in particular, see Jean M. O'Brien, *Firsting and Lasting: Writing Indians out of Existence in New England* (Minneapolis: Univ. of Minnesota Press, 2010). Margaret M. Bruchac's discussion of the ways Native people reacted to English colonization, ways that included "shift[s] in residence" away from English colonists, is very useful. Bruchac, "Revisiting Pocumtuck History in Deerfield: George Sheldon's Vanishing Indian Act," *Historical Journal of Massachusetts* 39, nos. 1–2 (2011): 31–77, esp. 68.

31 William Hubbard, *A Narrative of the Troubles with the Indians in New-England* (Boston, 1677), 128. Time did not soften colonial memories of the massacre. Summarizing the event some years later, Cotton Mather again showed his way with words, remarking that drowning the Indians was efficient: "it was found the quickest Way to feed the *Fishes* with 'em." *Magnalia Christi Americana*, bk. 7, p. 44.

32 This point is influenced by Edmund Morgan's attempt to understand why some Virginia colonists had felt authorized, nearly three decades before the Pequot War, to throw captive Indian children out of boats and then shoot them dead as they swam. Morgan observed, "When Englishmen at Jamestown throw Indian children in the water and shoot out their brains, we suspect they might not have done the same with French or Spanish children." Morgan, *American Slavery, American Freedom: The Ordeal of Colonial Virginia* (New York: W. W. Norton, 1975), 74, 130.

33 Hubbard, *Narrative of the Troubles*, 128.

34 Alden T. Vaughan, *New England Frontier: Puritans and Indians, 1620–1675* (Boston: Little, Brown, 1965), 150–51.

35 "Treaty of Hartford, 1638," Connecticut Archives, Connecticut State Library, digitized for the YIPP, 638.09.21.00, http://findit.library.yale.edu/catalog/digcoll:2389. On the Treaty of Hartford, see also Amy Ouden, *Beyond Conquest: Native Peoples an the Struggle for History in New England* (Lincoln: Univ. of Nebraska Press, 2005), 10–15.

36 "Hugh Peter to John Winthrop," *MHSC*, 4th ser., 6:95.

37 John Winthrop to William Bradford, 1637, in William Bradford, *History of Plymouth Plantation*, in *MHSC*, 4th ser 3:360.

38 *JJW*, 227; Michael L. Fickes, "'They Could Not Endure That Yoke': The Captivity of Pequot Women and Children after the War of 1637," *NEQ* 73, no. 1 (2000): 58–81.

39  The words of Jean-Paul Sartre on the seemingly natural progression toward brutality in colonization seem relevant. "Oppression," he observed, "justifies itself through oppression: the oppressors produce and maintain by force the evils that render the oppressed, in their eyes, more and more like what they would have to be like to deserve their fate. The colonizer can only exonerate himself in the systematic pursuit of the 'dehumanization' of the colonized by identifying himself a little more each day with the colonialist apparatus. Terror and exploitation dehumanize, and the exploiter authorizes himself with that dehumanization to carry his exploitation further. The engine of colonialism turns in a circle; it is impossible to distinguish between its praxis and objective necessity." Sartre, introd. to Albert Memmi, *The Colonizer and the Colonized*, trans. Howard Greenfeld (New York: Orion Press, 1965), xxvi–xxvii.

40  Bradford, *History of Plymouth Plantation*, in *MHSC*, 4th ser., 3:358.

41  Emanuel Downing to John Winthrop, Aug. 1645, *WP*, 5:38.

42  Ibid. It's ironic that he doubted the reproductive capacities of New England's colonists; they in fact increased at an amazing rate.

43  Craig Muldrew, *The Economy of Obligation: The Culture of Credit and Social Relations in Early Modern England* (New York: St. Martin's Press, 1998), 98–99.

44  John Easton, *A Narrative of the Causes Which Led to Philip's Indian War, of 1675 and 1676* (Albany, NY: J. Munsell, 1858), 21, 21–22n2. Easton was the son of Nicholas Easton, a former governor; John Easton himself would later serve as governor of the colony of Rhode Island. Both father and son were Quakers.

45  Easton, *Narrative*, 28.

46  Miller, *New England Mind*, 5.

47  "Petition of the Rev. John Eliot," 1675, *PCR*, 2:452.

48  Neal Salisbury, "Red Puritans: The 'Praying Indians' of Massachusetts Bay and John Eliot," *WMQ* 31, no. 1 (1974): 32.

49  Thomas Mayhew, *"To the Much Honored Corporation in* London, *Chosen to Place of Publick Trust for the Promoting of the Work of the Lord among the* Indians *in* NEW-ENGLAND," in John Eliot, *Tears of Repentance* (London, 1653), third page of Mayhew's letter (unpaginated).

50  John Eliot to Robert Boyle, Nov. 27, 1683, *MHSC*, 1st ser., 3:183.

51  "Transactions Remembrances Warrants of the Towne of Providence," *The Early Records of the Town of Providence* (Providence, RI, 1899), 15:155–56.

52  "Att a meeting of the councell of war for this jurisdiction," Aug. 1675, *PCR*, 5:173.

53  "Att a meeting of the councell of war for this jurisdiction," Sept. 1675, *PCR*, 5:173–74.

54  "An Account of the First Company of indians Sould And what is by us allready received," *Early Records of the Town of Providence*, 15:157–58. For a list of thirty-two children who surrendered to authorities—most, but not all, of whom were orphans—and were sent into English servitude until the age of twenty, see "List of Captive Indian Children, 1676," *CSMP*, 19:25–28. A brief

discussion of these sorts of dispersals is found in John Sainsbury, "Indian Labor in Early Rhode Island," *NEQ* 48, no. 3 (1975): 381–84.

55 "Excerpt from John Hull's Journal," in George Madison Bodge, ed., *Soldiers in King Philip's War*, 3d ed. (Leominster, MA, 1906), 479–80, cited in Mary Rowlandson, *The Sovereignty and Goodness of God*, ed. Neal Salisbury (Boston: Bedford Books, 1997), 145–46. On Hull, see also Mark Valeri, *Heavenly Merchandize: How Religion Shaped Commerce in Puritan America* (Princeton, NJ: Princeton Univ. Press, 2010), 84–85, 92–93. Margaret Newell notes that Hull "commissioned or shared in voyages to Virginia, Jamaica, Honduras, Curacao, Bristol, London, Ireland, Nevis, and Antigua, and received cargo from these port and more." Newell, *From Dependency to Independence: Economic Revolution in Colonial New England* (Ithaca, NY: Cornell Univ. Press, 1998), 92.

56 "Rev. James Noyes to John Allyn, 1676," *CCHS*, 21:255–57.

57 "Testimony of John Pell, 1697," MAC, 9:143a.

58 "Rev. James Noyes to John Allyn, 1676," *CCHS*, 21:255–56. This James Noyes, James Noyes II, was one of the first trustees of Yale College.

59 Noyes was careful to mention the transaction because Catapazet was concerned the authorities would invalidate the sale on the grounds that Catapazet had no right to sell her, since she, like all Indian war captives, remained under the legal control of the English. "Rev. James Noyes to John Allyn, 1676," *CCHS*, 21:255–57.

60 "To Governor John Winthrop, 21 June 1637," in *Correspondence of Roger Williams*, 1:86–87.

61 "To Governor John Winthrop, 30 June 1637," in *Correspondence of Roger Williams*, 1:88.

62 On Roger Williams, see Edmund S. Morgan, *Roger Williams: The Church and the State* (New York: W. W. Norton, 1967). On John Eliot's role, see Cogley, *John Eliot's Mission*, 47.

63 "To John Winthrop, 31 July 1637," in *Correspondence of Roger Williams*, 1:109.

64 Roger Williams, *A Key into the Language of America* (London, 1643), 29.

65 Ann Laura Stoler, *Carnal Knowledge and Imperial Power: Race and the Intimate in Colonial Rule* (Berkeley: Univ. of California Press, 2002), 8; Jacobs, *White Mother to a Dark Race*, 10–11.

66 "To Governor John Winthrop, 31 July 1637," in *Correspondence of Roger Williams*, 1:109.

67 "Richard Morris to John Coggeshall," May 1647, *WP*, 5:164.

68 "September 1676 Order of a General Court in Boston," *MHSC*, 4th ser., 8:689.

69 "Richard Morris to John Coggeshall," May 1647, *WP*, 5:164. On children of death, see also Joyce E. Chaplin, *Subject Matter: Technology, the Body, and Science on the Anglo-American Frontier, 1500–1676* (Cambridge, MA: Harvard Univ. Press, 2001), 227–28; and Jill Lepore, *The Name of War: King Philip's War and the Origins of American Identity* (New York: Alfred A. Knopf, 1998), 151.

70 "William Baulston to John Winthrop, Jr," May 1647, *WP*, 5:165.

71 "Will of Nicholas Easton" # 166, *Rhode Island Land Evidences*, vol. 1, *1648–1696* (Providence: Rhode Island Historical Society, 1921), 119–20.

72 "Plymouth, the 22nd of July, 1676," *PCR*, 5:207.

73 Providence, Aug. 14, 1676, *Early Records of the Town of Providence*, 15:154.

74 *ECCR*, 2:240.

75 Gallay, "Introduction," in *Indian Slavery in Colonial America*, 4. David Brion Davis has also observed that "in spite of a widespread tendency to differentiate the Negro from the Indian and to associate the latter with the freedom of nature, Negro slavery was in actuality imposed on top of a pre-existing Indian slavery; in North America, at least, the two never diverged as distinct institutions." Davis, *The Problem of Slavery in Western Culture* (Ithaca, NY: Cornell Univ. Press, 1966), 176.

76 In addition, even if, once on the island, slave owners perceived a distinction between Indian and African slaves, we should not assume that such a distinction meant much to the enslaved people who had been violently commodified. It was probably better to be enslaved and work as a hunter or fisher than to work as a harvester of sugar, but better can be a far cry from good.

77 "At a Meetinge of the ffree Inhabitants of the Towne of portsmouth," 1675, *The Early Records of the Town of Portsmouth* (Providence, RI: E. L. Freeman & Sons, 1901), 188. Rushforth, *Bonds of Alliance*, 119, finds a similar fear and response by French colonists in the Caribbean,

78 Dunn, *Sugar and Slaves*, 74, suggests some planters in Barbados were skeptical, pointing out that Indians who imported to the island from other colonies were considered poor workers.

79 See "An Act of Explanation to the Act of Negroes, and to prohibit the bringing of Indians to this Island," in Linford D. Fisher, "'Dangerous Designes': The 1676 Barbados Act to Prohibit New England Indian Slave Importation," *WMQ* 71, no. 1 (2014): 122–24.

80 On legislation requiring returns, see Linford Fisher, "'Dangerous Designes,'" 115–18.

81 "Gov. Leverett's Certificate," Sept. 12, 1676, Miscellaneous Bound Manuscripts, MHS. Some 70 came from Massachusetts Bay; another 110 came from Plymouth. Lepore, *Name of War*, 171. Whether the *Seaflower* slaves were sold in Jamaica is unclear.

82 "Att a General Court specially called in Boston, 6 September 1676," *MHSC*, 4th ser., 8:689.

83 John Taylor, *Jamaica in 1687: The Taylor Manuscript at the National Library of Jamaica*, ed. David Buisseret (Kingston, Jamaica: Univ. of the West Indies Press, 2009), 267.

84 Robert Roules, Deposition, MS 252, Edward E. Ayer Collection, Newberry Library, Chicago, reprinted in James Axtell, "The Vengeful Women of Marblehead: Robert Roules's Deposition of 1677," *WMQ* 31, no. 4 (1974): 650–52.

85 "Examination and Relation of James Quannapaquait, Alias James Runnymarsh," Jan. 24, 1675/6, YIPP, 1676.01.24.00, 2/35d; also transcribed in "The

Examination and Relation of James Quannapaquait," in Mary Rowlandson, *The Sovereignty and Goodness of God*, ed. Neal Salisbury (Boston: Bedford Books, 1997), 125.

86 Quentin Stockwell's account in Increase Mather, *An Essay for the Recording of Illustrious Providences* (Boston, 1684), 47.

87 "Examination and Relation of James Quannapaquait, Alias James Runnymarsh," YIPP, 3/35e.

88 Daniel Gookin, "An Historical Account of the Doings and Sufferings of the Christian Indians in New England, in the Years 1675, 1676, 1677," in *Archaeologia Americana: Transactions and Collections of the American Antiquarian Society* 2 (1836): 474, 485.

89 See Jace Weaver, *Red Atlantic: American Indigenes and the Making of the Modern World, 1000–1927* (Chapel Hill: Univ. of North Carolina Press, 2014), esp. 1–34. See also Paul Cohen's insightful article, "Was There an Amerindian Atlantic? Reflections on the Limits of a Historiographical Concept," *History of European Ideas* 34, no. 4 (2008): 388–410. On the Black Atlantic, see Paul Gilroy, *The Black Atlantic: Modernity and Double Consciousness* (Cambridge, MA: Harvard Univ. Press, 1993); Saidiya Hartman, *Lose Your Mother: A Journey along the Atlantic Slave Route* (New York: Farrar, Straus and Giroux, 2007); and *The Black Urban Atlantic in the Age of the Slave Trade*, ed. Jorge Cañizares-Esguerra, Matt D. Childs, and James Sidbury (Philadelphia: Univ. of Pennsylvania Press, 2013).

90 Rushforth, *Bonds of Alliance*, 66.

91 The best descriptions of Iroquoian captivity practices are in Daniel K. Richter, *The Ordeal of the Longhouse: The Peoples of the Iroquois League in the Era of European Colonization* (Chapel Hill: Univ. of North Carolina Press, 1992), esp. 33–37; and Rushforth, *Bonds of Alliance*, esp. 35–71.

92 Indeed, in most ways except perhaps the moment of capture, the unyielding Atlantic system was quite different from the local indigenous American model. A discussion of this idea is found in Rushforth, *Bonds of Alliance*, 65–66. On Native American forms of captivity and slavery, see also Christina Snyder, *Slavery in Indian Country: The Changing Face of Captivity in Early America* (Cambridge, MA: Harvard Univ. Press, 2010), esp. her chapter "Owned People," 127–51.

93 Snyder, *Slavery in Indian Country*, 5.

94 "Att the Court of his Majesty held att Plymouth," 1677–78, *PCR*, 5:253. See also "Indian Children Put to Service, 1676," *NEHGR*, 8:270–73.

95 "Memorial of Indian Peter," May 30, 1685, MAC, 5:477.

96 "Memorial of Peter Pratt," May 17, 1722, (1721.05.00.00), ed. Grant-Costa, Paul, and Tobias Glaza, YIPP. On Peter Pratt's position, see *The Memorial History of Hartford County, Connecticut, 1633–1884*, ed. James Hammond Trumbull (Boston: Osgood, 1886), 116.

97 For Indian population numbers, see Pulsipher, *Subjects unto the Same King*, 241. On the continued existence of Indians in the region, Jean O'Brien's subtitle admonishes historians to remember that conquest is not extermina-

tion; Indians continue to live in the region today and were certainly present throughout the eighteenth century. O'Brien, *Firsting and Lasting: Writing Indians out of Existence in New England.*

### Chapter 4: Visible Slaves

1 Samuel Maverick, *A Briefe Description of New England and the Severall Townes Therein: Together with the Present Government Thereof* (Boston: David Clapp and Son, 1885), 26; Daniel Neal, *The History of New-England, Containing an Impartial Account of the Civil and Ecclesiastical Affairs of the Country, to the Year of Our Lord, 1700,* vol. 2 (London, 1720), 587–90.

2 Philip Morgan calls this growth period the "frontier phase," a usefully evocative term. Morgan, *Slave Counterpoint: Black Culture in the Eighteenth-Century Chesapeake and Lowcountry* (Chapel Hill: Univ. of North Carolina Press, 1998), xviii–xix, xxi. A similar insistence on the importance of emphasizing temporality in studies of slavery can be found in Ira Berlin, "Time, Space, and the Evolution of Afro-American Society on British Mainland North America," *American Historical Review* 85, no. 1 (1980): 44–78, and in Walter Johnson, "Possible Pasts: Some Speculations on Time, Temporality, and the History of Atlantic Slavery," *Amerikastudien/American Studies* 45, no. 4 (2000): 485–99.

3 "Henry Winthrop to Thomas Fones," Aug. 22, 1627, in *MHSC,* 5th ser., 8:179–80.

4 Peter H. Wood describes this early period in South Carolina with the term "frontier colony," and draws similar conclusions about the fluidity that characterized early colonization. Slaves, he observed, "simply shared the calling of the white household to which they were annexed, participating fully in the colony's growing number of specialized trades." Wood, *Black Majority: Negroes in Colonial South Carolina from 1670 through the Stono Rebellion* (New York: Alfred A .Knopf, 1974), 47–48. See also Morgan, *Slave Couterpoint,* xvii. Other works on early colonization and slavery include T. H. Breen and Stephen Innes, *"Myne Owne Ground": Race and Freedom on Virginia's Eastern Shore, 1640–1676* (New York: Oxford Univ. Press, 1980); and Edmund S. Morgan, *American Slavery, American Freedom: The Ordeal of Colonial Virginia* (New York: W. W. Norton, 1975). See also Daniel Vickers, *Farmers and Fishermen: Two Centuries of Work in Essex County, Massachusetts, 1630–1850* (Chapel Hill: Univ. of North Carolina Press, 1994), 115–16.

5 Such blurriness has existed elsewhere. Seth Rockman has described a similar fluidity in early nineteenth-century Baltimore, where "employers constantly adjusted their workforces, shifting between and combining laborers who were enslaved, indentured, and free; black and white; male and female; young and old; native born and immigrant." Employers in that situation "were unlikely to deem a particular job suited only to men, only to adults, only to white people, or only to slaves." Rockman, *Scraping By: Wage Labor, Slavery, and Survival in Early Baltimore* (Baltimore: Johns Hopkins Univ. Press, 2009), 8. It has probably always been the case that working shoulder to shoulder with another does not presume or require equality, and it was certainly

true in early New England, where people who had been captured, sold, and purchased worked side by side with people who understood themselves to be free.

6  On the ubiquity of witchcraft in early New England, see John Demos, *Entertaining Satan: Witchcraft and the Culture of Early New England* (New York: Oxford Univ. Press, 1982).

7  *ECCR*, 7:329–30.

8  Ibid.

9  Oliver developed a bad reputation in Salem and was later accused in the famed Salem witch trials. See Carol F. Karlsen, *The Devil in the Shape of a Woman: Witchcraft in Colonial New England* (New York: W. W. Norton, 1987), 38; and Mary Beth Norton, *In the Devil's Snare: The Salem Witchcraft Crisis of 1692* (New York: Alfred A. Knopf, 2002), 112–13, 359n2.

10  But, of course, Wonn may have had his own ideas about witchcraft, may have interpreted Goody Oliver's apparitions by using a different cosmological framework. The absence in records of African religious references suggests that enslaved people knew how to mold their testimony to their audience, which perhaps makes their testimony a political act. On African witchcraft, see Diane Ciekawy and Peter Geschiere, "Containing Witchcraft: Conflicting Scenarios in Postcolonial Africa," *African Studies Review* 41, no. 3 (1998): 1–14, which hints that indigenous traditions predated European colonization; the older E. G. Parrinder, "African Ideas of Witchcraft," *Folklore* 67, no. 3 (1956): 142–50; Ronald Hutton, "Anthropological and Historical Approaches to Witchcraft: Potential for a New Collaboration?," *Historical Journal* 47, no. 2 (2004): 413–34; and E. E. Evans-Pritchard, *Witchcraft, Oracles and Magic among the Azande* (Oxford: Clarendon Press, 1937). Diana Paton addresses the problem of using a term such as "witchcraft," which has specific cultural meanings in English, to describe African cultural traditions in the Caribbean. Paton, "Witchcraft, Poison, Law, and Atlantic Slavery," *WMQ* 69, no. 2 (2012): 235–64. James H. Sweet makes a similar point in noting that "in most of Africa . . . the terms used to describe what Westerners call witchcraft were more ambiguous [and] in many societies, there was no discrete term that distinguished good rituals from malevolent rituals." Sweet, *Recreating Africa: Culture, Kinship, and Religion in the African-Portuguese World, 1441–1770* (Chapel Hill: Univ. of North Carolina Press, 2003), 161–62. In the Salem trials, one accused witch, an enslaved woman named Candy, disavowed indigenous African roots to witchcraft. When asked, "Candy! are you a witch?" she answered, "Candy no witch in her country. Candy's mother no witch. Candy no witch, Barbados. This country, mistress give Candy witch." The magistrate clarified: "Did your mistress make you a witch in this country?" Candy answered, "Yes, in this country mistress give Candy witch." "Examination of Candy," July 4, 1692," *Salem Witchcraft Papers*, vol. 1, ed. Paul Boyer and Stephen Nissenbaum (New York: Da Capo Press, 1977), 179. See also "The Examination of Mary Black (a Negroe)," 1692, during which observers answered positively when asked "Doth this Negroe hurt you?" Ibid., 113.

11  In 1694, Ingersoll's probate record listed a "negro man," valued at twenty

pounds, slightly less than market value. This may have been the now older
Wonn, though a later settlement between his wife and his son-in-law and
daughter calls the man "Dick." Whether one man or two, the Ingersoll family
held slaves for at least two decades. "Inventory of Estate of John Ingersoll,
late of Salem 22 January 1694," *Essex County Probate File Papers*; "Settlement
of Estate of John Ingersoll late of Salem, April 16, 1695."

12  Probate Record of John Ingersal, Salem, 1694, Case # 14577, NEHGS; Bond of
Administration of Estate of John Ingersoll late of sale Deceased, 1694, ibid.

13  A related argument about the many different iterations of chattel slavery in
the Atlantic world is contained in the subtitle of Robert Harms, *The Diligent:
A Voyage through the Worlds of the Slave Trade* (New York: Basic Books, 2002).
For another, theorized discussion of the local permutation of global move-
ments, see Joseph Fronczak, "Local People's Global Politics: A Transnational
History of the Hands Off Ethiopia Movement of 1935," *Diplomatic History* 39,
no. 2 (2015): 245–74.

14  On popular religious belief in seventeenth-century New England, see
David D. Hall, *Worlds of Wonder, Days of Judgment: Popular Religious Belief in
Early New England* (New York: Alfred A. Knopf, 1989), 6–20, and passim.

15  Carl Bridenbaugh and Juliette Tomlinson, eds., *The Pynchon Papers*, vol. 2,
*Selections from the Account Books of John Pynchon, 1651–1697* (Boston: Colo-
nial Society of Massachusetts, 1985), 482–83. On their marriage, see Josiah
Holland, *The History of Western Massachusetts* (Springfield, MA: Bowles and
Company, 1855), 198.

16  Arthur Anderson, "Recovery and Utilization of Tree Extractives," *Economic
Botany* 9, no. 2 (1955): 110. An overview of the uses of tar and turpentine is
Robert B. Outland III, "Slavery, Work, and the Geography of the North Car-
olina Naval Stores Industry, 1835–1860," *Journal of Southern History* 62, no.
1 (1996): 27–56. See also Stephen Innes, *Labor in a New Land: Economy and
Society in Seventeenth-Century Springfield* (Princeton, NJ: Princeton Univ.
Press, 1983), 90–91.

17  *The First Century of the History of Springfield*, ed. Henry M. Burt, vol. 2
(Springfield, MA: Henry M. Burt, 1899), 272. On boxing trees, see Mikko
Airaksinen, "Tar Production in Colonial North America," *Environment and
History* 2, no. 1 (1996): esp. 120–21.

18  The literature on rosin and turpentine and tar is extensive. A specialist overview is A. J. Gibson, "The Pine Forests of the Commonwealth as a Source of
Rosin and Turpentine," *Empire Forestry Review* 32, no. 2 (1953): 118–23.

19  David M. Powers, *Damnable Heresy: William Pynchon, the Indians, and
the First Book Banned (and Burned) in Boston* (Eugene, OR: Wipf & Stock,
2015), 91.

20  Robert Johnson, *The New Life of Virginea* (London, 1612), nineteenth page
(unpaginated), quoted in Peter Linebaugh and Marcus Rediker, *The Many-
Headed Hydra: Sailors, Slaves, Commoners, and the Hidden History of the
Revolutionary Atlantic* (Boston: Beacon Press, 2000), 43.

21  Samuel Wilson, *An Account of the Province of Carolina in America, together*

*with an Abstract of the Patent, and Several Other Necessary and Useful Particulars, to Such as Having Thoughts of Transporting Themselves Thither* (London, 1682), 7–8.

22  Linebaugh and Rediker, in *Many-Headed Hydra*, 43, comment, "The colonists were at first unfamiliar with the broadax and the felling ax, but after the Pequot War, which opened the way westward, they soon learned to saw, fell, cleave, split, and rive, making timber and its products the basis of an export economy to Barbados and other parts of the West Indies."

23  On clearing as colonizing, see Virginia DeJohn Anderson, *Creatures of Empire: How Domestic Animals Transformed Early America* (New York: Oxford Univ. Press, 2004), 81–82. On English clearing land for "fields and fences," see William Cronon, *Changes in the Land: Indians, Colonists, and the Ecology of New England* (New York: Hill and Wang, 1983), 127–55.

24  On enclosure, see Keith Wrightson, *Earthly Necessities: Economic Lives in Early Modern Britain* (New Haven, CT: Yale Univ. Press, 2000), 102–4; and Keith Wrightson, *English Society: 1580–1680* (New Brunswick, NJ: Rutgers Univ. Press, 1982): 157–88.

25  For an overview of early probate records, see Gloria L. Main, "Probate Records as a Source for Early American History," *WMQ* 32, no.1 (1975): 89–99.

26  "An Inventory of all such Goods Mr John Stoughton died possest of," *CSMP*, 29:46–47. A stone horse was one that had not been gelded.

27  *ECCR*, 5:64–65. The low price suggests the man was either an indentured servant or old or somehow undesirable. Either reading is possible; Price came from a merchant family (his father, Walter, was a merchant from Bristol, England, who emigrated in 1641 and had deals involving the West Indies). James Savage, A *Genealogical Dictionary of the First Settlers of New England*, 4 vols (Boston: Little, Brown, 1860–62), 3:484; Marsha L. Hamilton, *Social and Economic Networks in Early Massachusetts: Atlantic Connections* (University Park: Pennsylvania State Univ. Press, 2009), 82.

28  "Bond for Arbitration," Nicholas Davison of Charleston, Feb. 1678/9, in *Middlesex County in the Colony of the Massachusetts Bay in New England: Records of Probate and Administriation; March 1660/1–December 1670*, ed. Robert H. Rodgers (Boston: NEHGS, 2001), 234.

29  *Records of the Suffolk County Court, CSMP*, 29:232; *PREC*, 2:347–49.

30  *ECCR*, 8:416. Savage was closely related by marriage to the Hutchinson family. Bernard Bailyn, *The Barbarous Years: The Peopling of British North America: The Conflict of Civilizations, 1600–1675* (New York: Alfred A. Knopf, 2012), 491.

31  *ECCR*, 6:233–34; it also appears in *PREC*, 3:114–15.

32  Will of John Sanders, 1694, in Sarah Saunders Smith, *The Founders of the Massachusetts Bay Colony* (Pittsfield, MA: Press of the Sun, 1897), 61.

33  Estate of Benjamin Gibbs, Jan. 4, 1678, *MBCA*, 1:384.

34  Benjamin Gibbs Sale to Joshua Scottow, 1679, in *Suffolk Deeds*, ed. William Blake Trask et al., 14 vols. (Boston: Rockwell and Churchill, 1880–1906),

11:192–93. Scottow owned land in the center of town, at the foot of what is now Beacon Hill. It's unclear whether this land came from Gibbs, though there is some evidence that it did. "Joshua Scottow's Four-Acre Pasture," *Fifth Report of the Record Commissioners* [of the City of Boston], 2d ed. (Boston: Rockwell and Churchill, 1884), 65.

35 Joshua Scottow, *Old Mens Tears for Their Own Declensions* (Boston, 1691).

36 "An Inventory of the goods & Estate of Mr. Robert Cutt of Kittery," July 4, 1676, *Province and Court Records of Maine*, vol. 2, ed. Charles Thornton Libby (Portland: Maine Historical Society, 1931), 292.

37 That assessed values could fluctuate shows that New England heirs were able to assess relative value of human chattel. Consumers could be similarly savvy. Job Lane, a carpenter who lived in Malden in Middlesex County, bought from Boston's John Leverett, soon to become governor of Massachusetts Bay Colony, a "negro boy called mercury" for the sum of "thirty pounds of Currant monney of new Engld"—was it irony that he was named for the god of commerce? "Sale of Slave Mercury," 1667, *NEHGR*, 13:204. That was a large sum to spend on a slave, but a carpenter might have wanted a lifetime assistant. The sale by Samuel Phillips, a Boston bookseller, of a "negro boy" named Manual, for "Thirty Seaven pounds current silver money of New England," offers another example of a highly priced slave. Manual's name suggests non-English origins: was he linguistically skilled? Was he trained in some special way? "Slave sale," *Nathan Glover Papers*, Mss. 319, box 3, folder 3, NEHGS.

38 "The Will of George Clark," 1678, *Digest of the Early Connecticut Probate Records*, ed. Charles William Manwaring (Hartford, CT: R. S. Peck & Co., 1904), 2:42.

39 Deut. 21:16–17.

40 Ishmael in the Bible was the son of Abraham with Hagar, the slave/servant of Sarah, Abraham's wife. Gen. 16:1–16. Clarke, and most Puritans, would have known this story very well. Did Clarke's active interest in the boy, and the suggestive name, imply that Clarke had a role in his paternity? Such a relationship was common elsewhere in the history of slavery, of course.

41 "The Will of George Clark," Addendum 1688, *Digest of the Early Connecticut Probate Records*, 2:42.

42 "Estate of Samuel Moody of Newbury. March 22, 1675," *PREC*, 3:5–8. A more troubling case that may hint at the value of enslaved labor occurred in 1676, when Basto, "Negro slave to Robert Cox of Boston," was indicted on charges that he, "being Instigated by the Divill upon the 14th of Aprill last or thereabouts did Comitt a Rape upon the body of martha Cox daughter to his said master being a child about three yeares old." Basto pleaded not guilty, but evidence was found sufficient to convict him. For the crime of raping the child, he "had the sentenc of Death pronounced against him," in the form of hanging. Indictment of Basto, *MBCA*, 1:74. Amazingly, the child's father, Robert Cox, apparently appealed the decision, and in October 1676, the General Court acquiesced to his appeal, ruling that in lieu of death, "the said Bastian be severely whipt with thirty nine stripes, and allwayes to weare a roape

about his neck, to hang doune two Foot, that it may be seene, whilst he is in this jurisdiction, and when ever he is found without his roape, on complaint thereof, to be severely whipt with twenty stripes." That accomplished, and prison charges paid, Basto could be released. Basto kept his life; Robert Cox kept his property; Martha Cox, three-year-old rape victim, possibly saw her attacker every day. 5 Mass Recs. 116–17, Oct. 1676, cited in Helen Tunnicliff Catterall, ed., *Judicial Cases concerning American Slavery and the Negro,* vol. 4 (Washington, DC: Carnegie Institution of Washington, 1936), 473. The conviction and punishment suggest that the court believed that Basto had truly committed the crime. So, then, what can we make of Robert Cox, who asked for leniency for his slave who had raped his daughter? Did the additional financial loss of a slave make him request mercy for his child's rapist?

43 "Estate of Daniel Peirce," 1678, *PREC,* 3:210–11.

44 "Estate of John Knight of Newbury," 1678, *PREC,* 3:199–200.

45 "Will of Atherton Haugh, 1649," *Middlesex County Probate File Papers,* Case # 10755, NEHGS. It seems possible that these two people went on to parent two sons at least. The records state that "Francis and Mary Franseco" had a son named Jonathan in 1665, and that "Francis and Mary (Negroes)" has another named Samuel in 1668. *A Report of the Record Commissioners Containing Boston Births, Baptisms, Marriages and Deaths, 1630–1699* (Boston: Rockwell and Churchill, 1883), 96, 107.

46 Will of Antipas Boyse, 1669, *NEHGR,* 19:308–9.

47 "Will of John Winslow, 1674," *American Monthly Magazine, January to July, 1894,* vol. 4, ed. Ellen Hardin Walworth (Washington, DC: National Society, 1894), 43–45.

48 "Will of Peter George, 1694," John Osborne Austin, *The Genealogical Dictionary of Rhode Island* (Baltimore: Genealogical Publishing Co., 1978), 83.

49 Will of Richard Smith, 1691, *Genealogical Dictionary of Rhode Island,* 185. Ebed-Melech was a name of "the Ethiopian, one of the eunuchs," in Jer. 38:7–13, an allusion probably not lost on New England owners.

50 "Will of Elizeas Barron," *Massachusetts Probate Records,* Case 1291, NEHGS; "Will of Hannah Barron," ibid., Case 1292, NEHGS.

51 *ECCR,* 6:225. By the time White died, one year later, his probate inventory listed "1 Negrow, 30li" as a part of his estate. The pricing indicates the "negro" was an adult, owned for life. "Estate of Paul White of Newbury," Aug. 27, 1679, *Probate Records of Essex County,* 3:329–30. For a comprehensive overview of taxation in Colonial New England, see Alvin Rabushka, *Taxation in Colonial America* (Princeton, NJ: Princeton Univ. Press, 2008), esp. 144–98.

52 Taxation Act, 1695, *RICR,* 3:308.

53 Daniel Defoe, *The Political History of the Devil* (London, 1726), 269.

54 Jeanne Boydston has argued that "a thing can also, formally speaking, have a value without having a price; or, to put it another way, a labor form can also have a value without having a wage." Boydston, *Home and Work: Housework, Wages, and the Ideology of Labor in the Early Republic* (New York: Oxford Univ. Press, 1990), xviii.

55 "An Inventory of the goods & Estate of Andrew Sheppard," June 1676, *CSMP,*

30:731–33. Possession is a tricky thing; though technically and legally the property of the man of the house, the enslaved woman was also understood to owe service to Mrs. Sheppard to the point that she was thought of as "Mrs. Sheppard's Negro." In other words, though a servant's race and form of servitude (waged, indentured, or enslaved) did not dictate her or his labor, her or his gender might.

56 "Henchman v. Rock," 1672, *CSMP*, 29:195–98.

57 Kenneth Silverman, *Life and Times of Cotton Mather* (New York: Harper and Row, 1984), 20.

58 *ECCR*, 7:367–69.

59 Ibid., 366–75.

60 *Truelove* incident, Sept. 3, 1672, *MBCA*, 3:224.

61 Linebaugh and Rediker, *Many-Headed Hydra*, 163–73; W. Jeffrey Bolster, *Black Jacks: African American Seamen in the Age of Sail* (Cambridge, MA: Harvard Univ. Press, 1997), 3–5, and passim. A fascinating article that places enslaved people comfortably in aquatic environments is Kevin Dawson, "Enslaved Swimmers and Divers in the Atlantic World," *JAH* 92, no. 4 (2006): 1327–55.

62 *ECCR*, 8:297–98.

64 Ibid., 298.

65 On Keayne, see Bernard Bailyn, "The Apologia of Robert Keayne," *WMQ* 7, no. 4 (1950): 568–87. For more on Angola and his family, see Melinda Lutz Sanborn, "Angola and Elizabeth: An African Family in the Massachusetts Bay Colony," *NEQ* 72, no. 1 (1999): 119–29.

66 Will of Robert Keayne, *A Report of the Records Commissioners of the City of Boston, Containing Miscellaneous Papers* (Boston: Rockwell and Churchill, 1886), 25. Other "negro" Zipporahs appear in New England records. In 1726, one was warned out from Dorchester; the warning states, "May 16, Francis Negro and Ziporah his wife, house of Benjamin Everenden." "Dorchester, Mass., Warnings From the Town, from Original Papers," *NEHGR*, 50:68. Deriving meaning from names like Angola is very tricky; shiploads of Africans ostensibly from Angola might have been mixed with slaves from other African regions, and slaves identified as "Angolan" in the Caribbean may actually have come from another region entirely. Indeed, it is unclear whether an African from the region Europeans understood to be "Angola" would have labeled the area with the same term. Paradoxically, the name Angola may be an indicator that the man had not come from that area: thanks to early Portuguese contact, the Angolan coast had, after all, become largely Christian in the fifteenth century, and thus Africans in that region "used baptismal and saint's names, usually in a Portuguese form, from a period that antedated the transatlantic slave trade." Jerome S. Handler and JoAnn Jacoby, "Slave Names and Naming in Barbados, 1650–1830," *WMQ* 53, no. 4 (1996): 706. The name does connote a connection, perceived or real, with the continent of Africa, and would have served to demark Angola as different from English colonists, none of whom bore such a name. In contrast, Zipora (Zipporah) *was* a biblical name, belonging to the wife of Moses. That Moses famously led his

people out of slavery seems ironic, but it would be dangerous to assume that such allusions were lost on the Puritans.

67 The similarity of Kane and Keayne might hint at a prior connection—among the possibilities is that Kane had himself once been owned by the Keayne family, but sheer coincidence is also likely.

68 *Suffolk Deeds*, 2:297. Sanborn touches briefly on this deal, in "Angola and Elizabeth," 123.

69 Francis Vernon Note, *Suffolk Deeds*, 4:111.

70 Sebastian Kyne Sale, *Suffolk Deeds*, 4:113. A 1677 Dorchester church record lists a "Birst. Cane a free Negro" living where "Father Woods lived," having parted ways with Angola. *Records of the First Church at Dorchester, in New England, 1636–1734* (Boston: G. H. Ellis, 1891), 17.

71 "Depositions of James Pennyman, John Clough, Junior, and Meneno, Negro, Relative to [Angola]," *Fifth Report of the Record Commissioners*, 23–24

72 "Meneno Negro" Deposition, *Suffolk Deeds*, 8:298–99.

73 Angola did get a home. Three years before he died, his house was broken into by local Indians, known by name to authorities: "Francke Simon and John all Indians" were "convicted for breaking into Angola Negro's house which they confest." Though they do not appear to have stolen anything, they were found guilty of breaking and entering, and the court "sentanced them to bee whipt with twenty Stripes apeice paying fees of Court and prison Standing committed till the Sentance bee performed." That three Indians made trouble for "Angola Negro" is worth noting; to Indians, his may have been one more colonial house, part of a process of displacement and encroachment. "Indians Sentanced," 1672, *Records of the Suffolk County Court, CSMP*, 29:119.

74 Edmund Morgan called the relationship between freedom and slavery the "central paradox" of American history, and argued that the two were deeply connected. Morgan, *American Slavery, American Freedom,* 4. Eric Foner writes, "Whether Morgan's ingenious argument applies equally well to the northern colonies, where slavery was far less imposing a presence, may well be questioned." Foner, "The Meaning of Freedom in the Age of Emancipation," *JAH* 81, no. 2 (1994): 441.

75 Church Membership Records, 1641, and Vote on Dorcas, 1650, *Records of the First Church at Dorchester*, 5, 7; *JJW*, iii, 347.

76 Cotton Mather, *The Negro Christianized* (Boston, 1706), 26. In July 1652, "Matthew a negro sonne to Dorcas a Negro a sister of the Church of Dorchester" was admitted to church membership, perhaps still a slave. *The Records of the First Church in Boston, 1630–1868*, ed. Richard D. Pierce, 3 vols. (Boston: The Society, 1961), 1:323. "First Church" Records, *Report of the Record Commissioners Containing Boston Births, Baptisms, Marriages, and Deaths*, 39. For scholarship on slave baptism, see Rebecca Anne Goetz, *The Baptism of Early Virginia: How Christianity Created Race* (Baltimore: Johns Hopkins Univ. Press, 2012), 86–111; and Travis Glasson, "'Baptism Doth Not Bestow Freedom': Missionary Anglicanism, Slavery, and the Yorke-Talbot Opinion, 1701–1730," *WMQ* 67, no. 2 (2010): 279–318.

77 Nathaniel Hawthorne, "Alice Doane's Appeal," in *Tales and Sketches* (New

York: Literary Classics of the United States, 1982), 216; Perry Miller, *The New England Mind: From Colony to Province* (Cambridge, MA: Harvard Univ. Press, 1953), 476.

78 *Records of the First Church in Boston*, 1:74. This happened sporadically throughout the century. The same church in 1698/9 admitted "Jane Waters a negro" (p. 98). One presumes that, in the interim four decades, other people of African descent were also admitted, and that church membership had an immense impact on their individual lives. Such cases of course existed in southern colonies as well.

79 Anon., *New Englands First Fruits* (London, 1643), 5.

80 See, e.g., Breen and Innes, *"Myne Owne Ground,"* for a discussion of the contemporaneous possibilities of freedom in a southern colony. There were other New England marriages, too. In 1687 the First Church of Charleston saw the marriage of "Dan Smiths Negro Mingo" and "Mr. Soley Negro." *Records of the First Church in Charlestown, Massachusetts, 1632–1789*, ed. J. F. Hunnewell (Boston: D. Clapp and Son, 1880), 93.

81 Perry Miller, *Orthodoxy in Massachusetts, 1630–1650* (Cambridge, MA: Harvard Univ. Press, 1933), 292.

82 *JJW*, 586–88.

83 Winthrop was telling New England men to be women, and he assured them that this would not make them slaves. Winthrop's assurances against "bondage" aside, he was already asking New England men to endure too much indignity. Linda K. Kerber concludes, "Men understood the role Winthrop asked for as effeminate—the word also had pejorative connotations then—and refused to play it." Kerber, "Can a Woman Be an Individual? The Discourse of Self-Reliance," in *Toward an Intellectual History of Women: Essays* (Chapel Hill: Univ. of North Carolina Press, 1997), 203.

84 "Will of William Stitson," *Middlesex County Probate File Papers, 1648–1871*, Case # 21376, NEHGS.

85 MAC, 16:509.

86 On the hiring of slaves throughout the Americas, see Keith C. Barton, "'Good Cooks and Washers': Slave Hiring, Domestic Labor, and the Market in Bourbon County, Kentucky," *JAH* 84, no. 2 (1997): 436–60; Laird W. Bergad, *Slavery and the Demographic and Economic History of Minas Gerais, Brazil, 1720–1888* (New York: Cambridge Univ. Press, 1999), esp. 198–205; Clement Eaton, "Slave-Hiring in the Upper South: A Step Towards Freedom," *Mississippi Valley Historical Review* 46, no. 4 (1960): 663–78; Harlan Greene and Harry S. Hutchins Jr., with Brian E. Hutchins, *Slave Badges and the Slave-Hire System in Charleston, South Carolina, 1783–1865* (Jefferson, NC: McFarland, 2004); Sarah S. Hughes, "Slaves for Hire: The Allocation of Black Labor in Elizabeth City County, Virginia, 1782 to 1810," *WMQ* 35, no. 2 (1978): 260–86; and Jonathan D. Martin, *Divided Mastery: Slave Hiring in the American South* (Cambridge, MA: Harvard Univ. Press, 2004). On the distinction between renting indentured and free people in seventeenth-century Virginia, see John Ruston Pagan, *Anne Orthwood's Bastard: Sex and Law in Early Virginia* (New York: Oxford Univ. Press, 2003), 21–25.

87 Rif Winfield, *British Warships in the Age of Sail, 1603–1714: Design, Construction, Careers and Fates* (Barnsley, UK: Seaforth Publishing, 2009), 177. The *Sorlings* frigate sailed to New England in 1694.

88 MAC, 40:309.

89 Ibid., 309–10.

90 On the rise of Gullah, see Wood, *Black Majority*, 167–91.

91 *ECCR*, 5:141. There is a typo in the source here—1772, not 1672.

92 Ibid., 7:381–82.

93 Ibid., 3:54–55.

94 Ibid., 6:253–57.

95 Ibid.

96 In 1653, e.g., "A neager maide servant of John Barnes" had accused John Smith Sr., of Plymouth, "for receiveing tobacco and other things of her which were her said masters, att sundry times, in a purloineing way." Despite her confession, both the "neager maide servant" and Smith were released "for want of clearer evidence" with no more punishment than "admonission." *PCR*, 3:27, 39.

97 Orlando Patterson, *Slavery and Social Death: A Comparative Study* (Cambridge, MA: Harvard Univ. Press, 1982), 11; Walter Johnson, *Soul by Soul: Life inside the Antebellum Slave Market* (Cambridge, MA: Harvard Univ. Press, 1999), 78–79.

98 Bernard Bailyn, *The New England Merchants in the Seventeenth Century* (Cambridge, MA: Harvard Univ. Press, 1955), 192.

99 MAC, 36:446.

100 "Shrimpton's Plea," April 22, 1686, in Worthington Chauncey Ford, *The Case of Samuel Shrimpton* (Cambridge, MA: John Wilson and Son, 1905), 13.

101 For a discussion of the power of insults in early New England, and the ways they could be "unsaid," see Jane Kamensky, *Governing the Tongue: The Politics of Speech in Early New England* (New York: Oxford Univ. Press, 1997), 127–35.

102 Thomas Hobbes, *Leviathan* (London, 1651 "Head Edition"), 41–47. Orlando Patterson argues that an enslaved person "could have no honor because he had no power and no independent social existence, hence no public worth. He had no name of his own to defend. He could only defend his master's worth and his master's name." Patterson, *Slavery and Social Death*, 10–11. That seems an overstatement, but it is true that slaves were called upon to *perform* abjection and fealty.

103 For a fascinating discussion of the linkages between houses and bodies in colonial New England, and the targeting of houses as a proxy victim, see Robert Blair St. George, *Conversing by Signs: Poetics of Implication in Colonial New England Culture* (Chapel Hill: Univ. of North Carolina Press, 1998), 205–95, esp. 283–95. Samuel Shrimpton's son later owned slaves himself. He died in 1703 owning thirteen slaves. Peter Benes, "Slavery in Boston Households, 1647–1770," in *Slavery/Antislavery in New England* (Boston: Boston Univ., 2003), 15.

104 MAC, 36:443b, 444, 444a, 445.

105 Ibid., 446.

106 Of Shrimpton, Bernard Bailyn noted, "His assessed wealth in trade was 1.7 per cent of the total assessed mercantile property in Boston: his estimated real estate holdings in that town alone totaled .6 per cent of the entire value of the principality's land and buildings. And he owned property in Chelsea, Dorchester, and Brookline as well. He was the proprietor of Beacon Hill and both Noddles and Deer Island in Boston Bay. His trading operations extended into the logwood trade, the importation of manufactures, and the Newfoundland-to-Europe fish commerce." Bailyn, *New England Merchants*, 192.

107 "September 3, 1686," *SD*, 1:121.

108 Perry Miller, *Errand into the Wilderness* (Cambridge, MA: Belknap Press of Harvard Univ. Press, 1956), 190.

### Chapter 5: Intimate Slavery

1 Deposition of Hagar Blackmor/John Manning's Bond, 1669, April 15, Photostat Collection, MHS.

2 Ibid.

3 Ironically, though, three years later, an Irishman named Robert Collins used the law against forceful captivity to invalidate his contract of indenture, convincing the Suffolk County court that he had been kidnapped. See Edmund S. Morgan, *The Puritan Family: Religion and Domestic Relations in Seventeenth-Century New England* (New York: Harper and Row, 1966), 111.

4 His daughter was Mary Phipps, from whose house an enslaved African man escaped for a tryst with a servant. Manuscript files of Middlesex, MA, County Court, folder 99, group 3, cited in Morgan, *Puritan Family*, 129. Members of the Hannah Winthrop Chapter, National Society, Daughters of the American Revolution, *A Historic Guide to Cambridge*, 2d ed. (Cambridge, MA, 1907), 161.

5 Isa., 49:15. Hagar's name, taken from Gen. 16, seems oddly appropriate. Hagar was the "handmaid" of Abraham's wife Sarah, and when Sarah could not conceive, she prevailed upon her husband to impregnate Hagar instead. He did so, and she birthed Ishmael. Sarah later gave birth to Isaac, and Hagar and her son were sent away. The curious similarities between this biblical story of an impregnated handmaid and that of Hagar, the pregnant slave, in New England might not have been lost on any of the Puritan colonists who heard of it.

6 William Thaddeus Harris, "Notes on the Danforth Family," *NEHGR*, 7, no. 4 (1853): 317–21.

7 "Oct 5, 1669" Middlesex County, MA: Abstracts of Court Files, 1649–1675, (unpublished abstracts by Thomas Bellows Wyman, "Abstract of Middlesex court files from 1649," n.d.): 93–94, NEHGS. See also "Depositions of Anna Angier, Barbara Corlet, Elizabeth Bridges, and Anna Stedman," Middlesex Folio Collection, 49-viii, Mass. Arch., cited as such in Catherine Adams and Elizabeth H. Pleck, *Love of Freedom: Black Women in Colonial and Revolutionary New England* (New York: Oxford Univ. Press, 2010), 198. On this case, see also Michelle Jarrett Morris, *Under Household Government: Sex and Family in*

*Puritan Massachusetts* (Cambridge, MA: Harvard Univ. Press, 2012), 14–18. It may be that Hagar's accusations of John Manning made her an awkward slave to own; she does not appear in her owner's probate record some years later. Probate Record of John Manning, *Middlesex County Probate File Papers*, Case # 14585, NEHGS.

8   There were, of course, exceptions to the pattern of smallholdings. Remember the 1674 will of Robert Cutt, a Portsmouth (then in the Massachusetts Bay Colony) merchant with ties to the West Indies, which named eight slaves, though their combined value was only £111. James Savage, *A Genealogical Dictionary of the First Settlers of New England*, 4 vols. (Boston: Little, Brown, 1860–62), 1:495. On the more integrated nature of slavery in New England, see John Wood Sweet, *Bodies Politic: Negotiating Race in the American North, 1730–1830* (Baltimore: Johns Hopkins Univ. Press, 2003), 61–63; and Ira Berlin, *Many Thousands Gone: The First Two Centuries of Slavery in North America* (Cambridge, MA: Belknap Press of Harvard Univ. Press, 1998), 56–61. An older example of transitive reasoning that integration into a house-hold meant integration into a family is exemplified by William D. Piersen's point that slavery in New England was characterized by "a relatively mild form of servitude and a kind of household kinship." Piersen, *Black Yankees: The Development of an Afro-American Subculture in Eighteenth-Century New England* (Amherst: Univ. of Massachusetts Press, 1988), 146.

9   James Spaniard, according to Mayhew, was purchased by a "Gentleman in *Chilmark*, with whom he lived many Years, and was kindly used." After that man's death, Spaniard "purchased his Freedom from his Mistress" and, once free, married and had a son. Experience Mayhew, *Indian Converts; or, Some Account of the Lives and Dying Speeches of a Considerable Number of the Chris-tianized Indians of Martha's Vineyard* (London, 1727), 120–22. Alan Gallay has noted that Indians from Florida could be called "Spanish Indians," in *The Indian Slave Trade: The Rise of the English Empire in the American South, 1670–1717* (New Haven, CT: Yale Univ. Press, 2002), 304.

10  Scholarship on the "slave family" includes John W. Blassingame, *The Slave Community: Plantation Life in the Antebellum South* (New York: Oxford Univ. Press 1972), 149–91; Jacqueline Jones, *Labor of Love, Labor of Sorrow: Black Women, Work, and the Family from Slavery to the Present* (New York: Basic Books, 1985), esp. 3–43. On the reproductive labor asked of female slaves, see Jennifer L. Morgan, *Laboring Women: Reproduction and Gender in New World Slavery* (Philadelphia: Univ. of Pennsylvania Press, 2004); and Barbara Bush-Slimani, "Hard Labour: Women, Childbirth and Resistance in British Caribbean Slave Societies," *History Workshop* 36, no. 1 (1993): 83–99. James Sweet has recently complicated the notion of family, arguing that "the stabil-ity of African family or kinship, particularly in war-torn areas where slaving was frequent and sustained, should not be exaggerated. In these regions violence and unrest constantly threatened the survival of communal net-works." Sweet argues that given the slave trade–related violence enacted on African soil, individuals may have already developed strategies for building

new communities out of sundered individuals. He argues they "arrived with flexible and expansive notions of the social bonding patterns we call 'family.'" Sweet, "Defying Social Death: The Multiple Configurations of African Slave Family in the Atlantic World," *WMQ* 70, no. 2 (2013): 253–58. Some scholars of Native American history have made similar arguments against an essentialized notion of family and/or kinship. "Kinship is best thought of as a verb rather than a noun, because kinship, in most indigenous contexts, is something that's *done* more than something that simply *is*," and "kinship is adaptive" in native traditions, argues Daniel Heath Justice, though he also sees certainly continuous principles at work. Justice, "'Go Away Water!': Kinship Criticism and the Decolonization Imperative," in *Reasoning Together: The Native Critics Collective*, ed. Craig S. Womack, Daniel Heath Justice, and Christopher B. Teuton (Norman: Univ. of Oklahoma Press, 2008), 150, 159. See also Mark Rifkin, who sees a scholarly insistence on understanding certain norms of family as universal as one more manifestation of colonization; the insistence on heternormativity and certain forms of kinship as natural, he argues, "is a key part of the grammar of the settler state." Rifkin, *When Did Indians Become Straight? Kinship, the History of Sexuality, and Native Sovereignty* (New York: Oxford Univ. Press, 2011), 37.

11  "Negro womens children to serve according to the condition of the mother," Dec. 1662, in William Waller Hening, ed., *The Statutes at Large; Being a Collection of All the Laws of Virginia, from the First Session of the Legislature*, vol. 2 (Richmond, VA, 1810), 170, cited in Kathleen M. Brown, *Good Wives, Nasty Wenches, and Anxious Patriarchs: Gender, Race, and Power in Colonial Virginia* (Chapel Hill: Univ. of North Carolina Press, 1996), 132.

12  For foundational work that emphasizes this view of the New England Family, see John Demos, *A Little Commonwealth: Family Life in Plymouth Colony* (New York: Oxford Univ. Press, 1970); Philip Greven, *Four Generations: Population, Land, and Family in Colonial Andover, Massachusetts* (Ithaca, NY: Cornell Univ. Press, 1970); Morgan, *Puritan Family*; Norton, *Founding Mothers and Fathers*; and Laurel Thatcher Ulrich, *Good Wives: Image and Reality in the Lives of Women in Northern New England, 1650–1750* (New York: Alfred A. Knopf, 1982). More recent work that focuses more on non-English subjects includes Ann Marie Plane, *Colonial Intimacies: Indian Marriage in Early New England* (Ithaca, NY: Cornell Univ. Press, 2000); and Morris, *Under Household Government*.

13  William Gouge, *Of Domesticall Duties* (London, 1622).

14  On the importance of family and marriage in particular, see Norton, *Founding Mothers and Fathers*, 17, 56, 357.

15  Morgan, *Puritan Family*, 19.

16  William Bradford, *Of Plymouth Plantation* (New York: Modern Library, 1981), 133–34.

17  Sweet, "Defying Social Death," 261. On the distinction between free English and enslaved families, we might consider Lawrence Stone's provocative argument about the rise of affective families in the eighteenth century; it is

useful to consider that the idea of an affective family unit was racialized, and the chronology he posited did not hold for enslaved people. Stone, *The Family, Sex, and Marriage in England, 1500–1800* (New York: Harper and Row, 1977).

18  This is particularly true of the *colonial* slave family, which could be so fractured and separated owing to the very instability of the imperial system. Scholars have described other situations in slightly different, slightly more stable ways. See Blassingame, *Slave Community*, 149–91; Jones, *Labor of Love*, 11–43. Kirsten Fischer has a fascinating relevant discussion of female servants in colonial North Carolina in her *Suspect Relations: Sex, Race, and Resistance in Colonial North Carolina* (Ithaca, NY: Cornell Univ. Press, 2002), 101–22.

19  Walter Johnson has argued that this "chattel principle," the idea that slaves could be sold at their owner's will, eventually superseded physical coercion as the most effective method of controlling enslaved bodies, a "more displaced, systemic sort of violence that was registered in the (forcible) redistribution of those bodies over space." Johnson, "Introduction: The Future Store," in *The Chattel Principle: Internal Slave Trade in the Americas*, ed. Walter Johnson (New Haven, CT: Yale Univ. Press, 2004), 9. What he dates as beginning in the nineteenth century, I would argue, was a constitutive part of the chattel experience from the beginning of the Atlantic trade.

20  *ECCR*, 4:322.

21  "Keene contra Blighe," Oct. 29, 1672, *Records of the Suffolk County Court*, *CSMP*, 29:159.

22  For a similar observation on how the slave market created families in colonial Peru, see Rachel Sarah O'Toole, *Bound Lives: Africans, Indians, and the Making of Race in Colonial Peru* (Pittsburgh: Univ. of Pittsburgh Press, 2012), 35–63.

23  "The form of an Indenture for an Apprentice," Boston, 1692, quoted in Morgan, *Puritan Family*, 120–21. See also Norton, *Founding Mothers and Fathers*, 13. Such stipulations existed throughout the colonies; Lorena Walsh and Lois Green Car observed that a "servant woman could not marry unless someone was willing to pay her master for the term she had left to serve," in "The Planter's Wife: The Experience of White Women in Seventeenth-Century Maryland," *WMQ* 34, no. 4 (1977): 548.

24  For examples of Africans ("blackmoores" and "negros") getting married, see Connecticut Church Records Abstracts, "Private Records, Hampshire, Mass. Pynchon. Hadley, 224," Connecticut State Library, Hartford; "Marriage of Clement," Boston Records, *NEHGR*, 19:31.

25  Greene, *The Negro in Colonial New England, 1620–1776* (New York: Columbia Univ. Press, 1942), 211. A comparative discussion of the utility of marriage for enslaved people in colonial Latin America is Alexander L. Wisnoski III, "'It Is Unjust for the Law of Marriage to Be Broken by the Law of Slavery': Married Slaves and Their Masters in Early Colonial Lima," *Slavery and Abolition* 35, no. 2 (2014): 234–52.

26  Hannah Negro Womans Reason of Appeall, Suffolk Files 1832.3, Feb. 26,

1680, *Records of the Suffolk County Court, CSMP*, 30:1155. "Daniell Stone His Answer," Suffolk Files 1832.7, 1680, ibid.; Jury Verdict, Suffolk Files 1832.4, March 2, 1680, ibid., 1157.

27  Daniel Vickers, *Farmers and Fishermen: Two Centuries of Work in Essex County, Massachusetts, 1630–1850* (Chapel Hill: Univ. of North Carolina Press, 1994), 58–59.

28  Brown, *Good Wives, Nasty Wenches*, 133; *ECCR*, 1:196.

29  *ECCR*, 1:287.

30  Ibid., 323.

31  Ibid., 68, 154, 172.

32  Ibid., 285, 380.

33  Ibid., 2:247.

34  Ibid., 3:99, 101.

35  Fornication case of Christopher Mason and Bess, *Records of the Suffolk County Court, CSMP*, 29:185, 232.

36  *ECCR*, 6:256.

37  Court cases involving enslaved people are numerous. In 1674, the Hampton quarterly court, called the colonist John Clarke to respond to allegations made by an enslaved women that he was the father of her child. Six months later, the court confirmed the woman's accusation: "Jno. Clarke was declared to be the reputed father of the bastard child of Bess, the negro of Robert Smart, according to law." *ECCR*, 5:409, and 6:23. In April two years later (1677), "Miriam Negro Servant to John Pynchon junior" was convicted after confessing to "committing Fornication and having a bastard Childe" from an interracial relationship: she accused "one Cornish an English man to bee the Father." The court sentenced her to be whipped with ten stripes, or to pay forty shillings in fine. Forty shillings was beyond the reach of most slaves, of course, so the fine probably accrued to her owner. Unless an owner was willing to pay, those found guilty went under the lash. *Records of the Suffolk Country Court, CSMP*, 30:809. In January 1679, "Robert Corbet and George a Negro Servants unto Stephen French of Waymouth" confessed to committing "Fornication with Marea a Negro theire fellow Servant." They were sentenced to be whipped twenty lashes and to pay a fine. In this case, Marea had relationships with a fellow slave and an English servant. The penalty was the same for the two men. Ibid., 991. In 1673, Hope, a "negro servant of Mr. William Coddingon," was whipped for fornication with a colonist. Jane Fletcher Fiske, *Rhode Island General Court of Trials, 1671–1704* (Boxford, MA: J. F. Fiske, 1998), 22. In 1685, Plymouth's Hannah Bony was convicted of fornication with John Mitchell, and "with Nimrod, negro, and haveing a bastard child by said Nimrod." Nimrod and Hannah were sentenced to be whipped, and Nimrod further had to pay "18 *pence* per weeke to said Bonny towards the maintainance of said child for a year, if it live soe long." (Apparently there was some doubt about the health of the child.) The court also prepared for any potential delinquency on the part of Nimrod: "if he, or his master in his behalfe, neglect to pay the same, the said negro to be putt out to service by the Deputy Governor soe long time, or from time to time, soe as to procure the same." There was no mention of a

punishment for John Mitchell. Perhaps the complexion of the child assured colonial authorities as to paternity. *PCR*, 6:177. A court held in New Haven in 1692 charged "Cush, a Negro Servant," with fornication with Mary Potter. She had already delivered a "male child of a Negro complexion" and confessed to her father that Cush was the father. The court ordered Cush to be whipped forty lashes and then returned to his owner, who also was held liable for child support. The entry makes no mention of a punishment for Mary Potter. RG 003, vol. 1, p. 3, New Haven County Court Records, Connecticut State Library. A Plymouth County man, "Jo a Negro Servant to William Holbrooke of Scituate," was sentenced to be publicly whipped ten stripes for fornication with Sarah Curtice of Scituate. That affirmation involved Sarah's confessing publicly in court that Jo was the father of her child, and receiving a choice of sentences: whipping or a fine. David Thomas Konig, ed., *Plymouth Court Records, 1686–1859*, vol. 1 (Wilmington, DE: M. Glazier, 1978), 226.

38 June 1688, RG 003, vol. 1, p. 3, New Haven County Court Records, Connecticut State Library.

39 Cornelia Hughes Dayton, *Women before the Bar: Gender, Law, and Society in Connecticut, 1639–1789* (Chapel Hill: Univ. of North Carolina Press, 1995), 185.

40 *ECCR*, 7:419–20.

41 For a comparative discussion on this topic, see Herman L. Bennett, *Colonial Blackness: A History of Afro-Mexico* (Bloomington: Indiana Univ. Press, 2009), esp. 137–60.

42 Maria was owned by Francis Brinley, and George was owned by Mrs. Sarah Davis. "At the Generall Court of Tryalls Held for the Collony at Newport, 1673," Fiske, *Rhode Island General Court of Trials*, 21. See also the indictment against "Hope a Negro woman (servant to Mr. William Coddington for committing the act of fornication with James Parr," ibid., 22.

43 *ECCR*, 7:141.

44 Ibid., 411.

45 Manuscript files of Middlesex, MA, County Court, folder 99, group 3, cited in Morgan, *Puritan Family*, 129.

46 Jasper and Joan Fornication Case, 1672/3, *Records of the Suffolk County Court*, CSMP, 29:233.

47 *ECCR*, 5:411; "Marea Negro Sentenced," 1677, *Records of the Suffolk County Court*, CSMP, 30:809.

48 Grace Fornication Case, 1677, *Records of the Suffolk County Court*, CSMP, 30:841

49 Kathalina Fornication Case, 1679/80, *Records of the Suffolk County Court*, CSMP, 30:1164. In cases when such children lived, fines could be considerably higher (five to ten pounds). See, e.g., the case of Hanna Davis, fined five pounds or whipped twenty stripes (Nov. 23, 1675). *Records of the Suffolk County Court*, CSMP, 30:643.

50 *ECCR*, 5:316, 411, and 6:73, 135, 137. Regarding a reluctance to whip during pregnancy, see Dayton, *Women before the Bar*, 175–76.

51 *ECCR*, 6:138, 205, and 7:94.

52 Joshua Coffin, *A Sketch of the History of Newbury, Newburyport, and West Newbury, from 1635–1845* (Boston: Samuel G. Drake, 1845), 336.

53 *Records of the Superior Court of Judicature*, April 15, 1693, and May 10, 1700, Mass. State Archives, cited in Morris, *Under Household Government*, 180–82.

54 "Anna Negro Indictment and Sentence," 1674, *MBCA*, 1:29–30.

55 Rebecca Lynde was the widow of Thomas Lynde, who left to her in his will "my negro Peter and my negro girl Nan." It's possible Nan was a version of the name Anna; it's also possible that the Lynde family owned three slaves at some point; it's also possible that Peter was the father of the dead infant. Thomas Lynde was an innkeeper in Charlestown, who had migrated in 1634 to New England. Probate Record of Thomas Lynde, 1671, p. 340, file # 14433, NEHGS, *Middlesex County, MA: Probate File Papers, 1648–1871* (online database), *AmericanAncestors.org*, accessed 2014 (from records supplied by the Massachusetts Supreme Judicial Court Archives).

56 Two scholars have written on this case. Both refer to Zipporah as a free black servant; I did not find evidence to corroborate this. The threat to sell her away to Barbados certainly hints either that she was enslaved at the time of her pregnancy or that the threat of slavery hung over her head. See Melinde Lutz Sanborn, "The Case of the Headless Baby: Did Interracial Sex in the Massachusetts Bay Colony Lead to Infanticide and the Earliest Habeas Corpus Petition in America?," *Hofstra Law Review* 38, no. 1 (2009): 256; and Morris, *Under Household Government*, 191–208. The original indictment is found at Suffolk Files 5:27, # 605 (reel # 3), Mass. Arch.

57 On "blackish," see "Mrs. Parker's Testimony, Oct. 5, 1663," Suffolk Files 5:31, # 606, Mass. Arch.

58 "Testimony of Elizabeth Mellows," Suffolk Files 5:28, # 605, Mass. Arch.

59 Suffolk Files 5:28, # 605, Mass. Arch.

60 Suffolk Files 5:31, # 605, Mass. Arch.

61 Suffolk Files 5:28, # 605, Mass. Arch.

62 This Mary may have been the enslaved woman freed by Atherton Haugh's will, "Will of Atherton Haugh, 1649," *Middlesex County Probate File Papers*, Case # 10755, NEHGS. Morris, *Under Household* Government, 193.

63 *The Records of the First Church in Boston, 1630–1868*, ed. Richard D. Pierce, 3 vols. (Boston: The Society, 1961), 1:59.

64 Testimony of Hannah French, 1689, Suffolk Files, reel # 11, vol. 19, p. 123, Mass. Arch. For additional discussions of this case, see Plane, *Colonial Intimacies*, 96–99; and Morris, *Under Household Government*, 178–91.

65 Testimony of Sarah Pratt, 1689, Suffolk Files, reel # 11, vol. 19, p. 124, Mass. Arch.

66 Testimony of Hannah French, 1689, Suffolk Files, reel # 11, vol. 19, p. 123, Mass. Arch.

67 Frederick William Gookin, *Daniel Gookin: 1612–1687; Assistant and Major General of the Massachusetts Bay Colony* (Chicago: privately printed, 1912), 70–72. For a detailed and extensive account of the Warro affair, see Morris, *Under Household Government*, 20–27. For a concise synthesis of this case, see

Diane Rappaport, "Tales from the Courthouse: The Sale of Silvanus Warro," *New England Ancestors* 7, no. 4 (2006): 53–54..

68 Karen Ordahl Kupperman, "Errand into the Indies: Puritan Colonization from Providence Island through the Western Design," *WMQ* 45, no. 1 (1988): 96; Gookin, *Daniel Gookin*, 87–91.

69 Gookin, *Daniel Gookin*, 67, 75–76, 106, 196.

70 Silvanus first appears in court records accused of stealing his master's horse. *Records of the Suffolk County Court, CSMP*, 29:113. On the contract, see Covenant, 1682, Middlesex County Manuscript Collection, fol. 106, Mass. Arch.

71 Instructions to the prison keeper regarding Silvanus Warro's imprisonment, March 2, 1672, Miscellaneous Bound Manuscripts, MHS.

72 "Warro Sentanced," 1672, *Suffolk County Court Records, CSMP*, 29:113.

73 Ibid.

74 Henry S. Nourse, ed., *The Early Records of Lancaster, Massachusetts, 1643–1725* (Lancaster, 1884), 92–96.

75 "Court order to Deacon Parcke," April 29, 1673, *Records of the Suffolk County Court, CSMP*, 29:259.

76 Gookin, *Daniel Gookin*, 196. For a concise synthesis of this case, see Rappaport, "Tales from the Courthouse," 53–54.

77 Account of William Park's expenses relating to Sylvanus Warro, Nov. 15, 1682, Miscellaneous Bound Manuscripts, MHS.

78 Gookin, *Daniel Gookin*, 196.

79 An Answer to Some Articles Presented to the Court by Major Gookin, Miscellanous Bound Manuscripts, MHS.

80 Warning out of Silvanus Warrow, 1707, *A Report of the Record Commissioners of the City of Boston, Containing Miscellaneous Papers*, vol. 10 (Boston: Rockwell and Churchill, 1886), 113.

81 *CCR*, 4:375–76.

82 Cotton Mather, *Magnalia Christi Americana; or, The Ecclesiastical History of New-England* (London, 1702), bk. 2, p. 28.

83 Simeon E. Baldwin, "Theophilus Eaton: First Governor of the Colony of New Haven," in *Papers of the New Haven Colony Historical Society*, vol. 7 (New Haven, CT: New Haven Colony Historical Society, 1908), 1–20. This article also addresses, in typical turn-of-the-century fashion, Eaton's slaveholding. "He was a slaveholder; becoming such not long after he settled in New Haven. He belonged to his century and shared its opinions. Slavery was then an institution regarded as lawful throughout the world. He read also in his bible that it had always been recognized as such among the Hebrews, and his very reverence for the Old Testament led him, as it led so many other good men throughout the South, in later days, to accept, without question, whatever he found there, seeming to indicate a rule of social right and duty" (p. 31).

84 Isabel MacBeath Calder, *The New Haven Colony* (New Haven, CT: Yale Univ. Press, 1934), 146, 165–67. William Bradford, of the Plymouth Colony, was also fluent in Dutch. Bernard Bailyn, *The Barbarous Years: The Peopling of British North America: The Conflict of Civilizations 1600–1675* (New York: Alfred A.

Knopf, 2012), 333. Francis Bremer's *Building a New Jerusalem: John Daven-port, a Puritan in Three Worlds* (New Haven: Yale Univ. Press, 2012) offers an in-depth look at the New Haven Colony's political and religious scene.

85  Thelma Wills Foote, *Black and White Manhattan: The History of Racial Formation in Colonial New York City* (New York: Oxford Univ. Press, 2004), 36–39.

86  Christopher Moore, "A World of Possibilities: Slavery and Freedom in Dutch New Amsterdam," in *Slavery in New York*, ed. Ira Berlin and Leslie M. Harris (New York: New Press, 2005), 43–47; Foote, *Black and White Manhattan*, 39–40.

87  A witness, Brother Bradley, also heard her say that "the beer was bewitched, and that Mrs. Eaton would not let the neagar look into the tub of beer, for fear he should bewitch it." Newman Smyth, "Mrs. Eaton's Trial (in 1644); As It Appears upon the Records of the First Church of New Haven," in *Papers of the New Haven Colony Historical Society*, vol. 5 (New Haven, CT: New Haven Historical Society, 1894), 142. See also Norton, *Founding Mothers and Fathers*, 165–80, for an extensive discussion of Anne Eaton's life.

88  "Moreover of the children of the strangers that do sojourn among you, of them shall ye buy, and of their families that *are* with you, which they begat in your land: and they shall be your possession. And ye shall take them as an inheritance for your children after you, to inherit *them for* a possession; they shall be your bondmen for ever: but over your brethren the children of Israel, ye shall not rule one over another with rigour." Lev. 25:45–46.

89  Petition of Hannah Jones, 1691, vol. 2, fol. 1a, Connecticut Archives Miscella-neous Manuscripts, 1635–1789, Connecticut State Library, Hartford.

90  Will and Probate Inventory of Theophilus Eaton, vols. 1 and 2, fols. 68–75 (microfilm no. 3, reel 2), New Haven Probate Records, New Haven Colony His-torical Society, New Haven, CT.

91  "At a Court Held at Newhaven the 3d of January, 1659," *Ancient Town Records: New Haven Town Records 1649–1662*, vol. 1, ed. Franklin Bowditch Dexter (New Haven, CT: New Haven Colony Historical Society, 1917), 426.

92  "Upon a Complaint made by Mr. William Jones to the deputy Governor November 7th 1661," *Ancient Town Records*, 1:495.

93  Ibid. and "At a Court Held at Newhaven the 3d of December 1661," *Ancient Town Records*, 1:494–96.

94  Deposition of John How, vol. 2, fol. 7, Connecticut Archives Miscellaneous Bound, 1635–1789, Connecticut State Library.

95  Petition to the General Court, 1692, 1B: 1690–1701, Town Land Records, New Haven Ledger Book, New Haven City Hall, New Haven, CT.

96  Alfred A. Cave, *The Pequot War* (Amherst: Univ. of Massachusetts Press, 1996), 158–63. Isabel M. Calder, an early historian of the New Haven Colony, noted that in the 1630s, "The Pequot War was opening up territory beyond the limits of the colony of the Massachusetts-Bay." Calder, "John Cotton and the New Haven Colony," *NEQ* 3, no. 1 (1930): 85–86.

97  Testimony of Thomas Trowbridge, 1691, vol. 2, fol. 8, Connecticut Archives Miscellaneous Manuscripts, 1635–1789.

## Chapter 6: The Law of the Land

1 *ECCR*, 2: 421–22. A similar description of a suicide by a slave comes in Erskine Clarke, *Dwelling Place: A Plantation Epic* (New Haven, CT: Yale Univ. Press, 2005), 326.

2 "Wait Winthrop to Fitz-John Winthrop, 1682," *WP*, 8:427.

3 "Self-murther," in *The Colonial Laws of Massachusetts: Reprinted from the Edition of 1672 with the Supplements through 1686*, ed. William H. Whitmore (Boston: Rockwell and Church, 1890), 137.

4 Michael A. Gomez has a sustained discussion of suicide among enslaved African peoples, writing that, "without question, captives from all over West and West Central Africa reacted to enslavement and dislocation by committing suicide." Gomez is careful to highlight that the evidence for these acts is far from conclusive, but does note that in later years, "the belief [became] very strong within the African-based community that at death one returned to the land of one's birth. Thus flying via suicide was a sure way, perhaps the only way, to get back, at which point one could be reincarnated and live in the land of family and relations, far away from the experience called America." Gomez, *Exchanging Our Country Marks: The Transformation of African Identities in the Colonial and Antebellum South* (Chapel Hill: Univ. of North Carolina Press, 1998), 119–20. Other studies of suicide include Terri L. Snyder, "Suicide, Slavery, and Memory in North America," *JAH* (2010): 39–62; and idem, "What Historians Talk about When They Talk about Suicide: The View from Early Modern British North America," *History Compass* 5, no. 2 (2007): 658–74. A discussion of slave suicide in the context of abolition is offered in Richard Bell, "Slave Suicide, Abolition and the Problem of Resistance," *Slavery and Abolition: A Journal of Slave and Post-Slave Societies* 33, no. 4 (2012): 525–49.

5 Phyllis Whitman Hunter, *Purchasing Identity in the Atlantic World: Massachusetts Merchants, 1670–1780* (Ithaca, NY: Cornell Univ. Press, 2001), 37–38.

6 George Wells Bartholomew Jr., *Record of the Bartholomew Family: Historical, Genealogical and Biographical* (Austin, TX, 1885), 30, 43, 49–52. This source, like much nineteenth-century genealogical work, is both informative and problematic. In it we also learn that Henry Bartholomew "was broad minded and liberal in a bigoted age and among a narrow-minded people" (48).

7 This wasn't the only case of a slave suicide in the region, of course. Some years later, Increase Mather penned a cryptic, short entry in his diary on Oct. 17, 1689: "2 Negroes killed themselves on a Sabbath day." It is unclear which was worse to Mather, the self-murder or the breaking of the Sabbath. *Diary by Increase Mather, March, 1675–December, 1676*, ed. Samuel A. Green (Cambridge, MA: John Wilson and Son, 1900), 51. One wonders also whether the "negroes" knew about the Sabbath's theological meaning and so intended the extra insult, or whether it was simply a day when they could count on less surveillance.

8 On suicide, Ira Berlin has neatly summarized the threat to slavery: "For while slaveowners held most of the good cards in this meanest of all contests, slaves held cards of their own. And even when their cards were reduced to

near worthlessness, slaves still held that last card, which, as their owners well understood, they might play at any time." *Many Thousands Gone: The First Two Centuries of Slavery in North America* (Cambridge, MA: Belknap Press of Harvard Univ. Press, 1998), 2.

9  Militia Regulations, *MCR*, 3:268, 397. In the preceding decade, colonists had been strictly enjoined from selling guns to Indians; this policy shifted only as more Indians became captive or allied to the English. For laws prohibiting the sale of guns and ammunition, see *MCR*, 2:16. For early examples of colonists' being reprimanded for selling arms to Indians, see "The Humble Petition of Richard Parker of Boston merchant [1640?]" and "The Petition of Roger Toll Servant to Mr. Henry Webb of Boston," *Note-book Kept by Thomas Lechford, ESQ, Lawyer, in Boston, Massachusetts Bay from June 27, 1638 to July 29, 1641* (Cambridge, MA: John Wilson and Son, 1885), 409, 412.

10  Essex County Quarterly Court Records, WPA Transcripts, vol. 49, fols. 57-1, 57-2, Peabody Essex Museum, Salem, cited in Owen Stanwood, *The Empire Reformed: English America in the Age of the Glorious Revolution* (Philadelphia: Univ. of Pennsylvania Press, 2011), 171. See also Joshua Coffin, *A Sketch of the History of Newbury, Newburyport, and West Newbury, from 1635 to 1845* (Boston: Samuel G. Drake, 1845), 153–54.

11  "Persons exempted from training," 1693–94, *The Acts and Resolves, Public and Private, of the Province of the Massachusetts Bay*, 21 vols. (Boston: Wright and Potter, 1869–1922), 1:130.

12  For a sustained discussion of the history of arming slaves, see David Brion Davis, "Introduction," Hendrik Kraay, "Arming Slaves in Brazil from the Seventeenth Century to the Nineteenth Century," and Christopher Leslie Brown, "The Arming of Slaves in Comparative Perspective," in *Arming Slaves: From Classical Times to the Modern Age*, ed. Philip D. Morgan and Christopher Leslie Brown (New Haven, CT: Yale Univ. Press, 2006), 1–13, 146–79, 330–53. Some enslaved Africans might have had experience with guns before arriving in the Americas; Dutch and, increasingly, English traders sold guns to African buyers throughout the seventeenth century. See, e.g., R. A. Kea, "Firearms and Warfare on the Gold and Slave Coasts from the Sixteenth to the Nineteenth Centuries," *Journal of African History* 12, no. 2 (1971): 185–213.

13  "Robert Trayes, negro, indited this Court," 1648, *PCR*, 6:141–42.

14  Indictment of Robin Negro, *MBCA*, 1:304–5, 321.

15  "Nicholas Negro Setenced," 1677/8, *Suffolk County Court Records, CSMP*, 30:884.

16  For a discussion of arson in early modern England, see Keith Thomas, *Religion and the Decline of Magic: Studies in Popular Beliefs in Sixteenth and Seventeenth Century England* (London: Weidenfeld & Nicolson, 1971), 531–34; and Bernard Capp, "Arson, Threats of Arson, and Incivility in Early Modern England," in *Civil Histories: Essays Presented to Sir Keith Thomas* (Oxford, UK: Oxford Univ. Press, 2000), 197–214, esp. 198.

17  *JJW*, 352.

18  Anne Bradstreet, "Verses upon the Burning of Our House, July 10th, 1666,"

in *The Complete Works of Anne Bradstreet*, ed. Joseph R. McElrath Jr. and Allan P. Robb (Boston: Twayne Publishers, 1981), 236–37.

19 John Underhill, *Newes from America; or, A New and Experimentall Discoverie of New England* (London, 1638), 39. Underhill had some questionable traits. Winthrop noted of him that he had been admonished for "incontinency with a neighbor's wife"; they had been found several times "in private prayer together" behind a locked door. *JJW*, 264.

20 William Bradford, *Of Plymouth Plantation* (New York: Modern Library, 1981), 331.

21 Cotton Mather, *Magnalia Christi Americana; or, The Ecclesiastical History of New-England* (London, 1702), bk. 7, pp. 49–50.

22 Mary Rowlandson, *The Soveraignty & Goodness of God, together, with the Faithfulness of His Promises Displayed; Being a Narrative of the Captivity and Restauration of Mrs. Mary Rowlandson* (Cambridge, MA, 1682), 2–3.

23 Jill Lepore, *The Name of War: King Philip's War and the Origins of American Identity* (New York: Alfred A. Knopf, 1998), 88.

24 "Now away we must go with those barbarous creatures," she later wrote, "with our bodies wounded and bleeding, and our hearts no less than our bodies." Soon after came "the dolefullest night that ever [her] eyes saw," filled with the "roaring, and singing, and dancing, and yelling of those *black creatures* in the night, which made the place a lively resemblance of hell." Rowlandson, *The Soveraignty & Goodness of God*, 5–6 (emphasis added). Mary Beth Norton, *In the Devil's Snare: The Salem Witchcraft Crisis of 1692* (New York: Vintage, 2003), 58–59, explains that "black" was often used to refer to Indians, and relates it to a fear of the devil. I find it more compelling to believe that the adjective also connoted Africa and Africans. Our interpretations are not mutually exclusive. Africa was, after all, believed populated by heathens (who perhaps worshipped the devil), and its native inhabitants, many of whom were non-Christian, carried therefore a "devilish" stigma that would resonate in witchcraft cases.

25 "Excerpt from John Hull's Journal," in George Madison Bodge, ed., *Soldiers in King Philip's War*, 3d ed. (Leominster, MA, 1906), 479–80.

26 "Two petitions," 1646, *PCR*, 1:69.

27 Arson Law, 1652, cited in Abner C. Goodell Jr., "The Murder of Captain Codman," *MHSP* 20 (1883): 149.

28 Wyllys Papers, vol. 1, item 10B, Connecticut Historical Society, Hartford, CT. See also "Mrs. Elinor Howell to the General Assembly," 1663, in *CCHS*, 21:138.

29 *Diary by Increase Mather*, 52.

30 *JJW*, 352.

31 Proverbs 16:18.

32 *JJW*, 352.

33 Ibid.

34 John Brayne, *The New Earth; or, The True Magna Charta of the Past Ages, and of the Ages or World to Come: Called The Jews Commonweal* (London, 1653), 73. Also cited in Thomas, *Religion and the Decline of Magic*, 637.

35 "Maria Negro Indictment," 1681, *MBCA*, 1:198, cited in "Att A Court of Assistants held at Boston 6th September 1681," *CSMP*, 6:324.

36 Excerpt from Increase Mather's diary, cited in *CSMP*, 6:330.

37 A Court of Assistants Held at Boston 6th September, 1681, *MBCA*, 1:198–99. One is reminded here of Michel Foucault's discussion of the "disappearance of torture as a public spectacle" at the end of the early modern period. Clearly, Maria's execution was spectacle, and intended to be instructive to witnesses, some of whom presumably were enslaved. Foucault, *Discipline and Punish: The Birth of the Prison*, trans. Alan Sheridan (New York: Pantheon Books, 1979), 7.

38 See, e.g., Susan Dwyer Amussen, *Caribbean Exchanges: Slavery and the Transformation of English Society, 1640–1700* (Chapel Hill: Univ. of North Carolina Press, 2007), 160–61, 168, 169, for examples of slaves burned to death after alleged revolts.

39 "Ye have heard that it hath been said, An eye for an eye, and a tooth for a tooth: But I say to you, That ye resist not evil: but whosoever shall smite thee on thy right cheek, turn to him the other also." Matt. 5:38–39.

40 For examples of the punishment being enacted in seventeenth-century England, see Charles Cox, *Three Centuries of Derbyshire Annals*, vol. 2 (London: Bemrose and Sons, 1890), 39.

41 Edward Coke, *The Third Part of the Institutes of the Laws of England: Concerning High Treason, and Other Pleas of the Crown. And Criminal Causes* (London, 1669), 19–20; William Blackstone, *Commentaries on the Laws of England*, vol. 4 (Oxford: Clarendon Press, 1769), 93. An early commentator on this trial argued that the sentence could not have fallen under the petit treason charge, since it "is not probable that the relation of master and servants subsisted between the deceased [child] and Maria" but then admits that, without this framework, "how the court were satisfied of the legality of their sentence is to me inexplicable." Abner Cheney Goodell, *The Trial and Execution, for Petit Treason, of Mark and Phillis, Slaves of Capt. John Codman, Who Murdered Their Masters at Charlestown, Mass, in 1755* (Cambridge, MA: John Wilson and Son, 1883), 31–35. I suggest that the framework of chattel slavery helps provide an answer.

42 Eugene D. Genovese has argued that enslaved "arsonists usually worked alone or at most in groups of two or three; [and] their action usually represented retaliation for some private offense or injustice." Genovese, *Roll, Jordan, Roll: The World Slaves Made* (New York: Pantheon Books, 1974), 615. Bernard Capp, a scholar of arson in early modern England, made a similar point in "Arson, Threats of Arson, and Incivility in Early Modern England," in *Civil Histories: Essays Presented to Sir Keith Thomas*, 200–201.

43 What theorists call "intersectionality," the way that different forms of oppression might combine to doubly, triply, or infinitely damn a person, might have applied here. On intersectionality, see Kimberlé Crenshaw's foundational article, "Mapping the Margins: Intersectionality, Identity Politics, and Violence against Women of Color," *Stanford Law Review* 53, no. 6 (1991): 1241–99.

44 For a discussion of the "wonders" inhabiting the world of seventeenth-century English people, see David D. Hall, *Worlds of Wonder, Days of Judgment: Popular Religious Belief in Early New England* (New York: Alfred A. Knopf, 1989), 71–116.

45 *CCR*, 4:40.

46 Cotton Mather, *Rules for the Society of Negroes* (1693) (Boston, 1714).

47 Camp usefully invokes Edward Said's notion of "rival geography." Stephanie H. Camp, *Closer to Freedom: Enslaved Woman and Everyday Resistance in the Plantation South* (Chapel Hill: Univ. of North Carolina Press, 2004), 7. On the history of night movement, see Peter C. Baldwin, *In the Watches of the Night: Life in the Nocturnal City, 1820–1930* (Chicago: Univ. of Chicago Press, 2012), 2–13.

48 Mary Rowlandson, *The Soveraignty & Goodness of God* (Cambridge, MA, 1682), 71.

49 William Wood, *New Englands Prospect* (London, 1634), 37. See also Edward Johnson, *Wonder Working Providence, 1628–1651*, ed. J. Franklin Jameson (New York: Charles Scribner's Sons, 1910), 71–72.

50 Maria's Confession, 1681, in John Noble, "The Case of Maria in the Court of Assistants, 1681," *CSMP*, 6:326–27. The name Cheffaleer is unique among the records. It could be a mashing of the French word *chevalier*, meaning at the time "knight." The use of noble monikers for slaves, a sort of constant mocking (Caesar, Pompey, King, Duke), was not unusual. But there is no evidence of the name's origin in this case; it simply stands as an example of the heterogeneous enslaved population.

51 Noble, "Case of Maria," 326–28. Sentence of Cheffaleer negro servant and James Pembertons Negro, *MBCA*, 1:197–98.

52 Susannah Walker's Testimony, ccxii. 26: 559: 1, Suffolk Court Files, cited in Noble, "Case of Maria," 328–29; *MBCA*, 1:198–99.

53 Cotton Mather, *Pillars of Salt: An History of Some Criminals Executed in this Land, for Capital Crimes* (Boston, 1699), 71.

54 *MBCA*, 2:139 (original manuscript), cited in Noble, "Case of Maria," 324.

55 MAC, 39:697. See also Suffolk Court Files, xxiv. 2020:1 (original manuscript), cited in Noble, "Case of Maria," 325.

56 Wolcot's Testimony, *Colonial Justice in Western Massachusetts, 1639–1702: The Pynchon Court Record*, ed. Joseph H. Smith (Cambridge, MA: Harvard Univ. Press, 1961), 298.

57 Ibid.

58 "30 March 1675 Military Deferment, Anthony Dorchester," *Various Ancestral Lines of James Goodwin and Lucy (Morgan) Goodwin of Hartford Connecticut* (Hartford, CT, 1915), 66; Accounts of Anthony Dorchester, 1652, ibid., 61.

59 Smith, ed., *Colonial Justice in Western Massachusetts*, 298.

60 One nineteenth-century history of Northampton calls Jack a "vicious character, a forerunner of the great army of tramps now everwhere wearying the patience of the public." This author does not mention Samuel Wolcott's one hundred blows, but does include fascinating oral history regarding this story—namely, that Jack had "fastened the door on the outside so that no one

could escape," that William Clarke and his wife were injured by breaking down the door, that their toddler grandson was removed with great difficulty, and that all this was done in revenge for a wrong Clarke had allegedly done to Jack. James Russell Trumbull, *History of Northampton, Massachusetts, from Its Settlement in 1654* (Northampton, MA,1898), 1: 376–77.

61 *MBCA*, 1:198–99.

62 Ibid., 2:118.

63 *ECCR*, 7:425.

64 "An Act for the Better Discovery and more Effectual Suppressing of Unlicensed Houses, 1695," MAC, 47:162. See also *Acts And Resolves, Public and Private*, 1:154.

65 Hunting dogs were in use in seventeenth-century New England among both English and Indians. See references to the practice in David Silverman, "'We Chuse to Be Bounded': Native American Animal Husbandry in Colonial New England," *WMQ* 60, no. 3 (2003): 517; and Robert Walcott, "Husbandry in Colonial New England," *NEQ* 9, no. 2 (1936): 229. Jon T. Coleman covers the subject more in *Vicious: Wolves and Men in America* (New Haven, CT: Yale Univ. Press, 2004), 37–38, 45, 56.

66 For a recent discussion of the hunting of slaves with dogs, see Walter Johnson, *River of Dark Dreams: Slavery and Empire in the Cotton Kingdom* (Cambridge, MA: Harvard Univ. Press, 2013), 236–38.

67 Special Court and Charges Against Cush, Sept. 21, 1698, RG 003, vol. 1, p. 265, New Haven County Court Records. Cush was the same man who appeared in the preceding chapter having fathered a child of "a negro complexion" in 1692 with Mary Potter, an English servant in New Haven. The court made no mention of his child in this case. Someone, presumably a Potter, was taking enough care of the child that Cush's paternity did not trouble the court.

68 "Examination of Negro Will," MAC.

69 William Chauncey Fowler, *The Historical Status of the Negro in Connecticut* (Charleston, SC: Cogswell, 1900), 49.

70 General Sessions and Common Please, Oct. 26, 1686, in David Thomas Konig, ed., *Plymouth Court Records, 1686–1859*, vol. 1 (Wilmington, DE: M. Glazier, 1978), 189.

71 A long historiographical tradition holds that African slaves generally lived in their owners' houses in New England. Lorenzo Greene, *The Negro in Colonial New England, 1620–1776* (New York: Columbia Univ. Press, 1942), 223, argues that slaves "apparently were well-housed and their quarters did not differ much from the accommodations afforded servants today" and that "where there were only a few number of slaves, they usually lived in the masters' house." Richard S. Dunn has also argued that "Massachusetts servants and slaves generally had their own quarters *inside* the master's house," Dunn, *Sugar and Slaves: The Rise of the Planter Class in the English West Indies, 1624–1713* (Chapel Hill: Univ. of North Carolina Press, 1972), 270 (emphasis added). I have not found sufficient evidence to support or refute this statement—sometimes slaves appear to live in the attic, sometimes in another

room. More often there is simply no reference to where they slept. Given that state of affairs, I wish to highlight instances like that above, wherein the slave appears to have slept outside the family's home.

72 John Wood Sweet, *Bodies Politic: Negotiating Race in the American North, 1730–1830* (Baltimore: Johns Hopkins Univ. Press, 2003), 75, finds great significance in what slaves stole, noting that "if theft was always an act of resistance, it could express resentment as well as envy, mockery as well as emulation."

73 MAC, 40:311.

74 On the racialization of bodily punishments in the American slave system, see Diana Paton, "Punishment, Crime, and the Bodies of Slaves in Eighteenth-Century Jamaica," *Journal of Social History* 34, no. 4 (2001): 923–54. She observes that "punishments involving the bodily mutilation of individuals not sentenced to death had fallen out of use in Europe prior to the eighteenth century" (p. 941). But there were still cases in which courts imposed branding on English colonists late in the seventeenth century in New England.

75 Abraham Negro, Oct. 6, 1698, RG 001, vol. 53, p. 86, Connecticut Colonial Records, 1659–1700, Connecticut State Library, Hartford, CT.

76 Court of Assistants held at Hartford, May 8, 1699, in Helen Scharvet Ullmann, ed., *Colony of Connecticut, Minutes of the Court of Assistants, 1669–1711* (Boston: NEHGS, 2009), 231.

77 John Wood Sweet has pointed out that one of the most troubling discoveries from archaeological digs in the recently discovered African Burial Ground in New York was that the bones of those slaves found there, ostensibly engaged in urban, domestic work, were "enlarged and damaged by routine, heavy work and there is evidence of more malnutrition, less cultural autonomy, and more surveillance than slaves experienced on contemporary plantations in the Chesapeake region." Sweet, *Bodies Politic*, 62. Did New England slaves have similar stories, and does this explain the pilfering of food?

78 *ECCR*, 8:144–45.

79 Servis Negro, Nov. 1692, RG 003, vol. 1, p. 204, New Haven County Court Records.

80 Richard Cobb, *The People and the Police: French Popular Protest, 1789–1820* (Oxford, UK: Clarendon Press, 1970), 55. See also Jean-François Bayart, *The State in Africa: The Politics of the Belly*, 2d ed. (Cambridge, UK: Polity Press, 2009), esp. lxxxiii–lxxxvi.

81 Carl Bridenbaugh, "The Great Mutation," *American Historical Review* 68, no. 2 (1963): 320.

82 The stealing of food to supplement meager rations has been well documented in slavery studies. Genovese, *Roll, Jordan, Roll*, 603–4, has an extended discussion of food theft in the nineteenth-century American South, though he is fairly dismissive of the idea that slaves were hungry, saying that "plantation plunder occurred too often to be attributed mostly to underfeeding, not only because the evidence refutes the charge of widespread underfeeding but also

because the blacks so often rested their case elsewhere." He argues that food theft stemmed from a resentment of "the lack of variety" offered to slaves. Whether his argument is persuasive for the southern states, I leave to others to decide; in the case of New England, grain and meal and biscuits seem hardly enticing enough to steal simply for their variety. Walter Johnson has more recently argued, in *River of Dark Dreams*, 213–15, 472n15, that southern slaves were in fact often starved and that stealing food was a matter of survival and solidarity. He takes a dim view of Genovese's arguments about the nonnecessity of stealing food, and about the "shame" slaves might have felt even as they stole food; Genovese notes (pp. 608–9) that those who stole food "had to have mixed feelings and to experience some degradation."

83 For an initial count of runaways, derived from court cases and newspapers advertisements in seventeenth- and eighteenth-century Massachusetts, see Lawrence W. Towner, "'A Fondness for Freedom': Servant Protest in Puritan Society," *WMQ* 19, no. 2 (1962): 214. For a discussion of eighteenth-century runaways, see Robert E. Desrochers Jr., "Slave-for-Sale Advertisements and Slavery in Massachusetts, 1704–1781," *WMQ* 59, no. 3 (2002): 623–64.

84 On runaway slave notices, see David Waldstreicher, "Reading the Runaways: Self-Fashioning, Print Culture, and Confidence in Slavery in the Eighteenth-Century Mid-Atlantic," *WMQ* 56, no. 2 (1999): 243–72; and Antonio T. Bly, "A Prince among Pretending Free Men: Runaway Slaves in Colonial New England Revisited," *Massachusetts Historical Review* 14 (2012): 87–118.

85 William Tilly, *Advertisement. Ran Away the 13th of this Instant June . . .* (Boston, 1697), Early American Imprints, ser. 1, Evans 39326.

86 To Captain Cornelis Jacobs, [HCA 98, pt. 1, fol. 75], High Court of Admiralty Records, PRO.

87 For a discussion of Jack/John, see Dennis Maika, "Encounters: Slavery and the Philipse Family, 1680–1751," in *Dutch New York: The Roots of Hudson Valley Culture*, ed. Roger Panetta (Yonkers, NY: Fordham Univ. Press, 2009), 35–72. Special thanks to Patricia Bonomi for recognizing the story of Jack/John and directing me to Maika's work.

88 "Petition of Edward Bendall and Samuell Scarlet, 1649," Massachusetts Archives, 2:292292a, Mass. Arch. YIPP document # 1649.07.24.00.

89 *ECCR*, 8:59.

90 Herbert Aptheker noted that "slaves fled whenever havens of liberation appeared," but New England's slaves seldom had that opportunity. Aptheker, *American Negro Slave Revolts* (New York: Columbia Univ. Press, 1943), 140.

91 James H. Merrell has maintained, in regard to Indian and African encounters in the Southeast, that to native people "any physical or cultural differences [between Africans and English] must have been submerged beneath the newcomers' countless shared characteristics." Merrell, "The Racial Education of the Catawba Indians," *Journal of Southern History* 50, no. 3 (1984): 369.

92 James Axtell, "The White Indians of Colonial America," *WMQ* 32, no. 1 (1975): 67. See Edward Johnson, *Wonder Working Providence, 1628–1651*, ed. J. Franklin Jameson (New York: Charles Scribner's Sons, 1910), 150: "as for

beauty they esteeme black beyond any colour." Roger Williams offered some (probably) Narragansett words for people of African descent. "Mowesu, * Suckesu," he argued, were their words for *"Blacke or swarsish,"* noting that "hence they called a *Blackamore* (themselves are tawnie, by the Sunne and their annoyntings, yet they are borne white)." According to Williams, Indians had a still different word for a *"cole blacke man."* Williams, *A Key into the Language of America* (London, 1643), 52. Of course, such words may have existed before contact with Europeans and their chattel slaves, and were then applied to the Africans that Indians encountered.

93  "Description of Boston by an Anonymous Frenchman from Languedoc," cited in Nathaniel B. Shurtleff, *A Topographical and Historical Description of Boston* (Boston: City Council, 1871), 48.

94  N.S. [Nathaniel Saltonstall], "A Continuation of the State of New-England, 1676," in *Original Narratives of Early American History: Narratives of the Indian Wars, 1675–1699*, ed. Charles H. Lincoln (New York: Charles Scribner's Sons, 1913), 66.

95  Evan Haefeli and Kevin Sweeney, *Captors and Captives: The 1704 French and Indian Raid on Deerfield* (Amherst: Univ. of Massachusetts Press, 2003), 126.

96  John Williams, *The Redeemed Captive, Returning to Zion; or, A Faithful History of Remarkable Occurrences in the Captivity and the Deliverance of Mr. John Williams, Minister of the Gospel in Deerfield* (Boston, 1707), 4.

97  Williams, *Redeemed Captive, Returning to Zion*, 7.

98  Haefeli and Sweeney, *Captors and Captivity*, 126.

99  *CCR*, 4:40.

100  Oct. 20, 1680, MAC, 61:218. Maritime life seemed particularly prone to fostering interracial relationships. In 1668–69, "Franck Negro" was caught and charged for "aiding or assisting John Pottell in his escape out of the prison in Boston the 8th of December last." Pottell was in prison for "murdering of the Cooke of the ship Golden Fox." *MBCA*, 3:194.

101  1 Cor. 10:13.

### Chapter 7: The Selling of Adam

1  On Sewall's house, see Mark Valeri, *Heavenly Merchandize: How Religion Shaped Commerce in Puritan America* (Princeton, NJ: Princeton Univ. Press, 2010), 111.

2  Richard Francis, *Judge Sewall's Apology: The Salem Witch Trials and the Forming of an American Conscience* (New York: Fourth Estate/Harper Collins, 2005), 3, 7, 10, 14, 164–65, 181–83. On Sewall, see also David D. Hall, "The Mental World of Samuel Sewall," in *Worlds of Wonder, Days of Judgment: Popular Religious Belief in Early New England* (New York: Alfred A. Knopf, 1989), 213–38; Mary Adams Hilmer, "The Other Diary of Samuel Sewall," *NEQ* 55, no. 3 (1982): 354–67; and Valeri, *Heavenly Merchandize*, 111–77.

3  Perry Miller, *The New England Mind: From Colony to Province* (Cambridge, MA: Harvard Univ. Press, 1953), 442. Miller was talking about Cotton Mather, but his general point holds also for Samuel Sewall.

4 Samuel Sewall, *The Selling of Joseph: A Memorial* (Boston, 1700), 1.

5 Harry S. Stout, *The New England Soul: Preaching and Religious Culture in Colonial New England* (New York: Oxford Univ. Press, 1986), 131–35.

6 Morgan Godwyn, *The Negro's & Indians Advocate, Suing for Their Admission to the Church* (London, 1680).

7 Morgan Godwyn, *A Supplement to the Negro's [and] Indian's Advocate* (London, 1681), 10.

8 Jer. 2:34; Morgan Godwyn, *Trade Preferr'd before Religion, and Christ Made to Give Place to Mammon: Represented in a Sermon Relating to the Plantations* (London, 1685), 1 (of the preface), 1 (of the text).

9 Thomas Tryon, *Friendly Advcie to the Gentlemen-Planters of the East and West Indies* (London, 1684), 75–222. A thoughtful examination of Tryon is Philippe Rosenberg, "Thomas Tryon and the Seventeenth-Century Dimensions of Antislavery," *WMQ* 61, no. 4 (2004): 609–42.

10 "Germantown Friends' Protest against Slavery, 1688," in Jürgen Eichhoff, "The Three Hundredth Anniversary of the Germantown Protest against Slavery," *Monatshefte* 80, no. 3 (1988), prefatory material. On the Germantown community's antislavery stance, see Katharine Gerbner, "Antislavery in Print: The Germantown Protest, the 'Exhortation,' and the Seventeenth-Century Quaker Debate on Slavery," *EAS* 9, no. 3 (2011): 552–75.

11 Monthly Meeting of Friends of Philadelphia, *An Exhortation & Caution to Friends concerning Buying or Keeping of Negroes* (New York, 1693), 1, 2, 5.

12 *SD*, 1:432–33 (emphasis added).

13 Paul Bayne, *An Entire Commentary upon the Whole Epistle of the Apostle Paul to the Ephesians* (London, 1643), 695.

14 *SD*, 1:433.

15 *The Selling of Joseph* has received an abundance of scholarly attention. Lawrence W. Towner offered the first extensive discussion of the piece, in an article titled "The Sewall-Saffin Dialogue on Slavery," *WMQ* 21, no. 1 (1964): 40–52. Bernard Rosenthal placed Sewall in a wider context, seeing him as a nascent abolitionist, a remnant (in 1700) of the early "Puritan establishment" voicing the long-standing and embedded "intellectual opposition" to slavery that could be found in seventeenth-century New England. Rosenthal explained that inherent in orthodox Calvinism is the logic of antislavery, but that this logic remained latent and largely unexpressed for much of the early history. He writes, "And if puritan New England deservedly earns the stigma of having supported slavery, it is only fair to acknowledge that the principal intellectual opposition came from orthodox Puritans." Rosenthal, "Puritan Conscience and New England Slavery," *NEQ* 46, no .1 (1973): 62–81. David Brion Davis placed Sewall in a larger theological context, though he saw neither Puritanism nor early New England as being inherently antislavery. Davis argued that changes in late seventeenth-century New England, along with a petition Sewall had recently seen asking for freedom for an enslaved couple, caused the judge to write *The Selling of Joseph*. He saw Sewall as a uniquely sensitive man, already apologetic for his role in the infamous witch trials (and

therefore doubly aware of his capacity to err). What "distinguished Samuel Sewall," Davis held, "was a conscience sensitized to human injustice and to the woeful fate of an unrepentant America." Davis, *The Problem of Slavery in Western Culture* (Ithaca, NY: Cornell Univ. Press, 1966), 344–46. Mark A. Peterson more recently maintained, "In the closing decade of the seventeenth century and the first third of the eighteenth, rapidly changing circumstances within Boston and in the larger Atlantic community brought slavery and related issues to the forefront of public concern." Peterson sees *The Selling of Joseph* as an early intervention "in a complex conversation in which slavery took its place among a host of social and ideological issues animating the Protestant world." Peterson, "The Selling of Joseph: Bostonians, Antislavery, and the Protestant International, 1689–1733," *Massachusetts Historical Review* 4 (2002): 2, 14. On John Saffin and slavery, see Albert Von Frank, "John Saffin: Slavery and Racism in Colonial Massachusetts," *Early American Literature* 29, no. 3 (1994): 254–72, though Von Frank's skepticism about Saffin's (and New England's) familiarity with slavery is not echoed in this book.

16 *SD*, 1:18.

17 Ibid., 95.

18 Ibid., 77.

19 On Jamaican slave revolts in the mid to late seventeenth century, see Orlando Patterson, "Slavery and Slave Revolts: A Socio-Historical Analysis of the First Maroon War Jamaica, 1655–1740," *Social and Economic Studies* 19, no. 3 (1970): 297–300; and David Barry Gaspar, "A Dangerous Spirit of Liberty: Slave Rebellion in the West Indies in the 1730s," in *Origins of the Black Atlantic*, ed. Laurent Dubois and Julius Scott (New York: Routledge, 2013), 12–13.

20 On Cromwell's "Western Design," see Carla Gardina Pestana, "English Character and the Fiasco of the Western Design," *EAS* 3, no. 1 (2005): 1–31.

21 *SD*, 1:87.

22 Ibid., 306.

23 Ibid., 151.

24 Francis, *Judge Sewall's Apology*, 23. On Hull's owning and selling of "negros," see his 1682 letter to Robert Breck, in Herman Frederick Clarke, "John Hull— Colonial Merchant, 1624–1683," *Proceedings of the American Antiquarian Society* 46 (1936): 213–14. For a sober and fascinating account of Hull's life, see Valeri, *Heavenly Merchandize*, 74–110. For a fictitious account of Sewall's courtship of a purportedly portly Hannah Hull, see Nathaniel Hawthorne, "The Pine-Tree Shillings," in *The Whole History of Grandfather's Chair* (1840).

25 Mackerel is a fish that spoils quickly and was rarely preserved; we might imagine that the thirty barrels of mackerel being sent to the West Indies was not of top quality. A. R. Michell, "The European Fisheries in Early Modern History," *The Cambridge History of Europe from the Decline of the Roman Empire*, vol. 5, *The Economic Organization of Early Modern Europe*, ed. E. E. Rich and C. H. Wilson (London: Cambridge Univ. Press, 1977), 167–68; Samuel Sewall, "Letterbook," in *MHSC*, 6th ser., 1:2–4.

26 Gen. 37–50.

27  Sewall, *Selling of Joseph*, 1.

28  Ibid.

29  Cotton Mather, *A Good Master Well Served: A Brief Discourse on the Necessary Properties & Practices of a Good Servant in Every-Kind of Servitude: And of the Methods That Should Be Taken by the Heads of a Family, to Obtain Such a Servant* (Boston, 1696), 5. On Cotton Mather and slavery, see also Daniel K. Richter, "'It Is God Who Has Caused Them to Be Servants': Cotton Mather and Afro-American Slavery in New England," *Bulletin of the Congregational Library* 30, no. 3 (1979): 4–15.

30  Kenneth Silverman, *The Life and Times of Cotton Mather* (New York: Harper and Row, 1984), 3–6, 43–45. On the Mathers as a family, see Robert Middlekauff, *The Mathers: Three Generations of Puritan Intellectuals, 1596–1728* (Berkeley: Univ. of California Press, 1999).

31  On the black cap and the reason for it, see *SD*, 1:419n28.

32  This was a more important difference than it might seem, for Sewall took personal offense at wigs, deeming them offenses against God and writing sermons against their use. His diary is peppered with references to the fashion trend, including the story of his having "heard that Josiah Willard had cut off his hair (a very full head of hair) and put on a Wigg." Sewall marched to young Willard's house the very next morning and gave him a stern lecture, dismissing entirely Willard's explanation that his natural hair was lamentably straight. A chastened Willard agreed to "leave off his Wigg when his hair was grown." Sewall was not appeased, though, and later that year skipped a church service where Willard was to preach. *SD*, 1:448–49, 458. Josiah Willard's father was Samuel Sewall's minister. Mark Valeri, *Heavenly Merchandize*, 1. Sewall's distaste for wigs was shared. See also Nicholas Noyes, "Reasons against Wearing of Periwiggs," in Worthington C. Ford, "Sewall and Noyes on Wigs," *CSMP*, 20:120–28. Richard Godbeer discusses the significance of wigs in colonial Massachusetts, in "Perversions of Anatomy, Anatomies of Perversion: The Periwig Controversy in Colonial Massachusetts," *MHSP* 109 (1997): 1–23.

33  Cotton Mather, *The Declaration of the Gentlemen, Merchants, and Inhabitants of Boston, and the Countrey Adjacent* (Boston, 1689), 2. This same line appeared in a 1707 Mather publication, meaning that this comparison between sold and unsold slaves was one he pondered for some years. Philopolites [Cotton Mather], *A Memorial of the Present Deplorable State of New-England* ([London], 1707), 2.

34  Cotton Mather, *Diary of Cotton Mather, 1681–1708, MHSC*, 7th ser., 7:176.

35  Cotton Mather, "Rules for the Society of Negroes, 1693." These rules, eight in all, seem to have remained within the covers of Mather's diary until he published them as a broadside in 1706, with a ninth rule added. A copy of a 1714 reissue, now owned by the American Antiquarian Society, has, on the back in Samuel Sewall's hand, "Left at my house for me, when I was not at home, by Spaniard Dr. Mather's Negroe; March, 23 17/14." Cotton Mather, *Rules for the Society of Negroes, 1693* (Boston, ca. 1714), AAS, American Broadsides Collection.

36 Sewall, *Selling of Joseph*, 2

37 Cotton Mather, *A Pastoral Letter to the English Captives in Africa* (Boston, 1698), 4, 9.

38 Sewall, *Selling of Joseph*, 2. Unsurprisingly, the Mathers did not like Sewall's pamphlet against slavery. In part, this was because they were embroiled in another dispute at the time: Sewall had objected to Increase Mather's proposal to live in Boston while still the president of Harvard. Francis, *Judge Sewall's Apology*, 226–32. But also, the Mathers were not opposed to slavery as an institution; as already mentioned, Cotton Mather himself owned several Africans throughout his lifetime. A year after the publication, responding to a perceived slight from Sewall over an unrelated matter, Cotton Mather sniped in a public forum that, though "that one [Sewall] pleaded much for Negros," Sewall had treated Increase "worse than a Neger." A surprised and hurt Sewall sent Increase a gift to ease the rift: "October 9. I sent Mr. Increase Mather a Hanch of very good Venison; I hope in that I did not treat him as a Negro." *SD*, 1:454–55. Here Sewall's (out-of-character) sarcasm underscored the implicit understanding shared by all involved in the event that the acceptable ways of treating Africans and acceptable ways of treating European colonists differed dramatically.

39 In November 1665, he noted in his diary, "I was Joyned to the first Church in Boston. God in mercy makes me faithfull to his Covenant." John Saffin, *John Saffin, His Book (1665–1708); Collection of Various Matters of Divinity Law & State Affairs Epitomiz'd Both in Verse and Prose* (New York: Harbour Press, 1928), 2. Cotton Mather belonged to the Second Church, while Samuel Sewall was a member of the Old South (Third Church). For more on Saffin's trip to Virigina and for his wealthy status, see Von Frank, "John Saffin," 255, 257.

40 Von Frank, "John Saffin," 261.

41 "In reference unto a negro named Jethro," *PCR*, 5:216; also cited in Von Frank, "John Saffin," 255–56.

42 "John Saffin and Others to William Welstead, 1681," in Elizabeth Donnan, ed., *Documents Illustrative of the History of the Slave Trade to America* (Washington, DC: Carnegie Institution, 1932), 3:15–16.

43 John Saffin, "On the Deplorable Departure of the Honered and Truly Religious Chieftain John Hull Esqr Who Putt off His Earthly Tabernacle . . . ," in Harrison T. Meserole, ed. *American Poetry of the Seventeenth Century* (University Park: Pennsylvania State Univ. Press, 1993), 200.

44 Saffin has received much less attention than Sewall from historians. His response is difficult to find: half was republished in George Henry Moore's 1866 *Notes on the History of Slavery in Massachusetts*; the rest was summarized and excerpted in an 1895 publication of the Colonial Society of Massachusetts. Scholars have preferred to work with Sewall's piece, perhaps preferring its message, perhaps preferring its brevity.

45 Both Towner and Davis make this point. See, e.g., Davis, *Problem of Slavery in Western Culture*, 345; and Towner, "Sewall-Saffin Dialogue," 48–49.

46 John Saffin, "A Brief and Candid Answer to a Late Printed Sheet, *Entitled*, The Selling of Joseph," 1701, reprinted in George Henry Moore, *Notes on the His-*

*tory of Slavery in Massachusetts* (New York, 1866), 251–52. There were radical Protestants in England making this claim, though their views of Africans and Indians were less clearly stated. See Christopher Hill, *The World Turned Upside Down: Radical Ideas during the English Revolution* (New York: Viking, 1972), 107–50.

47 Saffin, "Brief and Candid Answer," 251.

48 Ibid., 252.

49 Ibid., 252–53.

50 Sewall, *Sellling of Joseph*, 3.

51 Ibid.

52 Saffin, "Brief and Candid Answer," 254.

53 Sewall, *Selling of Joseph*, 3.

54 Saffin, "Brief and Candid Answer," 254.

55 Ibid., 256; Von Frank, "John Saffin," 254.

56 John Saffin, *A Brief and Candid Answer to a Late Printed Sheet*, Entitled, *The Selling of Joseph Whereunto is annexed, A True and Particular Narrative by way of Vindication of the Author's Dealing with and Prosecution of his Negro Man servant for his vile and exorbitant Behaviour towards his Master, and his Tenant Thomas Shephard; which hath been wrongfully Represented to their Pejudice and Defamation* (Boston, 1701), in Abner C. Goodell, "John Saffin and His Slave Adam," *CSMP*, 1:104. See also MAC, 9:153.

57 Testimony of Thomas Shepherd of Bristol, Jan. 12, 1699, in Goodall, "John Saffin and His Slave Adam," 90–91.

58 Saffin, Brief and Candid Answer . . . *Vindication of the Author's Dealing*, 104.

59 Sarah Kemble Knight, "The Private Journal Kept by Madam Knight," in *The Journals of Madam Knight and Rev. Mr. Buckingham: From the Original Manuscripts, Written in 1704 and 1710* (New York: Wilder and Campbell, 1825), 40.

60 Saffin, *Brief and Candid Answer . . . Vindication of the Author's Dealing*, 105.

61 Ibid.

62 *SD*, 1:452.

63 Ibid., 474.

64 Ibid., 487.

65 Goodall, "John Saffin and His Slave Adam," 92.

66 "At Her Majestys Superiour Court of Judicature," Nov. 1703, *Acts and Resolves, Public and Private*, 8:266–71.

67 "An Act for the Regulating of Free Negroes, 1707," *The Charters and General Laws of the Colony and Province of Massachusetts Bay* (Boston: T. B. Wait, 1814), 386–87.

68 References to Adam Saffin, *A Report of the Record Commissioners of the City of Boston, Containing the Records of Boston Selectmen, 1701–1715* (Boston: Rockwell and Churchill, 1884), 73, 115, 137, 166, 210, 232.

69 John Saffin, "A brief Elegie on my Dear Son John the second of that name of mine," in Meserole, ed., *American Poetry of the Seventeenth Century*, 199.

70 Sewall was involved in arranging Bastian's marriage to "Jane, Mr. Thair's Negro," speaking to her on Bastian's behalf. *SD*, 1:408.

71 *SD*, 1:367.

72 Christopher Leslie Brown, *Moral Capital: Foundations of British Abolitionism* (Chapel Hill: Univ. of North Carolina Press, 2006), 40.

73 "Will of Increase Mather," *NEHGR* 1 (1851): 445-47.

74 Entry, 1706. Cotton Mather, *Diary of Cotton Mather, 1681-1708*, in *MHSC*, 7th ser., 7:579. *Onesimus* means useful in Greek; just as relevant to Mather's mind was probably the story of the slave who converted to Christianity under the influence of Paul, and was thus freed by his master.

75 Advertisement, *Boston News-Letter*, Sept. 13, 1714; also cited in Lorenzo Greene, *The Negro in Colonial New England, 1620-1776* (New York: Columbia Univ. Press, 1942), 41.

### Epilogue: A Thousand Such Fellows

1 Sarah Kemble Knight, "The Private Journal Kept by Madam Knight," in *The Journals of Madam Knight and Rev. Mr. Buckingham: From the Original Manuscripts, Written in 1704 and 1710* (New York: Wilder and Campbell, 1825), 36-38.

2 On obscure jokes, see Robert Darnton: "Our own inability to get the joke is an indication of the distance that separates us from the workers of preindustrial Europe." Darnton, *The Great Cat Massacre and Other Episodes in French Cultural History* (New York: Basic Books, 1984), 77-78.

3 Sarah Kemble Knight, "Journal," 46.

4 An excellent discussion of New England's slow road to abolition can be found in Joanne Pope Melish, *Disowning Slavery: Gradual Emancipation and "Race" in New England, 1780-1860* (Ithaca, NY: Cornell Univ. Press, 1998), 50-83.

5 On Quock Walker, see Emily Blanck, "Seventeen Eighty-Three: The Turning Point in the Law of Slavery and Freedom in Massachusetts," *NEQ* 75, no. 1 (2002): 24-25; John D. Cushing, "The Cushing Court and the Abolition of Slavery in Massachusetts: More Notes on the 'Quock Walker Case,'" *American Journal of Legal History* 5, no. 2 (1961): 118-44; A. Leon Higginbotham Jr., *In the Matter of Color: Race and the American Legal Process: The Colonial Period* (New York: Oxford Univ. Press, 1978), 91-99; William O'Brien, "Did the Jennison Case Outlaw Slavery in Massachusetts?," *WMQ* 17, no. 2 (1960): 219-41; and Arthur Zilversmit, *The First Emancipation: The Abolition of Slavery in the North* (Chicago: Univ. of Chicago Press, 1967).

6 "An Act Concerning Indian, Molatto, and Negro Servants and Slaves," 1784, in *Acts and Laws of the State of Connecticut in America* (New London, CT, 1784), 233-35; Gradual Emancipation Acts, *RICR*, 10:7, 132. On these acts, see David Menschel, "Abolition without Deliverance: The Law of Connecticut Slavery, 1784-1848," *Yale Law Journal* 111, no. 1 (2001): 183-222.

7 Melish, *Disowning Slavery*, 76.

8 Nathaniel Hawthorne, *The American Notebooks*, ed. Claude M. Simpson (Columbus: Ohio State Univ. Press, 1972), 111-12.

9 Ibid., 151.

10 A Peaceable Man [Nathaniel Hawthorne], "Chiefly about War-Matters," *Atlantic Monthly* 10, no. 57 (1862): 50.

# *Index*

Page numbers followed by *n* refer to endnotes. Page numbers in *italics* refer to figures and maps.

# About the Author

Wendy Warren is assistant professor of history and the Philip and Beulah Rollins Bicentennial Preceptor at Princeton University. She earned her PhD in history at Yale University and was a research fellow at Christ Church College, Oxford University. She lives in central New Jersey with her husband and three boisterous children.